MICROCOMPUTER
PROBLEM SOLVING USING PASCAL

Kenneth L. Bowles

MICROCOMPUTER
PROBLEM SOLVING USING PASCAL

Springer-Verlag

New York Heidelberg Berlin

Kenneth L. Bowles
Department of Applied Physics and Information Science
University of California
at San Diego
La Jolla, CA 92093
USA

AMS Subject Classifications: 68-01, 68-A05

Library of Congress Cataloging in Publication Data

Bowles, Kenneth L 1929-
(Microcomputer) problem solving using PASCAL.
1. PASCAL (Computer program language) 2. Microcomputers—Programming. I. Title.
QA76.73.P2B68 001.6'424 77-11959

Printed in the United States of America.

9 8

ISBN 0-387-90286-4 Springer-Verlag New York
ISBN 3-540-90286-4 Springer-Verlag Berlin Heidelberg

PREFACE

This book is designed both for introductory courses in computer problem solving, at the freshman and sophomore college level, and for individual self study. An earlier version of the book has been used seven times for teaching large introductory classes at University of California San Diego (UCSD). This preface is intended for the instructor, or for anyone sophisticated enough in contemporary computing practice to be able to advise the prospective student.

The amount of material presented has been completed by about 55 percent of all students taking the course, where UCSD schedules 10 weeks of classes in a quarter. We have taught the course using Keller's Personalized System of Instruction (PSI), though the organization of the book does not require that plan to be used. PSI methods allow slightly more material to be absorbed by the students than is the case with the traditional lecture/recitation presentation. PSI allows grading according to the number of chapter units completed. Virtually all students who pass the course at UCSD do complete the first ten essential chapters and the Exercises associated with them. For a conventional presentation under the semester system, the 15 chapters should present an appropriate amount of material. For a conventional course under the quarter system, one might not expect to complete more than the first 12 chapters except on an extra credit basis.

Whereas most introductory textbooks attempt to reach students who will do their program debugging work on a wide variety of host machines and operating systems, this one does not, at least for the near future. One of our primary objectives has been to reach the large proportion of all college students who arrive with inadequate preparation in mathematics at the high school level. In general, we have found these students to be nearly as adept in learning to write programs and solve problems on the computer as are the students to arrive with a stronger mathematics background. The basic methods of programming differ very little between science and engineering applications on the one hand, and business or arts and humanities applications on the other. We have found it possible to motivate and to teach students across this entire spectrum using problem examples with a non-numerical orientation. Earlier versions of this book have accomplished this using manipulation of text strings wherever possible. In this version, we use graphics to enhance the motivational value, in many cases borrowing from the "Turtle Graphics" approach originated by Seymour Papert of MIT.

To reach students who have never programmed before using examples based on graphics and on string manipulation requires that the PASCAL implementation include built-in procedures and functions to work with those kinds of data. "Standard" implementations of PASCAL, meaning generally those which adhere closely to the definition of PASCAL described in the "<u>User Manual and Report</u>" of Jensen & Wirth (Springer-Verlag, 1975), do not contain the necessary built-in functions and procedures.

At UCSD, we have implemented a complete single-user software system based on PASCAL, and this system embodies extensions to the standard which include the necessary functions and procedures for handling graphics and strings. In most other respects, the system adheres closely to the standard. This software system is interpreter based, and is intended for interactive use on a variety of the single user microcomputers now being sold in profusion. It is assumed that the microcomputer the student will use has provision for displaying graphic images, even if they are only of the crude variety made possible by a "bit-map" scheme used with standard television receivers. By the time this book is available for distribution, copies of this software system will be available from UCSD for use on small computers based on the Digital Equipment LSI-11 (or any small PDP11 machine), for the Zilog Z80, and for certain machines based on the 8080 microprocessor. It is likely that implementations will also be available for the widely used 6800 and 6502 microprocessors as well, probably by early 1978. Inquiries to the author will be welcomed regarding requests for copies of this software system for microcomputers already supported.

Clearly, the extensions to PASCAL, needed to use this book in environments where larger shared computers are employed, are not extremely difficult to make. To the greatest degree possible, the extensions have been done in such a way as to avoid requiring extensive compiler changes. The author and his colleagues will be pleased to cooperate, within the limited resources available, with other groups who wish to implement these changes in PASCAL for other operating systems.

At UCSD, the course based on this book will be supported increasingly by interactive quizzes, by course management software, and by supplementary materials on paper. In general, we will be happy to share these materials with other campuses.

I wish to acknowledge with gratitude the assistance given to me, and influence on this work, from roughly 50 graduate and upper division students at UCSD. They have contributed most of the work that has made the underlying software system successful, and their efforts and suggestions have made the PSI course format a big success with the students taking the course. Special recognition is due Mark Overgaard, who has assisted me as a colleague from the inception of the project, and to Robert Hofkin, Richard Kaufmann, Keith Shillington, Roger Sumner, and John Van Zandt, all of whom have contributed in major ways. Shawn Fanning has assisted in preparation of the Glossary and Index. Dale Ander has assisted in editing the plot files for many of the drawings. None of these people are to be blamed for the errors that inevitably will be found in this preliminary edition, and for which I am myself responsible. Errors in editing and typesetting are mine alone, as I have done all of that work myself using a word processing editor which runs under the same software system on which the teaching materials are based. As often happens, the available time schedule has been somewhat too short for the task at hand.

August, 1977

Kenneth L. Bowles
University of California
San Diego
La Jolla, California 92093

CONTENTS

Chapter 0

INTRODUCTION

The main objective of this book is to teach you an orderly approach to solving problems using computers. As an inseparable second objective, you must learn to write computer programs. Very little attention will be given to describing computers, or to surveying the vast number of ways in which they are used.

The subject material has been chosen to be understandable to all students at about the college freshman level, with almost no dependence on a background in high school mathematics beyond simple algebra. In spite of our non-numerical approach, the methods taught are the same as those taught traditionally using problem examples founded in mathematics. Students oriented to the sciences, humanities, arts, or professional studies should all perform about equally well in preparing to use computers in their chosen fields. Those who will not make later use of computers should find benefit in using the same general approach to solving problems in other contexts.

This chapter describes the environment in which you as a student are assumed to be working. The fundamental basis of the approach we use is broadly applicable to the use of computers in science, business, industry, the arts, communications, and many other fields. For practical reasons, no book can convey this approach without handling many specific details that may not apply unmodified in the environment you will encounter after completing the work in this book. The computing field is changing so rapidly that all students are sure to encounter environments quite different from the ones in which they first learn to use computers. We have found that most students who complete the material in this book have little difficulty in shifting to another programming language, or to a very different method of interacting with the computer.

1. Problem Examples

Problem solving is an inexact art involving a substantial measure of style that can only be learned by practice in working out many sample problems. This book contains many problem "Exercises" intended, in most cases, to be worked out using the computer. "Problems" given at the end of most chapters are for pencil and paper solution. We attempt in the text to provide guidance on the approaches to solving problems that have worked best for others. However, unless you make the substantial effort to work out most of the Exercises yourself on a computer, you will miss the main message this book has been written to convey.

The subject material of most of the Examples and Problems in the earlier parts of the book is based on the processing of line-drawings, and of "strings" of English text. These are both frequently used applications of computers. Both involve use of most of the same basic techniques that apply also to the computer solution of mathematical problems. Drawings and text examples are familiar to all students. Many students who need to use computers, and will enjoy doing so, have had unpleasant experiences with mathematics at the high school level. Our choice of examples very largely avoids the need for them to cope further with mathematics.

The book starts by presenting a repetoire of the basic tools one uses in solving problems on a computer. In the early Examples, many detailed suggestions are made on approach, and the objective is for you to to build confidence on the use of the tools through practice. In the later chapters, fewer and fewer suggestions are made on approach, and the Examples become progressively more difficult. Eventually you should be able to synthesize the complete solution to a problem with nothing more than the specification of what needs to be done as information given in advance.

As the problems become more complex, you will find it best to subdivide each problem into component steps, each of which can be carried out independently. This "divide and conquer" approach is a theme that will reappear many times in this book, and in many different contexts. Sometimes you will find it best to subdivide each component of the main problem in order to reduce the steps to manageable size.

The solution of problems using computers requires the translation of a conceptual method and framework into abstract terms. Some students seem to regard the need to use abstract terms as equivalent to working with mathematics, and hence just as difficult. It may help to regard the abstractions needed in computer work as closer to the abstractions needed in everyday conversation than those needed in mathematics.

In conversation, we constantly use abstract terms intended to refer to some complex concept without describing that concept to the listener. For example, if you make plans with a friend to go to "the movies", there is no need to spend time describing the use of a projection screen and projector, the fact that moving pictures are really composed just of samples of the story being told, and so on. In this case, the term "the movies" is intended to refer to a substantial fund of information with which you assume your listener is already familiar. In the same way, the solution of a problem on a computer often involves the use of terms that you invent to apply to independent components of the problem. While you are concentrating on one aspect of the problem, it helps to refer to the other aspects by their names rather than worrying about the details.

2. Algorithms, Data, and Programs

An "Algorithm" is a statement of a sequence of actions one can go through to accomplish some task. "Data" is the information on which an algorithm "operates", i.e. the information which is used by the sequence of actions to achieve the desired result. An algorithm is similar to a cooking recipe in which the ingredients are data items. Unlike many recipes, it often makes sense to use the same algorithm to operate on, or "process", many different items of data having similar characteristics.

A "Program" is an abstract statement of an algorithm, and a description of the data to be processed by the algorithm. Usually it is understood that the program is to be expressed in terms suitable for interpretation by a computer without further human intervention. A "programming language", like a "natural language" such as English, is a vocabulary of terms, and the set of conventions on connecting those terms together for the purpose of communicating one's thoughts. In the case of a programming language, one usually wishes to communicate the details of a program to a computer. Quite often, an important secondary objective is to communicate to other humans, since most programming languages allow much more concise, and precise, expression of an algorithm than is possible with a natural language.

For your purposes in studying the early chapters of this book, it will be sufficient for you to have just a rough idea of the distinction between an algorithm and a program. Starting in Chapter 6, we will see that it sometimes is useful, for comprehension and clarity, to describe an algorithm in terms of a diagram understandable to humans but not to the computer.

3. The Choice of PASCAL as our Programming Language

At present, the most widely used programming languages are BASIC, COBOL, and FORTRAN. Somewhat less popular, but also widely used, are APL, PL/1, and to a lesser degree ALGOL. Why then have we chosen to use PASCAL for use with this book, which is intended to be used at the introductory level?

PASCAL is a more recent development than the other languages cited. It was created to avoid many of the pitfalls that had already been experienced in using those languages by the late 1960's. PASCAL was introduced, by Niklaus Wirth of the Engineering University at Zurich, to serve as an improved basis for teaching a systematic approach to computer problem solving and programming. PASCAL also has excellent facilities for handling complex data. These facilities have led increasingly to its use in large programming projects in industry.

In mid 1977, PASCAL was in use for teaching at roughly 400 universities and colleges, and its use was spreading rapidly. At least one large state university, where PASCAL has been in general use for about 4 years, reports that the popularity of PASCAL has become comparable to that of FORTRAN. It was recently reported that PASCAL has now been made available for use on at least 50 different makes and models of computers.

PASCAL is clearly the best language now in widespread use for teaching the concepts that have come to be known in the industry as "<u>structured programming</u>" at the introductory level. Structured Programming is a method designed to minimize the effort that the programmer has to spend on finding and correcting logical errors in programs. Put more positively, it is a method designed to allow a program to produce correct results with a minimum amount of effort on the part of the programmer. Most large employers who analyze the productivity of their computer programmers now insist that their employees use the disciplined approach of Structured Programming. It is possible to use this approach with any of the popular languages cited earlier in this section, but one must avoid using those languages to do certain things that have been found generally to lead to errors.

We have found that students who learn to program first using PASCAL have very little difficulty in shifting to use FORTRAN. In doing so, they are led naturally to use the structured approach. Students who have shifted to COBOL have had to spend several weeks in learning the new language. They would have spent this extra time even had they started learning to program directly in COBOL, mostly because COBOL has more fussy rules that must be followed before one can write successful programs. The shift to BASIC can be accomplished within a few hours. However, the result is likely to be that the student will then realize that BASIC does not have facilities for doing easily many of the things that PASCAL allows with minimal effort.

In practice, it seems best to learn to program first using PASCAL, and then to shift over to one of the other languages if there are practical reasons for doing so. Those reasons might include a need to communicate on one's programming activities with a group of people who already make very extensive use of one of the other languages. If one tries to learn the discipline of Structured Programming while also learning to program for the first time in one of the other languages, the experience is a little like learning to walk for the first time in an area where a chance mis-step could lead to falling off a precipice.

The version of PASCAL used in this book includes virtually all of the features of the language as it was originally designed by Professor Wirth. His definition did not provide facilities to make it easy for beginning students to work with line drawings and strings of text, which are the principal focus of this book. Accordingly, we have extended PASCAL to provide those facilities. When you reach the stage of wanting to use PASCAL on a computer other than the one you use in learning with this book, it will be useful to review Appendix A which lists the differences between our extended PASCAL and Wirth's original version.

4. Equipment - Micro, Mini, and Maxi Computers

The jargon of the computer industry has come to describe the small machine, typically capable of serving only one user at a time and costing only a few thousand dollars, as a "Micro-computer". A machine big enough to be shared by several dozen people working simultaneously on programs of moderate size, and costing typically from $50,000 to $100,000 is called a "Mini-computer". The larger machines, capable of handling more people and large programs, and costing substantially more than a Mini, will be called "Maxi-computers" in this book. The industry jargon is somewhat less standardized on the third of these terms than on Micro's and Mini's.

Current trends in the computer industry make it increasingly likely that you will use a Micro computer, both while studying this book and later. Until recently, most colleges and universities have used Maxi or Mini computers shared by many people simultaneously for instruction. However, the growth in use of Micro's is extremely rapid in mid 1977, and expected still to increase. By the mid 1980's, it is clear that most people will have contact with Micro's rather than with Mini's or Maxi computers. The reason for this rapid growth is that new techniques for producing electronic components, and associated large volume production line efficiencies, are reducing the cost of individual Micro computers to the point where a mass market is beginning to evolve.

The extensions to PASCAL needed to study the material in this book without modification can be made available, in principle, on any computer for which PASCAL is already available. In practice, a substantial amount of work is needed to install the extensions in PASCAL on the larger machines. At UCSD we have found it possible to provide the extended PASCAL for most of the present generation of Micro computers with only a moderate amount of effort. Unless you are using a version of PASCAL derived from the version we have developed at UCSD, you should be on the lookout for differences between the version you are using and the version used in this book.

5. Graphic Display Devices

Most of the illustrations in this book are copies of line drawings made by a Micro computer with PASCAL programs. There is a wide variety of devices being used to display graphic output from computers. One of the main reasons for this variety is that one can obtain high quality images only with a device costing many thousands of dollars, while simple approximations to those images can be made with a home television set and electronic equipment costing only a few hundred dollars. Between these extremes there are many different devices which produce images of quality sufficient for most educational uses, and which cost from $1000 to $3000 per unit. In addition to the devices used to "display" an image on a viewing screen, similar to the screen on a television receiver, there are also many devices available to record the images in "hard-copy" form, i.e. on paper.

Virtually all of the illustrations in this book have been recorded on paper using either of two hard copy recording devices made by Tektronix Corporation. One draws lines with pen and ink. The other records on paper the image stored on the screen of a display device designed for interacting with computers. Many of the Tektronix display terminals are in use at educational institutions for instructional computing. We are indebted to Tektronix for the loan of this equipment during the period the book has been in preparation.

On many of the Micro computers you may be using in connection with this book, the appearance of line drawings generated by your machine may differ slightly from the appearance of the drawings shown in the book. Figure 0-1 shows the reason for this difference. Many devices do not draw lines directly on the screen. Rather, they create the appearance of a line by plotting a sequence of dots at regular intervals. Usually the dots can only be placed at the intersection points of the grid lines of an imaginary sheet of graph paper. Figure 0-1 shows both the dots, the lines they are intended to simulate, and the grid lines defining the graph paper. It costs much less to produce a device which allows the dots to be placed only at the grid intersection points, instead of at any location on the screen that you might wish. The result is a line that in some cases has a stair-step appearance. The coarser the imaginary graph paper, the more apparent will be the stair-step appearance of the lines plotted by your computer. With only a little bit of imagination, you should be able to ignore the stair-step appearance of the lines plotted, and to visualize the plotted lines as if they were continuous.

6. Organization of the Book

There seems to be no ideal order in which to present the repertoire of basic tools one must learn in order to write computer programs. Until you learn to write simple programs, it will be difficult to understand the reasons for the structured approach to solving problems. The approach used in this book is to start with very simple problem examples using a selection of the basic tools. In successive chapters, the problems are made progressively more difficult to

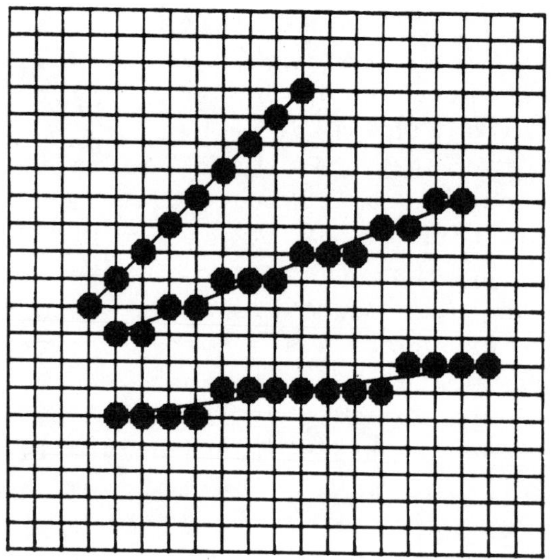

Figure 0-1

give you practice at synthesizing complete problem solutions. In each succeeding chapter, it is assumed that you have mastered the material from all of the preceding chapters. For this reason alone, it is suggested that you proceed through the book in the order of presentation, rather than trying to alter that order for reasons of personal preference.

For many students, one of the more troublesome aspects of learning to use computers is the need to learn a large number of details about the working environment which usually are not described in the textbook associated with the course of instruction. Chapter 1 of this book goes into more detail on these matters than is usual, and assumes that you will be using some variant of the UCSD software system for PASCAL. If you are not using that system, a supplement representing a replacement for Chapter 1 should be available to you for the system you are using.

Chapters 2 through 6 present basic tools for programming and for expressing algorithms. Chapters 7 through 10 add tools for working with data transmitted to the computer from external devices, and for working with complex data. Chapter 11 covers the controversial GOTO statement and its relatives. Chapters 12 through 15 provide illustrations of complex problems of types that are frequently encountered by virtually all programmers. The appendices at the end of the book are provided for reference purposes.

7. Computer Jargon

In computer work, many concepts that have become familiar have been given names or abbreviations that are commonly known. Quite often the name or word that is used sounds like a word used in everyday English to describe a slightly different set of concepts. The terms that computer people use to communicate with each other allow descriptions to be much shorter than they would otherwise be. This relates back to the example of "the movies" already cited.

In this book, we attempt to define each specialized term in the jargon of computers using quotation marks and underlining at the place in the text where the term is first introduced. If you forget what a term means when it appears later in the text, refer to the Glossary in Appendix B. The Glossary gives a very brief definition or description of the term, as well as a reference to the chapter and section where the term first appeared in the book. Once introduced, we will use each term freely in the later text. Some students object to this practice because it requires them to remember a large number of unfamiliar words in a short time. This is unfortunate but necessary. Without using these terms, the book would be much longer and it would be harder to read.

8. The Goals Statements

Each chapter in this book starts with a brief statement of the objectives you should attain before proceeding to the next chapter. Many students get bogged down in details without understanding the main points of a book or course of study. Usually, an author intends the outline of chapter and section headings to imply the general framework in which the detailed material is being presented. The goals statements differ slightly from the outline in that they summarize the points that should be mastered by combining all of the sections in a chapter.

Many of the students who have used early versions of this book have found the Goals statements to be extremely useful. We suggest that you should read the Goals first fairly quickly. Following that, read the chapter as a whole and work out the problem Examples. Then, before proceeding to the next chapter, go back and read the Goals statement again for the chapter you have just finished. This should help to place in your mind the relevance of the several detailed points in the chapter to the subject as a whole.

9. Study Habits

The solution of problems using a computer involves both creative activity, and a willingness to follow a set of very precise and unbending rules. Some students find it hard to adjust to this need to use precise rules, and feel that the computer somehow should be able to understand what they wish to do even if they stray a little from the rules. If you feel that way, try to understand that the computer really has almost no intelligence. All it can do is to follow a set of logical steps (an algorithm) that someone else has previously programmed it to follow. As the course proceeds, you will come to understand how difficult it is to predict all of the possible ways in which a human might choose to ask the computer to perform even the simplest conceivable task. The size and complexity of the program needed to cope with human variability gets out of hand quite rapidly. Until we find ways of making computers more intelligent with less programming effort, you will have to put up with the need to be precise if you wish to use computers productively.

One consequence of the need to be precise is that this book must be written in a way that packs a substantial amount of detailed information into relatively few pages. You cannot read material written in this way as if it were a novel, to be skimmed by speed reading techniques, and expect to derive much benefit from the reading effort.

In some cases, failure to obey the rules for programming is readily detected by the large program (called a "compiler") that translates the programming language into a form the machine itself can understand. In other cases, the failure is manifested by incorrect, and unexpected, results from running the program. The errors detected by the compiler are relatively easy to correct in most cases, since the compiler displays messages giving you a good clue to what went wrong. The errors in program logic are harder to find, and often require a systematic approach for solution. Development of such a systematic approach should be one of your goals in studying the material in this book.

Psychologists who have studied computer programming activities have suggested several approaches to program development that work well for many people. Caution: No one approach works best for everyone. Some of the following suggestions will be easier to understand on re-reading, after several of the following chapters have been completed.

9a. Team solution of Exercises

Explain your work on a program design to a friend before trying it on the computer. If there are errors, you are more likely to find them yourself in the midst of this explanation than is your friend, even if the friend understands the material thoroughly. Often you will find errors much more quickly by this approach than by checking for results directly on the computer. Remember that the computer does what you *instructed* it to do, not necessarily what you *meant* it to do.

9b. Document in Advance

Write out a description in words of what you intend a program to accomplish. Draw diagrams or tables to accompany this "*document*" to help in the explanation. Even if the document consists only of rough notes to serve as a reminder for you in the future, the effort to put the notes on paper helps you to work out the logic of a program correctly the first time.

9c. Check and Re-check your work

Write out the initial solution to a programming problem, then lay it aside for several days. Before trying to run the solution on the computer, go over what you have done once again to see if you understand the logic. The process of having to think through what you have done once again will quite often reveal logical inconsistencies that can easily be corrected with pencil and paper. In some cases, the same errors could take days to discover using the computer directly.

9d. Experiment

Be willing to experiment (with very simple illustrative programs) on the computer if written descriptions on how it should work are not clear to you. If the written descriptions covered all of the possible misconceptions of all possible readers, all descriptive documents would be too long for most people to read. In general, you can create a very simple example to test your understanding of how a point described in a book or manual really works. It saves time to try out an example or two of this type, rather than guessing how things work, and then burying your guesses deeply in a complicated program.

9e. Building Block Design

Use a building block approach in designing algorithms and programs. This is a theme repeated over and over throughout this book. Make sure that each building block is correct before you use it to fit together with other building blocks to create a complete structure. Sometimes, to do this you have to create some special test data to be used only in testing the building block alone. A little effort spent on this advance testing may save a lot of effort in testing the complete program.

9f. Analyze - Don't Conjecture

Don't try to resolve difficulties in a complex program by randomly trying various conjectured solutions. We call this the "dart board approach". It is one of the most common ways in which students waste large amounts of their time. Analyze what your program really does to determine whether it produces the intended results. If you make a change in a program, have a logical reason for doing so. Check to make sure that the results obtained from the change agree with the results you expected.

Chapter 1

GETTING STARTED

1. Goals

Our main purpose in this chapter is to acquaint you with the computer, the manner in which we use it, and the methods we will use to describe how the computer is used.

1a. Run the TURTLE program and use it to draw pictures on the computer's display screen.

1b. Learn to use the computer's Editor to read and modify the programs GRAPH1 and STRING1.

1c. Compile and Run the sample programs, returning to step 1b several times until you have a rough understanding of what these programs do, and how you can change them to obtain different results.

1d. Learn to use syntax diagrams as a concise way to understand the rules for constructing programs using the PASCAL programming language. Learn to construct an <identifier>, and a complete <program> consisting of several <statement>s.

1e. Intentionally introduce several different kinds of syntax errors into a program, try to compile it, and observe how the compiler attempts to inform you what went wrong.

1f. Run one of the programs you have already tested, now under control of the Debugger. Execute one statement at a time and observe how the action accomplished relates to the part of the program being executed.

2. Commands to the Computer

The computer equipment that you can see and touch, called the "hardware" in computer jargon, is capable of carrying out only quite primitive actions which change in some way the data stored in its memory. What allows the computer to carry out very complex sequences of actions is its capability to store sequences of instructions, each of which tells the computer to perform some primitive action. These stored sequences of instructions are called "programs", and they are stored in the computer's memory just as data is stored there. In this book we will give only slight attention to details of the primitive instructions that the hardware itself understands. Instead, we will be more concerned with the use of several large programs that have already been provided for your use. These large programs allow the computer hardware to appear to be capable of carrying out very complex and sophisticated instructions. However, even these large programs can be changed relatively easily, if you know how, and for that reason they have come to be known as "software". Most people who use computers don't have to concern themselves with the details of how the hardware works, and they are content to use the software provided by a few specialists who do need to be concerned with the hardware.

The software that you will use to work with this book is designed so that you may "converse" with the computer. As a first step to see what this means, someone who knows how to use this software should give you a brief demonstration of how to place the software "system" in operation. We will use the term "system" quite often to refer to the collection of large programs constituting the software provided for your use. In most cases, you will be using a computer that requires the software to be loaded into the computer's memory from some removable medium such as a floppy disk. The method you will need to use to initiate this loading process is different on almost every different model of computer. If no-one familiar with your computer is available, you will need the short manual of instructions for that computer to substitute for the demonstration.

When the software system first starts running, something resembling the following lines will appear on the display screen (or typewriter terminal) connected to the computer:

```
Command: E(dit), R(un), F(ile), C(ompile), X(ecute)

U.C.S.D. PASCAL SYSTEM II.3B
```

The second of these lines simply informs you that the system has started running on the computer, and is waiting for instructions on what to do. The first line, called the "Prompt Line", is displayed to inform you what part of the software is currently running ("Command:" in this case), and to inform you which instructions you can "command" the system to perform starting from this point. You send such a command to the system by pressing the key corresponding to the command's initial letter on the typewriter-like keyboard provided with the computer. For example, to cause a program called MYPROG to start executing (We'll be using the terms "execute" and "run" to mean the same thing for most purposes in this book.) you press the "X" key. The system will respond by displaying a message which asks you to type in the name of the program to be executed. After typing the name, you complete your response by pressing the RETurn key. If the indicated program is available in the disk library currently connected to the computer, that program will then be placed in execution, i.e. it will start running.

We'll explain more about each of the commands shown on the Command: prompt-line above a little later. The important point for you to understand here is that the computer has no intelligence of its own. You cause it to carry out some action by telling it to start running an appropriate program, or part of a program. In the conversational software system you

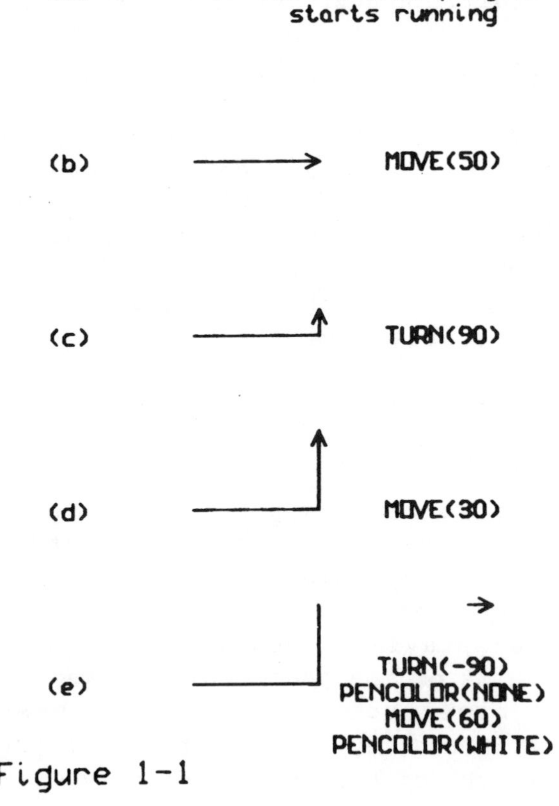
(a)
Turtle when program starts running
(b)
MOVE(50)
(c)
TURN(90)
(d)
MOVE(30)
(e)
TURN(-90)
PENCOLOR(NONE)
MOVE(60)
PENCOLOR(WHITE)

Figure 1-1

will be using, you do this by selecting one of several commands that have been programmed into the system. To tell the system which command you have selected, you press the keyboard key corresponding to the command you want to use.

3. Drawing Simple Pictures with Commands

If you are working with a computer capable of displaying line drawings, a program called TURTLE is available in the library provided with the software system. (If your computer cannot display line drawings, then study the printed text as given, then try working out the exercises using the sample program described in Section 11 of this chapter.) To start this program from the "Command:" level, press the "X" key (for eX(ecute), the "E" is reserved for E(dit)), then type in:

```
TURTLE
```

followed by pressing the RETurn key. The program will replace the "Command:" prompt line with its own, and it will display a marker resembling an arrow near the center of the display screen. An example of such a marker is shown in panel (a) of Figure 1-1. This marker is called the "Turtle" because it can be used in some of the same ways that one can use a computer controlled mechanical turtle built several years ago by a research group at Massachusetts Institute of Technology. On some display devices, it may be difficult for you to discern the direction in which the Turtle is pointing based on its appearance on the screen. In those cases, you should remember that the Turtle points horizontally toward the right side of the screen when the program first starts running.

The TURTLE program responds to commands designed to allow you to construct drawings on the screen using an appropriate sequence of those commands. The method you must employ to tell the program which command to use differs from the method described in the previous section, which applies at the "Command:" level and in other parts of the main software system. The system commands respond to pressing a single key on the keyboard. The TURTLE program requires that you spell out the entire command word. The program is designed in this way to provide you practice and insight that you will need very shortly for writing computer programs yourself using the PASCAL language. As an example, try the following command on your computer (after starting the TURTLE program with the "X" command):

```
MOVE(50)<RET>
```

where <RET> indicates that you should press the RETurn key. The result you should get is illustrated in panel (b) of Figure 1-1. In subsequent references to MOVE, and to other Turtle commands, we will omit the reminder about using <RET> to avoid cluttering the illustrations more than necessary.

If you make a typing error, the program will display a message indicating that it did not understand the command message that you sent to it by typing on the keyboard. The TURTLE program is forgiving in this respect, and you can try again without any harm being done. In fact, the system does not send the command message to the program until you press the <RET> key, and you can erase characters typed in error, starting with the last character typed, by using either the <Backspace> or <Rubout> key. The <Backspace> key will erase one character at a time. The <Rubout> key, sometimes marked as <DELete>, will erase the entire command.

The number 50 tells the TURTLE program how long the line to be displayed should be. The larger the number, the longer the line. The exact length of line you will obtain by using 50 will depend on characteristics of your display screen that vary from one brand of computer to another. A little experimentation should indicate whether you should increase or decrease the numbers suggested in this section in order to obtain lines of a size that seems reasonable to you. The TURTLE program requires that you place the number, indicating how long the line should be, inside matched parentheses.

At any location on the screen, you can command the Turtle to change its direction by using the TURN command, as in panel (c) of Figure 1-1. A subsequent MOVE will cause it to draw a line in the new direction, as in panel (d). The number used with the TURN command is measured in <u>degrees</u>, and gives the angle between the old direction and the new one going counterclockwise. If you wish to turn 45 degrees to the right, i.e. clockwise, then use TURN(-45). Either TURN(180) or TURN(-180) causes the Turtle to reverse direction completely. TURN(270) is equivalent to TURN(-90). There is no point in using numbers larger than 359, since TURN(360) causes the Turtle to rotate its direction one full circle, returning to the same direction from which it started. If you have forgotten, or never studied, the points of the compass, then let the Turtle itself teach you what to do by experimenting with TURN, giving it different numbers of degrees ranging from -180 to +180 degrees.

Two other Turtle commands will be of use to you in experimenting with this program. First, you can think of the mechanical turtle as having a ball point pen which draws on paper on the floor over which the turtle is commanded to move. On the display screen you are probably using, the turtle will draw a bright ("white") line on a black background. If you wish to move the turtle to a new location on the screen without drawing a line, use the command

```
PENCOLOR(NONE)
```

followed by appropriate MOVE and TURN commands. You can then cause subsequent Moves to draw lines again by using:

```
PENCOLOR(WHITE)
```

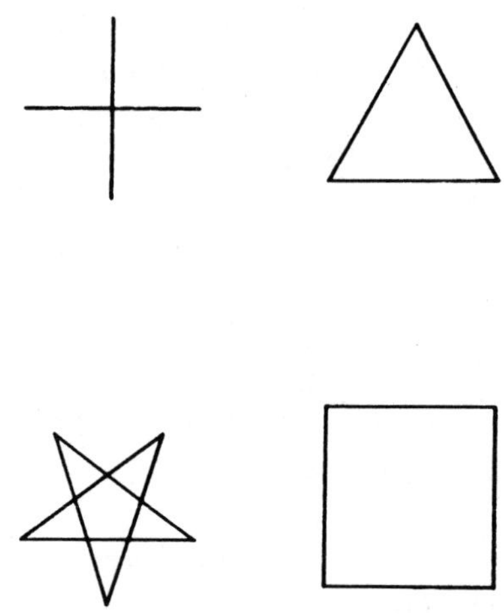

Figure 1-2.

(even if your screen draws green lines!). On some screens you will be able to erase points already drawn on the screen using:

```
PENCOLOR(BLACK)
```

The second additional command is simply:

```
CLEARSCREEN
```

which erases everything drawn since the program started, and allows you to begin again.

Exercise 1.1:

Refer to Figure 1-2. Use the TURTLE program and its associated commands to draw the shapes shown in the illustration. Don't be afraid to experiment with the Turtle until you get the desired effect.

4. A PASCAL Program Using the Turtle

Instead of using the Turtle commands in a conversational manner, as in the previous section, we can write and save a computer program which will execute a sequence of Turtle commands. A sample of such a program is reproduced below as "PROGRAM GRAPH1". There should be a copy of this program in the library of programs supplied to you with the software system. As a first step, try executing this program using the "X" command at the "Command:" level. When the "X" command requests a program name, type:

```
GRAPH1<RET>
```

The program should display one of the figures illustrated in Figure 1-2. You should have no trouble in associating the successive commands in the program with the figure that is displayed when the program runs.

```
 1: PROGRAM GRAPH1;
 2: BEGIN
 3:    MOVE(100);
 4:    TURN(120);
 5:    MOVE(100);
 6:    TURN(120);
 7:    MOVE(100);
 8:    READLN  (*prevents display from getting*)
 9:            (* wiped out until <RET> typed *)
10: END.
```

The first "command" executed by this program is the MOVE in line 3. Those in lines 4, 5, 6, 7, and 8, are then executed in that order. When used in a program, we call each command an "executable Statement". The READLN statement (Read a line) is used in this instance to cause the program to wait at line 8 until you press the <RET> key, signifying the end of a line. This is necessary to keep the figure displayed by this program on the screen until you are ready to terminate the program and to go back to the "Command:" level of the system. To avoid confusion on later commands, the system clears the screen automatically when each program terminates.

Notice that each statement in this program is separated from the next by a semicolon character ";". The semicolon has an effect similar to the effect you invoked by using the <RET> key when these statements appeared instead as commands sent to the TURTLE program.

The numbers appearing at the left of each line are not part of the program text. Rather, they are included in the program illustrations shown in this book to allow us a convenient means to refer to specific items in a program.

The notation between the symbols "(*" and "*)" on lines 8 and 9 in the GRAPH1 program is a "comment" which explains the purpose of a statement, but is not part of the executable program itself.

5. Modifying a Program with the Editor

Next, use the "E" for E(dit) command at the "Command:" level, which will start the Editor program supplied with the software system. The Editor will ask for the name of the "file" you wish to use. In response, enter "GRAPH1" followed, as usual, by <RET>. After a short delay for loading the text of the program GRAPH1 into the computer's memory, the Editor will display its own prompt line followed by as many lines of GRAPH1 as will fit on your display screen.

The Editor uses a place marker, called a "cursor", which is similar in some ways to the Turtle. There are commands which allow you to move the cursor to point to any character in the text of the program. In most cases, your keyboard has four directional arrow keys which point to the right, left, upwards, and downwards. If your keyboard does not have these keys, equivalent commands are available and described in a supplementary document associated with the model of computer you are using. To move the cursor down one line, press the arrow pointing downwards. To move one position to the right, press the arrow pointing to the right, and so on. If the cursor is in the bottom or top line currently displayed on the screen, use of the down or up arrow respectively will shift the portion of the text seen through the screen as a "window" in such a way as to keep the cursor on the screen.

On some keyboards, it is possible to make the cursor move rapidly over many lines or character positions by simply holding the appropriate arrow key down as long as necessary. (On some other keyboards, there is a special <Repeat> key which you hold down before pressing the key to be repeated.) If your keyboard lacks either of these features, you can cause any command to be repeated a specific number of times by typing a number followed by the command key.

Two other commands provide you with the means to modify any program, that is to "Edit" the PASCAL text of the program. After pressing "I", for I(nsert), you can type new lines into the program, or insert characters into the middle of existing lines. The characters to be inserted start immediately before the location of the cursor at the time the "I" command is entered. The portion of the program starting with the character pointed to by the cursor is moved on the screen to give you room into which more characters can be typed. When you have completed typing in the new information, you can leave the control of the I(nsert) command by holding down the <Control> key, and pressing the "C" key. This will cause the information typed in to be retained as part of the program text. If, after typing in many characters, you decide not to retain the result, you can return to the condition of the text as it was immediately before you entered I(nsert) by pressing the <ESCape> key.

The other principal command for modifying a program is "D" for D(elete). After you enter the D(elete) command, the normal cursor positioning commands are available. The portion of the text to be deleted lies between the cursor position at the time D(elete) is entered, and the position it reaches just before the command is terminated with <RETurn>. As you move the cursor under control of D(elete), the characters to be removed from the text are blanked out on the display. As with the I(nsert) command, you can use <ESCape> to terminate the D(elete) command in such a way as to return to the status that existed just before D(elete) was entered.

In either I(nsert) or D(elete) commands, you can back up one character at a time using the <Backspace> key, reversing the effect of your previous actions.

Exercise 1.2:

Use the Editor to modify the program GRAPH1 in such a way that it should draw a square, cross, star, or some other figure different from the one the program draws as shown.

6. Running the Modified Program

In order to Run (effectively execute) a program you have written or modified with the Editor, you must first return to the "Command:" level. To do this use the "Q", for Q(uit) command of the Editor. After a short delay, the "Command:" prompt line should reappear. Now press the "R", for R(un), key. After a short delay, the message "compiling..." should appear on the screen.

To understand what happens next, you need to know that the PASCAL program you modified with the Editor must be translated into a form the computer's hardware can understand. Part of the system software is a translator program called a "compiler" in computer jargon. Before your program can be run, it must be translated by the PASCAL Compiler into executable form. In executing the R(un) command, the system first checks to see whether you have just modified your program. If so, it calls for the Compiler to translate the PASCAL program into executable form. To keep you informed of what is happening, the Compiler displays messages showing the progress it is making. For a program as short as GRAPH1, the whole process of compiling should only consume two or three seconds. Most of that time is used in reading the compiler into the computer's memory from the disk library.

If the compiler finds no errors in your edited PASCAL program, the system will start executing your program as soon as the compiler completes its work. You will be notified that this is happening when the message "running..." appears on the screen. What happens after that will depend upon how the program is written.

Unfortunately one can easily make editing changes in a program that the Compiler cannot understand. We'll explain more about how you can determine whether your changes are correct starting in section 8. Although the compiler is a large and sophisticated program, it is not very smart and cannot recognize what you <u>intended</u> to do even if you make simple errors that any human would be able to overlook. When the Compiler finds an error, it cannot proceed further in the translation process until you fix that error. Instead, a message is displayed with an <u>approximate</u> description of the error that was found. In addition, the software system returns you automatically to the Editor, and displays the portion of the program text where the error was found, with the cursor pointing at the place where the error was found. When you progress to work with larger programs, you may prepare a program that contains several errors, requiring you to go through this sequence of E(dit)-R(un) followed by automatic return to the Editor several times. A method is provided for experienced users to allow the compiler to uncover all of the errors in a program in one use of the R(un) command.

<u>Exercise 1.3:</u>

> Modify the GRAPH1 program to produce a different displayed figure, as in Exercise 1.2, then R(un) the program to check your results. Repeat this process for several different figures.

7. Disk Library and Workfile

The software system provides a means to save, and later retrieve, programs on the magnetic disk device connected to your computer. (As an alternative to disk, you may be using a magnetic tape cassette or cartridge device.) The items stored in the disk library are called "files". When the Editor asks what file you wish to use, or when the "X" command asks for a program name, the response you give causes the named file to be retrieved from the disk library and loaded into the computer's memory.

When you modify a named file with the Editor, a temporary working copy is made of the program and kept in a special file on the disk called the "Workfile". If, when you start the Editor with the "E" command, there is already a Workfile on the disk, then the Editor will display the first part of the Workfile on the screen rather than asking for the name of the file you wish to use.

Now that you know about the Workfile, it is possible to understand the distinction between the R(un) and X(ecute) commands. R(un) is designed to work exclusively with the Workfile, and assumes that you want the program in the Workfile (if any) to be executed. If there is no Workfile on the disk when you use the R(un) command, an error message will be displayed. X(ecute) requires that you give the name of the program you want executed. X(ecute) assumes that the named program has already been successfully compiled, i.e. without errors, and then saved in the disk library under an appropriate descriptive name. A successfully compiled program kept in the Workfile can be executed multiple times using R(un) without requiring the compiler to be used each time.

In order to save a program in the Workfile under some name in the disk library, you must use the "F", for F(ile) command at the "Command:" level. After a short delay, the prompt-line for F(ile) commands will appear on the screen. You can then use the "S", for

S(ave), command which will ask you to respond with the name you want assigned to the program.

To get a list of the names of the files already saved in the disk library, use the L(ist) command at the "File:" level. Notice that most files have the suffix ".TEXT" or the suffix ".CODE". The ".TEXT" files are in the form that can be read or modified using the Editor. The ".CODE" files are the result of the Compiler's translation of the corresponding ".TEXT" file into the form that the hardware understands.

The "File:" level provides several other commands for working conveniently with the library of disk files. R(emove) allows a named file to be deleted from the disk library, thereby making space available for other uses. N(ew) creates a new Workfile with which you can start a new program using the Editor. G(et) replaces the current Workfile with a copy of a named file already in the library. C(hange) allows you to change the name of a library file to a new name. Most of these commands request you to respond by typing in file names when needed. If a command will have the effect of destroying the current workfile, you will be informed of that fact and asked whether you wish to continue or abandon the command. Respond with "Y", for Y(es), if you wish to continue. Any other response will be assumed to mean "No".

Exercise 1.4:

After checking to make sure that the program in your Workfile produces the desired results on the screen, as in Exercise 1.3, save that program in your disk library under a name you invent for it. After doing this, list the disk directory to verify that the desired result has been achieved. Now create a new Workfile, then edit and run a new small program. Having done this, return to the "File:" level, remove the new program from the disk, and verify that R(un) at the "Command:" level refuses to work.

8. Syntax Diagrams

Thus far, we have depended upon your being able to infer how an error free program should be written by reference to the sample program GRAPH1. Very soon you will know enough about writing PASCAL programs that inference from examples will no longer be sufficient. Even with only a few of PASCAL's programming tools, you will be able to create programs never written before quite easily. The number of possible error free programs is so great that a more precise method than the use of examples is needed to explain how a "legal" or "correct" program can be constructed. We will use "Syntax Diagrams" for this purpose.

English, and all natural languages, are described by rules of grammar telling how "correct" sentences can be constructed. The rules telling the order in which different classes of words (nouns, verbs, adjectives, adverbs, ...) may be used, as well as the rules of punctuation, are called "Syntax" rules. Similarly the rules that describe how you can write computer programs are called syntax rules. In English you can violate the syntax rules and still be understood. With a few exceptions, computers are not intelligent enough, nor flexible enough, to understand program statements that violate the syntax rules. We humans who wish to use computers have to learn to express our thoughts in ways that conform to the syntax rules of the programming languages we use.

An advantage of the PASCAL programming language, relative to some other languages, is that its syntax rules can be described in a clear and simple way using Syntax Diagrams. In this chapter, we'll start with a few examples which help to describe the sample programs. Some of these examples represent simplified versions of the complete Syntax Diagrams printed as the last appendix of this book.

In a PASCAL program, you can assign names to various cells in the computer's memory. While the computer keeps track of these cells merely by numbering them, it is much easier for humans to use a name for each cell which tells something about the purpose for which the cell is to be used. The names are an aid to memory, and to understanding how a program works. One of the main tasks of the compiler is to keep a dictionary of these names, and to translate each name into the number of its corresponding memory cell when it produces an executable ".CODE" file. These names are called "identifiers" in computer jargon. In words, the syntax rules state that an identifier may be constructed as follows:

1) Start with any letter "A" through "Z".
2) Follow the first letter with any sequence of letters (A..Z) and/or digits (0..9).

Here are some examples of character sequences that you could use as identifiers in a PASCAL program:

```
X
ABC
SHORT
BIGLONGIDENTIFIER
P27
L914PDK
```

Here are some examples of character sequences that would not be acceptable as identifiers, since they do not conform to the syntax rules:

```
3RD
(714)452-4050
UNIT-1
I 12.34
TWO WORDS
Lowercase
```

Figure 1-3 gives a statement, in the form of a diagram, of the syntax rules for forming identifiers. Something not stated in the diagram is that only the first 8 characters of an identifier are significant to the PASCAL compiler you will use. You can use identifiers longer than 8 characters, but only the first 8 characters will be used by the compiler to distinguish any identifier from any other. Thus the compiler will judge the following two identifiers to be identical, even though they look different to us:

```
TURBOINCABULATOR  TURBOINCINERATOR
```

In the rest of this book, we will often refer to an object described by the syntax rules using broken brackets, for example <identifier>. If you see a reference to some object written with broken brackets in this way, the brackets should be a clue to look for a description of the object in the syntax diagrams. Inside the boxes of a syntax diagram, we will generally omit the broken brackets, but will still use lower-case characters for items that are defined by other syntax diagrams. A word appearing in UPPER CASE letters in a syntax diagram is a "Reserved Word" having special significance to the compiler. A reserved word should appear in a program with the same spelling, and in the same relative position, as in the syntax diagram. Punctuation characters with special significance in the syntax appear within circles in the diagrams.

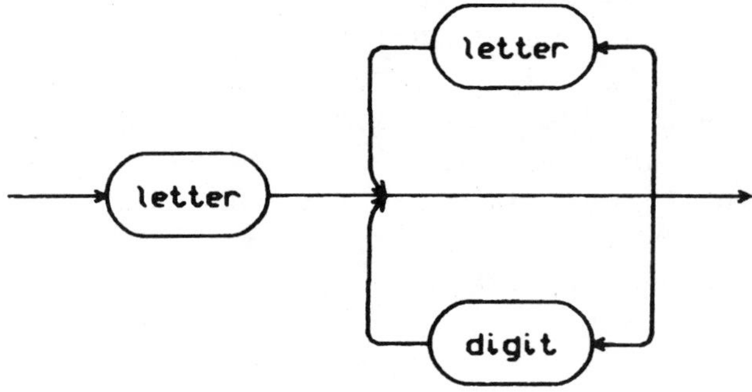

Fig. 1-3 Syntax Diagram for <identifier>

9. Syntax for <program> and <block>

Refer now to Figure 1-4, which shows simplified syntax for <program> and <block>. Compare the program example GRAPH1 with this diagram and satisfy yourself that you understand the relationship between the program and the diagram. (Once again: Notice that the line numbers printed with the sample programs in this book are not part of those programs, and not described by the syntax. They are used only to allow us an easy means to refer, within the written text, to specific items in a program.) Line numbers in the following discussion refer to program GRAPH1.

The diagram tells us that every program should start with a line:

```
PROGRAM <identifier> ;
```

as in Line 1. The <identifier> names the program to the compiler, and for future reference to the text of the program, but it does not automatically establish the name of the ".TEXT" file. You can assign any legal <identifier> as the name of a program.

The diagram tells us that a complete program consists of the PROGRAM line terminated by a semicolon (";"), and followed by a <block> which in turn is followed by a period ("."). The period is essential. As you will soon see, a program may contain END many times. The period notifies the compiler that the last END has been reached, and hence the end of the complete program.

To see what <block> means, you refer to part (b) of the diagram in Figure 1-4. This shows that a <block> starts with the reserved word BEGIN, and terminates with the reserved word END. Between these two reserved words, there may be any number of <statement>'s separated by semicolon characters.

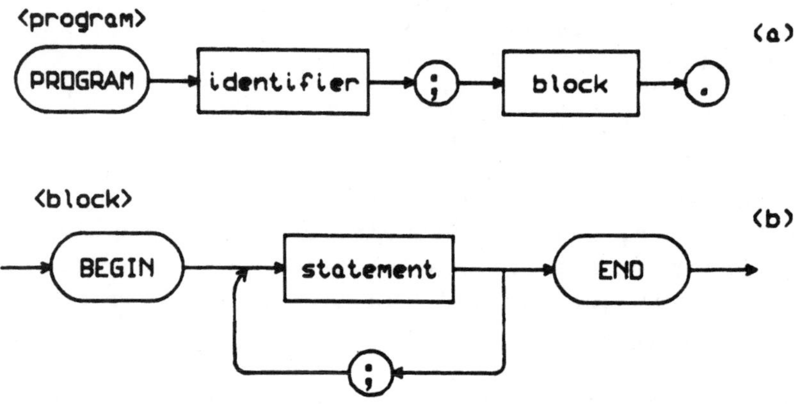
<program>
(a)
PROGRAM
identifier
;
block
.
<block>
(b)
BEGIN
statement
END
;

Figure 1-4.

<statement>

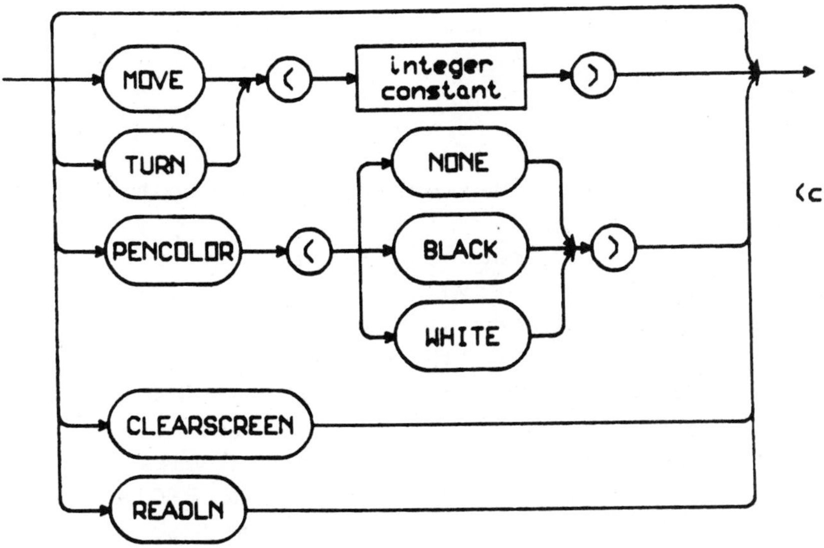

MOVE

TURN

(

integer constant

)

PENCOLOR

(

NONE

BLACK

WHITE

)

CLEARSCREEN

READLN

(c)

Part (c) of Figure 1-4 provides a simplified (and temporary) definition of <statement>. This shows that you can use any of the reserved words MOVE, TURN, PENCOLOR, CLEARSCREEN, or READLN as the basis of a <statement>, or that a <statement> can be completely "<u>empty</u>". The device of the empty statement appears to have been invented to make the semicolon optional just after the last <statement> before END at the end of a <block>. The rules of PASCAL would be a little easier to understand without this empty statement. The empty statement device makes it easier for programmers who know an older, but similar, language called ALGOL to write programs in PASCAL.

<u>Exercise 1.5:</u>

Try modifying some working version that you have made starting from the GRAPH1 program, by intentially introducing several specific syntax errors. Then observe what the compiler reports back on the error that it has found by using the R(un) command in the "Command:" level. For example, remove the left or right parenthesis in a MOVE or PENCOLOR statement; leave out the semicolon separating two statements; mis-spell one of the reserved words; leave out the BEGIN; leave out the period following END; and so on. You should notice that the error message displayed by the compiler does not always agree exactly with the reason you think it should have found for the error. There are thousands of ways in which syntax errors can be introduced into a program, and only room for about 300 error messages. The programmer who wrote the compiler was not able to predict all possible combinations of circumstances that might have led to a specific violation of the syntax rules that might be relevant to you.

10. The Debugger

When a programmer introduces an error into a program that makes the program produce the wrong results, we say that a "bug" has been introduced in computer jargon. The act of removing bugs from a program is called "debugging". Since there is no program capable of determining whether your program does what you intended it to do (in the manner that the compiler finds syntax errors and notifies you of them), you must determine whether a program works correctly in other ways. As you will soon see, the number of possible ways in which a program might run can be so great that you never will have enough time to check for correct operation of each way. Nevertheless, it is possible to check on the correct operation of small parts of a program separately, and then to treat those parts as building blocks to obtain a more complex result. If each building block works correctly, then the entire program should generally work correctly, assuming that the building blocks have been designed to work together correctly.

The software system you will use with this book includes a utility program called the "Debugger" for use in assisting you to check a program for correct operation, and in finding bugs. In this section we will be concerned only with one simple aspect of the Debugger. Other aspects will be introduced later.

When in the "Command:" level, you can run a program under control of the Debugger by using the "D", for D(ebug), command in place of R(un). Instead of "running...", the Debugger's prompt line will appear along with some additional information describing your program. You can now proceed to execute the program by using the "J", for J(ump), command of the Debugger. Each time J(ump) is used, one statement of the program will be executed. That statement will be displayed on the screen. In most cases, you will also be able to observe the computational action accomplished by the execution of the statement. It is often very helpful in understanding how a program works, to execute the program in this "single-step" mode.

For the simple example programs discussed in this chapter, you can probably follow the action of single step execution using handwritten notes containing the complete program. It is not possible to display the entire program on the screen while the Debugger is operating, since the space is needed for other information. When you progress to larger programs, it will often be desirable to have available a printed "listing" of the program you are working with. You can then make notes in the margin of the listing to help after going back to the Editor. In general, a printer suitable for obtaining such listings should be available to you in connection with the study of this book. The rules for using such printers vary greatly from one model of computer to another. For that reason, you will have to obtain directions from someone who knows how to use the printer locally available to you.

Exercise 1.6:

> Try your hand at using the Debugger by running one of the programs you have been working with using the D(ebug) command. Make sure that you can identify the action achieved after executing the statement displayed on the screen. (In most cases, both the previous and next statements are shown.)

11. Sample Program Using <string>'s

If your computer does not provide a way to display line drawings, the following sample program can be used to understand most of the points presented in this chapter. This program displays "strings" of characters in the manner one finds in normal English text. We will be working with both line drawings and strings of text throughout this book, since both are important in practical uses of computers. By working with both types of information, as well as with numbers starting with Chapter 5, you will have a more thorough understanding of computer problem solving than by using any one of those types alone.

```
1: PROGRAM STRING1;
2: BEGIN
3:   WRITE('HI');
4:   WRITE(' ','THERE');
5:   WRITELN; (*moves to start of next line*)
6:   WRITE('HI THERE');
7:   WRITELN(' THIS IS A DEMONSTRATION');
8:   WRITELN('OF PROGRAM EXECUTION')
9: END.
```

Simplified syntax for the WRITE and WRITELN statements used in this program may be found in Figure 1-5. These statements cause the data within parentheses to be presented as a message on your display screen. In combination, lines 3 and 4 have the same effect as line 6, i.e. they display:

```
HI THERE
```

on the screen. The reason for presenting them differently in this example is to show that successive messages sent to the screen by WRITE simply follow the previous messages already sent.

In every case where a message is sent (lines 3..8, except for line 5), the data consists of one or more <string constant>'s. Syntax for <string constant> is also shown in Figure 1-5. A <string constant> consists of any sequence of displayable characters presented between a single quote character (') on the left, and one on the right. These quote characters are said to "*delimit*" the <string constant> and are known as "*delimiters*". Note that the quote characters themselves are not displayed by WRITE or WRITELN, and they are not considered to be part of the data enclosed within the <string constant>.

<write statement>

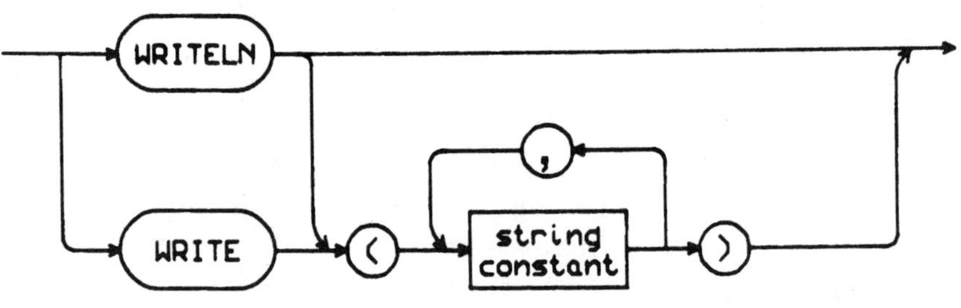

<string constant>

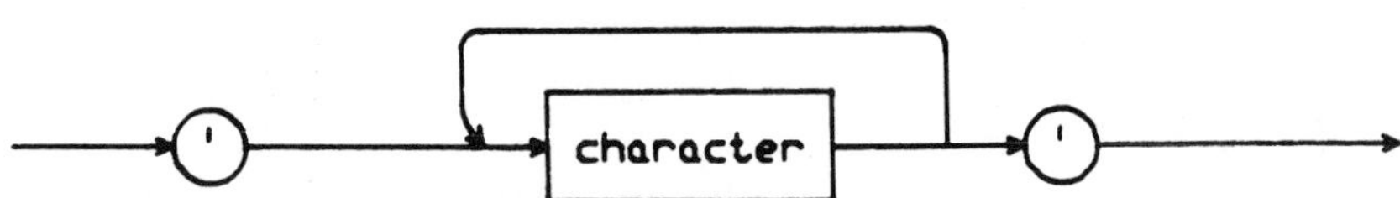

Fig. 1-5 Simplified syntax for WRITE and WRITELN

Note also that the <string constant> ' ' encloses a single blank character. If you want a blank character to be displayed, then you must tell the computer to do so.

Before reading on, consider how you might arrange to display a message containing a single quote, i.e. an apostrophe symbol (').

The WRITELN statement is similar to WRITE, except that following a WRITELN statement the next WRITE will commence placing characters at the beginning of the next line below. Thus the sample program STRING1 should display the following complete message:

```
HI THERE
HI THERE THIS IS A DEMONSTRATION
OF PROGRAM EXECUTION
```

The answer to the puzzle about displaying a single quote character is that you use <u>two</u> quotes in succession for every <u>one</u> quote that you want displayed. For example WRITE('''') will display a single quote symbol. The middle two quotes stand for the character to be displayed. The first and last are delimiters as usual.

<u>Exercise 1.7:</u>

Modify and run the STRING1 program to make it display the following:

```
HI THERE FRIENDS
THIS IS A DEMONSTRATION
OF 'PASCAL' PROGRAM EXECUTION
```

Chapter 2

PROCEDURES AND VARIABLES

1. Goals

In this chapter you will learn how to subdivide a program into primitive action units called "procedures", and to give names to computer memory locations where data can be stored under names that you designate, called "variables".

1a. Declare and use procedures which draw simple figures such as triangles, squares, stars, etc. Draw complex figures by calling these procedures several times.

1b. Use parameters to control the size of the figures drawn by your procedures, and to control where on the screen those figures are drawn.

1c. Declare and use variables of type CHAR, INTEGER, and STRING to save and later re-use various items of data.

1d. Learn to use the built-in procedures and functions designed to make computational changes on character strings.

1e. Use simple arithmetic expressions to compute new integer values by combining integer variables and constants.

1f. Develop familiarity with the syntax rules of PASCAL by locating errors in several program examples.

2. Background

You have already seen enough about programming to realize that writing a program to draw a complex figure could become quite tedious. PASCAL has facilities, as do most programming languages, which allow breaking a program up into small manageable units, and for repeating the same actions over and over where appropriate. This chapter and the next introduce the main features of PASCAL for this purpose.

To see the need for breaking a program up into small manageable chunks, try to remember the following two strings of 10 characters each:

```
BIGTENTEAM                         YCSHWMCDTE
```

Flip over this page after concentrating on these strings for just a moment, and then see how long you can remember each one. Chances are pretty strong that you had little trouble remembering the first string. Unless you are a wizard with photographic memory, you probably would have to expend some real effort to memorize the second string.

If you study psychology, you will no doubt learn of explanations for this difference involving short versus long term memory, and involving the number of independent items we can relate in memory directly to another item. A simple explanation of this is as follows: Because of the way you have learned to read, you automatically break up the first string into three familiar smaller strings on a second level.

```
     BIGTENTEAM
    /    ¦    \
 BIG    TEN  TEAM
```

Each of the smaller second level strings is a familiar word to you. With the other string there are really no familiar sub-strings to use as an aid to memory. Of course we could break it up:

```
          YCSHWMCDTE
         /     ¦     \
      YCS    HWMC   DTE
```

But these new short groupings of letters are not very helpful in remembering the whole string, because none of the short groupings has any meaning for us.

The point of all this is that a program should be broken up into small groups of statements (sometimes called "modules" or "sub-routines"), each of which can be thought of as performing a single action. Inside such a group, several statements must be performed in order to cause the required action to take place. However, once the group has been written, you can think of it as one unit and forget the fact that it really consists of several independent statements. When you write a program containing more lines than will fit easily on one page, say 25 to 50 lines, it gets too complicated to think of as a simple unit. Then it is time to think of breaking the program up into separate modules.

3. Procedures

A "procedure" is really a small program that appears inside another program. Consider the four squares displayed in Figure 2-1. Before proceeding, imagine how you would construct a program to plot these four squares using the methods introduced in Chapter 1. It should occur to you that the statements you write get pretty repetitious after the first square is completed and you are working on the second or third.

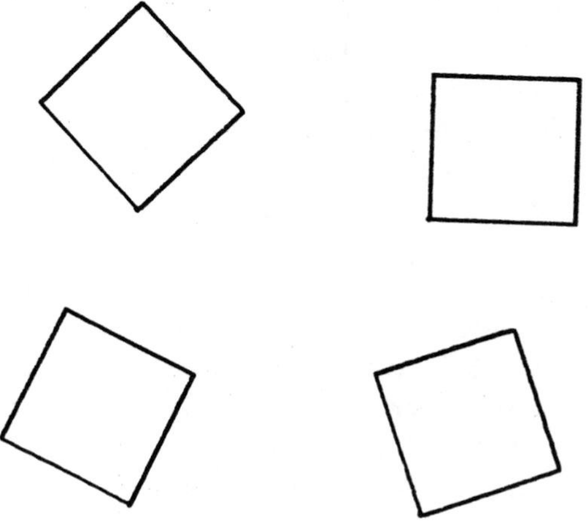

Figure 2-1

Now refer to the sample program SQUARES which performs the same action. In fact this program was used to plot Figure 2-1. Lines 3 through 15 constitute the procedure ONESQUARE. As you can see, if those lines were to be used as the basis of a complete program, with the word PROCEDURE changed to PROGRAM, that program would plot one square on the screen. (If you don't yet see why a square should be plotted, it may be time to run a small experiment to observe what happens.)

Now refer to lines 17 through 31, which constitute the main program SQUARES. In line 20, the turtle is moved to a point 150 screen units to the right, and 150 screen units upward from center screen. MOVETO is similar to MOVE, in that it moves the turtle to a new point on the screen. MOVETO must be given two numbers, the first measuring how far to the right of center screen the turtle should be moved, the second how far above center it should move. If the first number is negative, as in line 22, then the turtle moves to the left, i.e. the reverse of going to the right. If the second number is negative, as in line 28, then the turtle moves downward below center screen, i.e. the reverse of upward. Whereas MOVE causes the turtle to move the indicated number of screen units starting from its present position, MOVETO causes it to move to a position measured starting from the center of the screen. (If this explanation isn't clear to you, take the time to experiment with MOVETO using the TURTLE program as in Chapter 1, Section 3.)

Having moved the Turtle to the upper right portion of the screen in line 20, we now "<u>call</u>" the procedure ONESQUARE in line 21. Line 21 instructs the computer to transfer the order of processing to line 5, which is the first "<u>executable</u>" statement of the procedure. By "executable", we mean that it is the first line where some action is called for directly. Processing continues through line 14, i.e. until the END is reached in line 15. The statements in lines 5 through 14 cause the square to be plotted in the

```
PROGRAM SQUARES;
PROCEDURE ONESQUARE;
BEGIN
  PENCOLOR(WHITE);
  MOVE(150);
  TURN(90);
  MOVE(150);
  TURN(90);
  MOVE(150);
  TURN(90);
  MOVE(150);
  TURN(90);
  PENCOLOR(NONE);
END (*ONESQUARE*);
BEGIN (*MAIN PROGRAM*)
(*NOTE:MOVE VALUES APPLY TO TEKTRONIX 4006*)
(*  CHANGE FOR OTHER TERMINALS             *)
  MOVETO(150,150);
  ONESQUARE;
  MOVETO(-150,150);
  TURN(45);
  ONESQUARE;
  MOVETO(-150,-150);
  TURN(20);
  ONESQUARE;
  MOVETO(150,-150);
  TURN(-45);
  ONESQUARE;
END.
```

upper right portion of the screen, as shown in Figure 2-1.

Having reached line 15, the procedure ONESQUARE terminates, just as it would have done had it been a complete program. In this case, however, the control of processing returns to the point immediately following the point where ONESQUARE was called, i.e. to line 22. Line 21 instructs the computer to process the procedure until it finishes. Having finished, processing continues to the next statement as usual.

Upon reaching line 22, the turtle is moved to the upper left portion of the screen. In line 23 it is turned 45 degrees to the left in preparation for whatever follows. What follows is another call to ONESQUARE which causes yet another square to be plotted. Line 24 once again transfers the control of processing to line 5, as before. This time, when the procedure terminates, processing continues at the point following line 24, since that was the point where the procedure was called on this occasion.

Notice that we have now gone through the statements contained in the procedure ONESQUARE twice so far in processing the program. In fact the complete program does so a total of four times, once for each square plotted in Figure 2-1. Notice also that the procedure appears in the PASCAL program <u>before</u> the main part of the program appears. It may be helpful for you to know that the compiler translates your PASCAL program into the language of the machine by reading in the same order that we humans read, i.e. starting at the top and then working on each successive line. However, the program begins processing after the BEGIN line corresponding to the main program's <block>, i.e. line 17 in this sample program. When the compiler reaches line 21, it is necessary for it to know all about the procedure ONESQUARE so that arrangements can be made for processing to continue in the procedure. This is one reason why, in PASCAL, a procedure appears earlier in the program than does the main program itself. We say that the procedure is "declared" in lines 3 through 15. This means that we describe in advance the actions that the procedure will perform when, and if, it is called from the main program.

This is the first point where it is important for you to understand the distinction between the stage when a program is compiled, and the later stage when it is processed (i.e. "run" or "executed"). Remember that the compiler must first translate the PASCAL statements into a form the computer itself can understand. The compiler has its own requirements for keeping track of the various parts of the program, and this accounts for some of the rules on the order in which those parts are written into the program. After the program has been successfully compiled, it can then be executed. The order of execution is not exactly the same as the order in which the statements appear when procedures are used. In the next chapter we will see several other ways for altering the order of execution.

In summing up the content of this section, you have seen that a procedure can be used to accomplish two objectives. First, it can be used to isolate, from the main program, the steps needed to perform some primitive action (plotting one square in the sample program). You can concentrate on how those steps fit together while considering the procedure itself, then ignore those details while working on the main program. While working on the main program, it is sufficient to remember what the procedure does in a rough conceptual way. It helps considerably to give the procedure an <identifier> as its name which serves directly as a reminder about what the procedure is supposed to do when called.

As a second objective, a procedure can be used to reduce the amount of writing you have to do. In the sample program SQUARES, writing down the steps needed to plot a square just once was sufficient to plot a square on four different occasions, each time by simply naming the procedure in a one line statement.

4. Calling One Procedure from Another

Quite often it is helpful to be able to call one procedure from within another. The main thing to remember in this case is that the name of the procedure you call must already be known to the compiler at the point where the call occurs. The sample program PROCDEMO should help you to see how this works. Here is what this program displays:

```
START MAIN PROGRAM
PROC-P
BACK FROM P
START PROC-Q
PROC-P
STOP PROC-Q
STOP MAIN PROGRAM
```

The main point of this program is to illustrate the order of processing when one procedure calls another, as compared with calling the latter procedure from the main program as before. The WRITELN statements in this program provide a means of "tracing" the order of execution. If you are in doubt about the order in which a program of yours is executing, it would be a good idea to add WRITELN statements which display brief messages to tell you where the program is at strategic points. When the program has been fully debugged, you can take out these trace statements to obtain the desired final result.

Notice that the call to P in the second line of the main program works in the same manner as the calls to the procedure ONESQUARE in the previous section. This accounts for the first line displayed with the legend "PROC-P". Following this, the procedure Q is called, and it displays the line saying that it has started. Next, P is called again in line 11, this time from within the procedure Q. Once again P processes its only executable line, and the legend

```
PROGRAM PROCDEMO;

PROCEDURE P;
BEGIN
  WRITELN('PROC-P');
END (*P*);

PROCEDURE Q;
BEGIN
  WRITELN('START PROC-Q');
  P;
  WRITELN('STOP PROC-Q')
END (*Q*);

BEGIN (*MAIN PROGRAM*)
  WRITELN('START MAIN PROGRAM');
  P;
  WRITELN('BACK FROM P');
  Q;
  WRITELN('STOP MAIN PROGRAM');
END.
```

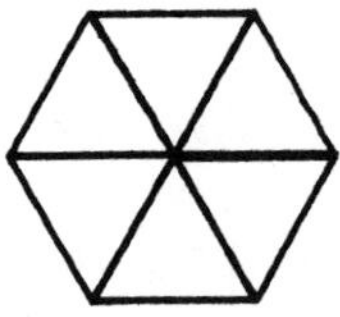

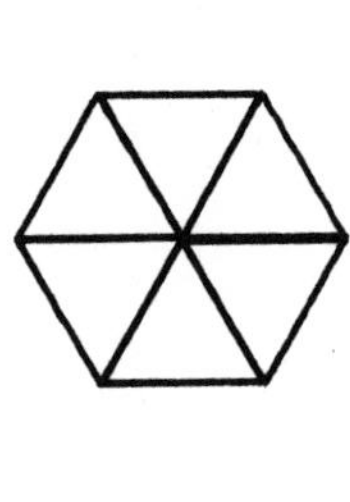

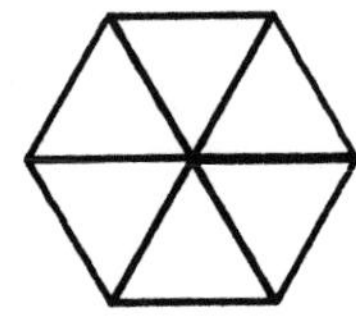

Figure 2-2

"PROC-P" appears again. This time, when P terminates, control returns to line 12, the line immediately following the line where P was called on this occasion. The next statement executed is in line 12, announcing that the procedure Q is going away. Finally, Q terminates leaving only one more statement, line 20, to be processed in the main program.

An important point to note is that the order of appearance of the procedures P and Q could not be reversed in PROCDEMO without some other change being made. If they were reversed, then the call to P which appears inside Q would occur before the compiler would have seen the declaration of "P" as the name of another procedure. This would leave the compiler confused, and a syntax error message would appear notifying you that the identifier "P" is undeclared.

Exercise 2.1:

Refer to Figure 2-2. Write and test a program which displays this figure. Hint: First write a procedure TRIANGLE which plots one of the six triangles in each of the three hexagonal figures. Now write a second procedure HEXAGON which plots one of those figures by calling TRIANGLE six times. Between calls to TRIANGLE it will be necessary to turn the turtle 60 degrees each time. Before completing the program, it would be very desirable to make sure that the procedure HEXAGON works as planned! Now you can plot the three hexagons by writing the rest of the main program, moving the turtle to a different part of the screen before each call to HEXAGON.

5. Parameters

By now, it might have occurred to you that the figures we have been plotting would be more interesting were it possible to tell a procedure how big we want it to make the primitive figure that is to be plotted. This can be done with something called a "parameter" as illustrated in the sample program GRAFPROCS. There are in fact two kinds of parameters, but this is a complication we can put off until Chapter 4. GRAFPROCS displays the figures illustrated in Figure 2-3.

As a first step to understand this program, concentrate on the procedure SQUARE, from line 14 through line 26, which is very similar to the procedure ONESQUARE used previously in the program SQUARES. The difference in this case is that the length of the sides of the square, specified in each MOVE statement (lines 17,19,21,23), is given by the identifier SIZE rather than by a number. SIZE refers to a location in the computer's memory where a numeric value has been previously stored.

To understand how the numeric value gets stored in SIZE, notice that SIZE is also mentioned in the first line of the procedure, line 14. The appearance of the notation "SIZE:INTEGER" within parentheses notifies the compiler that the <identifier> SIZE will be used as a parameter. The notation ":INTEGER" tells the compiler to mark that parameter as being capable of storing a value of "type" INTEGER. This means that the value can be a whole number (no fractions or decimal point). On the small microcomputer you may be using, an integer value can be any whole number between -32767 and +32767, including -1, 0, 1, 2, 3, ... and so on. On larger machines, the largest and smallest allowable integer values may include more digits.

```
PROGRAM GRAFPROCS;

PROCEDURE TRIANGLE(SIZE:INTEGER);
BEGIN
  PENCOLOR(WHITE);
  MOVE(SIZE);
  TURN(120);
  MOVE(SIZE);
  TURN(120);
  MOVE(SIZE);
  TURN(120);
  PENCOLOR(NONE);
END (*TRIANGLE*);
PROCEDURE SQUARE(SIZE:INTEGER);
BEGIN
  PENCOLOR(WHITE);
  MOVE(SIZE);
  TURN(90);
  MOVE(SIZE);
  TURN(90);
  MOVE(SIZE);
  TURN(90);
  MOVE(SIZE);
  TURN(90);
  PENCOLOR(NONE);
END (*SQUARE*);
BEGIN (*MAIN PROGRAM*)
(*NOTE:Parameters apply to Tektronix 4006    *)
(* terminal.  Change for others if necessary *)
  MOVETO(200,200);
  TRIANGLE(100);
  TURN(120);
  TRIANGLE(150);
  TURN(120);
  TRIANGLE(50);
  MOVETO(-250,-250);
  TURNTO(0);
  SQUARE(200);
  MOVETO(150,-200);
  TURN(30);
  SQUARE(120);
END.
```

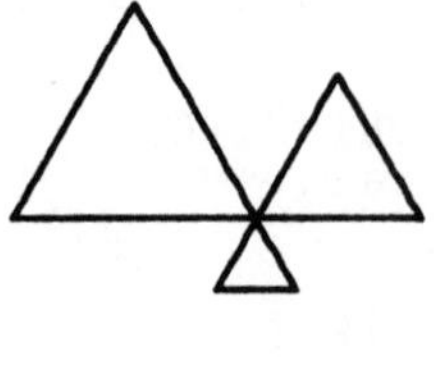

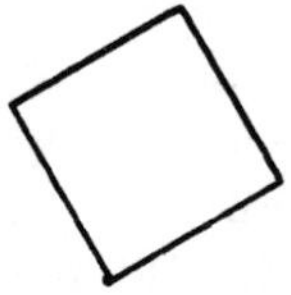

Figure 2-3

Now refer to line 38 where the procedure SQUARE is first called from the main program. The "integer constant", i.e. whole number, 200 tells the compiler to arrange the program so that SIZE will be set to the value 200 when SQUARE starts executing. This value will be used in place of SIZE in each of the four MOVE statements within the procedure.

Next, notice that the call to SQUARE in line 41 uses a different value, namely 120. This time, when the procedure is executed, that value will be used in place of SIZE in each of the MOVE statements within the procedure. This accounts for the difference in size of the two squares plotted in Figure 2-3. Similarly, a parameter, also called SIZE, is used in the procedure TRIANGLE. TRIANGLE is called three times, each time using a different value for the parameter. Notice that the three triangles plotted in the figure are of three different sizes.

Since we use the term "parameter" both when a procedure is declared, as in lines 3 and 14 of GRAFPROCS, and when it is called, as in lines 31 and 38, it is helpful to have terminology to distinguish these two uses. In lines 3 and 14, SIZE is referred to as a "formal parameter", implying that the identifier will be used in place of the value it represents. In lines 31 and 38 (also 33,35 and 41), the values "passed" to the procedure for its use are called "actual parameters", implying that the formal parameter should actually be set to the value given during execution of the procedure.

6. Syntax for Procedures

Figure 2-4 shows revised syntax for <block>, incorporating what we have done so far with procedures. The reference to <type identifier> in <parameter list> is expanded in Figure 2-5. We will define the meanings of type STRING and type CHAR in the next few sections.

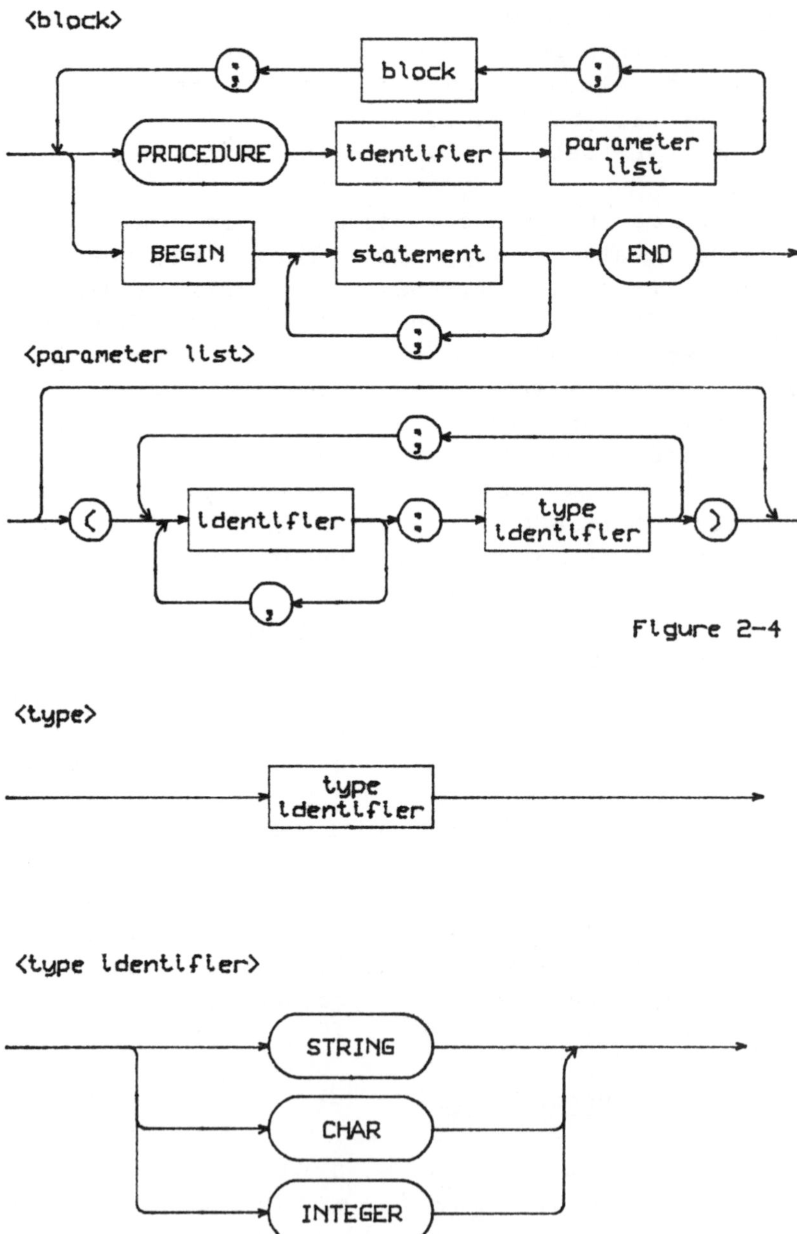

Figure 2-4

Figure 2-5

Notice that the syntax for <block> requires that all procedures be declared before the BEGIN ... END part constituting the main body of the <block>. Notice also that the reference to <block> as part of a procedure declaration means that it is possible to declare a procedure inside another procedure. We will have more to say about this issue in Chapter 4.

Within a <parameter list>, the syntax shows that several identifiers of the same <type> can be listed together, separated by commas (","). Each identifier is the name of a parameter. We could also have parameters of several different <type>'s declared in the same procedure "heading" line. We'll expand on this idea after describing the use of STRING and CHAR types in later sections. Notice also that the syntax allows an "empty" parameter list, lacking even the enclosing parentheses. This covers the case of the procedure we used in the sample program SQUARES, where no parameters are used.

Exercise 2.2:

Test your ability to draw general conclusions from the syntax diagrams by revising your program from Exercise 2.1 in the following ways: Design the program to draw each of the hexagon figures with a different value for the length of the side of each triangle. Instead of moving the turtle to the starting position of each hexagon using MOVE or MOVETO statements in the main program, declare and use two additional parameters with the HEXAGON procedure to define where on the screen the hexagon should be plotted. The associated MOVE or MOVETO statements should now be placed inside the procedure rather than in the main program. The two parameters, which define the starting position, could be either a radial distance from center screen and an angle, or they could be the horizontal and vertical distances from center screen. The result of these changes should be a shorter program than the one you wrote in Exercise

2.1, since repeated setting of the starting position is now handled using the parameters.

7. Variables

A "variable" is a name given to a location in the computer's memory where a data value (or in some cases a group of associated data values) may be stored for later use. A variable must be declared to have some data <type> associated with it. In these respects, a variable is similar in concept to a parameter. A variable differs from a parameter in that there is no automatic assignment of value to a variable when a procedure is called. Each location referred to by a simple variable, such as those we use in this section, has room to store only one value at a time. You can think of a variable as similar to a post office box which is only big enough to store one letter at a time.

For a simple illustration of the use of a variable, see sample program STARS, which displays the drawing in Figure 2-6. In this program, the variable SCALE is declared in line 2 to be of type INTEGER. As with a parameter of type INTEGER, this means that SCALE can be used to store a whole number whose value ranges from -32767 to +32767 if you have a microcomputer (or a wider range on larger machines).

In STARS, the variable SCALE is "assigned" a value of 30 in line 24. The symbol (":=") indicates that the value of whatever appears on the right of that symbol should be assigned to the variable appearing on the left. Line 24 is an example of an "assignment statement". Thereafter, unless a new value is assigned later, the identifier SCALE will have the value 30 wherever it appears, as in lines 28, 29, 33, 34, 38 and 39. If a new value had been assigned later, that value would have replaced the original value of 30, since the variable has room for only one value at a time. Each time an assignment statement is executed, the value it assigns to the

```
PROGRAM STARS;
VAR SCALE:INTEGER;

PROCEDURE STAR(SIZE:INTEGER);
BEGIN
  TURN(-18);  (*BALANCE THE STAR ON BRANCH*)
  PENCOLOR(WHITE);
  MOVE(SIZE);
  TURN(144);
  MOVE(SIZE);
  TURN(144);
  MOVE(SIZE);
  TURN(144);
  MOVE(SIZE);
  TURN(144);
  MOVE(SIZE);
  TURN(144);
  PENCOLOR(NONE);
  TURN(18);
  (*RESTORE TURTLE TO ORIGINAL DIRECTION*)
END (*STAR*);

BEGIN (*MAIN PROGRAM*)
  SCALE:=30;  (* 30 FOR TEKTRONIX 4006,*)
     (* USE 10 FOR TERAK, ?? FOR OTHERS*)
  PENCOLOR(WHITE);
  TURN(45);
  MOVE(SCALE*8);
  STAR(SCALE*4);
  MOVETO(0,0);
  TURNTO(165);
  PENCOLOR(WHITE);
  MOVE(SCALE*4);
  STAR(SCALE*8);
  MOVETO(0,0);
  TURN(150);
  PENCOLOR(WHITE);
  MOVE(SCALE*6);
  STAR(SCALE*6);
END.
```

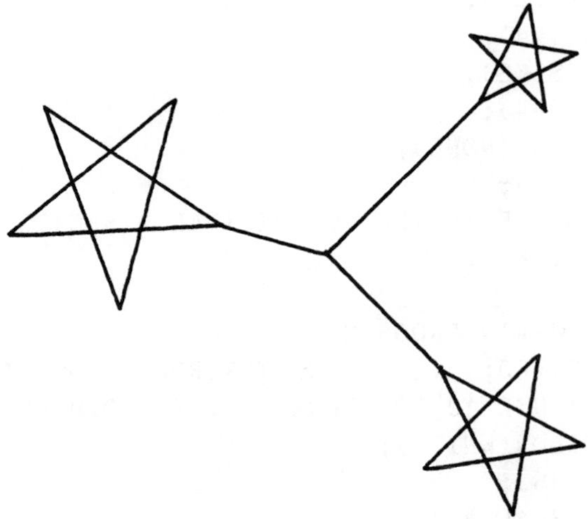

Figure 2-6

variable on the left replaces the value previously stored in that variable, and the old value is lost for any further use.

In this case, SCALE is used to specify how many screen display units there should be along each line drawn by the program. The value of 30 used in the program as printed in this book is appropriate for displaying figures on the Tektronix 4006 graphic terminal. If you are using a different display device, then a different value of SCALE may well apply. For example, on the Terak model 8510A microcomputer, the appropriate value would be 10 instead of 30 to give a figure of the same size as seen on the Tektronix device. The difference arises because the number of dots per centimeter (or per inch) used to simulate a line, as in figure 0-1, varies from one display device to another.

If the value of SCALE were of interest by itself, then it might appear alone as an actual parameter, or in other contexts. In the sample program STARS, we use SCALE to change the value of an "<u>integer constant</u>" (i.e. a whole number given explicitly) in order to control the line length specified by that number. For example, in line 28, the MOVE is expected to cover 30 times 8, i.e. 240, screen units. The "asterisk" character ("*") indicates that SCALE should be multiplied by 8. This is an example of an "<u>arithmetic expression</u>", a topic that we will expand on later in this chapter.

8. Syntax for Variables

As a first step to understand the syntax of variables, refer to Figure 2-7 showing expanded syntax for <block>. This shows that a block may begin with a sequence of variable declarations introduced by the reserved identifier "VAR", which occurs just once. All of the variables in a block must be declared before the first procedure within that block is declared. As in a parameter list, you

<block>

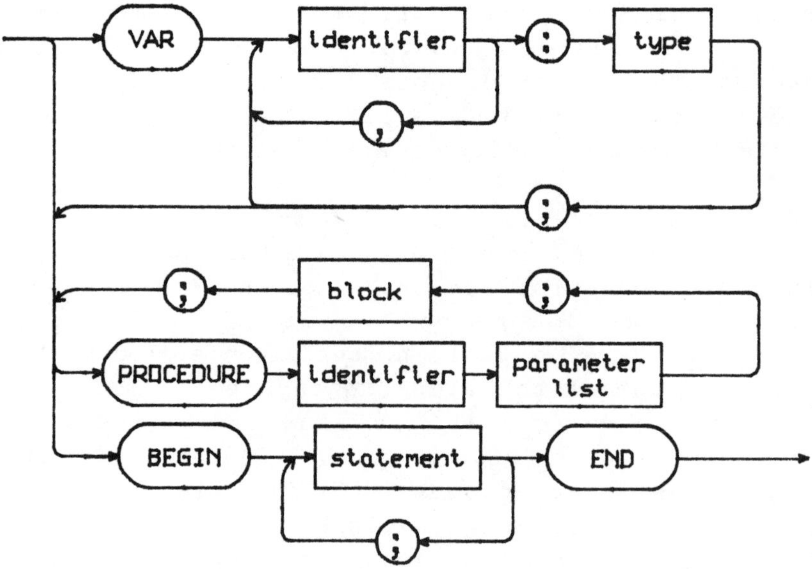

VAR
identifier
:
type
,
;
;
block
;
PROCEDURE
identifier
parameter list
BEGIN
statement
END
;

Figure 2-7

can declare that all identifiers in a list separated by commas are to be associated with a single <type>.

If you declare a variable following VAR inside a <block> which is part of a procedure declaration, that variable is said to be "local" to that block, and it cannot be referred to from the main program or from any other procedure. We will discuss this issue in detail in Chapter 4. A variable declared in the <block> of the main program is said to be "global", and it can be referred to from either the main program or from almost any procedure. The one case where a global variable cannot be used inside a procedure occurs when a variable of the same name is also declared to be local in that procedure.

Figure 2-8 shows syntax for the <assignment statement> in general form. What the diagram does not explicitly say is that the entity on the right side of the "assignment operator" (":=") must be of the same type as the variable on the left. This restriction will be relaxed slightly in Chapter 5 when we begin dealing with numbers of two different types. Temporarily, you should assume that each item in the syntax of <assignment statement> should be prefixed by "integer". We will comment on the syntax of <expression> in the following sections.

9. Working with STRING variables

Thus far, our work with strings of characters has been confined to writing out <string constant> values as described in Chapter 1. Now, having introduced the concept of a <variable> we can begin working with variables which store whole strings, and variables intended to store only a single character each. Before showing how you can use strings for some interesting computations, it is necessary to set the stage by showing the relationship between variables of type CHAR and type STRING. The sample program POINT provides an example from which we can begin. This program should display the following lines:

<assignment statement>

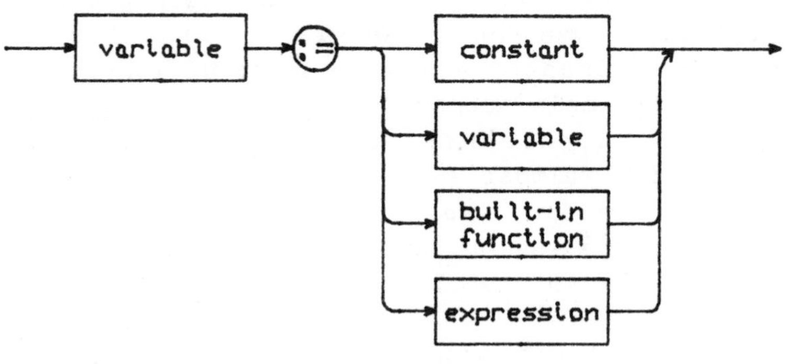

<constant>

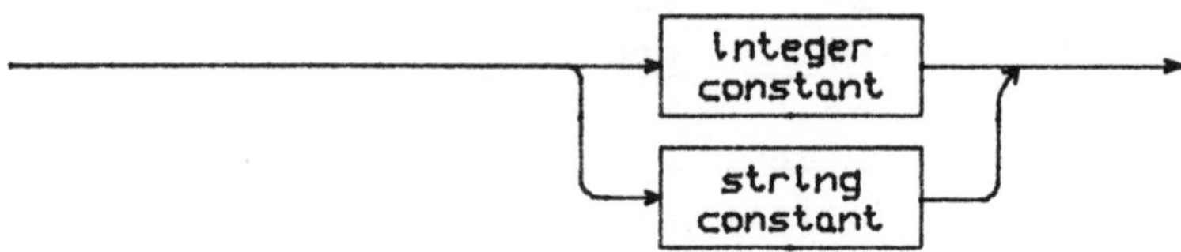

<integer constant>

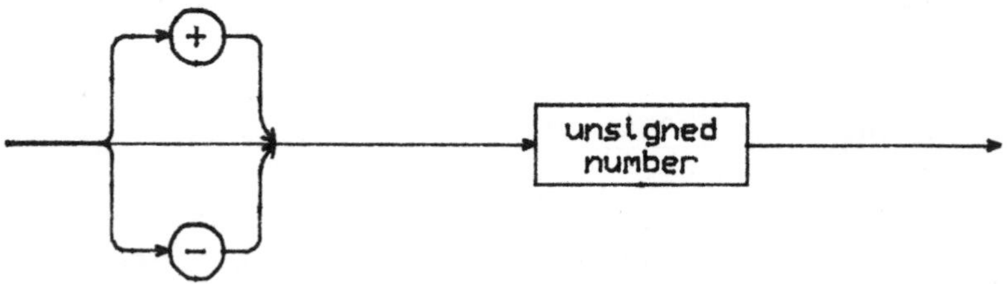

Figure 2-8

```
PROGRAM POINT;
(*pointing to specific characters in a string*)
VAR S:STRING;
   CH:CHAR;
    I:INTEGER;
BEGIN
  S:='EVEN IF HE SAW ME';
  WRITELN(S); (*trace*)
  CH:=S[7]; (*7th character of S*)
  WRITELN(CH);
  I:=12;
  WRITELN(S[I],S[12]);
      (*they'd better be the same!*)
  CH:='X';
  S[4]:=CH;
  WRITELN(S); (*trace following the change*)
  CH:=S[I-3];
  WRITELN('S[', I-3, ']=', CH);
END.
```

```
EVEN IF HE SAW ME
F
SS
EVEX IF HE SAW ME
S[9]=H
```

The variable CH may hold a value which is any single character that can be displayed. (A variable of type CHAR can also hold a character that cannot be displayed. Unless you are very brave or very smart, we suggest avoiding this issue until much later.) In line 14, the variable CH is assigned the value 'X', i.e. the single letter "X". The constant on the right side of line 14 is a single character string constant. CH must be assigned a value of <type> CHAR.

The STRING variable S is assigned the value of a <string constant> in line 7. A STRING variable may hold a value that varies from zero to 80 characters long. Means are available to alter the "<u>default</u>", i.e. assumed, value of the maximum number of characters in a string variable to some other value. More of that later.

Each character stored in a STRING variable is in fact itself a variable of <type> CHAR. This allows us to refer to a specific character in the variable S as in line 9. The number which selects the desired character within the STRING variable follows the identifier of that variable, and is placed within square brackets. The first character stored in a STRING variable is number 1, i.e. the value stored in S[1] is 'E' in the example. Thus "S[7]" refers to the seventh character in S. The quantity within the brackets needs only to have a value of <type> INTEGER. It does not need to be an integer valued constant such as "7". In line 11, we assign the value 12 to the INTEGER variable I. Then in line 12 we show that S[I] and S[12] refer to the same character in S, since the value of I remains equal to 12 in that line.

As with other variables, one can either use a character value stored in a specific location in a STRING variable, or one can assign a new value to that location. In line 15, the value currently stored in CH is assigned to location 4 in S. The WRITELN statement, used as a trace in line 16, shows that the fourth character has thus been changed to 'X' by that action.

In lines 17 and 18, we illustrate the use of an <arithmetic expression>, in this case "I-3". The effect here is that the value 3 is subtracted from the value of I, yielding 9 in this instance, and the resulting integer value is then used. In line 17, this value points to location 9 in the STRING variable S. In line 18, the value of the expression is printed out. Notice that two quoted <string constant>'s are used to make the displayed line appear to be a reference to "S[9]=".

10. Preliminaries on Arithmetic Expressions

In this chapter and the next two we will have occasion to make use of simple <arithmetic expression>'s several times. Since arithmetic expressions provide a means for manipulating numbers on the computer, we wish to defer detailed consideration of this subject until Chapter 5. The preliminary discussion given in this section should be sufficient for you to understand how to use simple arithmetic expressions for problem examples occurring before Chapter 5.

Simplified syntax for <arithmetic expression> and its associated constructs appears in Figures 2-9 and 2-10. Ignore the box labelled <integer-valued built-in function> until the next section. The syntax shows that you can use an integer valued constant, an integer variable, or a <term>, at each of several positions in an <arithmetic expression>, each position being separated from the next by "+" or "-". The "<u>operator</u>" "+" signifies addition of the

<arithmetic-expression>

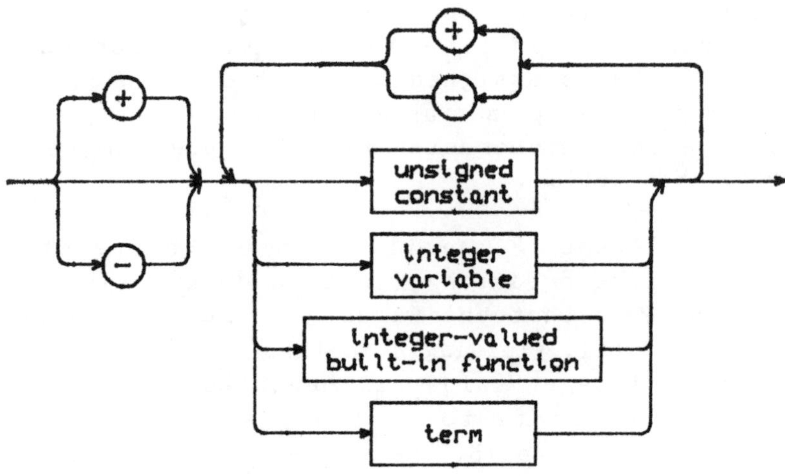

<term>

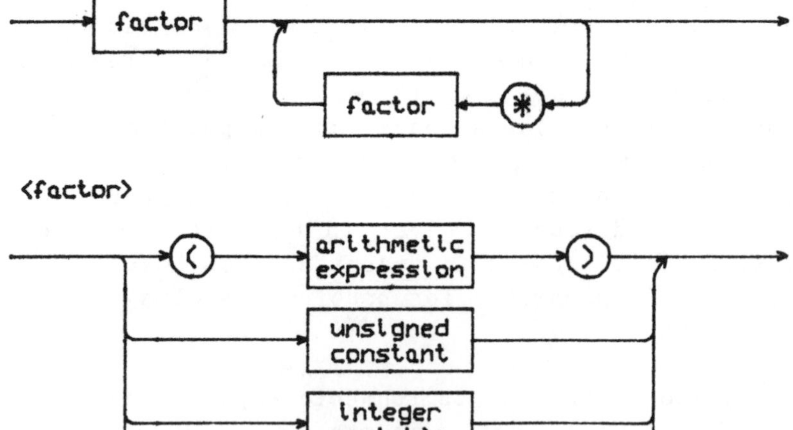

Figure 2-9

<variable>

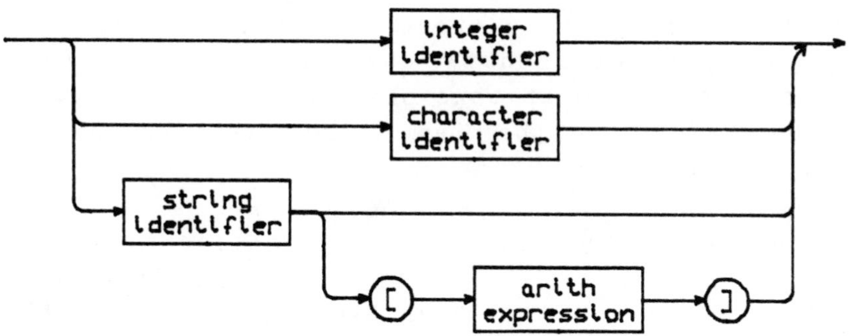

Figure 2-10

quantities on either side of the symbol, while "-" signifies that the second quantity is to be subtracted from the first. The symbols "+" and "-" are optional before the first item in an <arithmetic expression>. When present, they imply that the integer constant 0 is on the left of the symbol. Thus "-10" is equivalent to writing "0 - 10". Space characters are optional between successive symbols, but not inside an identifier or integer constant.

The entity called <term> in the syntax is a device to be used in connection with the multiplication symbol "*" (and later with the symbols which signify division). The syntax shows that a term is to be constructed from one, two, or more <factor>'s. If there is more than one factor, then each is to be separated from the next by the symbol "*". Thus "A * B" represents a <term> in which the variable A is to be multiplied by the variable B. This multiplication must take place in order for a value to be obtained for the <term>. The effect is that in the expression:

```
A * B + C * D - E
```

the evaluation proceeds by first carrying out the multiplications. Only after the multiplication is complete is the addition carried out, followed by the subtraction. Processing proceeds from left to right in handling the "+" and "-" operators within an <arithmetic expression>, and in handling successive "*" operators within a <term>. We say that the multiplication operator "*" has higher "<u>precedence</u>" than the addition and subtraction operators because the multiplication comes first. In other words, the multiplication operation must precede the addition and subtraction operations in an <arithmetic expression>.

Notice that provision is made in the definition of <factor> to allow you to force addition or subtraction to take place before multiplication, through the use of parentheses. When you enclose part of an expression between matched (left and right) parentheses, the part which is enclosed will be evaluated first, before the part outside the parentheses is evaluated. To see this in operation, consider the following simple example:

If A has the value 1, B=2, and C=3 then

A + B * C has the value 7

(A + B) * C has the value 9

In the first case, B is multiplied by C before addition to A because of the precedence rule. In the second case, the value of A added to B is first computed because of the parentheses, then the result is multiplied by C.

Exercise 2.3:

The drawing portrayed in Figure 2-11 can be displayed by a main program containing the following four statements, and one other to set the value of the size or scale of the drawing in screen units.

```
RECT(5,5);
RECT(10,3);
RECT(3,10);
RECT(2,12);
```

RECT is a procedure which draws a rectangle whose height is given by the first parameter, and whose width is given by the second parameter.

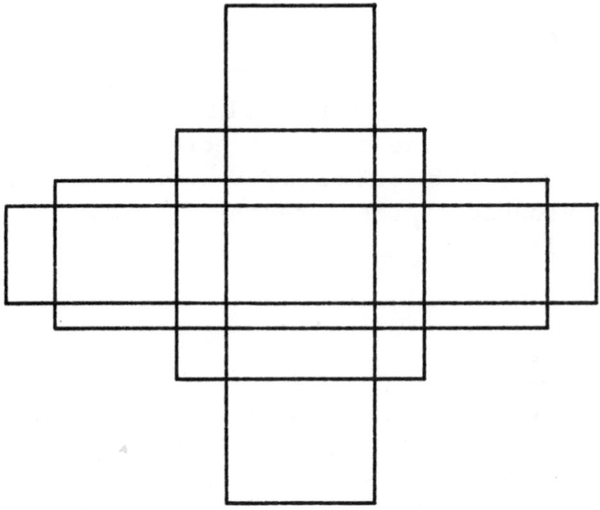

Figure 2-11

Write and test a complete program, including the procedure RECT, which draws this figure. Make sure that different values of the size factor give figures of differing size but having similar appearance otherwise. In other words, one variable SIZE should control the relative size of all parts of the entire drawing. It should only be necessary to alter one statement to change the size of the whole drawing.

11. Built-in Procedures and Functions for Strings

A "function" (in the jargon of computer people) is a special kind of procedure. One calls a function by placing its identifier, plus any list of actual parameters, within an expression. When the steps taken to evaluate the expression reach the function identifier, the function is placed in execution. When the function's execution terminates, a value is left in place of its identifier in the expression, and evaluation of the expression continues once again. We say that a function "returns" a value to be used in the expression. The <type> of the value returned by a function depends upon how the function is declared, and the manner in which it performs its computations. Chapter 4 includes a description of how you can declare your own functions as well as procedures.

As a convenience to programmers, the PASCAL compiler provides facilities for you to call various procedures and functions that have been made part of the system, i.e. they are "built-in" so that you do not have to declare them. You have already met the built-in procedures MOVE, TURN, MOVETO, PENCOLOR, and CLEARSCREEN, all of which are designed for working with turtle graphics problems. In this section, we introduce two built-in procedures, and four built-in functions, designed for working with STRING variables. Syntax to cover these is shown in Figures 2-12, 2-13 and 2-14.

<built-in procedure>

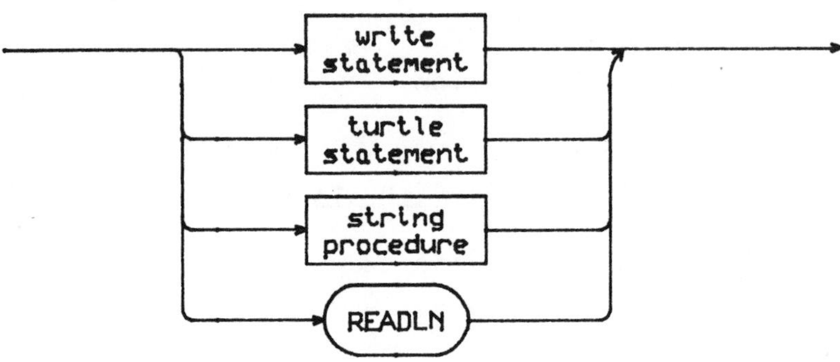

<string procedure>

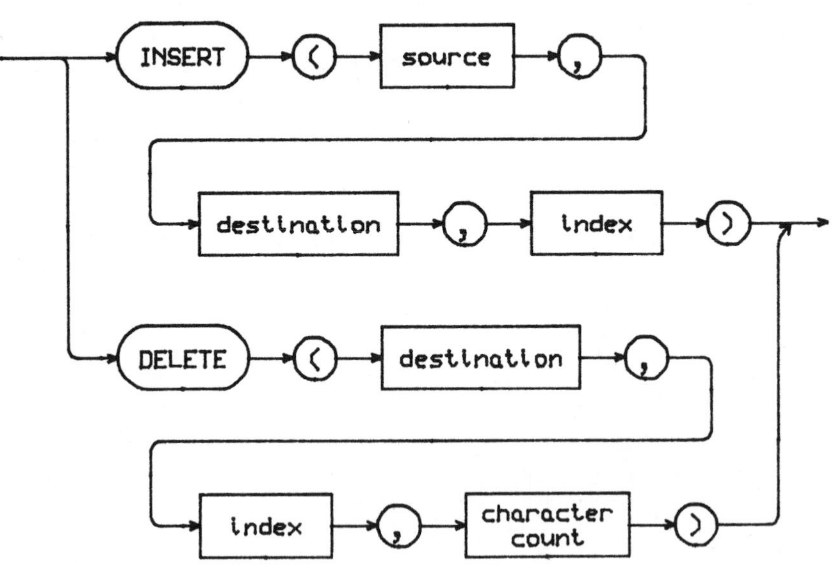

Figure 2-12

<built-in function>

part (a) - string valued

CONCAT (source ,)

COPY (source ,

index , character count)

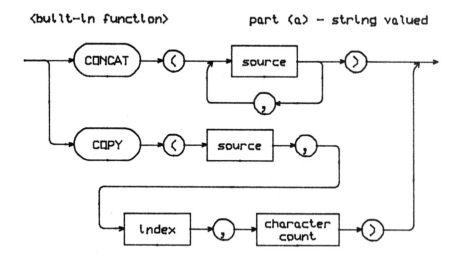

part (b) - integer valued

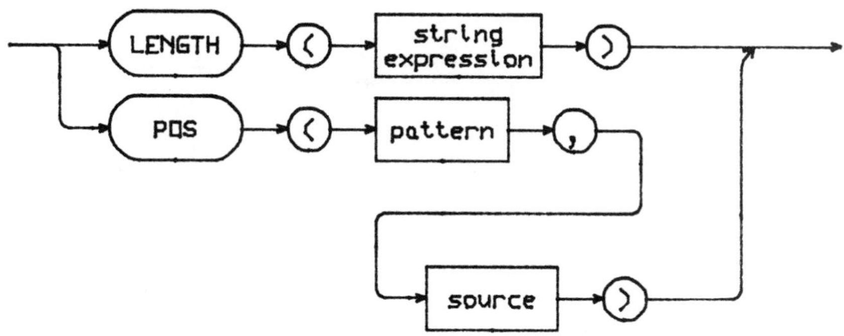

Figure 2-13

<source>, <destination>, <pattern>

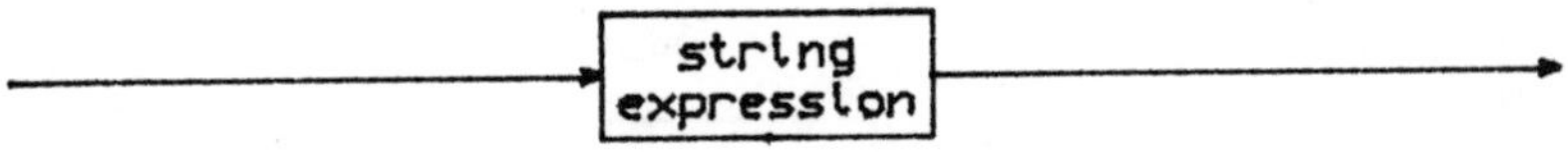

<string expression>

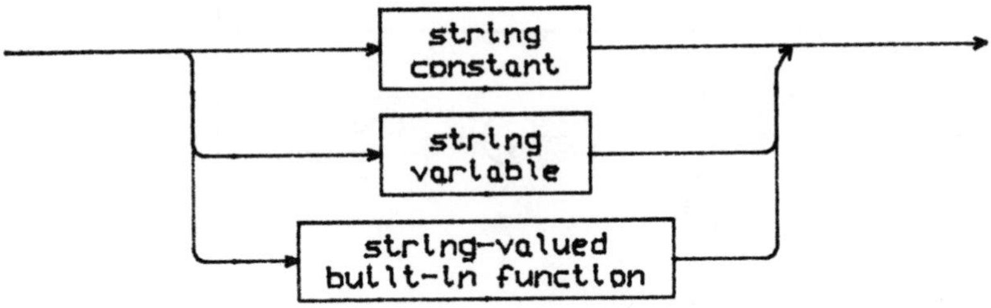

<index>

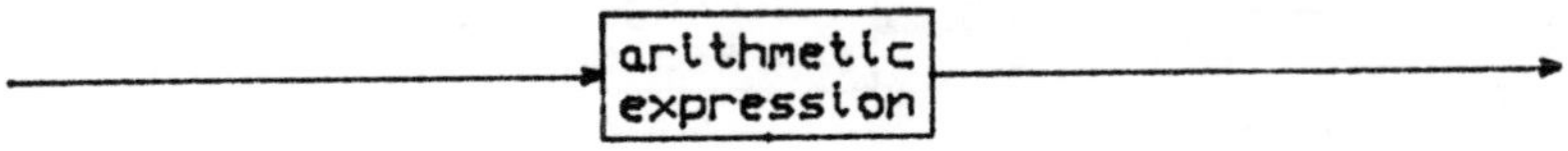

Figure 2-14

Let us first illustrate the operation of each of these procedures and functions with the sample program INTRINSIC. We will then show several examples with more interesting data. This program displays the following lines:

```
POSITION OF SAW IS:12
LENGTH OF PATTERN IS:3
BEFORE DELETE:EVEN IF HE SAW ME
AFTER DELETE:EVEN IF HE  ME
AFTER INSERT:EVEN IF HE HEARD ME
AFTER CONCAT:EVEN IF HE HEARD MEI WILL DENY IT
1ST COPY:EVEN IF HE HEA
2ND COPY:RD MEI WILL DENY IT
```

In line 9, the function POS searches for an occurrence, within the string variable DEST, of a string of characters matching the content of the "pattern" variable PAT. The value returned is an integer representing the first character position where the matching string is found. As you can readily verify by counting the characters, "SAW" starts with the "S" in position 12 of DEST, as shown by the display. If no matching string is found for the pattern, then POS returns a value of 0 (zero), which does not correspond to one of the allowable character positions in a STRING variable.

In line 14, the function LENGTH returns the number of characters stored in the STRING variable PAT. As the display shows, and you can readily verify, "SAW" contains 3 characters.

In line 21, the procedure DELETE removes LP (i.e. the value stored in LP) characters from the STRING variable DEST starting at character location NB. DELETE reduces the number of characters stored in the <destination>. If you try to execute DELETE with a value of the <character count> corresponding to more characters than are currently stored in the <destination> STRING variable, your program will terminate abnormally and a message saying why will be displayed by the system.

```
PROGRAM INTRINSIC;
(*illustrate built-in procedures & functions*)
VAR SRC,DEST,PAT,SCRATCH: STRING;
    LP,NB,NE: INTEGER;
BEGIN
  DEST:='EVEN IF HE SAW ME';
  PAT:='SAW';
  (*find POSition of PAT in DEST*)
  NB:=POS(PAT,DEST);
  WRITELN('POSITION OF ', PAT, ' IS:', NB);
      (* used for trace *)

  (*now determine number of characters to delete*)
  LP:=LENGTH(PAT);
  NE:=NB+LP;
       (*save end of pattern in NE for later use*)
  WRITELN('LENGTH OF PATTERN IS:',LP);
  WRITELN('BEFORE DELETE:',DEST);

  (*delete pattern before inserting substitute*)
  DELETE(DEST,NB,LP);
  WRITELN('AFTER DELETE:',DEST);
  INSERT('HEARD', DEST, NB);
  WRITELN('AFTER INSERT:',DEST);

  (*concatenate new string to end of DEST*)
  SRC:='I WILL DENY IT';
  DEST:=CONCAT(DEST,SRC);
  WRITELN('AFTER CONCAT:',DEST);

  (*now make copies of beginning and end of DEST*)
  SCRATCH:=COPY(DEST,1,NE-1);
  WRITELN('1ST COPY:',SCRATCH);
  SCRATCH:=COPY(DEST,NE,LENGTH(DEST)-NE+1);
  WRITELN('2ND COPY:',SCRATCH)
END.
```

In line 23, the procedure INSERT opens up a space within the <destination> variable DEST starting at character number NB (i.e. the value stored in NB), and then moves the string 'HEARD' into that space. As the syntax in Figure 2-14 shows, the <source> could have been a <string constant>, as in this case, a <string variable>, or it could have been <a string valued built-in function> meaning either CONCAT or COPY. The result of using INSERT is to leave more characters stored in the <destination> STRING variable, as can readily be verified using LENGTH.

In line 28, the function CONCAT first builds a new STRING variable containing the current contents of DEST followed by those of SRC. It then assigns the content of this new variable, which is hidden by the system, to DEST, thus replacing the original value that was stored in DEST. As the syntax shows, you can "concatenate" more than two strings using CONCAT. For example, if DEST, BEFORE and AFTER are STRING variables, then

```
BEFORE:='THIS ';
AFTER:=' LIFE';
DEST:=CONCAT(BEFORE, 'IS THE', AFTER);
```

leaves DEST containing 'THIS IS THE LIFE'.

In line 32, the function COPY returns a <string> value consisting of the (NE-1) characters from DEST starting at location 1. Similarly, in line 34, COPY returns all the characters in DEST starting at location NE, and going to the end. As a short exercise, verify that the expression

```
LENGTH(DEST)-NE+1
```

does in fact produce the number of characters actually in the string value shown in the display following "2ND COPY:".

Notice that the result of using the CONCAT is that two words are displayed without an intervening space as presumably might have been intended, i.e. "MEI". The program runs, but does not produce quite the intended result. Can you revise the program so as to make it display "ME I" at this point?

12. Sample Programs Using Strings

Refer now to the program CHOP, which displays the following lines:

```
EVEN IF HE SAW ME, I WILL DENY IT
IF HE SAW ME, I WILL DENY IT
HE SAW ME, I WILL DENY IT
SAW ME, I WILL DENY IT
ME, I WILL DENY IT
I WILL DENY IT
```

This program depends on the procedure CHOPAWORD to remove one word from the beginning of the string variable SUBJ each time it is called. Within the procedure, the first step is to scan for a single blank space character. In line 8, all characters up to and including the space are deleted. In line 9 the new contents of SUBJ are again displayed.

Exercise 2.4:

Rewrite the program CHOP to make it display each successive line of the original value of SUBJ with the first remaining blank space removed. For example, after the first call to the procedure, SUBJ should contain:

```
EVENIF HE SAW ME, I WILL DENY IT
```

```
PROGRAM CHOP;
VAR SUBJ:STRING;
    NSPACE: INTEGER;

PROCEDURE CHOPAWORD;
BEGIN
  NSPACE:=POS(' ',SUBJ);
  DELETE(SUBJ,1,NSPACE);
  WRITELN(SUBJ);
END (*CHOPAWORD*);

BEGIN (*MAIN PROGRAM*)
  SUBJ:='EVEN IF HE SAW ME, I WILL DENY IT';
  WRITELN(SUBJ);
  CHOPAWORD;
  CHOPAWORD;
  CHOPAWORD;
  CHOPAWORD;
  CHOPAWORD
END.
```

Now revise the original program to put <u>two spaces</u> in place of every one in the original. Thus:

```
EVEN  IF  HE  SAW  ME,  I  WILL  DENY  IT
```

Now refer to the program CHANGE, in which the procedure SUBST is used to substitute one string, the second parameter, for another in the first parameter. This program displays the following lines:

```
TOO WISE YOU ARE
TOO SMART YOU ARE

TOO SMART YOU BE
```

In line 7, POS is used to scan for a match with the pattern string. If it is found, the pattern is then deleted. Note that the program will terminate abnormally if the pattern is not found. We'll have to defer consideration about what to do in this circumstance until the next chapter. Assuming the pattern was found and deleted, the substitute string SNEW is then inserted where the pattern was deleted. The result is then displayed.

<u>Exercise 2.5:</u>

Revise the program CHANGE so that it first displays the following two lines:

```
TOO WISE YOU ARE, TOO WISE YOU BE
I SEE YOU ARE TOO WISE FOR ME
```

then alters each occurrence of "WISE" by substituting 'SMART' (or 'CLEVER', or 'DUMB', or whatever pleases you) and then displays the resulting lines again. The program should use a procedure like SUBST to make the changes. Do not solve the problem the lazy way by simply

```
PROGRAM CHANGE;
VAR SUBJ:STRING;

PROCEDURE SUBST(PAT,SNEW:STRING);
VAR NP: INTEGER;
BEGIN
  NP:=POS(PAT,SUBJ);
  DELETE(SUBJ,NP,LENGTH(PAT));
  INSERT(SNEW,SUBJ,NP);
  WRITELN(SUBJ)
END (*SUBST*);

BEGIN (*MAIN PROGRAM*)
  SUBJ:='TOO WISE YOU ARE';
  WRITELN(SUBJ);
  SUBST('WISE', 'SMART');
  WRITELN; (*put blank line in display*)
  SUBST('ARE', 'BE');
END.
```

displaying two lines that you assign to SUBJ explicitly setting its value to the desired new result.

Problems

Problem 2.1:

The program BLEWIT, which is reproduced below, is intended to display the following four lines:

```
      X
     XXX
    XXXXX
   XXXXXXX
```

```
PROGRAM BLEWIT
VAR: S,XS,X2; STRING;
     N; INTEGER;
BEGIN
  S='          '; (*ten blank spaces*)
  XS:='X';
  X2:='XX';
  S:=CONCAT(S,XS)
  WRITELN(S);
  XS=CONCAT(X2,XS);
  INSERT(XS,S,N);
  WRITELN(S);
  XS:=CONCAT(XS,XS);
  INSERT(XS,S,N-2)
  WRITELN(S);
  XS:=CONTAC(X2,XS);
  INSERT(XS,S,N-3)
END.
```

Unfortunately, the program was prepared by a student who was a little too late to meet the required homework deadline, and it contains a few errors. As a first step, correct the syntax errors. You should be able to find 9 syntax errors in this program without resorting to use of the compiler to help you. None of them involve any ambiguity about what the program should be expected to do after the syntax errors are corrected.

Even after the syntax errors are corrected in this program, the resulting display will not be quite what was expected, as shown above. As a next step, analyze what the program really does do, and write out the display it will produce <u>without using the computer to help you</u>. Quite frequently the fastest way to find errors in a program is to use this approach.

Finally, alter the program to make it produce the expected result. At this point, if you have the opportunity, you might try the revised version of the program on the computer. For a problem of this level of difficulty, you should be able to get the correct program before ever trying it on the computer. Assume that you will be graded "barely passing" if you have to make two tries, and "failing" if you need more than two tries!

<u>Problem 2.2:</u>

In some programs for editing text, one can display a line of text on a TV-like screen for possible alteration, quite possibly similar to the display screen you may be using. To point to a place where a change is wanted, a variety of methods are available for pointing. One method is to split a line of text at the point where the logical text pointer is currently located. For example

```
THE QUICK BROWN FOX
```

becomes:

```
THE QUICK
          BROWN FOX
```

The point where the line jumps is where a change might be wanted. The program below is intended to illustrate this. Add PASCAL statements and declarations to those given in order to complete this program. Correct any syntax errors you may find in the portion of the program that is given. The program should print out the split line.

```
PROGRAM TRANSFER;
VAR TOP,BOTTOM,BLANKS,PAT:STRING;
BEGIN
  BLANKS:='                    ';
  TOP:="THE QUICK BROWN FOX";
  PAT:='BROWN';
  NP:=POS(PAT,TOP);
  BOTTOM:=COPY(TOP,NP,LENGTH(TOP)-NP+1);
     . . .
     . . .
```

Problem 2.3:

The names of typical American people are constructed in the form:

<first name><SP><middle initial>.<SP><last name>

For example John Q. Public. Notice that this is really a simple statement of syntax. The item <SP> stands for a single blank space character. Quite often, it is desired to order the parts of the name with the last name first, so as to allow alphabetic ordering yielding the form:

<lastname>,<firstname><SP><middle initial>.

as in: Public,John Q. The program which has been started below is intended to reorder any American name from the first form to the second. The statement assigning a value to SOURCE substitutes for the reading of an arbitrary name from the keyboard or from some other external device. (We describe how you can do that in Chapter 7.) Correct any syntax errors you may find, and write the remainder of the program in such a way as to leave the desired final form of the name in DEST. It should then display the value left in DEST.

```
PROGRAM LASTFIRST;
VAR SOURCE,DEST,PATTERN:STRING;
  NL:INTEGER;
BEGIN
  SOURCE:='MARY W. JONES';
    (*make it work for any name!*)
  PATTERN:='.';
  NL:=POS(PATTERN,SOURCE);
  DEST:=SOURCE;
    . . .
    . . .
```

Problem 2.4:

In your own words, give short answers to the following:

What is a procedure?

Describe three reasons why one might use procedures in a program designed for almost any purpose.

What is a parameter, and how is it used?

What is a variable, and how is it used?

What is a <type>? Name 3 <type>'s used in this chapter.

For what purpose does one use an <arithmetic expression>?

Problem 2.5:

Assume that the following variable declarations appear in the heading of a program:

```
VAR I,J:INTEGER;
    CH1,CH2:CHAR;
    SA,SB:STRING;
```

Indicate which of the following statements violate the rules of PASCAL and which are "legal":

```
I:=-1;
J:=I;
J:='3';
I:=LENGTH(SA);
I:='1234';
CH1:=1;
CH1:='Q';
CH2:=SA[J];
CH2:=27;
CH1:=CH2;
SA:='any string';
SA:=5;
SB:=CH2;
SA:=I;
SB:=SA;
SB:=CONCAT(SB,SA);
SA:='R';
```

Indicate what is wrong with each statement that you mark as not legal.

Chapter 3

CONTROLLING PROGRAM FLOW, REPETITION

1. Goals

In this chapter, you will learn to make a program repeat specified actions over and over again, and to make it decide whether certain actions will be performed or not, depending upon values of specified data items.

1a. Learn to use the WHILE and REPEAT statements to to control the number of times certain statements are repeated based on data values.

1b. Use the FOR statement to control repetition a predetermined number of times, and to simplify the assignment of new values to a control variable which increases (or decreases) by 1 on each loop.

1c. Learn to use the IF statement, with one or two branches, to decide whether a statement (or group of statements) will be executed, depending on the values of specified data items.

1d. Use the Compound statement to allow related groups of statements to be treated as one statement for control purposes.

1e. Use Boolean variables to save, and re-use, the TRUE or FALSE values needed to control IF, WHILE, and REPEAT statements.

1f. Learn to read simple flow charts which show the path of execution of sections of program which have branches or loops.

1g. Introduce simple data values into your programs using READ and READLN statements to obtain information typed into the keyboard.

1h. Employ various of the new programming tools of this chapter to create more complex graphic figures, and to perform more complex string operations, than were possible heretofore.

1i. Begin to use indentation to help visualize and explain the stucture of a program.

1j. Debug program examples in which the control variables are not correctly set to initial values, or are not left with correct values when repetition terminates.

2. Background

On several occasions in Chapter 2, we had reasons for repeating the same statement, or group of statements, over and over again. For example, the procedure ONESQUARE is called several times in the program SQUARES. CHOPAWORD is used similarly in the program CHOP. These are simple programs, and you may have wondered how one would write a program in which the same procedure has to be called hundreds of times (or even millions!). The WHILE, REPEAT, and FOR statements introduced in this chapter are designed to handle these situations quite easily with very little writing needed.

You may also have wondered how a program might handle a special situation that arises only occasionally during repeated calculations, but which requires special calculations to be performed when it does arise. For example, a calendar program designed to display the month and day, based on the count of days since 1 January, would have to take special action at the end of February on a leap year. Similarly, a line drawing program, such as the TURTLE program that you have already used, may need to decide whether to draw a line or not based on computing whether the length of the line is going to be too long to fit on the display screen. Decisions like these can easily be handled with the IF statement.

Quite often, you will have reasons for controlling not just one statement, but a whole group of statements, with the same IF, WHILE, REPEAT or FOR statement. PASCAL syntax rules allow this to be done by enclosing the statements in such a group within a "Compound statement".

The IF, WHILE, REPEAT and FOR statements all depend upon the fact that a digital computer can be programmed to "jump" from one place in a program to another if some test condition is found to be satisfied. In the traditional method of introducing a programming language, students are shown rather early how to use the GOTO statement to control jumps directly. However, use of the GOTO statement without considerable caution has been found to lead to logical errors, and to large amounts of time spent in debugging programs. The four statements mentioned above are all ways of using the jump feature of the computer's hardware in a software way that avoids many of the chances for programming errors. We will delay, until Chapter 11, discussion of the few situations in which use of the GOTO proves very useful. In those cases it may even be used to avoid errors. Until then, we have arranged the PASCAL system to prevent you from using the GOTO statement.

3. The WHILE Statement

The program WHILEPLOT illustrates the use of the WHILE statement. The program produces the drawing shown in Figure 3-1. Starting at the center of the screen, a line 10 units long is drawn in the initial direction of the turtle. A turn of 89 degrees is made, and the DISTANCE variable is increased from 10 to 13 units. Another line DISTANCE units long is then drawn, another 89 degree turn takes place, and

```
PROGRAM WHILEPLOT;
VAR
  DISTANCE,ANGLE:INTEGER;
  CHANGE:INTEGER;

PROCEDURE NEXTLINE;
BEGIN
  MOVE(DISTANCE);
  TURN(ANGLE);
  DISTANCE:=DISTANCE+CHANGE;
END (*NEXTLINE*);

BEGIN (*MAIN PROGRAM*)
  PENCOLOR(WHITE);
  DISTANCE:=10;
  ANGLE:=89;
  CHANGE:=3;
(*DISTANCE & CHANGE correct for Tektronix 4006*)
(*use 4 and 1 for Terak 8510A;  ??? for others*)
  WHILE DISTANCE<=600 DO NEXTLINE;
END.
```

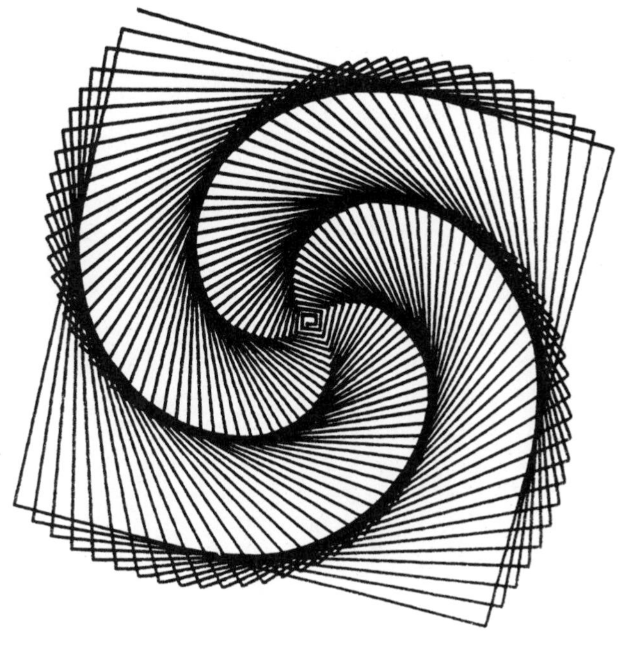

Figure 3-1

```
PROGRAM WHILE1;
  VAR S:STRING;
BEGIN
  WRITELN('TYPE ANY STRING FOLLOWED BY <RET>');
  READLN(S);
  WRITELN(S);
  WHILE LENGTH(S)>0 DO
  BEGIN
    DELETE(S,1,1); (*REMOVE 1ST CHAR*)
    WRITELN(S);
  END (*WHILE*);
END.
```

so on. Drawing stops when a value of DISTANCE greater than 600 units is reached. This prevents the drawing from attempting to go off the screen.

The WHILE statement in line 20 first determines whether the value of DISTANCE is less than or equal to 600. If it is, then the procedure NEXTLINE is called. Since NEXTLINE may, and does, have an effect on DISTANCE, the heading of the WHILE statement again compares DISTANCE to 600. If DISTANCE is still less than or equal to 600, NEXTLINE is again called. This process continues until DISTANCE is larger than 600, at which time NEXTLINE is not called and the entire WHILE statement terminates.

The program WHILE1 illustrates the use of the WHILE statement, and the Compound statement, and also introduces the READLN statement in a simple form. In line 4, this program displays a message asking whoever runs it to type a string on the keyboard. When the return key, <RET>, is struck, the READLN statement assigns the characters entered from the keyboard (and also displayed on your screen) to the STRING variable S. The last character assigned to S is the one typed immediately before <RET> is pressed.

Now let's assume that you type the string "GOING AWAY" in response the the prompt message displayed in line 4. The result should be the display of the following lines:

```
GOING AWAY
OING AWAY
ING AWAY
NG AWAY
G AWAY
 AWAY
AWAY
WAY
AY
Y
```

Notice that the line displayed on the screen while you were typing is also still displayed on the screen. When execution reaches line 7, the value of LENGTH(S) is compared with 0 (zero). If it is greater than zero, then lines 8 through 11 are executed.

To understand better what the WHILE statement does, refer to Figure 3-2, showing both syntax diagrams and flow charts which apply to the WHILE1 program. Part (a) of Figure 3-2 is a "<u>flow chart</u>" expressing in general terms how the WHILE statement operates. A <Boolean expression> is an expression which may take on one of only two possible values, i.e. either TRUE or FALSE. Upon first entering the statement, a test is made to determine whether the <Boolean expression> evaluates as TRUE. If so, then the <statement> is executed once. This <statement> may be of any of the statement types that we have already discussed, and any of those introduced in this or later chapters. After the <statement> is executed, the value of the <Boolean expression> is again tested. Execution of the <statement> continues until a test evaluates the <Boolean expression> to be FALSE. The WHILE statement then terminates. In a flow chart, the rectangular boxes are meant to contain statements which perform one or more actions. The diamond shaped boxes contain <Boolean expression>'s, and are used in connection with tests of the kind discussed here.

Part (b) shows a flow chart depicting the WHILE1 program with a minor change. In the first action box, a specific string constant is assigned to S. This is the same value for S that we used in the illustration above. You could exercise the program as given using different string values typed from the keyboard.

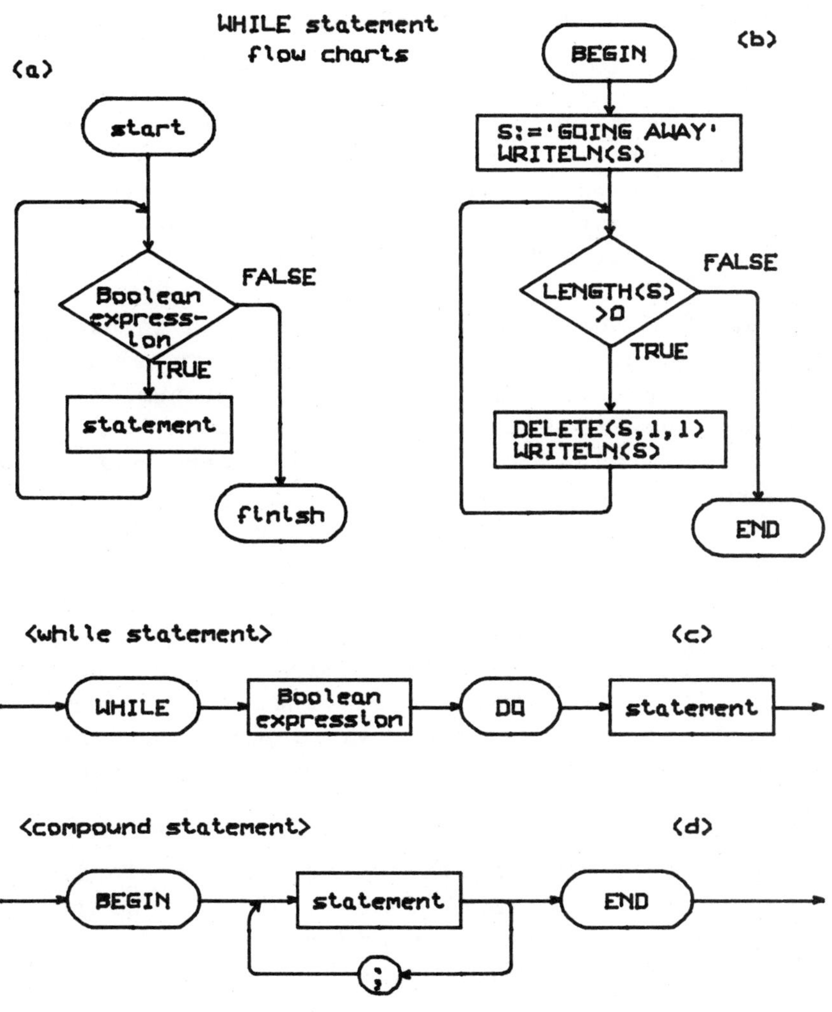
WHILE statement
flow charts
<a>
start
Boolean
express-
ion
FALSE
TRUE
statement
finish
BEGIN
<b>
S:='GOING AWAY'
WRITELN(S)
LENGTH(S)
>0
FALSE
TRUE
DELETE(S,1,1)
WRITELN(S)
END
<while statement>
<c>
WHILE
Boolean
expression
DO
statement
<compound statement>
<d>
BEGIN
statement
;
END

Figure 3-2

Both parts (a) and (b) of Figure 3-2 illustrate a bit of the familiar jargon of computer people. If you follow the arrows from the "start" box downward through the diamond of the test, and the action box below it, the arrow emerging from the action box then loops back and rejoins an arrow that has already been passed. This is the kind of program control path that computer people describe as a "loop".

Part (c) of Figure 3-2 shows syntax for the WHILE statement. In addition to "WHILE", "DO" is a reserved identifier known to the compiler in this context. The <statement> controlled by the WHILE statement in this case is in fact a "Compound statement".

Syntax for <compound statement> is shown in part (d) of the figure. As you can see, the executable part of a <block> is in fact a <compound statement>. We can use the BEGIN and END symbols, which also are reserved identifiers, as if they were enclosing parentheses for a group of program statements. If there were enough truly distinct symbols for enclosing information, PASCAL would probably use those symbols rather than BEGIN and END. A <compound statement> may be used at any place in a program where it is legal to use any other statement. The <compound statement> is a convenient way to group together several statements which you want always to be executed together, if any of them will be executed at all.

The program WHILE2 provides yet another example of the use of the WHILE statement, and the Compound statement. Analyze the program yourself before reading on to see what it does.

```
PROGRAM WHILE2;
VAR S:STRING;
    L,N:INTEGER;
BEGIN
  WRITELN('TYPE ANY STRING FOLLOWED BY <RET>');
  READLN(S);
  N:=1; (*initialize N pointing to start of S*)
  L:=LENGTH(S);
  WHILE N<L DO
    BEGIN
      WRITE(S[N],'-');
      N:=N+1
    END;
  WRITELN(S[L]);
    (*display last char without trailing dash*)
END.
```

WHILE2 again accepts a string typed from the keyboard and assigns it to the STRING variable S. Suppose you were to type "DASHITALL" in response to the prompt message. The result should be that the following gets displayed:

```
D-A-S-H-I-T-A-L-L
```

Do you see why there is no dash displayed after the final "L"?

4. The IF Statement

Refer now to the sample program IFDEMO1, which is similar in concept to the program CHOP of section 2.12, but differs in many details. You should compare the two programs before proceeding further.

In IFDEMO1, we call the procedure ONEWORD repeatedly with a WHILE statement. On each call, the subject string in S is reduced by one word, assuming that at least one blank remains in S when ONEWORD is called. If we typed "IS NOW THE TIME FOR ACTION?" in response to the prompt displayed by line 16 in IFDEMO1, the resulting display should be:

```
NOW THE TIME FOR ACTION?
THE TIME FOR ACTION?
TIME FOR ACTION?
FOR ACTION?
ACTION?
```

The line typed-in will remain on the screen just above the first of these lines. In both programs, elimination of the last blank character from the subject STRING variable will result in POS returning a value of 0 (zero). In CHOP this will prevent the last word in the string from being deleted, and further calls to CHOPAWORD will only result in that last word being displayed again. In IFDEMO1, a value of zero in N will be detected in line 11 by the IF statement, causing all of the remaining characters in

```
PROGRAM IFDEMO1;
VAR SPACE,S:STRING;
  N:INTEGER;

PROCEDURE ONEWORD;
BEGIN
  N:=POS(SPACE,S); (*find 1st blank in S*)
  IF N>0 (*check whether space was found*)
    THEN DELETE(S,1,N);
         (*don't delete if no space found*)
  IF N=0 THEN DELETE(S,1,LENGTH(S));
  WRITELN(S)
END (*ONEWORD*);

BEGIN (*MAIN PROGRAM*)
  WRITELN('TYPE ANY STRING FOLLOWED BY <RET>');
  READLN(S);
  SPACE:=' ';
  WHILE LENGTH(S)>0 DO ONEWORD;
END.
```

S to be deleted (i.e. LENGTH(S) characters). In this instance, the test for N>0 in line 8 will evaluate as FALSE, and the DELETE statement in line 9 will not be executed. Computer people sometimes say, in a case like this, that the false test (as in line 8) causes the program to "fall through" to the point following the end of the statement controlled by the IF (as in line 11).

5. Two-way IF Statement, Syntax for IF Statements

You may have noticed that in IFDEMO1, it was necessary to test the value of N twice, once in line 8 to see if it had a value greater than zero, and once in line 11 to see if it were exactly equal to zero. (POS does not return a value less than zero under any circumstances.) This calls for more writing than is really needed, and might lead to confusion or errors in a more complex program.

A somewhat better way of handling the problem at hand is shown in the sample program IFDEMO2. The logic as far as lines 8 and 9 is the same as in IFDEMO1. In line 10, the reserved identifier ELSE refers back to the test in line 8 just as THEN did. The statement following ELSE is executed if the result of the test is FALSE. The program logic has also been changed slightly to display a message "NO MORE SPACES" to verify that the end of processing has been reached.

Figure 3-3 shows syntax and flow diagrams for the IF statement. As seen in part (a), the ELSE and its associated statement (i.e. the "ELSE clause") are optional in the syntax. The flow charts in parts (b) and (c) show that the main difference between the two forms of IF statement is that in the single branch IF (part (a)) the controlled statement may be avoided entirely. In the two-branch form (part (b)), either one statement or the other must be executed. You will have occasion to use both forms many times as you proceed through this book.

```
PROGRAM IFDEMO2;
VAR SPACE,S:STRING;
  N:INTEGER;

PROCEDURE ONEWORD;
BEGIN
  N:=POS(SPACE,S); (*find 1st blank in S*)
  IF N>0 (*check whether space was found*)
    THEN DELETE(S,1,N)
    ELSE
      BEGIN
        WRITELN('NO MORE SPACES');
        DELETE(S,1,LENGTH(S));
      END;
  WRITELN(S)
END (*ONEWORD*);

BEGIN (*MAIN PROGRAM*)
  WRITELN('TYPE ANY STRING FOLLOWED BY <RET>');
  READLN(S);
  SPACE:=' ';
  WHILE LENGTH(S)>0 DO ONEWORD;
END.
```

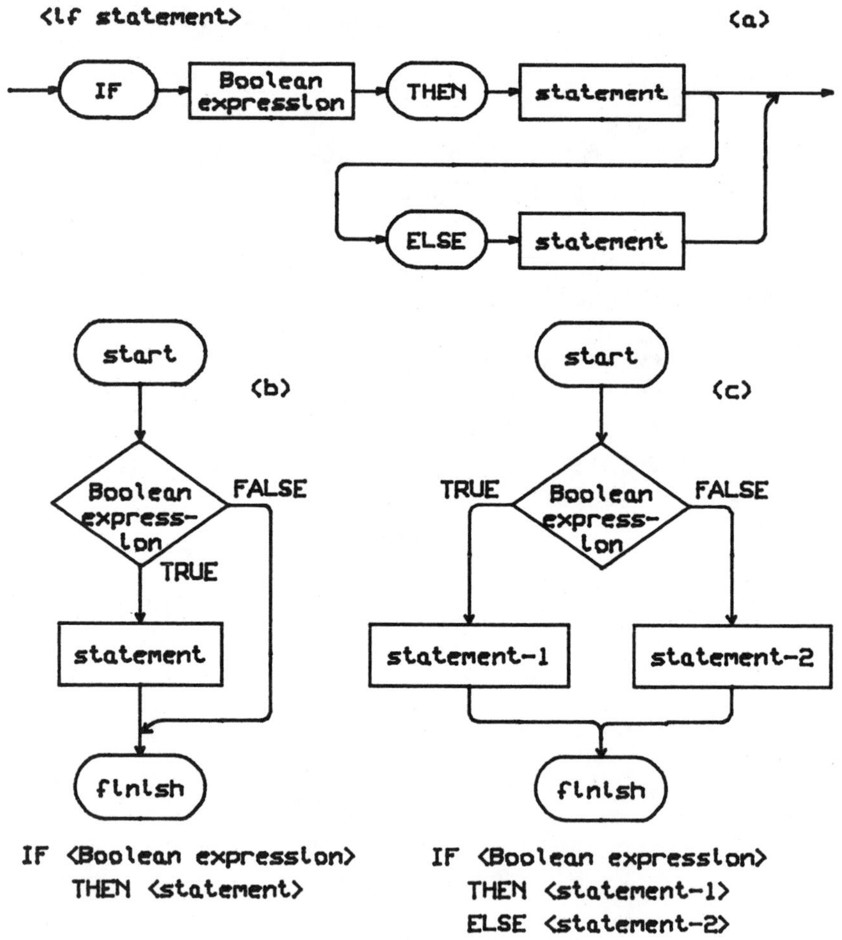
<if statement>
(a)
IF
Boolean expression
THEN
statement
ELSE
statement
start
(b)
Boolean expression
FALSE
TRUE
statement
finish
IF <Boolean expression>
THEN <statement>
start
(c)
TRUE
Boolean expression
FALSE
statement-1
statement-2
finish
IF <Boolean expression>
THEN <statement-1>
ELSE <statement-2>

Figure 3-3

The sample program PLOTNAME provides an example of the use of the IF statement in a graphics context. If, in response to the prompt "TYPE ANY NAME", you type in "John Q Public" followed by <RET>, the drawing shown in figure 3-4 will appear on your screen. The drawing is dependent upon the name typed in, and in a sense is a "signature" created by the computer. Try typing in your own name to this program to see what signature results. (If you are using a Tektronix 4006 terminal for display, enter the integer 20 following the prompt "DELTA:". Use 6 instead of 20 for the Terak 8510A display unit. Some other value may be needed if you are not using one of these two devices for display of graphics.)

PLOTNAME differs in several respects from previous sample programs regarding the entry of data from the keyboard to the program. The READLN in line 8 establishes conditions, to convert the integer you type into the internal "computational" form that the computer uses for integer values, because the compiler knows that the identifier DELTA has been declared to be of <type> INTEGER. The READ statements in line 11 and line 20 similarly expect a single value of <type> CHAR. READ differs from READLN in that READ does not require the <RET> key to be struck before it terminates. PLOTNAME introduces the built-in function ODD(X) which returns TRUE if the value of the integer parameter X is an odd number, i.e. 1, 3, 5, 7, ...

PLOTNAME also introduces the use of the integer-char conversion functions ORD and CHR. ORD(CH) returns the integer equivalent of the character value of CH. CHR(<integer expression>) returns the character which is equivalent to the value of the expression. Each character displayed, and many of those which are not displayed but serve for control purposes, has an equivalent integer value. These type conversion functions allow one to compute a new character value using <arithmetic expression>'s. The <RET> key corresponds to the integer 13. For reasons we will explain in Chapter 7, the character which is returned

```
PROGRAM PLOTNAME;
VAR SIZE,DELTA:INTEGER;
  CH:CHAR;
BEGIN
  WRITELN('PLOTNAME');
  PENCOLOR(WHITE);
  WRITE('DELTA:');
  READLN(DELTA);
  SIZE:=DELTA;
  WRITE('TYPE ANY NAME:');
  READ(CH);
  WHILE CH<>CHR(127(*DEL*)) DO
    BEGIN
      MOVE(SIZE);
      IF ODD(ORD(CH)) THEN
        TURN(-90)
      ELSE
        TURN(90);
      SIZE:=SIZE+DELTA;
        READ(CH);
    END;
END.
```

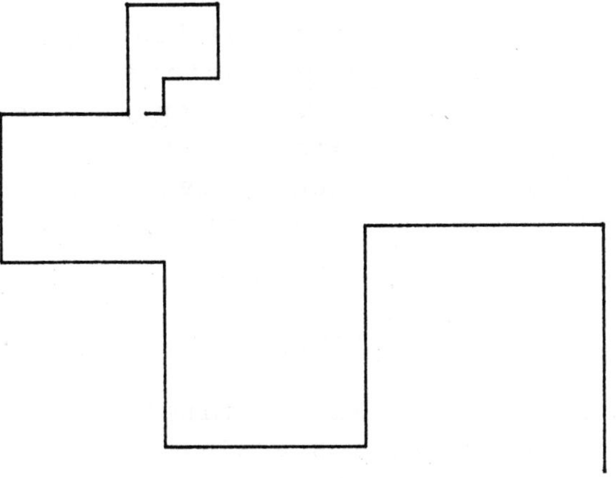

Figure 3-4

to the program when you type <RET> is equal to <space>, and has an integer value of 32. There is a way to determine whether <RET> or <space> (the space-bar) has been struck, but we will not discuss that complication until Chapter 7.

As a way to avoid this complication, yet to have a suitable character to use to stop the REPEAT action, we use <DEL> (called "RUBOUT" on some keyboards) instead. <DEL> has an integer equivalent value of 127, and this is used in line 12 of the program. The program will terminate when you strike the <DEL> key, not when the <RET> key is struck. Neither <RET> nor <DEL> can appear explicitly within a quoted <string constant>, as they are non-printing characters. However we can cause these, and other "<u>control characters</u>" to be transmitted to the display device by converting from the equivalent integer value to the character using the CHR function.

<u>Exercise 3.1:</u>

The program PLOTNAME as printed above does not provide any protection against the turtle going off the screen. Just how many characters must be typed in to cause that effect will depend upon the name typed in.

Modify PLOTNAME to cause it to terminate when the turtle attempts to go off the edge of the screen, and to count the characters entered and "displayed" as lines up until that happens. The character count should be displayed before the program terminates, but after the REPEAT statement is completed. Instead of entering names, you might create a competitive word game by trying to find the longest correctly spelled English word whose graph will still fit on the screen. Note that the turtle always turns either 90 degrees clockwise or counterclockwise. Thus you can keep track of where the turtle is at any time by keeping position counters (in integer variables) for its horizontal and vertical movement away from the center of the screen. Either the horizontal or the vertical counter will change as a result of plotting each new line, but both will not change at once.

6. Syntax of Boolean Expressions

Refer to Figure 3-5 for simplified syntax covering the use of <Boolean expression>'s in PASCAL. The word "Boolean" is capitalized because it is used in honor of a well known mathematician named George Boole. As the diagram shows, there are six possible symbols you can use for comparison of two <simple expression>'s to obtain a TRUE/FALSE result. Both simple expressions being compared must be of the same <type>, in practice either INTEGER or CHAR for the present. The symbols are defined as follows:

```
=    Equal
<>   Not equal
<    Less than
>    Greater than
<=   Less than or equal
>=   Greater than or equal
```

In the last two of these, it is essential that the equal sign ("=") appear after the broken bracket. In the second case of Not equal, the order of the two brackets may not be reversed.

You can combine two or more <Boolean expression>'s using the connective operators AND and OR. For example, if W=1, X=2, Y=3, Z=4 then

```
(X > 0) OR (Y > 10)
```

evaluates as TRUE because X is greater than zero, even though Y is not greater than 10. The expression would be TRUE if *either* comparison were TRUE, and only FALSE if *both* were FALSE. Similarly

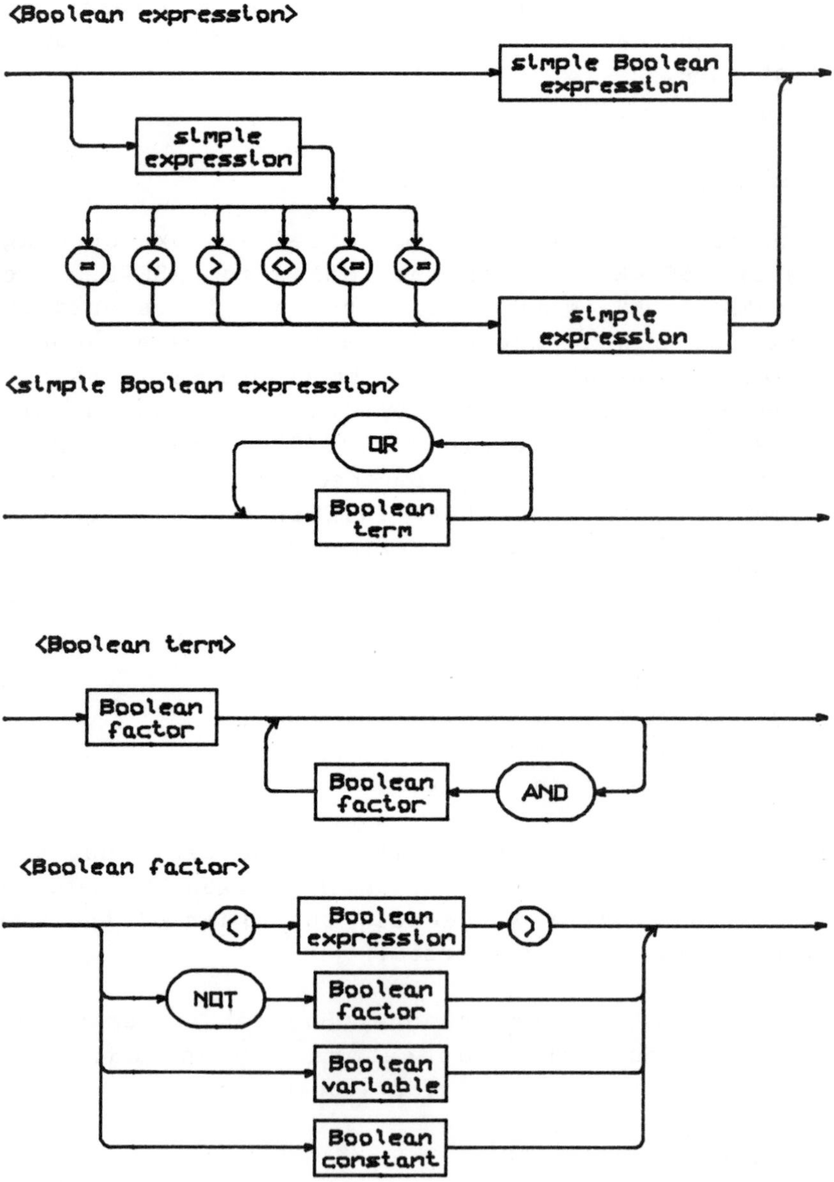

<Boolean expression>

simple Boolean expression

simple expression

= < > <> <= >=

simple expression

<simple Boolean expression>

OR

Boolean term

<Boolean term>

Boolean factor

Boolean factor

AND

<Boolean factor>

(Boolean expression)

NOT

Boolean factor

Boolean variable

Boolean constant

Figure 3-5

```
( (W-X) < 0) AND ( (Z-X) > 0)
```

evaluates as TRUE because both comparisons are TRUE. It would evaluate as FALSE if either comparison were FALSE. The syntax shows that when either AND or OR is used, it is necessary to enclose each comparison within parentheses, but not otherwise.

We will discuss the syntax of Boolean expressions further at the end of this chapter in connection with Boolean variables.

Exercise 3.2:

> Modify the program PLOTNAME (either the original form or the form you obtained in Exercise 3.1) to plot lines only when alphabetic characters are typed. To do this you need to know that all of the upper case characters 'A' thru 'Z' are greater than or equal to 'A' and at the same time less than or equal to 'Z'. Similarly no lower case character is less than 'a' nor greater than 'z'.

7. The FOR Statement

The WHILE statement, and its companion the REPEAT statement, can be used as the basis for any repetition control you may wish. The FOR statement has been provided to simplify control of one type of repetition that occurs so frequently that a special statement was justified in PASCAL. Quite often in designing a program, you need to have a simple way to do both of the following:

1) Cause a <statement> to be repeated a definite number of times.

2) Cause some INTEGER <variable> to increase (or decrease) by 1 on each repetition.

For example, you might wish to have the variable K take all of the following values in uniform progression:

1,2,3,4,5,6,7,8,9,10

A frequent use in handling STRING variables might be to check whether each character in a STRING variable satisfies some condition. One application would be to count the total number of vowels ('a', 'e', 'i', 'o', or 'u') in a line of text. In such a case, you would like to have the "<u>control variable</u>" K take on values equal to all of the possible position numbers from 1 up to the LENGTH of the STRING variable.

The FOR statement is illustrated in the sample program POLYGONS, which suggests the manner in which you can draw a figure looking very much like a circle using only straight lines. The drawings which result from this program are shown in Figure 3-6. The procedure POLY draws NSIDES lines that are LGTH long. Following each line, the turtle turns through ANGLE degrees. In relative terms, the starting location for drawing each polygon is at (X,Y) relative to the center of the screen, where X is the horizontal distance and Y the vertical. The heading of the FOR statement is in line 9, while the statement controlled by the FOR statement is in lines 10 through 13. In this case, the simple variable I is used to control the number of repetitions, running from 1 to NSIDES inclusive. I is not used within the controlled statement, though it could have been used there and often is used in statements controlled by the FOR statement.

Syntax and a flow chart for the FOR statement are shown in Figure 3-7. As you can see from the flow chart, the internal workings of the FOR statement are very similar to the WHILE statement. The FOR statement provides a shorthand way to set the control variable to an initial value, i.e. to "<u>initialize</u>" it, and to change the control variable by 1 on each

```
PROGRAM POLYGONS;
VAR SCALE:INTEGER;

PROCEDURE POLY(NSIDES,LGTH,ANGLE,X,Y:INTEGER);
VAR I:INTEGER;
BEGIN
  MOVETO(X*SCALE,Y*SCALE);
  PENCOLOR(WHITE);
  FOR I:=1 TO NSIDES DO
  BEGIN
    MOVE(LGTH*SCALE);
    TURN(ANGLE);
  END;
  PENCOLOR(NONE);
END (*POLY*);

BEGIN (*MAIN PROGRAM*)
  SCALE:=9; (*9 FOR TEKTRONIX 4006;*)
  (* USE 3 FOR TERAK; ?? FOR OTHERS*)
  POLY(5,16,72,-30,-30);
  POLY(10,8,36,20,-30);
  POLY(20,4,18,20,6);
  POLY(40,2,9,-30,6);
END.
```

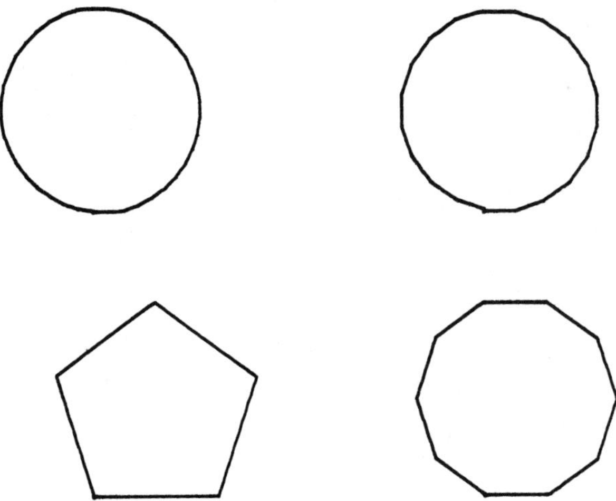

Figure 3-6

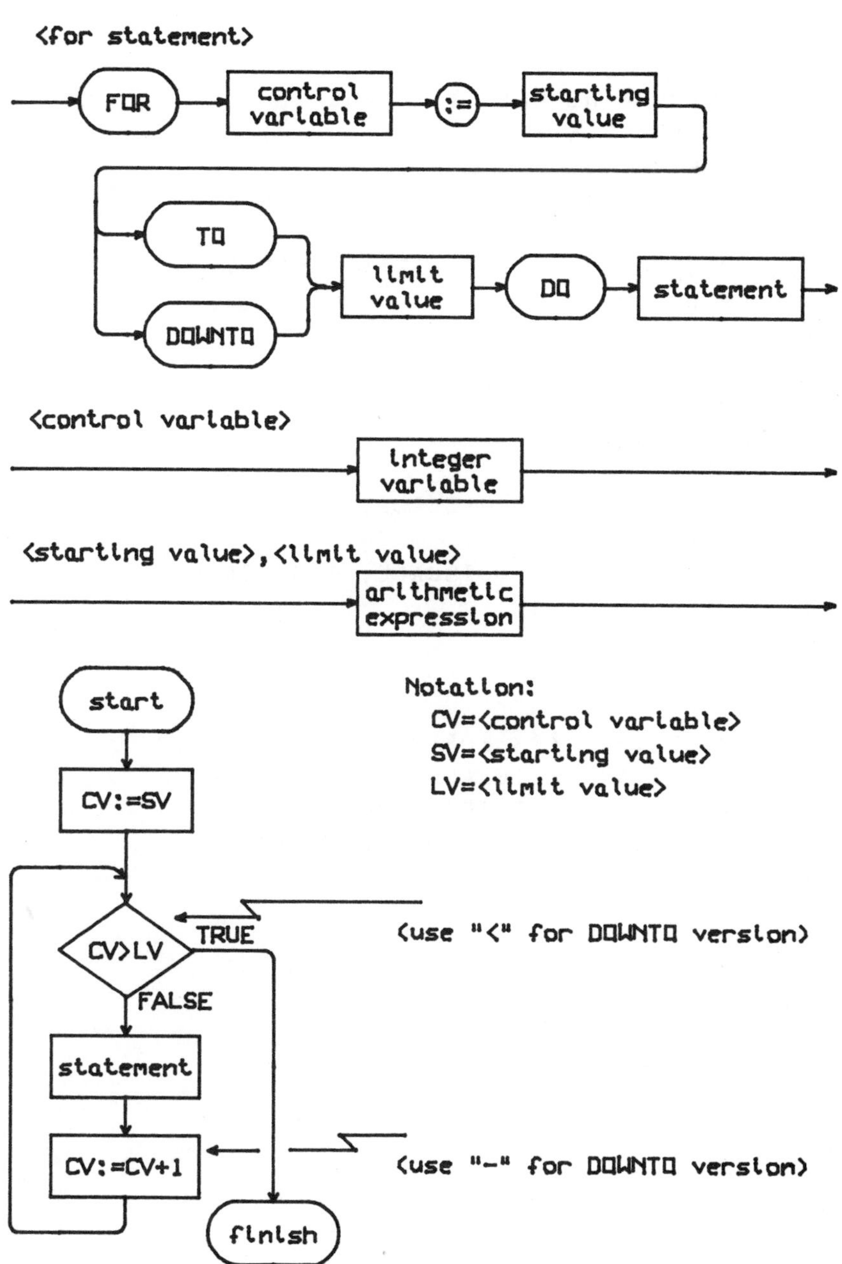
<for statement>
FOR
control variable
:=
starting value
TO
DOWNTO
limit value
DO
statement
<control variable>
integer variable
<starting value>,<limit value>
arithmetic expression
start
CV:=SV
CV>LV
TRUE
FALSE
statement
CV:=CV+1
finish
Notation:
CV=<control variable>
SV=<starting value>
LV=<limit value>
(use "<" for DOWNTO version)
(use "-" for DOWNTO version)

Figure 3-7

```
PROGRAM GRAPHPAPER;
VAR SCALE,X,Y:INTEGER;

PROCEDURE HLINE(HGT:INTEGER);
VAR I:INTEGER;
BEGIN
  MOVETO(-100*SCALE,HGT*10*SCALE);
  PENCOLOR(WHITE);
  MOVETO(100*SCALE,HGT*10*SCALE);
  PENCOLOR(NONE);
END (*VLINE*);

PROCEDURE VLINE(XDIST:INTEGER);
VAR I:INTEGER;
BEGIN
  MOVETO(XDIST*10*SCALE,100*SCALE);
  PENCOLOR(WHITE);
  MOVETO(XDIST*10*SCALE,-100*SCALE);
  PENCOLOR(NONE);
END (*HLINE*);

BEGIN
  SCALE:=3; (*3 FOR TEKTRONIX 4006;*)
 (* USE 1 FOR TERAK OR OTHER DISPLAYS*)
  FOR X:=-10 TO 10 DO VLINE(X);
  FOR Y:=-10 TO 10 DO HLINE(Y);
END.
```

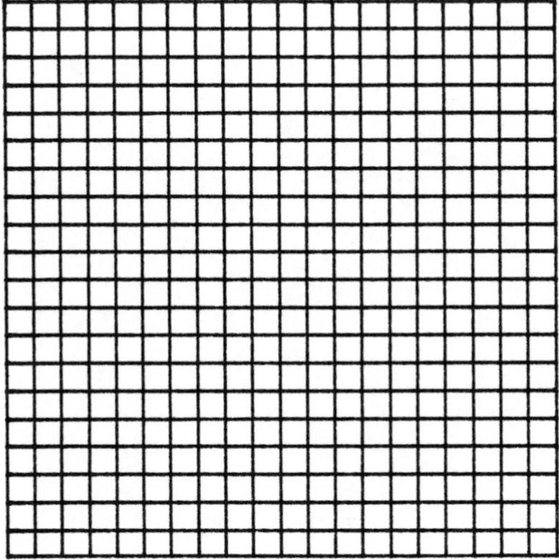

Figure 3-8

```
PROGRAM FOR1;
VAR S,W:STRING;
    N:INTEGER;
BEGIN
  W:='HEAP*';
  S:=W;
  FOR N:=1 TO 6 DO
  BEGIN
    WRITELN(S);
    S:=CONCAT(S,W);
  END;
  WRITELN(S);
END.
```

```
PROGRAM FOR2;
VAR S:STRING;
  K,N:INTEGER;
BEGIN
  WRITELN('TYPE ANY STRING FOLLOWED BY <RET>');
  READLN(S);
  N:=LENGTH(S);
  FOR K:=N DOWNTO 1 DO WRITELN(' ':K,S[K]);
END.
```

loop. When "TO" appears between the <starting value> and <limit value>, the control variable is increased by 1 on each loop. When "DOWNTO" appears, the control variable is decreased by 1 on each loop.

The program GRAPHPAPER provides a second graphics example of the use of the FOR statement. The associated drawing is shown in Figure 3-8. In this program, the control variables X and Y are used within the controlled statement, and they control the position of the lines that are drawn by each of the two simple procedures. Notice also that the control variable does not need to begin at 1, as is the case in some other programming languages.

A point to be cautious about with the FOR statement is the value of the <control variable> after the FOR statement completes its work. The flow chart suggests that the final value of the <control variable> will be either one greater (the TO version) or one less (the DOWNTO version) than the <limit value>. This action is not guaranteed, and the rules of PASCAL state that the value of the control variable is "<u>undefined</u>" after the FOR statement terminates. It is very bad programming practice to depend upon the value of the control variable being as the flow chart suggests after the FOR statement is completed. In some PASCAL systems, it will be explicitly changed to an undefined value before the next statement can be executed. You can use the same variable for other purposes later in the program as long as you again initialize that variable to some new value.

The sample programs FOR1 and FOR2 provide string oriented examples of the use of the FOR statement. FOR1 displays the following lines:

```
HEAP*
HEAP*HEAP*
HEAP*HEAP*HEAP*
HEAP*HEAP*HEAP*HEAP*
HEAP*HEAP*HEAP*HEAP*HEAP*
HEAP*HEAP*HEAP*HEAP*HEAP*HEAP*
HEAP*HEAP*HEAP*HEAP*HEAP*HEAP*HEAP*
```

All but the last line are displayed by line 9 of the program. The CONCAT statement in line 10 tacks a new "HEAP*" at the end of S on each loop.

If, in response to the prompt message displayed in line 5 of FOR2, you type the word "DIAGONAL", the program will display the following (where the top line is displayed as part of the READLN action while you are typing):

```
DIAGONAL
       L
      A
     N
    O
   G
  A
 I
D
```

Notice here that the control variable K is used inside the loop controlled by the FOR statement, but that no new value is assigned to K inside the controlled statement. <u>It is essential that you not assign a new value to the control variable within the statement controlled by FOR</u>, since that would make it difficult or impossible to predict in advance how many loops would be executed.

This program illustrates a feature of the WRITE and WRITELN statements that we have not shown earlier. The phrase ' ':K states that K columns will be filled with blank characters. If you follow any item within the list of items to be displayed by a WRITE or WRITELN statement by a colon (":") followed by an

<arithmetic expression>, the minimum number of columns to be occupied will be given by the value of that expression. If the quantity to be displayed is not a blank, and does not fill at least K columns, then extra blank columns will be inserted on the left to make the item fill up K columns. If the item fills more than K columns, then that larger number of columns will be displayed, and no blanks will be inserted on the left.

<u>Exercise 3.3:</u>

Modify the program FOR1 to make it display the following lines:

```
                         HEAP*
                    HEAP*HEAP*
               HEAP*HEAP*HEAP*
          HEAP*HEAP*HEAP*HEAP*
     HEAP*HEAP*HEAP*HEAP*HEAP*
HEAP*HEAP*HEAP*HEAP*HEAP*HEAP*
```

Note that there are only 6 repetitions of HEAP* on the bottom line.

Now go one step further and modify the program to produce the same displayed result without using CONCAT, INSERT, COPY or DELETE. Hint: You can do this by putting a second FOR statement inside the one already in the program. Then control WRITE('HEAP*') with this inner FOR statement. Clearly the inner FOR statement has to use a different <control variable> than the variable used to control the outer FOR statement (N in the sample printed above).

Finally, to see clearly the order in which the two control variables are changed, add WRITE statements to trace the values of the two control variables as they change in this program. The outer control variable (N in FOR1) should be shown only once per displayed line using something like:

WRITE('N:',N). If the inner FOR statement is controlled by the variable K, then use something like WRITE('K:',K) for each time around the inner loop. The tracing output should be displayed interspersed with the repetitions of HEAP*.

8. The REPEAT Statement

The REPEAT statement is a close cousin of the WHILE statement. Refer first to sample program REPEAT1 for an example. If you respond to the prompt displayed by line 5 with the string "GROWING BIGGER", the program will display the following lines:

```
G
GR
GRO
GROW
GROWI
GROWIN
GROWING
GROWING
GROWING B
GROWING BI
GROWING BIG
GROWING BIGG
GROWING BIGGE
GROWING BIGGER
```

Syntax and flow charts for the REPEAT statement are presented in Figure 3-9. Note that the order of the controlled <statement> and the test of the <Boolean expression> are reversed compared with the WHILE statement. Where the WHILE statement tests before executing the controlled <statement>, the REPEAT statement makes its test after executing the controlled statement. This means that the REPEAT statement will always execute the controlled statement at least once. The WHILE statement may not execute the controlled statement at all if the test evaluates as FALSE on the first try.

```
PROGRAM REPEAT1;
VAR S,SG:STRING;
    L,N:INTEGER;
BEGIN
  WRITELN('TYPE ANY STRING FOLLOWED BY <RET>');
  READLN(S);
  N:=1;
  L:=LENGTH(S);
  REPEAT
    SG:=COPY(S,1,N);
    WRITELN(SG);
    N:=N+1
  UNTIL N>L
END.
```

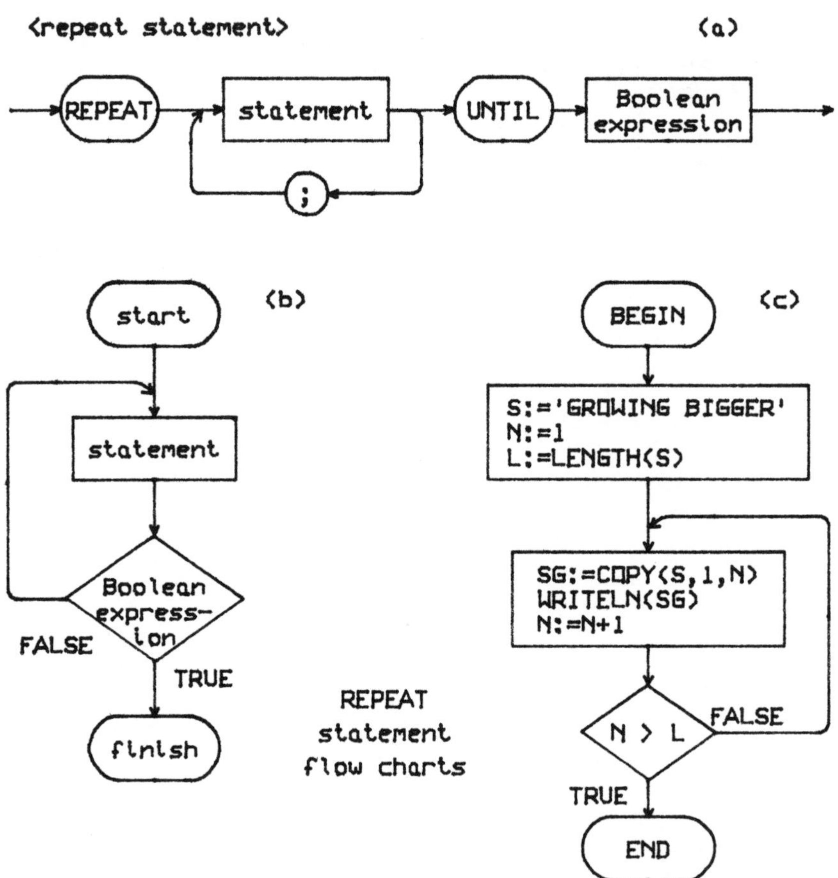
<repeat statement>
(a)
REPEAT
statement
;
UNTIL
Boolean expression
(b)
start
statement
Boolean express-ion
FALSE
TRUE
finish
REPEAT statement flow charts
(c)
BEGIN
S:='GROWING BIGGER'
N:=1
L:=LENGTH(S)
SG:=COPY(S,1,N)
WRITELN(SG)
N:=N+1
N > L
FALSE
TRUE
END

Figure 3-9

Notice that the body of the REPEAT statement looks very much like a Compound statement, except that BEGIN and END are missing. The reserved identifier REPEAT serves both to tell the compiler what kind of statement will be executed next, and also as a left program bracket in the same manner as the BEGIN serves in the Compound statement. Similarly, UNTIL serves both to introduce the <Boolean expression> that will be tested, and also in place of the END that otherwise would be needed in the Compound statement. Note that there is no harm in controlling a Compound statement with a REPEAT statement, as in:

```
REPEAT
  BEGIN
    statement-1;
    statement-2
  END
UNTIL <Boolean expression>;
```

In this case the BEGIN and END are redundant, and not needed, but they do no harm.

In general, a WHILE statement can be converted into a REPEAT statement that has the same effect if you invert the <Boolean expression>. In other words, if the <Boolean expression> yields TRUE in the WHILE statement, it should yield FALSE in the REPEAT statement, and vice versa. Here are two simple programs which produce the same result:

```
PROGRAM WHILEDEMO;
VAR I:INTEGER;
BEGIN
  I:=1;
  WHILE I<=5 DO
    BEGIN
      WRITELN(I);
      I:=I+1;
    END;
END.
```

```
PROGRAM REPEATDEMO;
VAR I:INTEGER;
BEGIN
  I:=1;
  REPEAT
    WRITELN(I);
    I:=I+1;
  UNTIL I>5;
END.
```

Each program should display a column of the five integers from 1 through 5. Notice that the test following WHILE, i.e. I<=5, is the "inverse" or the opposite of the test following UNTIL, i.e. I>5.

As a final illustration of the REPEAT statement, consider the program SPIROLATERAL. This program was suggested by Martin Gardner in his regular column "Mathematical Games" in Scientific American, November 1973. Figure 3-10 shows several figures displayed by the program which are similar to those printed in Gardner's column involving a turn angle of 90 degrees, and right hand (clockwise) turns in all cases. Figures 3-11 and 3-12 show figures with angles in some cases other than 90 degrees, and with mixed right and left hand turns. Some of these drawings are similar to those in Gardner's column, and others differ. All were plotted using the program SPIROLATERAL.

The program first asks for a size factor in line 8. The amount you type in will depend upon the display device you are using, and a little experimentation will show what factors should be used to get drawings of pleasing size. The program then asks for the angle to use. At each step, the turtle will turn either to the left (positive angle) through ANGLE degrees, or to the right (negative angle) through ANGLE degrees. Finally the program prompts for "SEQUENCE:", to which you respond with a sequence of the characters "R" and "L" terminated by <RET>. For example, Figure 3-10 part (a) was produced with the sequence

RRR

followed by <RET>. The program responds immediately by plotting three lines. The first line is SIZE units long, the second 2*SIZE, the third 3*SIZE. If more than three characters had been typed in the SEQUENCE, then additional lines would have been plotted, each one being SIZE longer than the previous line.

```
PROGRAM SPIROLATERAL;
VAR SEQ:STRING;
  SIZE,ANGLE,I:INTEGER;
  CH:CHAR;
BEGIN
  WRITELN('SPIROLATERALS');
  PENCOLOR(WHITE);
  WRITE('SIZE:');
  READLN(SIZE);
  WRITE('ANGLE:');
  READLN(ANGLE);
  WRITE('SEQUENCE:');
  READLN(SEQ);
  REPEAT
    I:=1;
    REPEAT
      MOVE(SIZE*I);
      IF SEQ[I]='R' THEN
        TURN(-ANGLE)
      ELSE
        TURN(ANGLE);
      I:=I+1;
    UNTIL I>LENGTH(SEQ);
    READ(CH); (*ANY KEY: USE <DEL> TO*)
           (* AVOID DISPLAY ON SCREEN*)
  UNTIL CH=CHR(127(*DEL*));
END.
```

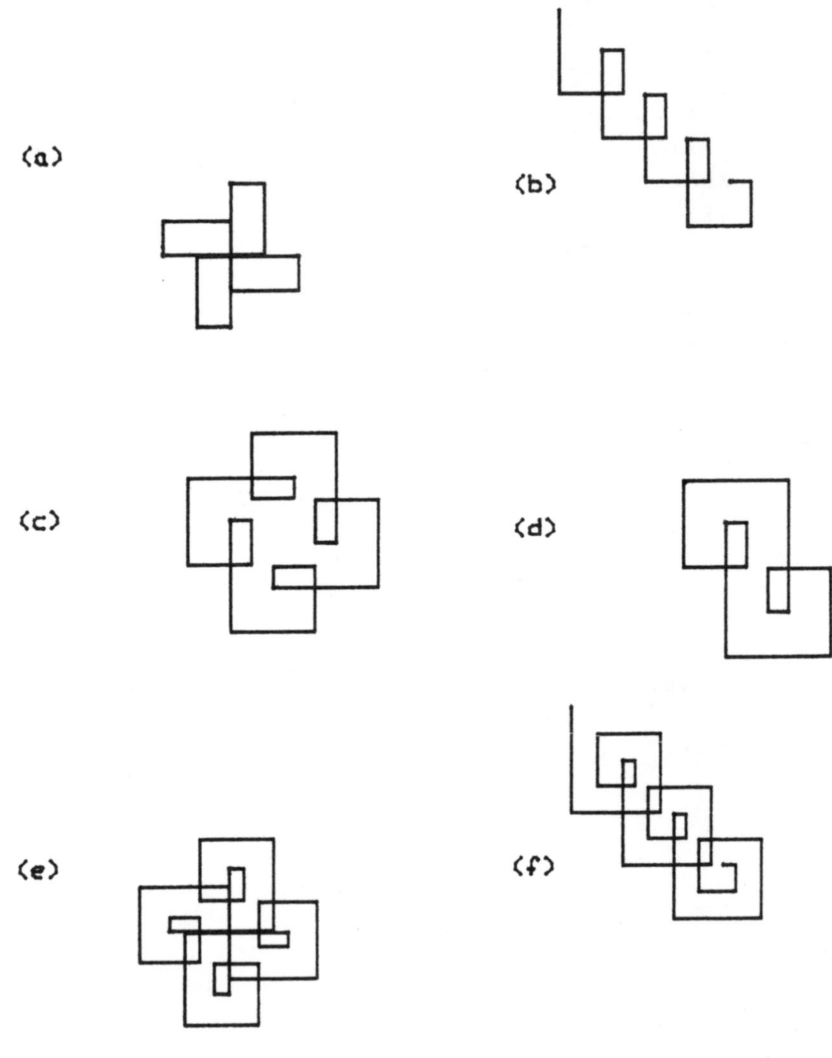

Figure 3-10

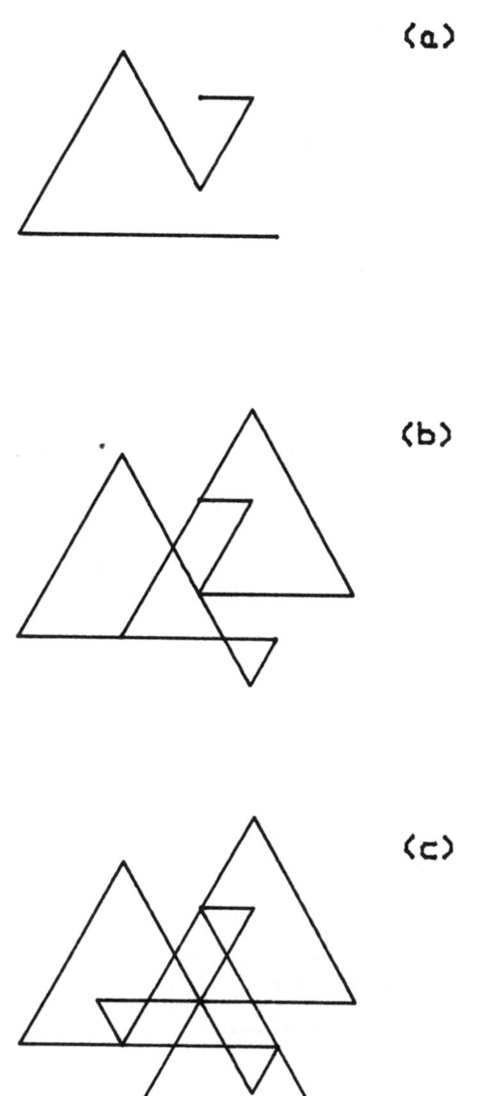

Figure 3-11

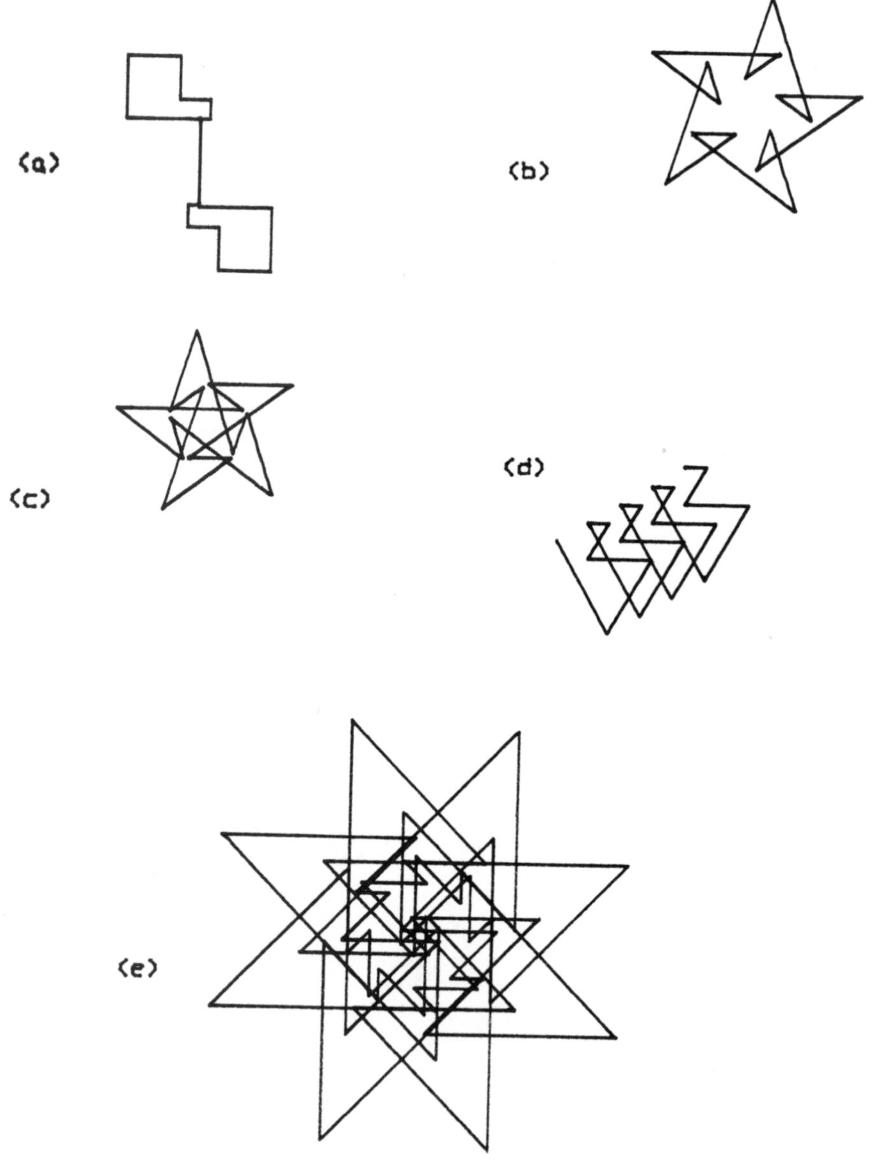

Figure 3-12

Having gone through the sequence once, the program waits in line 24 for you to type in any character. If that character is not equal to <DEL>, the REPEAT in line 14 returns for another loop in which the sequence is again followed from the beginning. This time, the sequence begins from the point where the turtle was left resting at the end of the previous inner REPEAT loop (lines 16 thru 23). In parts (a), (c), (d), and (e), the turtle eventually reaches the point from which it originally started and further repetitions simply retrace the drawing already on the screen. In parts (b) and (f), the turtle slowly wanders off the screen if you repeat the inner loop enough times. Part (a) was obtained with 3 R's, part (b) with 4, part (c) with 5, and so on. As we did with the program PLOTNAME, this program can be told to terminate normally by using the <DEL> key to stop the outer REPEAT statement.

All three parts of Figure 3-11 were obtained from this program using the SEQUENCE "RRLLR" and an ANGLE of 120 degrees. Part (a) was drawn with just one inner loop, part (b) with two, and part (c) with three.

Figure 3-12 provides examples of additional kinds of drawings all of which can be made with the same simple program. In effect, the SEQUENCE that you type in is a new kind of "program" which is interpreted by the SPIROLATERAL program acting as if it were a special kind of computer. Computer people frequently write programs known as "<u>interpreters</u>" which make a real hardware computer appear to be a different software computer with its own properties. The PASCAL system you are using to work with this book depends upon a fairly complex interpreter program capable of running on a variety of small computers. The sequences and angles used to produce the drawings of Figure 3-12 are given in the following table:

Part	Angle	Sequence
a	90	LLRLLLRR
b	144	RRR
c	144	RRL
d	120	RLRRR
e	135	RLRRLLL

Exercise 3.4:

Use the SPIROLATERAL program to create at least one drawing not shown in Figures 3-10 through 3-12. The SEQUENCE you use should contain at least 5 characters including both "L" and "R", and the figure should not be a mirror image of one of the drawings shown in the book. Your figure should be arranged to repeat after at least one inner REPEAT loop. To accomplish this, note that the drawing can only repeat itself if the result of all TURN statements, after several inner loops have been executed, is that ANGLE becomes 0 (zero) or some multiple of 360 degrees.

Exercise 3.5:

Rewrite the programs REPEAT1 and SPIROLATERAL replacing all REPEAT statements with WHILE statements, yet keeping the program logic otherwise the same as shown in this book. Test these revised programs on the computer to make sure you have accomplished the conversion correctly.

Exercise 3.6:

Rewrite the programs WHILEPLOT, WHILE1, WHILE2, and PLOTNAME replacing all WHILE statements with REPEAT statements, yet keeping the program logic otherwise the same as shown in this book. Test these revised programs on the computer to make sure that you have accomplished the conversion correctly. Caution: the requested conversion may require that you change the positions of one or more READ statements in order to keep the logic intact.

Exercise 3.7:

Rewrite the programs FOR1 and POLYGONS to use the WHILE statement instead of the FOR statement, and the programs FOR2 and GRAPHPAPER to use the REPEAT statement instead of the FOR statement. The program logic should be kept otherwise the same as in the printed programs. Test these revised programs to make sure that they perform the same actions as described in the book.

Exercise 3.8:

The sample program REPEAT2 is intended to reverse the order of the characters in the STRING variable S. The program requests that you type in any string from the keyboard, and is intended to loop repeatedly asking for additional strings to be reversed. As you can readily verify, the program will respond to the string:

BACKWARDS

with

SDRAWKCAB

Unfortunately the program contains a logical error which causes it to terminate abnormally if you type in the string:

EVENWORD

```
PROGRAM REPEAT2;
VAR S:STRING;

PROCEDURE REVERSE;
  (*reverse the order of characters in S*)
VAR NB,NE:INTEGER; (*Begin & End pointers*)
  SAVE:CHAR;
BEGIN
  NB:=1;
  NE:=LENGTH(S);
  REPEAT
    (*exchange char's NB &NE, shift NB & NE*)
    SAVE:=S[NE];
    S[NE]:=S[NB];
    S[NB]:=SAVE;
    NB:=NB+1;
    NE:=NE-1;
  UNTIL NB=NE;
END (*REVERSE*);

BEGIN (*MAIN PROGRAM*)
  WRITELN('TYPE ANY STRING FOLLOWED BY <RET>');
  READLN(S);
  WHILE LENGTH(S)>0 DO
  BEGIN
    REVERSE;
    WRITELN(S);
    WRITELN;
    WRITELN('TYPE ANOTHER STRING');
    READLN(S);
  END;
END.
```

Find the error, and make the program work correctly with strings containing either even or odd numbers of characters.

9. Boolean Variables

Sometimes you may find it convenient to save the value of a <Boolean expression> for later use. Of course it would be possible to set an integer variable to 1 if the expression were TRUE, or to 0 if it were FALSE. Or you could set a character variable to 'T' or 'F'. However it has proven more convenient to have a <type> for variables designed explicitly for saving the values of <Boolean expression>'s, and the <type> is called BOOLEAN.

Program BOOLDEMO provides a simple example of one situation in which a Boolean variable can be useful. This program first initializes the STRING variable S to contain a list of names (identifiers) separated by commas. The program's task is to "scan" across S, separating the names, and displaying each name on its own line. This task is similar to the task performed by the PASCAL compiler when it separates the identifiers declared in a list such as that shown in line 5 of the program. In this sample program, we stop the scanning action when the program encounters a blank <space> character. The compiler must use more complex logic to determine when to stop scanning, since you are allowed to separate each symbol in a program from the next with an arbitrary number of blank characters. This program should display the following lines:

```
ALICE
BARBARA
CHARLIE
DORIS
ED
FRANK
```

```
PROGRAM BOOLDEMO;
VAR CH:CHAR;
  NAME,S:STRING;
  BCOMMA:BOOLEAN;
  NAMEPTR,LS,KS:INTEGER;
BEGIN
  S:='ALICE,BARBARA,CHARLIE,DORIS,ED,FRANK    ';
  KS:=1;
  NAMEPTR:=1;
  LS:=LENGTH(S);
  REPEAT
    WHILE (S[KS]<>',') AND (S[KS]<>' ') DO
      KS:=KS+1;
    BCOMMA:=(S[KS]=',');
    NAME:=COPY(S,NAMEPTR,KS-NAMEPTR);
    WRITELN(NAME);
    KS:=KS+1;
    NAMEPTR:=KS;
  UNTIL (NOT BCOMMA) OR (KS>LS);
END.
```

The variable KS serves as a "pointer" to the characters in S, while NAMEPTR is placed at the beginning of a name during each loop of the REPEAT statement. These variables are initialized to point to the 'A' in 'ALICE' before looping starts. The WHILE statement in lines 12 and 13 then advances KS until either a comma (",") or a blank character (' ') is found. Having found one of these, the Boolean varible BCOMMA is set TRUE in line 14 if the character S[KS] is in fact a comma, otherwise it is set to FALSE. Note that this assignment statement is a more efficient way to write what amounts to:

```
IF S[KS]=',' THEN BCOMMA:=TRUE ELSE BCOMMA:=FALSE
```

In lines 17 and 18, the pointers are advanced to point now to the beginning of the next name in the list. The REPEAT is terminated in line 19 if BCOMMA is FALSE, or if KS has increased to be greater than LS, which stores the LENGTH of S. The same result could have been obtained using "LENGTH(LS)" instead of "LS", but this would have required calling the built-in procedure LENGTH many times to return the same result. Calling a procedure takes substantially more time for execution than does a reference to a simple variable (of <type> INTEGER, CHAR, or BOOLEAN). Thus the method shown would operate more efficiently in a program long enough to make the execution time a matter of importance.

To understand the rationale in using the Boolean variable BCOMMA, try to revise the program to operate by comparing the appropriate character in S with a comma in line 19. There are of course a number of ways of doing this, but most of them are more awkward than the technique used here.

Having introduced the idea of a Boolean variable, it is now appropriate to return to the logic of <Boolean expression>'s to see what the effects of AND, OR, NOT, and parentheses will be. Consider the following "truth table" in which A and B are both assumed to have been declared to be BOOLEAN:

A	B	Expression	Resulting Value
TRUE	TRUE	A OR B	TRUE
TRUE	TRUE	A AND B	TRUE
TRUE	FALSE	A OR B	TRUE
TRUE	FALSE	A AND B	FALSE
FALSE	TRUE	A OR B	TRUE
FALSE	TRUE	A AND B	FALSE
FALSE	FALSE	A OR B	FALSE
FALSE	FALSE	A AND B	FALSE
TRUE		NOT A	FALSE
FALSE		NOT A	TRUE
TRUE	FALSE	A AND NOT B	TRUE

Restated: The expression (A OR B) is TRUE if either is TRUE, but not if both are FALSE. The expression (A AND B) is TRUE only if both are TRUE, otherwise it is FALSE. NOT followed by a TRUE value creates a FALSE value, the "inverse", and vice versa.

10. Hints on Boolean Expressions and IF Statements

When Boolean expressions or IF statements become complex, involving many terms to be evaluated as TRUE or FALSE, it is often easy to become confused. This section presents a small collection of strategies you can employ to help straighten out the confusion.

The syntax for <Boolean expression>, Figure 3-5, shows that there is an order of precedence similar to that which applies to the precedence of the multiply operator ("*") over the addition ("+") and subtraction ("-") operators. Thus NOT is executed before AND, while AND is executed before OR. If A=TRUE, B=FALSE, C=FALSE, and D=TRUE, then the expression

```
A AND NOT B OR C AND D
```

evaluates as TRUE because A AND NOT B evaluates as TRUE. Thus it does not matter that C AND D evaluates as FALSE because C is FALSE. Similarly if X=2 and Y=1, then

```
NOT A OR (X > Y) AND C
```

evaluates as FALSE because NOT A is FALSE, and C being FALSE forces (X > Y) AND C also to be FALSE even though (X > Y) is TRUE.

If you find either of the Boolean expressions shown above to be confusing, you are not alone! It often helps to use parentheses to group sub-expressions in such a way as to make the order of execution more obvious. As the syntax shows, the presence of *matched* parentheses forces the expression within the parentheses to be evaluated first. That value then replaces the entire parenthesized expression, including the parentheses, and the evaluation of the outer expression continues. As with arithmetic expressions, Boolean expressions are evaluated by scanning from left to right within any single level of "*nesting*" of parentheses. Thus we can clarify the expressions shown above as follows:

```
(A AND (NOT B)) OR (C AND D)

(NOT A) OR ((X > Y) AND C)
```

without changing the values obtained. On the other hand you could change the meaning of the first of these expressions by using:

```
A AND ((NOT B) OR C) AND D
```

in which the outer group of parentheses has been used to force the OR operation to take place before either of the AND operations.

Now turning to the IF statement, you may sometimes find it preferable to "nest" several IF statements rather than using a single complicated Boolean expression in a single IF statement. However you have to be cautious in doing this. For example:

```
IF A AND B THEN statement-1
```

is equivalent to

```
IF A THEN
  IF B THEN statement-1
```

However

```
IF A AND B THEN statement-1 ELSE statement-2
```

is not the same as

```
IF A THEN
 IF B THEN statement-1 ELSE statement-2
```

The first arrangement will cause statement-2 to be executed if either A or B is FALSE. However, the second arrangement will cause statement-2 to be executed only if A is TRUE and B is FALSE. If A is FALSE, the second arrangement will cause neither statement to be executed.

In the same philosophy that leads to using parentheses to group expressions that you want to be executed first, it can be helpful with IF statements to use BEGIN ... END for a similar purpose. For example:

```
IF A THEN
  BEGIN
    IF B THEN statement-1;
  END ELSE
    statement-2;
```

adds a Compound statement to alter the effect of the nested IF statement above. Now, if A is FALSE then statement-2 will be executed. Statement-1 will be executed only if both A and B are TRUE. If A is TRUE but B is FALSE, then neither statement will be executed. To cover this situation with the IF statement logic, you would have to use:

```
IF A THEN
  BEGIN
    IF B THEN statement-1
         ELSE statement-2;
  END ELSE
    statement-2;
```

in order to be sure that one of the two statements would be executed in all possible situations.

Judicious use of IF statements in this way can sometimes make a program run substantially faster than would be possible using complex Boolean expressions. The reason for this is that the PASCAL system evaluates all items in a complex <Boolean expression> even if the value of the expression could be determined by going through only part of the scan process. One can argue whether it should do this, or should stop the evaluation as soon as the value of the final expression is known. There are reasons for doing it either way.

Regardless of whether you use complex Boolean expressions or nested IF statements when dealing with a complicated decision problem, it is highly desirable to make a <u>truth table</u> similar to the one used in Section 9 to illustrate the values of expressions combining Boolean values with AND, OR and NOT. The table should contain one entry for every <u>possible</u> combination of the values of the components of an expression. There are 4 possible combinations of A and B, 8 combinations of A, B and C, 16 combinations of 4 variables, and so on. It is best to analyze what your IF (or WHILE or REPEAT) statement will do in the case of <u>every</u> one of these combinations individually before concluding that the program is correct. Things can be materially simplified if you know that the <u>same</u> action should result if one of the variables, say B, has a value of FALSE, and that other actions will only take place if it is TRUE. It is then safe to isolate the test for B into a simple IF statement such as:

```
IF B THEN
  BEGIN
    other-actions-including-IF
    .. .. ..
  END ELSE
    alternate-action;
```

11. Note on Indentation

Notice that in many of the examples that we have been using, we "<u>indent</u>" a line from the left margin by an amount that depends upon what we are doing. For example, we indent two more columns for all statements between BEGIN and END in a Compound statement. We indent two additional columns for all lines contained in a statement controlled by a WHILE, REPEAT, FOR, or IF statement. When the controlled statements are completed, we reduce the indentation by an equal amount. This allows one to visualize the structure of the program much more easily than would be possible without using any indentation at all.

Many people who fail to bother with indentation spend large amounts of time finding simple logic errors in their programs because they cannot easily "see" how the program is organized simply by looking at it. To avoid problems it is helpful to follow these rules:

a) Use the same indentation for BEGIN and the END matched with it. Do not put BEGIN or END anywhere except as the first non-blank item on a line. This way you can avoid problems of not knowing which END is matched with which BEGIN.

b) Unless you can fit an entire IF statement on one line, put the statement controlled by THEN and the statement controlled by ELSE at the same indentation. Both should be indented two columns further to the right than the IF itself.

c) Except where a group of short statements are all closely related to each other, and where the order of those statements is not significant, you should never put more than one statement on a line.

Exercise 3.9:

Write and test a program that displays a geometric pattern like the following, using the characters '*', '-', and '¦'. Hint: Use statements of the form WRITE('*'), or WRITE('-'), within loops using any of the control statements discussed in this chapter. You could also assign a long string of blank spaces to a string variable S, and then use statements of the form S[N]:='*'. After "formatting" the content of S, you could display its content with WRITELN(S).

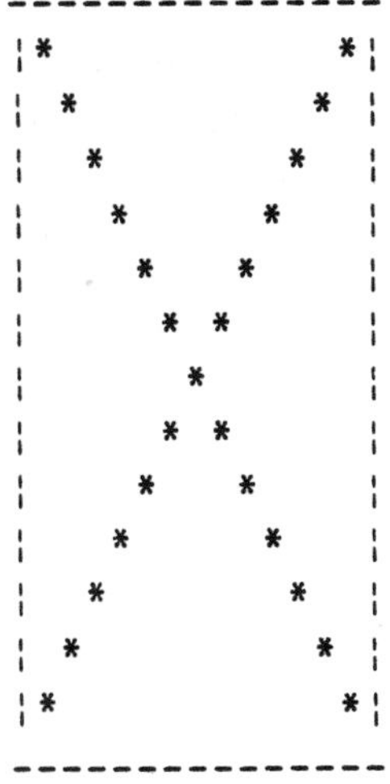

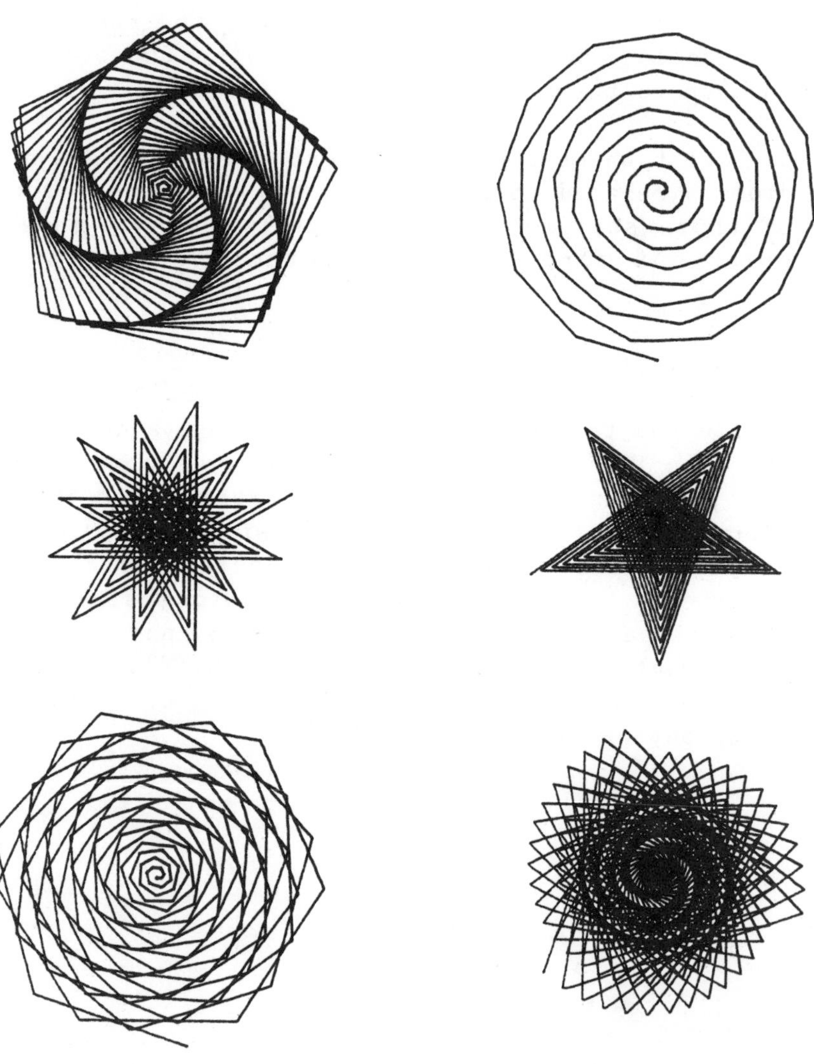

Figure 3-13

Exercise 3.10:

All of the drawings in Figure 3-13 were produce by one small program similar to a program shown earlier in this chapter. The differences among the drawings result from typing different values in response to READLN statements. Write a program capable of producing these drawings, and experiment with it to obtain different drawings in addition to those shown in Figure 3-13.

Problems

Problem 3.1:

Each of the programs POLYBUG1, POLYBUG2, and POLYBUG3 contains a logical error which will prevent it from plotting a 5-sided polygon (same as the lower left drawing of Figure 3-6). Find the error(s) in each program, and state what that program will in fact do as it is written.

```
PROGRAM POLYBUG1;
VAR SCALE,K:INTEGER;

BEGIN
  SCALE:=60; (*60 FOR TEKTRONIX 4006;*)
         (* 20 FOR TERAK; ?? FOR OTHERS*)
  PENCOLOR(WHITE);
  WHILE K<=5 DO
  BEGIN
    MOVE(SCALE);
    TURN(72);
    K:=K+1;
  END;
END.
```

```
PROGRAM POLYBUG2;
(*This program should draw 5 sided polygon*)
VAR SCALE,CNT:INTEGER;

BEGIN
  SCALE:=60; (*60 FOR TEKTRONIX 4006;*)
       (* 20 FOR TERAK; ?? FOR OTHERS*)
  PENCOLOR(WHITE);
  CNT:=1;
  WHILE CNT<5 DO
  BEGIN
    MOVE(SCALE);
    TURN(72);
    CNT:=CNT+1; (*CNT IS NUMBER OF LINES DRAWN SO FAR*)
  END;
END.
```

```
PROGRAM POLYBUG3;
(*This program should draw 5 sided polygon*)
VAR SCALE,CNT:INTEGER;

BEGIN
  SCALE:=60; (*60 FOR TEKTRONIX 4006;*)
       (* 20 FOR TERAK; ?? FOR OTHERS*)
  PENCOLOR(WHITE);
  CNT:=1;
  REPEAT
    MOVE(SCALE);
    TURN(72);
    CNT:=CNT+1;
      (*CNT IS NUMBER OF LINES DRAWN SO FAR*)
  UNTIL CNT=5;
END.
```

Problem 3.2:

Write out what the procedures VERSIONA and VERSIONB will display when called using the parameter values shown in the following table (one call to each procedure for each line in the table):

X	Y	Z
1	10	100
5	5	5
10	10	10
5	8	10

```
PROCEDURE VERSIONA(X,Y,Z:INTEGER);
VAR W:INTEGER;
BEGIN
  IF X < 10 THEN
    BEGIN
      W:=1;
      IF Y > 5 THEN
        IF Z = 10 THEN
          WRITELN('Y=',Y)
        ELSE
          WRITELN('Z=',Z)
    END;
  WRITELN('W=',W, ', X=',X, ', Y=,Y, ', Z=',Z);
END (*VERSIONA*);
```

```
PROCEDURE VERSIONB(X,Y,Z:INTEGER);
VAR W:INTEGER;
BEGIN
  IF X < 10 THEN
    BEGIN
      W:=1;
      IF Y > 5 THEN
        BEGIN
          IF Z = 10 THEN
            WRITELN('Y=',Y)
        END ELSE
          WRITELN('Z=',Z)
    END;
  WRITELN('W=',W, ', X=',X, ', Y=',Y, ', Z=',Z);
END (*VERSIONB*);
```

In principle, PASCAL should be implemented so that an attempt to use the value of any variable that has never had a value assigned to it will cause the program to terminate abnormally. Indicate whether this situation would apply to any of the four conditions given in the table above. Modify these procedures to prevent this situation from arising. (Values are assigned to each of the three parameters when the procedure is called.)

Chapter 4

MORE ON PROCEDURES

1. Goals

In this chapter we add several important details to the discussion on Procedures. An understanding of these details will help you to write programs that are both simpler and more likely to run correctly with a minimum of effort. The concepts involved also apply to many non-computer problem solving situations.

1a. Learn to use the rules on the scope of identifiers to limit the possibility that a variable might be used erroneously.

1b. Use procedures whose declarations are nested to several levels.

1c. Develop the ability to design procedures so that they communicate no more than necessary with other parts of a program.

1d. Learn to use recursive procedures as a way to make simple certain problems that otherwise would be very complex. Conversely, learn when not to use recursion, even though the program that results may seem simpler.

1e. Write and use your own functions.

1f. Learn the distinction between value parameters (the kind we have used so far) and variable parameters.

1g. Learn to use the CASE statement.

2. Background

For problems of the complexity we have dealt with so far, it has not been necessary or desirable to complicate matters with several important characteristics of procedures designed for working with complex problems. These characteristics are the subject of this chapter, as we will need to use them in later chapters.

Two general ideas permeate the characteristics discussed in this chapter. First, the concept of using procedures to break a problem solution into independent primitive parts implies that one should minimize the amount of information that needs to be handled in common by distinct procedures. This makes it easier to forget about details of variables and other named items that are external to a procedure when working with the details of that procedure. Similarly, when working in one part of a program, you should not have to worry about the effects a procedure, that might be called from elsewhere in the program, will have on variables you may happen to be working with currently. Computer people call these inadvertent changes in a variable "side-effects" of a procedure.

The second general idea is the use of a logical device called a "stack", which simplifies retention of data values that are specific to a particular situation or context, particularly when you expect to leave that context but have to return later. A stack is a list of data values bearing a logical similarity to a stack of books in a library, or stack of cans in the supermarket. As the number of items on the stack grows large, it is certainly easiest to remove the top item before any other item. A logical stack has the same property, i.e. the last item to be added to the stack is the first one to be taken off. "Recursive" procedures allow you to manipulate a stack of data values with very little effort. This is why "recursion" is considered a very important tool in computer science, and in other problem solving situations.

3. Scope of Variable Identifiers

Refer to the program SCOPEDEMO, and to the page on which the lines displayed by this program are shown. The variables S and LEVEL, declared in lines 2 and 3 respectively, are said to be "global" as they may be used throughout the entire program. The variable S, declared in line 15, is said to be "local" to the procedure Q is it may only be used within that procedure. Although they have the same name, the two declarations of S refer to completely different cells in the computer's memory, and the compiler does not confuse one of them with the other.

The use of the same <identifier> to refer to two different <variable>'s may seem strange at first, but there are often important reasons for doing this. This particular program is not intended to do any more than illustrate how the rules work, and it is difficult to make a strong case for the use of this rule in a small program that will fit on one page. If you are concentrating on the details of a procedure, such as Q, and have no occasion to refer within that procedure to a global variable such as S, then you save mental effort by not having to worry about possible conflicts of names used locally within the procedure and names used elsewhere in the program.

To see what this rule implies, refer to the Display associated with SCOPEDEMO. Lines 3 thru 5 of the display are generated by the call to P in line 39 of the program. We use the global variable LEVEL in this program to illustrate, through indentation, how many procedures are in execution at any time. In this case, we indent one level (2 columns) to show that only the procedure P is currently active. The indentation is accomplished by adding 1 to LEVEL immediately after each procedure is entered, and subtracting 1 from LEVEL as the last thing done

```
PROGRAM SCOPEDEMO;
VAR S:STRING;
  LEVEL:INTEGER;

PROCEDURE P;
BEGIN
  LEVEL:=LEVEL+1;
  WRITELN(' ':LEVEL*2, 'ENTER P');
  WRITELN(' ':LEVEL*2, S);
  WRITELN(' ':LEVEL*2, 'EXIT P');
  LEVEL:=LEVEL-1;
END (*P*);

PROCEDURE Q;
VAR S:STRING;
BEGIN
  LEVEL:=LEVEL+1;
  WRITELN(' ':LEVEL*2, 'ENTER Q');
  S:='HI THERE';
  WRITELN(' ':LEVEL*2, S);
  P;
  WRITELN(' ':LEVEL*2, 'EXIT Q');
  LEVEL:=LEVEL-1;
END (*Q*);

PROCEDURE R;
BEGIN
  LEVEL:=LEVEL+1;
  WRITELN(' ':LEVEL*2, 'ENTER R');
  S:='WATCH ME NOW!';
  WRITELN(' ':LEVEL*2, S);
  WRITELN(' ':LEVEL*2, 'LEAVE R');
  LEVEL:=LEVEL-1;
END (*R*);

BEGIN (*MAIN PROGRAM*)
  S:='MAIN PROGRAM';
  LEVEL:=0;
  P;  WRITELN(S);
  Q;  WRITELN(S);
  R;  WRITELN(S);
END.
```

```
Display associated with SCOPEDEMO

  ENTER P
  MAIN PROGRAM
  EXIT P
MAIN PROGRAM
  ENTER Q
  HI THERE
    ENTER P
    MAIN PROGRAM
    EXIT P
  EXIT Q
MAIN PROGRAM
  ENTER R
  WATCH ME NOW!
  LEAVE R
WATCH ME NOW!
```

before the procedure terminates. Each WRITE statement in the procedures displays 2*LEVEL blank spaces before its non-blank message. Line 6 of the Display listing is generated by the WRITELN statement in line 39 of the program, and is shown without indentation to represent LEVEL=0, i.e. no procedures currently in execution.

In line 40 of the program, Q is called. This immediately results in the next two lines being displayed by the WRITELN statements in lines 18 and 20 of the program. Line 20 displays "HI THERE" since that value is assigned to S in line 19. The S involved here is local to the procedure, having been declared in line 15. It is not the same as the S used everywhere in the program <u>except</u> within procedure Q. Thus when we call P in line 21, that procedure displays exactly the same three lines that it did before, except that the indentation has been increased by one level. In particular, line 10 of the display contains "MAIN PROGRAM" showing that the value of the global variable S has not been changed. This is further emphasized after Q terminates, displaying line 12, because the WRITELN in line 40 of the program produces "MAIN PROGRAM" in line 13 of the display.

Now, in line 41 of the program, R is called. The content of R is very similar to the content of P, except that a new value is assigned to S in line 30. Thus the procedure R displays "WATCH ME NOW!" as the value of the global variable S in line 15 of the display. Since there is no local variable S declared in R, the compiler refers to the global variable S when it translates lines 30 and 31 in R. Therefore, the value of the global S is permanently changed by this process. As a result, when the last statement in the program is executed, i.e. the WRITELN in line 41, the legend "WATCH ME NOW!" is again displayed.

To visualize how the rule works, and what the compiler does, refer to the "window diagram" in Figure 4-1. This diagram provides a simplified representation of the program SCOPEDEMO. There is one closed box, or "window", corresponding to each <block> in the program. The largest window corresponds to the main program, and is seen to enclose all the other windows, as well as the main program part at the bottom. No one of the other windows encloses any other. These windows allow viewing in only one direction. For example, in procedure P, the appearance of the identifier S causes the compiler to look outwards through the window for P in order to "see" the global identifier S. The same is true for R. If there were a unique local identifier declared in the procedure P, it would be necessary to look inward through the window for P in order to see that identifier from anywhere else in the program. But this is not allowed, since the window is made of one-way "glass".

In procedure Q, the reference to S is satisfied without having to look through a window since there is a local variable declared with that identifier. The compiler always looks in its directory for a record of a local declaration of an identifier, before looking out through the window of the block for a declaration of the same identifier outside. Similarly, the reference to S in the main program leads to the global declaration of S, and there is no need to look through a window in that case.

Also in procedure Q, the procedure P is called. This causes the compiler to look for the identifier P locally first. Since none is found there, it looks out through Q's window and finds that the identifier P has been declared (as the name of a procedure) in the main program's <block>.

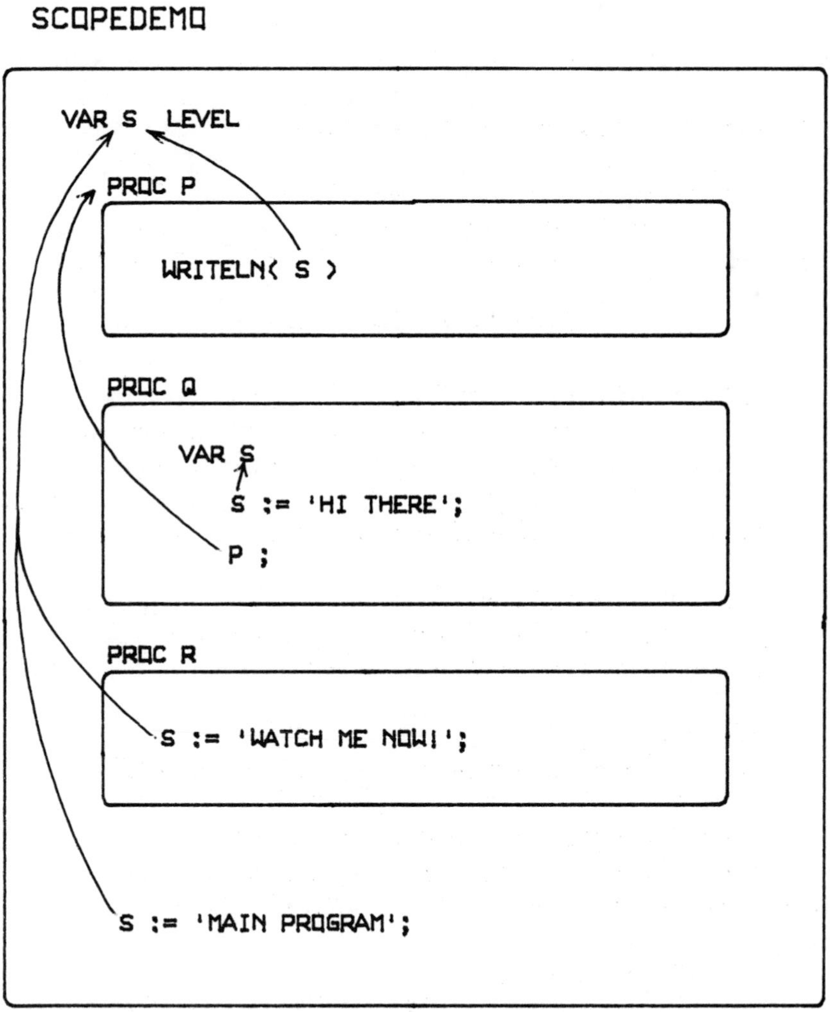

SCOPEDEMO

```
VAR S  LEVEL

PROC P
    WRITELN( S )

PROC Q
    VAR S
      S := 'HI THERE';
      P ;

PROC R
    S := 'WATCH ME NOW!';

S := 'MAIN PROGRAM';
```

Figure 4-1

As a final point regarding operation of the compiler, note that just one "pass" is made over your program starting at the beginning, and not terminating until END. is reached. Thus, when procedure P is being translated, the identifiers for procedures Q and R are not yet known to the compiler. This means that you cannot call either R or Q from within P, at least unless something special is done to provide for this situation.

There are some cases where it is convenient to be able to call a procedure from a point in the program which occurs before the procedure itself is declared. This can be done with a "FORWARD" declaration. For example, to call R from within P in SCOPEDEMO, without having to move the declaration of R earlier in the program, insert the following at line 4 in the program:

```
PROCEDURE R; FORWARD;
```

This FORWARD declaration line should contain any declaration of parameters for the procedure, and the parameter list should be omitted from the declaration line of the procedure declaration itself.

Exercise 4.1:

Analyze how the lines displayed by the program SCOPEDEMO would be changed if the variable declaration in line 15 of the program were simply removed. If necessary, run the revised program on the computer to see what happens. Then explain why the changes that occur do occur.

Exercise 4.2:

Try using the FORWARD declaration arrangement described above by calling procedure R from within procedure P. After showing that this works on the computer, now try the same tactic to call procedure Q from within P. What kind of problem do you get into? Can you think of a way to prevent this problem from getting out of hand?

4. Nested Procedures

As the syntax for <block>, shown in Figure 2-7 has already implied, it is possible to declare a procedure to be local within another procedure. This process is known as "<u>nesting</u>". The sample program NESTDEMO is an illustration in the form of a program designed specifically to show how the nesting rules work. The lines displayed by this program are shown on a separate page.

As in the illustration with the program SCOPEDEMO, the variable LEVEL is used to keep track of how many procedures are currently active. In NESTDEMO, LEVEL takes the form of the single parameter used by each procedure. Thus each occurrence of LEVEL in a procedure declaration heading line establishes a new variable local to the procedure, which happens to be a parameter, and whose name happens to be the same as that of several other parameters. Each time one of the procedures is called from within another procedure, the actual parameter used is (LEVEL+1). The effect of this is that each time a procedure is entered, the value of LEVEL within that procedure is 1 higher than the value of LEVEL within the calling procedure. The procedure DOTS is used to emphasize this by displaying one additional dot for each procedure activated.

```
PROGRAM NESTDEMO;

PROCEDURE DOTS(N:INTEGER);
VAR I:INTEGER;
BEGIN
  FOR I:=1 TO N DO WRITE('. ');
END (*DOTS*);

PROCEDURE P1(LEVEL:INTEGER);
BEGIN
  DOTS(LEVEL);
  WRITELN('P1 RUNNING');
END (*P1*);

PROCEDURE P2(LEVEL:INTEGER);
  PROCEDURE P2A(LEVEL:INTEGER);
    PROCEDURE P2A1(LEVEL:INTEGER);
    BEGIN
      DOTS(LEVEL); WRITELN('P2A1 RUNNING');
    END (*P2A1*);

  BEGIN(*P2A*)
    DOTS(LEVEL); WRITELN('ENTER P2A');
    P1(LEVEL+1);
    P2A1(LEVEL+1);
    DOTS(LEVEL); WRITELN('LEAVE P2A');
  END (*P2A*);

BEGIN (*P2*)
  DOTS(LEVEL); WRITELN('ENTER P2');
  P1(LEVEL+1);
  P2A(LEVEL+1);
  DOTS(LEVEL); WRITELN('LEAVE P2');
END (*P2*);

BEGIN (*MAIN PROGRAM*);
  WRITELN('MAIN PROGRAM');
  P1(1);
  WRITELN('MAIN PROGRAM AFTER P1');
  P2(1);
  WRITELN('MAIN PROGRAM AFTER P2');
   (*NOT LEGAL TO CALL P2A FROM HERE*)
END.
```

```
Display associated with NESTDEMO

MAIN PROGRAM
. P1 RUNNING
MAIN PROGRAM AFTER P1
. ENTER P2
. . P1 RUNNING
. . ENTER P2A
. . . P1 RUNNING
. . . P2A1 RUNNING
. . LEAVE P2A
. LEAVE P2
MAIN PROGRAM AFTER P2
```

As an example, in line 31 of the program, P1 is called, leading to line 7 of the display which shows "P1 RUNNING" with two levels of indentation. The value of LEVEL within P2 is 1, as shown by line 6 of the display. Thus the value passed as an actual parameter to P1 in line 31 is LEVEL+1, i.e. 2, leading to the two levels of indentation in line 7.

In line 32, P2 calls P2A (where the "A" is used to suggest that P2A is the first subsidiary procedure within P2) which leads to lines 8 thru 11 in the display. P2A calls P1 again in line 24, but this time the value of LEVEL passed to P1 is 3, leading to the 3 levels of indentation in line 9. The same is true in line 10, although P2A1 is declared as local within P2A.

The window diagram illustrating NESTDEMO may be found in Figure 4-2. The diagram shows that the rule about looking only outward through a window applies in the case of procedure identifiers just as it does to variables. In each case of a parameter LEVEL, it occurs within the window of the procedure in whose heading it is declared. The rules covering the scope of parameter identifiers are the same as the rules covering variables declared following VAR within the <block> belonging to the same procedure. In fact each of the parameters in this program is in reality a local variable having the special characteristic that its value is initialized by the statement in which the associated procedure is called. We will discuss a different kind of parameter, having somewhat diferent properties, later in this chapter.

Notice that the indentations of lines 8 and 11 in the display are the same, indicating that LEVEL had the same value of 2 in line 23 of the program and again in line 26. Meanwhile, both P1 and P2A1 were called in lines 24 and 25 respectively. Line 11 of the display shows that the value of the instance of LEVEL local to P2A remained unchanged while the other procedures were in operation, just as any other local variable would have done. During the activation of

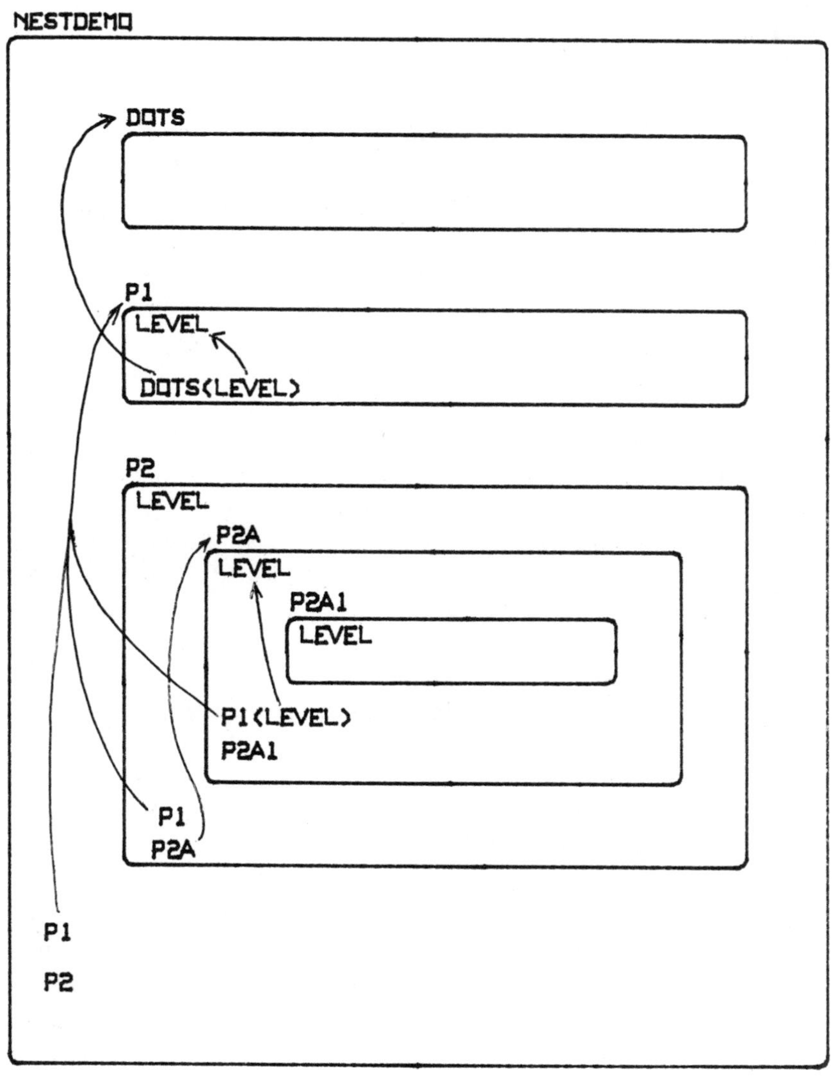
NESTDEMO
DOTS
P1
LEVEL
DOTS(LEVEL)
P2
LEVEL
P2A
LEVEL
P2A1
LEVEL
P1(LEVEL)
P2A1
P1
P2A
P1
P2

Figure 4-2

P1, it is not possible to refer to any variable which is declared local to P2A as the calling procedure, because of the one way window rule. During the activation of P2A1 it would have been possible to refer to a variable in P2A, P2, or to a global variable in the main program, since this would have involved looking outward through one or more windows.

Study the displayed lines for NESTDEMO carefully, and satisfy yourself that you understand why each line is displayed when it is, and why the indentation is as it is. An understanding of this demonstration is essential to understanding the remainder of this chapter.

Exercise 4.3:

Add local STRING variables to each of the procedures in the program NESTDEMO, giving them names which associate them with the parent procedure. For example use S2 for the variable which is local to procedure P2, S2A for procedure P2A, and so on. Also declare a global variable S.

Now add a statement to each <block> assigning a unique value to each variable that can be "seen" from that <block>. At the beginning of each <block>, add statements which display the current values of all STRING variables that can be seen from that <block> AND that have already had values assigned to them. If you assign a short string constant to each variable, then all of the values visible at a particular point can be displayed on a single line of the screen, allowing you to review what happens easily after making these changes. Trace through the program and account for the values that are actually displayed.

5. Case Study - Using Nested Procedures

Consider Figure 4-3a showing a simple "plant", with two flowers, drawn by the turtle. Note that the flowers are of different sizes, and that there are two leaf petals connected to the main stem of the plant. Before you read further, try to devise a strategy that would allow writing a simple program to draw this figure.

Since the two flowers are of identical shape, except for the size, one obvious simplification would be to write a procedure that draws a flower. Similarly one procedure can be used to draw the two leaf petals connected to the stem. Finally, the program can draw the stem, calling the appropriate procedures when the places where the leaf petals and the flowers are to be connected. Now stop reading again, and consider how you would design the procedure to draw the flower.

Let us concentrate on the question of the flower by using Figure 4-3b. Note that each flower petal sprouts from the main stem on a short straight stem of its own. Moreover, each petal seems to consist of two identical sides drawn as an arc (portion of a circle). This suggests arranging a procedure whose duty is to draw an arc. In this case an arc covering 90 degrees, by making ten steps of 9 degrees each, was sufficient to give the desired appearance. The effect is similar to the circle drawn by the program POLYGONS in Chapter 3, except that one-fourth as many steps are needed to draw one quarter-circle. Now stop reading again, and make notes on the general appearance of the program you might write to draw the flower.

Refer now to the program FLOWER, which drew Figure 4-3b, and is designed along the lines just described. Notice that ARC is a procedure local to PETAL, since it is used only by PETAL. ARC can refer to SIZE, which is local to PETAL, since that variable (parameter) is local to an enclosing block. Had ARC

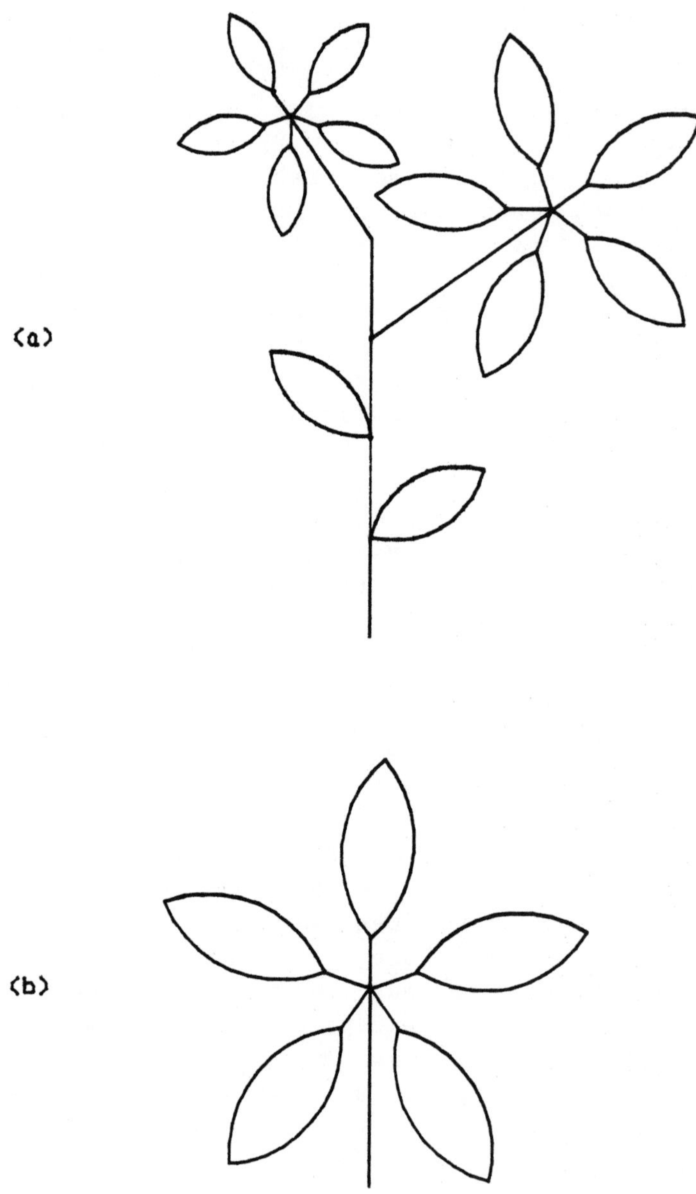

Figure 4-3

```
PROGRAM FLOWER;
VAR SCALE:INTEGER;

PROCEDURE BLOSSOM;
VAR I:INTEGER;

  PROCEDURE PETAL(SIZE:INTEGER);
    PROCEDURE ARC;
    VAR I:INTEGER;
    BEGIN
      PENCOLOR(WHITE);
      FOR I:=1 TO 10 DO
      BEGIN
        MOVE(SIZE*SCALE);
        TURN(9);
      END;
      PENCOLOR(NONE);
    END (*ARC*);

  BEGIN (*PETAL*)
    TURN(-45);
    ARC;
    TURN(90);
    ARC;
    TURN(135);
  END (*PETAL*);

BEGIN (*BLOSSOM*)
  FOR I:=0 TO 4 DO
  BEGIN
    PENCOLOR(WHITE);
    MOVE(5*SCALE);
    PETAL(2);
    MOVE(-5*SCALE);
    TURN(72);
  END;
END (*BLOSSOM*);

BEGIN (*MAIN PROGRAM*)
  SCALE:=12; (*12 FOR TEKTRONIX 4006;*)
        (* 4 FOR TERAK; ?? FOR OTHERS*)
  PENCOLOR(WHITE);
  MOVETO(0,-20*SCALE);
  MOVETO(0,0);
  TURN(90);
  BLOSSOM;
END.
```

been declared outside PETAL, it would have been necessary to give ARC a parameter SIZE also.

PETAL in turn is local to BLOSSOM since it is called only by BLOSSOM. BLOSSOM simply calls PETAL 5 times, in each case moving 5 scale units to create the stem of the petal. In this illustration, SCALE has been made a global variable rather than a parameter of BLOSSOM. If we were to make this entire program into a procedure to draw a flower, we probably would make SCALE into a parameter also. The principal duties of the main program in this case are to initialize the SCALE, and to draw the main stem of the flower.

Notice that at the level of each procedure, we can ignore virtually all of the details of the others. Having devised an overall strategy for writing the program, we can write the main part of the program by simply including a call to BLOSSOM, ignoring for the moment what the internal workings of BLOSSOM will have to be. Next we can declare BLOSSOM, including a call to PETAL, as in line 33. The only detail we need to carry over into PETAL from BLOSSOM is the question of the size of the petal to be drawn, which we decide to communicate to the procedure in the form of a parameter.

Next, we concentrate on PETAL, realizing that it will consist mainly of two calls to ARC. Since the arc will cover 90 degrees, we need to start by turning the Turtle -45 degrees (to the right in this case) in order to make the petal appear to be balanced on the end of the stem. At the remote end, a turn of 90 degrees then positions the Turtle symmetrically to make the return arc. Finally, the turn of 135 degrees in line 25 is needed to return the Turtle to its original direction. This is needed to avoid complicated record keeping in the calling procedure (BLOSSOM). To return the Turtle to its original direction simply requires that we assure that the sum of all turns is either 0 (zero) degrees, or some integer multiple of 360 degrees. In this case, we have decided that the arc will use up 90 degrees each time it is called. Thus twice 90, or 180 degrees, is to be added to the sum of the turns embodied within PETAL.

As a last step, we fill in the details of ARC. As already noted, ARC is very similar to POLYGONS in that it draws a sequence of short line segments separated by small turns.

Note that the simple variable I is used for quite distinct purposes both in ARC and in BLOSSOM. Since I is declared to be local to each procedure separately, we do not need to concern ourselves with the question of whether the use of I in ARC will interfere in any way with the use of I in BLOSSOM. Of course it would have been possible to use different identifiers in these two cases to avoid the possibility of interference entirely. However the "lazy way" is the best way in this case. By making sure that the control variable of the FOR statement is declared locally in the <block> where the FOR statement appears, we can be sure that there will be no interference. Thus, we can forget about the need to check on interference when working with the other <block>'s in the program.

As a general rule, you should get into the habit of declaring variables as close to local as you can in a nested procedure situation. In some cases, the same variable will be used for similar or identical purposes at several levels of procedure nesting, as with SCALE in this example program. As long as we do not assign new values to such a variable from several of the procedures, we can get in no trouble from placing it in the <block> which encloses all the procedures that use the variable.

However, you can get into real trouble in debugging a program if you decide to take a shortcut by using the same variable, declared at an enclosing level, for different purposes in different procedures. Thus, procedure A might assign one value to the variable, procedure C another value. Then if procedure B uses the value of that variable, you have to know whether the value was assigned by A or C before the program can make sense. All too often, a programmer will assign a value to a global variable, say X, in a procedure A, and use that value in procedure B. Later, it becomes necessary to declare procedure C for a new purpose, and "convenience" leads to the use of X within C for some new task. The programmer assumes that, following assignment to X within A, B will always be called before C. Thus, the programmer assumes, there can be no problem in re-using the variable and avoiding the small effort needed to make a new declaration.

Unfortunately, it often happens that a new task has to be added to the program at a still later stage. That later stage is often encountered after the programmer has forgotten that X is used for two different purposes. The new task may require calling A followed immediately by C before B is called. At this point X has been assigned a value that has no relevance for B, and the program cannot run correctly.

<u>MORAL</u>: Use each variable you declare for only one purpose, and keep it as close to local in the <block> where it is used as you can. This is what we mean by saying that the "<u>communication</u>" between <block>'s should be minimized. For similar reasons, you will probably want to assign tasks to each of your procedures in such a way as to keep the number of parameters that are needed as small as possible. Lest we be misunderstood, let us hasten to add that this rule about minimizing communication between <block>'s should not lead you to put all of the logic of the program into one giant <block>. The point of breaking the program into separate blocks is to avoid the need to keep track of communications between distinct parts of the program which handle tasks that are conceptually distinct.

Exercise 4.4:

Complete the design of the program to draw a complete "plant", as illustrated in Figure 4-3a. Note that the requirement to draw leaf petals sprouting from the main stem of the plant will require a re-design of the procedure nesting relationships if you start with the program FLOWER in the role of a procedure. Do not solve this problem by using two different procedures to draw petals! One of the main points of this exercise is to give you experience in seeing that program design will occasionally require certain amounts of re-design, even after you have reached a fairly advanced stage in solving the problem.

6. Declaring Your Own Functions

As noted earlier in the book, a "Function" in PASCAL is really a special kind of Procedure. You call a procedure by giving its name in a separate statement containing only that name, plus a list of parameters. You call a function by using its identifier within an expression, just as if it were an ordinary variable except that any list of parameters must be included. When called, a function performs its calculations just as a procedure does, but it also "returns" a value which takes the place of the function's identifier when the function finishes execution.

With this background, the sample program COUNTWORDS should be easy to understand. The program requests that you type in a one line sentence. It then assumes that the number of words in the sentence can be computed by adding up the number of blank spaces in the sentence, and adding 1 for the last word. Of course you could be perverse and type in a sentence using more than one blank to separate successive words, and the result computed by this program would then be wrong. This is a complication that we can avoid temporarily for the purpose of illustrating how

```
PROGRAM COUNTWORDS;
VAR S:STRING;

FUNCTION COUNTEM(S:STRING):INTEGER;
VAR CNT,K:INTEGER;
BEGIN
  CNT:=0;
  FOR K:=1 TO LENGTH(S) DO
      IF S[K]=' ' THEN CNT:=CNT+1;
  COUNTEM:=CNT+1;
END (*COUNTEM*);

BEGIN (*MAIN PROGRAM*)
  WRITELN('COUNTWORDS');
  WRITELN('TYPE ANY ONE LINE SENTENCE');
  READLN(S);
  WHILE LENGTH(S)>0 DO
    BEGIN
      WRITELN(COUNTEM(S),' WORDS');
      WRITELN;
      WRITELN('TYPE ANOTHER');
      READLN(S);
    END;
END.
```

functions work.

The declaration of the function COUNTEM commences in line 4 of the program. Line 4 differs from a procedure declaration heading line in two respects. First, the reserved word FUNCTION appears in place of PROCEDURE. Second, the <type> of the value that the function will return must be given following the parameter list. The syntax, as shown in Figure 4-4, specifies that a colon (":") must appear between the parameter list and the <type identifier>. The <type identifier> must refer to a simple type, i.e. one containing only one value, such as INTEGER, CHAR, or BOOLEAN. You cannot return a STRING as the value of a function. A function or procedure can return the value of a STRING via a variable parameter, something we will discuss in a later section of this chapter.

In addition to the heading line, a function differs from a procedure in the requirement that a value be assigned to the function's identifier somewhere within the <block> belonging to the function. This is the manner in which the value to be "returned" by the function will be made available within the expression where the function is called. For example, COUNTEM is assigned a value in line 10 of the program. Although COUNTEM appears to be used as if it were an ordinary identifier in this context, this appearance is deceptive. Within the function's own <block>, you cannot put the identifier of the function itself on the right of the assignment operator, or elsewhere where an expression would be appropriate, without causing the function to call itself!. This is called "recursion", a subject we will discuss later in this chapter. There is no problem associated with assigning values to the identifier of a function in several different places within the function's <block>. This might be done inside a complex of nested IF statements to assign different values to the function's identifier depending upon differing conditions.

The program COUNTWORDS calls the function COUNTEM in line 19 as the first of two items to be displayed by the WRITELN statement.

Exercise 4.5:

> Write and debug a program containing a function which scans an input line of text and reports how many non-alphabetic characters appear in that line. Remember that all of the alphabetic characters are greater than or equal to 'A' AND less than or equal to 'Z', OR they are greater than or equal to 'a' AND less than or equal to 'z'. Test your program using any five lines of text from this book which contain several punctuation characters such as '.', ';', ':', '<', and so on, making sure that the program's displayed result agrees with the result you get by scanning by eye.

7. Variable Parameters

Occasionally it is desirable to have a procedure or function return two or more values after completing its work. This can be done with "*variable parameters*" as distinguished from the parameters you have been using so far. The parameters you have been using are known as "*call-by-value parameters*" or simply "*value parameters*". This implies that a value parameter can only *receive* a value when the procedure or function is called.

The sample program PARAMDEMO is a simple illustration of the difference between value parameters and variable parameters. Syntax covering both is shown in part (b) of Figure 4-4, which describes <parameter list>. The procedure DISPLAY is used at each step in the program to trace the results of that step as they affect the global variables X and Y. The program consists of 5 main parts, separated by blank lines for clarity, in addition to the initialization in

```
PROGRAM PARAMDEMO;
VAR X,Y:INTEGER;

  PROCEDURE PV(X: INTEGER);
  BEGIN
    WRITELN('ENTER PV, X=', X);
    X:=X+5;
    WRITELN('LEAVE PV, X=', X);
  END (*PV*);

  PROCEDURE PN(VAR N: INTEGER);
  BEGIN
    WRITELN('ENTER PN, N=', N);
    N:=N+1;
    WRITELN('LEAVE PN, N=', N);
  END (*PN*);

  PROCEDURE DISPLAY;
  BEGIN
    WRITELN('X=',X, ', Y=',Y);
    WRITELN
  END (*DISPLAY*);

BEGIN (*MAIN PROGRAM*)
  X:=1;
  Y:=2;
  DISPLAY;

  PV(Y);
  DISPLAY;

  PV(X);
  DISPLAY;

  PV(3*Y + X);
  DISPLAY;

  PN(X);
  DISPLAY;

  PN(Y);
  DISPLAY
END.
```

```
Display associated with PARAMDEMO
X=1, Y=2
ENTER PV, X=2
LEAVE PV, X=7
X=1, Y=2
ENTER PV, X=1
LEAVE PV, X=6
X=1, Y=2
ENTER PV, X=7
LEAVE PV, X=12
X=1, Y=2
ENTER PN, N=1
LEAVE PN, N=2
X=2, Y=2
ENTER PN, N=2
LEAVE PN, N=3
X=2, Y=3
```

<block>

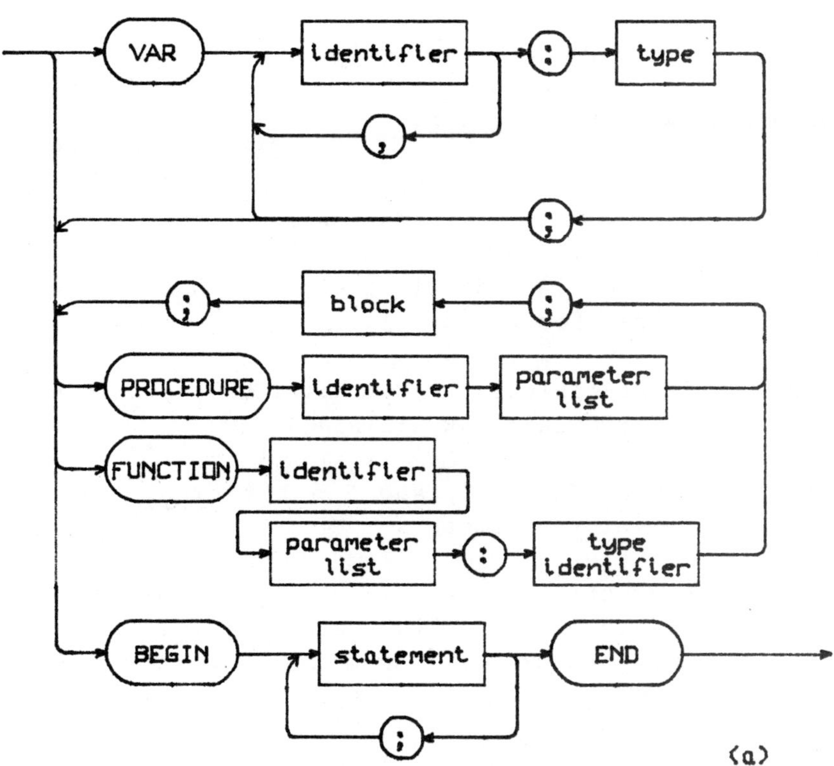

(a)

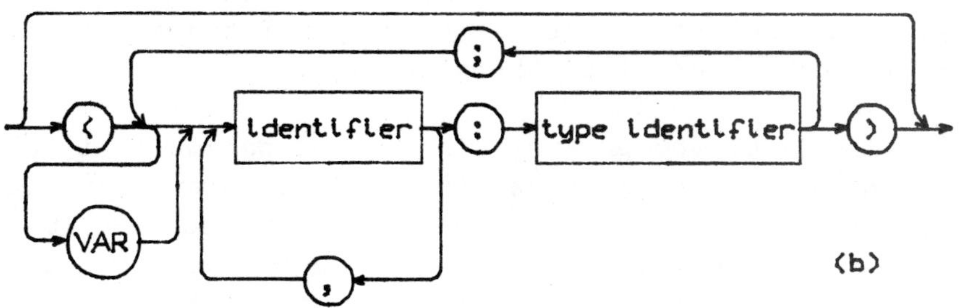

(b)

Figure 4-4

lines 25 and 26. A separate page shows the displayed lines associated with PARAMDEMO.

The procedure PV has one value parameter X. The procedure PN has one variable or "call-by-name" parameter N. The syntax requires that the reserved identifier VAR appear before any list of identifiers which are to be variable parameters. VAR must not appear before identifiers which are to be call-by-value parameters. This requires that VAR appear once for each distinct <type> associated with the parameters. For example, in:

```
PROCEDURE P(A:INTEGER; VAR B,C:INTEGER; D:INTEGER;
     VAR E:BOOLEAN; VAR S:STRING);
```

the parameters B, C, E, and S are variable whereas A and D are value parameters.

In line 29 of the program, PV is called using Y as its actual parameter. Y is evaluated, and its value of 2 is assigned to the parameter X within PV as shown by line 5 of the display. The procedure then adds 5 to X in line 7, and displays the resulting value of 7 in line 6 of the display. Notice that line 7 of the display shows that this process has made no change in the global variables X or Y. Only the local variable X in the procedure, i.e. the parameter, was changed. Similarly, the call to PV with the global X as its actual parameter, in line 32, produces no change in the value of the global X, as shown by line 11 of the display.

In line 35 of the program, the actual parameter is an arithmetic expression rather than a simple reference to a variable. One can use an expression for the actual parameter if the associated formal parameter (in the procedure or function declaration line) is call-by-value and of the same <type> as the expression. Thus line 13 of the display shows that the parameter X has been set to 7 when the procedure PV was called. You can easily verify that this is the value of 3*Y+X at this point. Once again the call to

PV has not affected the values of the global variables X and Y.

In line 38 of the program, PN is called with an actual parameter of X. Lines 17 and 18 of the display show that the parameter N is changed, as expected, by the addition in line 14 of the program. This time however, the display line 19 shows that the global variable X has taken on a new value, i.e. the value that the parameter N had when PN terminated. This is because a variable parameter masquerades within the procedure for the actual parameter used when the procedure is called. The actual parameter is substituted for the formal parameter in this case. Thus the call PN(X) in line 38 of the program should be read as causing every reference to N in the procedure PN to be re-named X. However the call PN(Y) in line 41 causes every reference to N in the procedure to read as Y instead. Thus, both calls to PN have the effect of making permanent changes in the global variables used as actual parameters.

In general, when you want only to communicate information INTO a procedure or function, you should use value parameters. When you need to communicate information back OUT of the procedure or function, and it is not convenient to use the function value return mechanism, then variable parameters must be used. In the latter case, the compiler generates instructions which translate each reference to the formal variable parameter into references to the location of the actual parameter in memory. For simple variables it is generally best to use the value parameter mechanism. For complex data structures, such as we will encounter in Chapters 8, 9 and 10, the value parameter mechanism uses substantial amounts of processing time that may not be necessary. In those cases the variable parameter mechanism will generally be preferable. Notice that the substitution mechanism associated with variable parameters means that they may be used both to communicate information INTO and OUT of a procedure or function.

Exercise 4.6:

Revise the program you wrote to count alphabetic characters in Exercise 4.5 to use a procedure with a variable parameter, rather than using a function. Debug and test the program to verify that it works correctly, again with at least 5 lines of text.

Exercise 4.7:

A very common task for programmers is to arrange a procedure which scans a line of text, starting at some specified position, and returns as its value the <string> associated with the next "token" of text. For the purposes of this exercise, a token will be either a single English word, or any other non-blank character.

Write and debug a program which prompts for and accepts an arbitrary string of characters from the keyboard, and then displays each token in the input line on a separate line of its own. For assistance in debugging this program, it will be helpful to display also the value of the variable you use to point to the current scanning position in the STRING variable containing the input line, at the time when each token is displayed. You might also display the number of characters that your program "thinks" are associated with the token which is displayed. Be sure that this count does not include any blank characters.

For your program to be able to handle non-alphabetic characters which are not blanks, you will have to use IF statements for scanning rather than using the built-in POS function. However, COPY and DELETE may be of assistance in handling the substrings which you scan off for each successive token. To test your program, use as input lines 11 and 13 of the PARAMDEMO program. Check the results that the program returns by visually scanning for tokens in those lines.

8. Recursive Procedures

A "recursive" procedure is one which calls itself. This conceptually simple mechanism is one of the most powerful tools of computer science. It is very similar to the principle used by mathematicians in describing relationships that would otherwise be very complex. We discuss recursive procedures at this point in the book for two reasons. First, it has been our experience that you need to understand recursive procedures in order to develop an understanding of how procedures in general really work. Second, recursion is so fundamental to problem solving methods that you should learn to use the concept, even if you will have relatively few occasions for working with complex computer programs after finishing this book. Recursion is sometimes considered to be too complicated a topic to include in a beginning course on programming. We have not found recursion to be too complex for most students. However, a little extra effort spent in understanding the material on recursion in this chapter will be well worth your while.

As a first step, refer to the program RCOUNT, which performs the same task in counting words that the program COUNTWORDS performed, as we have already described. Now, instead of using a FOR statement to control looping, we call COUNTEM in line 9 of the program if the value of the actual parameter string S contains at least one blank space character. The value passed to the new instance of COUNTEM as its parameter is a COPY of all characters in S following the first blank character. Thus the next instance of COUNTEM receives, as its value of S, a string with one fewer blanks. Eventually, an instance of COUNTEM will be called in which S contains no blanks. The ELSE clause in that instance of COUNTEM will then cause CNT to be assigned the value 1 in line 11, and the function will return a value of 1, indicating

```
PROGRAM RCOUNT;
VAR S:STRING;

PROCEDURE DOTS(N:INTEGER);
VAR I:INTEGER;
BEGIN
  FOR I:=1 TO N DO WRITE('. ');
END (*DOTS*);

FUNCTION COUNTEM(S:STRING;
                 LEVEL:INTEGER):INTEGER;
VAR CNT,K,L:INTEGER;
BEGIN
  K:=POS(' ',S); L:=LENGTH(S);
  DOTS(LEVEL); WRITELN(S, ', L=',L);
  IF K>0 THEN
      CNT:=1
        +COUNTEM(COPY(S,K+1,LENGTH(S)-K),LEVEL+1)
    ELSE
      CNT:=1;
  COUNTEM:=CNT;
  DOTS(LEVEL);
  WRITELN('LEAVE, CNT=',CNT, ', L=',L);
END (*COUNTEM*);

BEGIN (*MAIN PROGRAM*)
  WRITELN('COUNTWORDS');
  WRITELN('TYPE ANY ONE LINE SENTENCE');
  READLN(S);
  WHILE LENGTH(S)>0 DO
    BEGIN
      WRITELN(COUNTEM(S,0),' WORDS');
      WRITELN;
      WRITELN('TYPE ANOTHER');
      READLN(S);
    END;
END.
```

```
Display associated with RCOUNT

NOW IS THE TIME FOR ACTION
NOW IS THE TIME FOR ACTION, L=26
. IS THE TIME FOR ACTION, L=22
. . THE TIME FOR ACTION, L=19
. . . TIME FOR ACTION, L=15
. . . . FOR ACTION, L=10
. . . . . ACTION, L=6
. . . . . LEAVE, CNT=1, L=6
. . . . LEAVE, CNT=2, L=10
. . . LEAVE, CNT=3, L=15
. . LEAVE, CNT=4, L=19
. LEAVE, CNT=5, L=22
LEAVE, CNT=6, L=26
6 WORDS
```

that only one word is left in S.

The last instance of COUNTEM will now terminate, leaving a 1 in its place in line 9 of the next previous instance (from which the last instance of COUNTEM had been called). The addition then takes place, and the next-to-last instance of the function returns a value of 2. This value is substituted for COUNTEM in line 9 of the next previous instance, and the process continues until all instances have terminated except for the first one. The first instance of COUNTEM was called from line 32 of the program within the WRITELN statement. When this instance terminates, the program continues processing the WRITELN statement just as it did in the COUNTWORDS program.

It is important to realize that each _instance_ or _activation_ of a function or procedure is like having a new copy of that function or procedure declared in your program with a slightly different name. You might think of each instance as having a different color to keep them distinguished. Thus, when the "black" instance of COUNTEM calls the "brown" instance into execution, the "brown" function must eventually return to the point from which it was called in line 18. That point is within the "black" instance, not in line 32 of the main program. Each new instance has its own local variables and parameters which are totally different from all of the parameters and variables of all the other instances. This is just like having a new "window" in the window diagrams for each instance of the function or procedure, even though every instance appears to have the same name.

For further illustration of the operation of RCOUNT, refer to the display listing for that program. Line 3 represents the line of text typed into the program. Line 4 repeats the same information, and is displayed by the WRITELN in line 15 within the COUNTEM procedure the first time it is called. This first instance of COUNTEM is called by the reference to

COUNTEM in the WRITELN statement in line 32 within the main program. Notice that the WRITELN in line 32 does not get around to displaying its output until COUNTEM has been called an additional 5 times, creating 5 additional instances of the procedure which have to terminate before the program can continue.

In RCOUNT, as in the program NESTDEMO, we have used the device of showing dots and indenting the lines displayed by a procedure as a way to illustrate how many procedures are currently activated. Lines 5 through 9 of the display listing are all generated by the calls to DOTS and WRITELN(S) in line 15 of the function COUNTEM, each line being displayed by a new instance of the function. Thus each line shows the value of the parameter S, which is one word shorter on each successive instance of the function. Having reached the sixth instance of COUNTEM, for which the value of the parameter LEVEL is 5 (5 dots), the value assigned to K by POS in line 14 becomes zero since there are no blanks in the string 'ACTION'. In this instance of the function, the ELSE side of the IF statement is executed, setting CNT to 1 but not calling COUNTEM once again. This breaks the cycle of repeated calls to COUNTEM from within itself, and line 10 of the display is generated as the last instance of the function is terminating.

This is the point where many students seem to lose track of what happens, and we urge careful study of the program and display listings until you feel you understand why the display is generated as it is. The main point to remember is that each <u>instance</u> of the function COUNTEM must terminate normally just as it would have had it been a completely distinct procedure in the PASCAL program.

Since COUNTEM is a function, it must return a value which is then used to complete the calculation of the value of the expression within which the function is called. Thus the sequence of actions, starting when line 10 of the display is generated, is that CNT in lines 17 and 18 of the program is assigned a value of 2 (1 is a constant in the expression, 1 is the value returned by the last instance of COUNTEM as shown by line 10 of the display), then COUNTEM is assigned the value of 2 in line 21, then line 11 of the display is generated. Next, the next-to-last instance of COUNTEM terminates, causing a value of 2 to be added into the expression in lines 17 and 18, so that 3 is the value assigned to CNT in the previous instance of COUNTEM. The process continues from there, each instance of COUNTEM terminating and leaving its value for use in the next previous instance of the function.

To further illustrate the operation of this program, we have added a local variable L in the function COUNTEM whose only purpose is to help in understanding the trace of the program execution. Each time COUNTEM is entered, L is assigned the value of the LENGTH of S within the current instance of COUNTEM. This value is then displayed along with S by the WRITELN in line 15, and again as the function terminates in line 23. In the first instance of COUNTEM, L is assigned a value of 26, as may be seen in line 4 of the display. Later, after all the other instances have finished their work, processing returns to the first instance of COUNTEM, and line 15 of the display is generated. This line shows that L still has the value of 26 in that instance of the function, since there are no further statements in the function where L is assigned any new value. Notice that this is evidence that <u>each instance of the function has its own separate set of local variables</u>, which are not shared with any other instance, even though the program statements within each instance are the same.

Exercise 4.8:

The recursion mechanism just described applies to both procedures and to functions. Revise the program RCOUNT making the function COUNTEM a procedure. For the value of CNT, you will have to add a value computed in the next instance of COUNTEM. To return this value to the instance of the procedure within which you are working, you will have to use a variable parameter, since the function value return mechanism will not apply. Note that there is a way to return this value, from one instance of the procedure to the instance which called it, by using a global variable. The use of a global variable for this purpose happens to work in this simple case of recursion, but often will not work when recursion is used. Thus the variable parameter mechanism is the one you should use for this exercise.

9. Misuses of Recursion in PASCAL

While the program RCOUNT gave us an example to use in explaining how recursion operates, the program COUNTWORDS is really a better way to solve the problem involved in both programs. Our main reason for taking this approach was a desire to avoid additional complications in the problem until you see how the mechanism works. The sample programs shown in this section will allow you to develop insight on how recursion operates, but they too can be programmed quite readily to operate more efficiently in a non-recursive manner.

In general, recursion will be used appropriately in cases where the algorithm requires one instance of a procedure to call itself, or a companion procedure, at least two times. The local variables in the procedure then serve to save information from the time the first new instance is called until that instance returns and preparations are made to call the next one. In the next section, we illustrate that principle in several sample programs. Another appropriate use may arise when it is necessary to save each member of a sequence of data values for later additional uses which will arise in the reverse of the initial order of processing.

The program FACTORIAL illustrates the example of recursion that is probably most often (mis)used in introductory programming texts. The factorial function has a simple definition in mathematics, namely:

```
factorial(N) = N * factorial(N-1)
```

An additional provision is that factorial(1) is defined to have a value of 1. For example:

```
factorial(2) = 2 * 1
factorial(3) = 3 * 2 = 6
factorial(4) = 4 * 6 = 24
factorial(5) = 5 * 24 = 120
```

and so on. Our program computes the value of the factorial function for an "argument", i.e. a data value to be used as an actual parameter, which you type in from the keyboard. The program allows the argument to be any digit from 0 through 7. Larger values will result in a value being computed which is too large to be held in one memory cell of the microcomputer you are probably using. Larger values can be computed exactly on larger computers, or approximately on a microcomputer as we will see in the next chapter.

The page showing what the FACTORIAL program displays contains examples for arguments of 1, 2, 3, and 4. One of the main points of showing the four illustrations is to show that the program determines how many instances of the function RFACT will be called depending upon the values of the data it works with. When the parameter N is not greater than 1, then the function returns a 1 rather than calling RFACT with a value of N-1 for the actual parameter.

```
PROGRAM FACTORIAL;
VAR X,RESULT:INTEGER;

PROCEDURE DOTS(N:INTEGER);
VAR I:INTEGER;
BEGIN
  FOR I:=1 TO N DO WRITE('. ');
END (*DOTS*);

FUNCTION RFACT(N,LEVEL:INTEGER):INTEGER;
VAR RF:INTEGER;
BEGIN
  DOTS(LEVEL);
  WRITELN('ENTER, N=',N);
  IF N>1 THEN RF:=RFACT(N-1,LEVEL+1)*N
         ELSE RF:=1;
  RFACT:=RF;
  DOTS(LEVEL);
  WRITELN('LEAVE, N=',N, ', RF=',RF);
END(*RFACT*);

FUNCTION FACT(N:INTEGER):INTEGER;
VAR I,X:INTEGER;
BEGIN
  X:=1;
  FOR I:=N DOWNTO 2 DO X:=X*I;
  FACT:=X;
END (*FACT*);

BEGIN (*MAIN PROGRAM*)
  WRITELN('FACTORIAL');
  WRITELN('TYPE ANY DIGIT 0 THRU 7, THEN <RET>');
  READLN(X);
  WHILE (X>=0) AND (X<=7) DO
    BEGIN
      RESULT:=RFACT(X,0);
      WRITELN('X=',X, ', RFACT=', RESULT,
                       ', FACT=',FACT(X));
      WRITELN;
      WRITELN('TYPE ANOTHER');
      READLN(X);
    END;
END.
```

```
Display associated with FACTORIAL

TYPE ANOTHER
1
ENTER, N=1
LEAVE, N=1, RF=1
X=1, RFACT=1, FACT=1

TYPE ANOTHER
2
ENTER, N=2
. ENTER, N=1
. LEAVE, N=1, RF=1
LEAVE, N=2, RF=2
X=2, RFACT=2, FACT=2

TYPE ANOTHER
3
ENTER, N=3
. ENTER, N=2
. . ENTER, N=1
. . LEAVE, N=1, RF=1
. LEAVE, N=2, RF=2
LEAVE, N=3, RF=6
X=3, RFACT=6, FACT=6

TYPE ANOTHER
4
ENTER, N=4
. ENTER, N=3
. . ENTER, N=2
. . . ENTER, N=1
. . . LEAVE, N=1, RF=1
. . LEAVE, N=2, RF=2
. LEAVE, N=3, RF=6
LEAVE, N=4, RF=24
X=4, RFACT=24, FACT=24
```

We use the local variable RF to hold the value that the function will return so that this value can be used within the tracing WRITELN statement in line 19 without causing the function to be called once again. Otherwise, it would have been possible in lines 15 and 16 to assign values to RFACT directly.

Now turn your attention to the function FACT. As the display clearly shows, FACT computes the same value as does RFACT when the value of the parameter is the same. FACT is based on the observation that the table shown above can be rewritten as follows:

```
factorial(2) = 2 * 1
factorial(3) = 3 * 2 * 1
factorial(4) = 4 * 3 * 2 * 1
factorial(5) = 5 * 4 * 3 * 2 * 1
```

and so on. The use of the FOR statement to compute this result is simple enough that one does not need to resort to the less efficient device of the recursive function or procedure. If all we need to do is to compute the value of the factorial function occasionally for one value, the difference in efficiency is probably of little concern. However, one often needs to write a procedure or function that will be used a large number of times. In that case it is important to avoid the extra processing time needed to call a procedure or function if doing so does not imply that the program will become harder to debug.

To make this point more forcefully, we will now analyze recursive and non-recursive functions for computing the members of a sequence of numbers of importance in mathematics called the "Fibonacci" sequence. Each successive member of the sequence equals the sum of the previous two members. Thus we obtain the following:

0 1 1 2 3 5 8 13 21 34 55 89

and so on, where the first two members, 0 and 1 are defined to start the sequence. Thus we can say that

fib(N) = fib(N-1) + fib(N-2)

where the argument is the number of the member of the sequence starting from 0 (zero). For example:

fib(3) = fib(2) + fib(1) = 1 + 1 = 2

fib(6) = fib(5) + fib(4) = 5 + 3 = 8

and so on. The program TRACEFIB contains both recursive (RFIB) and non-recursive (FIB) functions for computing the Nth member of this sequence. The display lines obtained for N values of 2, 3, and 4 are shown on a separate page. The main thing to notice here is that RFIB gets called more than once to compute the value of the lower numbered members of the sequence. For example, in lines 32, 37, and 41 of the display, the trace tells us that RFIB was called to compute RFIB(1), all in the course of handling the computation for just one member of the sequence, RFIB(4). The number of times RFIB will be called in this recursive solution to the problem will become exceedingly large very quickly. For example RFIB(11) will require RFIB to be called 1024 times for subsidiary values of N!

In contrast, the function FIB uses a simple FOR loop which saves the values of two members of the sequence for use in computing the next member. Once the new member of the sequence has been assigned to X, new values can be assigned to XBACK1 and XBACK2 for use in the next loop. The amount of computation required rises in proportion to the value N passed to FIB, whereas it rises in proportion to 2 raised to the power (N-1) in the recursive case! Obviously, the non recursive solution to this problem works much better than the recursive solution.

```
PROGRAM TRACEFIB;
VAR X,RESULT:INTEGER;

PROCEDURE DOTS(N:INTEGER);
VAR I:INTEGER;
BEGIN
  FOR I:=1 TO N DO WRITE('. ');
END (*DOTS*);

FUNCTION RFIB(N,LEVEL:INTEGER):INTEGER;
VAR RF:INTEGER;
BEGIN
  DOTS(LEVEL);  WRITELN('ENTER, N=',N);
  IF N>1 THEN
      RF:=RFIB(N-1,LEVEL+1) + RFIB(N-2,LEVEL+1)
    ELSE
      IF N=1 THEN RF:=1
        ELSE RF:=0;
  RFIB:=RF;
  DOTS(LEVEL);
  WRITELN('LEAVE, N=',N, ', RF=',RF);
END(*RFACT*);

FUNCTION FIB(N:INTEGER):INTEGER;
VAR XBACK1,XBACK2,SAVE,X,I:INTEGER;
BEGIN
  IF N<=1 THEN FIB:=N ELSE
  BEGIN
    XBACK1:=1; XBACK2:=0;
    FOR I:=2 TO N DO
      BEGIN
        X:=XBACK1 + XBACK2;
        (*now prepare for next time around*)
        SAVE:=XBACK1; XBACK1:=X; XBACK2:=SAVE;
      END;
    FIB:=X;
  END;
END (*FIB*);

BEGIN (*MAIN PROGRAM*)
  WRITELN('FIBONACCI');
  WRITELN('TYPE ANY DIGIT 0 THRU 7, THEN <RET>');
  READLN(X);
  WHILE (X>=0) AND (X<=7) DO
    BEGIN
      RESULT:=RFIB(X,0);
      WRITELN('X=',X, ', RFIB=', RESULT,
                           ', FIB=', FIB(X));
      WRITELN;
      WRITELN('TYPE ANOTHER');
      READLN(X);
    END;
END.
```

```
Display Associated with TRACEFIB
TYPE ANOTHER
2
ENTER, N=2
. ENTER, N=1
. LEAVE, N=1, RF=1
. ENTER, N=0
. LEAVE, N=0, RF=0
LEAVE, N=2, RF=1
X=2, RFIB=1, FIB=1
TYPE ANOTHER
3
ENTER, N=3
. ENTER, N=2
. . ENTER, N=1
. . LEAVE, N=1, RF=1
. . ENTER, N=0
. . LEAVE, N=0, RF=0
. LEAVE, N=2, RF=1
. ENTER, N=1
. LEAVE, N=1, RF=1
LEAVE, N=3, RF=2
X=3, RFIB=2, FIB=2
TYPE ANOTHER
4
ENTER, N=4
. ENTER, N=3
. . ENTER, N=2
. . . ENTER, N=1
. . . LEAVE, N=1, RF=1
. . . ENTER, N=0
. . . LEAVE, N=0, RF=0
. . LEAVE, N=2, RF=1
. . ENTER, N=1
. . LEAVE, N=1, RF=1
. LEAVE, N=3, RF=2
. ENTER, N=2
. . ENTER, N=1
. . LEAVE, N=1, RF=1
. . ENTER, N=0
. . LEAVE, N=0, RF=0
. LEAVE, N=2, RF=1
LEAVE, N=4, RF=3
X=4, RFIB=3, FIB=3
```

Although RFIB does require saving the value of N locally in the function so that it may be used in computing the values N-1 and N-2 when calling new instances of RFIB, the program never has to save more than two values from the sequence in order to arrive at the next value. When recursion is the best solution, it is usually true that the program needs to save an indefinitely large number of values for later use. The programs shown in the next section all have this property, and they would be much more difficult to write without recursion.

Exercise 4.8:

Write and debug a program which contains a recursive procedure REV designed to reverse the order of appearance of the characters in an arbitrary string. In words, the general logic of the procedure should be as follows: Use a single value parameter of <type> STRING, that might be called "SOURCE" to refer to the original value of the string to be reversed. Within REV, if the length of SOURCE is longer than one character, save the first character in a local STRING variable, then call REV again with a copy of the SOURCE string containing all of its original characters except for the first. Following the call to REV, concatenate or insert the saved character at the end of a global STRING variable DEST. If the length of SOURCE is found to be just one character on entering REV, then initialize DEST by assigning to it the value of SOURCE.

Add WRITELN statements to trace the value of SOURCE each time REV is entered, and to show the values of SOURCE,DEST, and the saved character just before REV terminates. Test the program with strings of varying length entered from the keyboard. Analyze your tracing display to be sure that you understand how each line is derived by the program. Try to implement essentially the same algorithm in a non-recursive way, after you have the recursive version working.

10. Applications of Recursion

In this section, we present three programs which are representative of the complexity of problems which can be solved with quite simple programs. All three are graphics oriented, and for that reason may be used to give you a time sequenced view of recursion that is very difficult to express in a textbook. We will analyze only one of these programs in detail. It uses an algorithm which is a close relative of a very important family of algorithms used in a wide variety of applications in computer science. These algorithms, which use a logical device called a "tree", are also being used increasingly in business applications of computers.

Refer to the program GROWTREE, and to Figure 4-5 which shows examples of the figures displayed by this program. As a first step to explaining the program, we need to explain the "CASE statement" which appears in lines 10 thru 19 of the program. In effect, the CASE statement is like an IF statement which gives more than two possible choices of action. As with the IF statement, only one of the possible choices is executed, following which execution continues after the end of the CASE statement. Figure 4-6 shows syntax and a flow chart illustrating the CASE statement.

Within the "range" of the case statement, there are several independent statements, each one being marked by one or more constants followed by a colon (":") character. Only one statement within this range is executed. That statement is selected from the entire group by the value of the <expression> in the heading line of the CASE statement, which must equal one of the marker constants. If the value of the <expression> does not correspond to one of the markers, then the action to be taken is left undefined by the standard definition of PASCAL. In

```
PROGRAM GROWTREE;
VAR SCALE,ORDER:INTEGER;

PROCEDURE TREE(X,Y,LGTH,DIR:INTEGER);
  PROCEDURE CHANGEXY;
  VAR DX,DY:INTEGER;
  BEGIN
    IF DIR<0 THEN DIR:=DIR+8;
    IF DIR>=8 THEN DIR:=DIR-8;
    CASE DIR OF
      0: BEGIN DX:=1; DY:=0; END;
      1: BEGIN DX:=1; DY:=1; END;
      2: BEGIN DX:=0; DY:=1; END;
      3: BEGIN DX:=-1; DY:=1; END;
      4: BEGIN DX:=-1; DY:=0; END;
      5: BEGIN DX:=-1; DY:=-1; END;
      6: BEGIN DX:=0; DY:=-1; END;
      7: BEGIN DX:=1; DY:=-1; END
    END (*CASES*);
    X:=X+SCALE*LGTH*DX;
    Y:=Y+SCALE*LGTH*DY;
  END (*CHANGEXY*);
BEGIN (*TREE*)
  PENCOLOR(NONE);
  MOVETO(X,Y);
  TURNTO(DIR*45);
  PENCOLOR(WHITE);
  CHANGEXY;
  MOVETO(X,Y);
  IF LGTH>1 THEN
  BEGIN
    TREE(X,Y,LGTH-1,DIR+1);
    TREE(X,Y,LGTH-1,DIR-1);
  END;
END (*TREE*);

BEGIN (*MAIN PROGRAM*);
  WRITE('SCALE:');
  READLN(SCALE);
  WRITE('ORDER:');
  READLN(ORDER);
  TREE(0,-SCALE*ORDER-100,ORDER,2);
END.
```

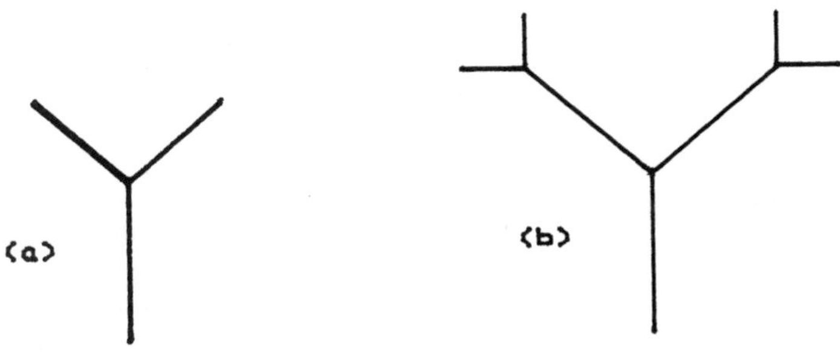

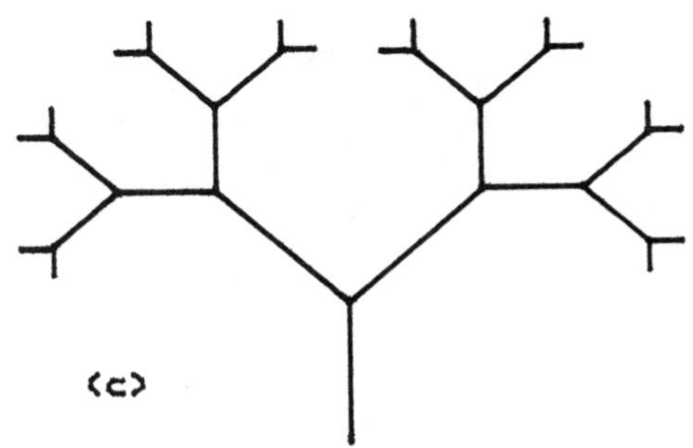

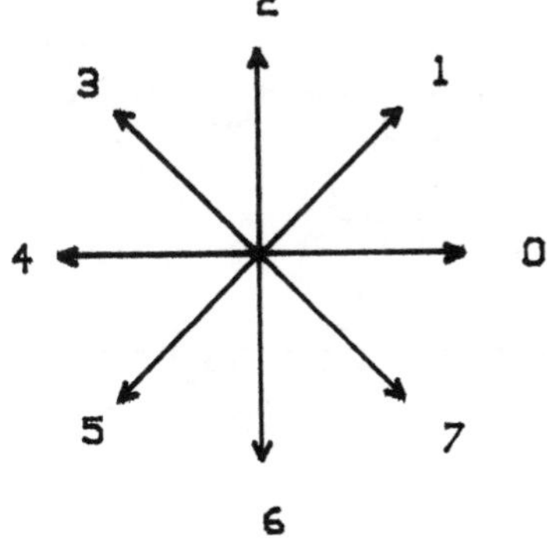

Figure 4-5

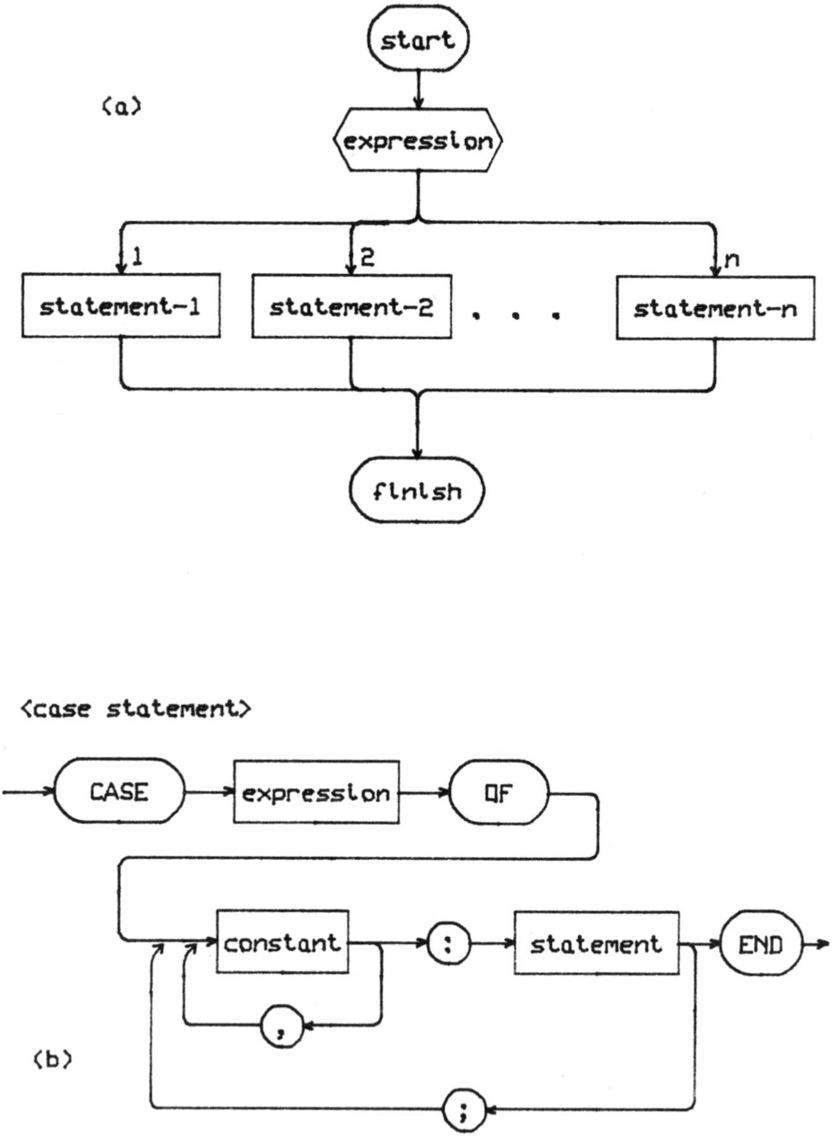

(a)

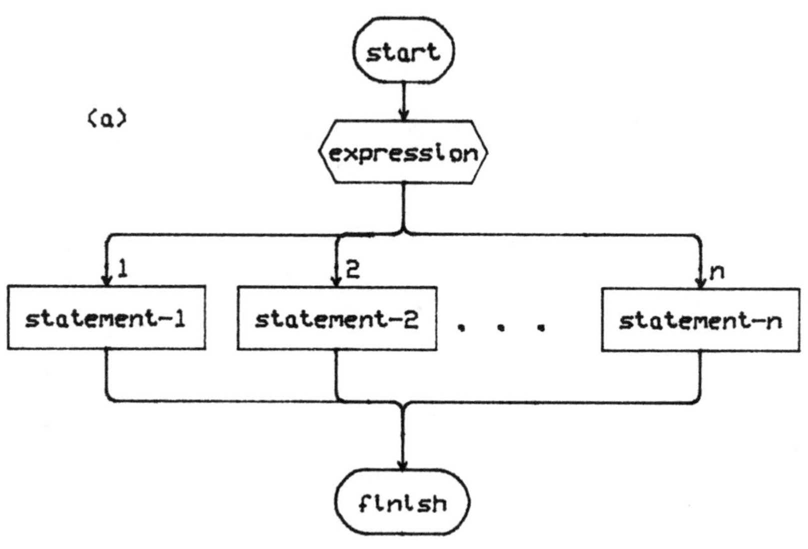

<case statement>

CASE
expression
OF
constant
:
statement
END
,
;

(b)

Figure 4-6

general, it is best to use IF statements just before the heading line of a CASE statement whose purpose is to assure that the value of the selector <expression> lies within the range of the marker constants. There should be a statement within the range of those markers to correspond to every possible value of the <expression> not rejected by the IF statements. The compiler will indicate a syntax error if the last statement within the range of the CASE statement is terminated with a semicolon (";").

In the program GROWTREE, the CASE statement is equivalent to the following:

```
IF DIR=0 THEN
  BEGIN DX:=1; DY:=0; END
  ELSE IF DIR=1 THEN
    BEGIN DX:=1; DY:=1; END
    ELSE IF DIR=2 THEN
      BEGIN DX:=0; DY:=1; END
      ELSE IF DIR=3 THEN
        BEGIN ...
          etc...
```

The CASE statement is simpler to write and read than is a long sequence of nested IF statements like this. On the average, the CASE statement will usually execute substantially faster than the equivalent nest of IF statements.

Figure 4-5 part (d) illustrates the purpose of the procedure CHANGEXY in the sample program, which contains the CASE statement. The drawing associates an integer in the set 0,1,2,...,7 with each of the eight Turtle pointing directions shown. CHANGEXY computes new position coordinate values for use by the MOVETO statement in line 29 of the program. The effect of lines 25 through 29 of the program, including the call to CHANGEXY, is to cause the Turtle to draw a line in one of those 8 directions, as specified by the value parameter DIR of the TREE procedure. The length of the line is specified by LGTH. The lines in the four sloping directions

(DIR=1, 3, 5, or 7) are longer than those in the horizontal or vertical directions because both DX and DY have an absolute value of 1.

The principal drawing action of the program is accomplished by the two calls that the recursive procedure TREE makes to itself in lines 32 and 33. This action is illustrated in part (a) of Figure 4-5 in which the variable ORDER was initially set to 2 by the READLN in line 41. TREE was then called in line 42, which assigned the value 2 to the parameter LGTH. Lines 24 and 25 then caused the Turtle to move, without drawing a line, to the position on the screen indicated by the values of X and Y. Lines 27 thru 29 then caused the vertical line, forming the "trunk" of the two-branch tree in the figure to be drawn. Since LGTH had a value greater than 1, TREE was then called twice: once in the direction to the left of the trunk's direction (DIR+1); once in the direction to the right of the trunk's direction (DIR-1). In both cases, the new LGTH was specified to be one unit shorter, i.e. 2 - 1 = 1. Thus the two "branches" of the tree are half as long as the trunk.

Part (b) of Figure 4-5 shows the tree drawn by this program when ORDER is initialized to 3, while part (c) shows the tree for ORDER=5.

<u>Exercise 4.9:</u>

Implement (i.e. type in and run) the program GROWTREE on your computer. First check to make sure that the display you get is the same as shown in Figure 4-5 for each of the three values of ORDER 2, 3, and 5 illustrated there. Now, place a READLN statement between lines 29 and 30 in the program. When you run this modified program, the result should be that the trunk of the tree will appear on your screen, and then the program will wait for further instructions. Press <RET> once, satisfying the READLN statement, and observe that one more line will be drawn. Each time you press

<RET>, one more line will appear.

Now operate the program with a value of ORDER (entered from the keyboard) of 2. Observe the action on a line by line basis, and make sure that you understand what the program is doing at each step. Now operate the program with a higher value of ORDER, say 5 or 6. Again observe the action on a line by line basis and notice the order in which the various lines are drawn. Notice that each of the two lines drawn by the calls to TREE (lines 32 and 33 of the program), from any one <u>instance</u> of tree, "sprout" from the same location, i.e. from the same values of X and Y. Since many small branches are drawn during the interval between the time when the first main branch is drawn, and the time when the second is drawn, it is clear that the X and Y values corresponding to the main branches had to be saved without alteration by the first instance of the TREE procedure. In the larger trees, the same comment applies to each higher level branching point, corresponding to higher level instances of the procedure.

If this demonstration is not yet sufficient to explain the operation of the program, then we suggest putting WRITELN statements, which display values of all the parameters of TREE, just before lines 24 and 35 respectively. On some display devices this may not be too practical if the display device cannot separately and simultaneously handle both graphics and alphanumeric characters.

<u>Exercise 4.10:</u>

Modify the GROWTREE program to display the trees illustrated in 4-7. The principal change is that three branches sprout from each branching point. Notice that the middle branch in each case does not itself branch into smaller branches. Note: This modification will be very simple to make if

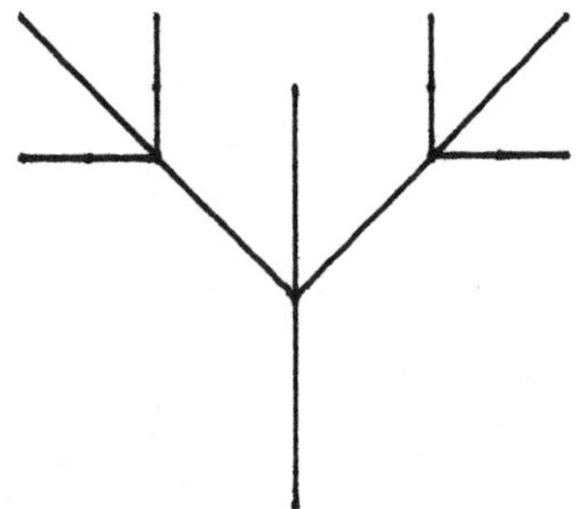

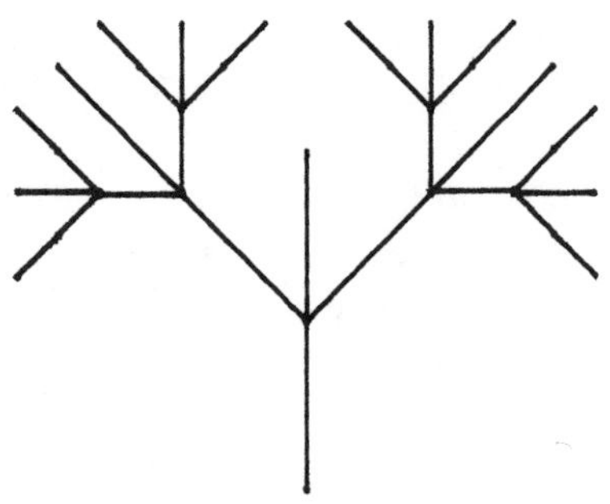

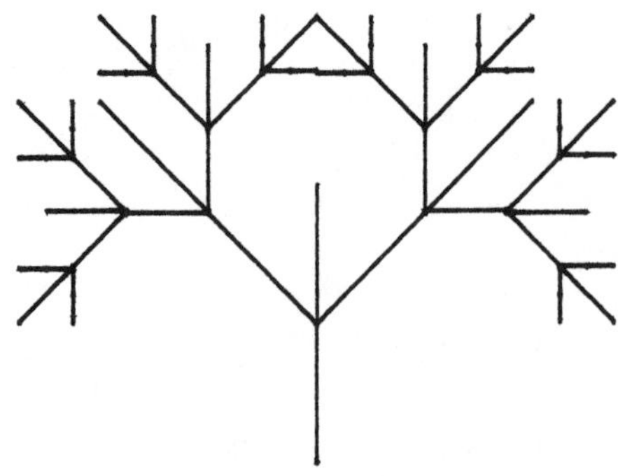

Figure 4-7

you understand the algorithm. No more than a few lines need to be added or changed.

Exercise 4.11:

Modify the GROWTREE program to display the "apple tree" shown in Figure 4-8. This modification should also be very simple to make.

Now refer to the sample program DRAGONS, which is shown to illustrate the complexity of an interesting drawing that can be made with a very simple program. The "dragon" shown in Figure 4-9 resulted from responding to the prompt for a "size" with the digit 8. The algorithm calls for a line to be drawn only when the value of the parameter LENGTH of the DRAGON procedure is zero.

Exercise 4.12:

Practically the only effective way to get an intuitive understanding of how the simple DRAGONS program works is to execute the program on a single step, line-by-line basis. Implement the program on your computer, adding a READLN statement between lines 5 and 6. If your display unit will allow both graphics and alphanumeric characters to be superimposed, then also add WRITELN('L:',LENGTH) at the same point. Now run the program several times with different values of SIZE starting with 1. Follow the action step by step, keeping track of what happens by comparing with the printed program, or with a program listing from your computer center.

When you think that you understand how the dragon is drawn, try modifying the program to draw a mirror image of the dragon shown in Figure 4-9, i.e. make the "dragon" face toward the right rather than toward the left. Try to perform this

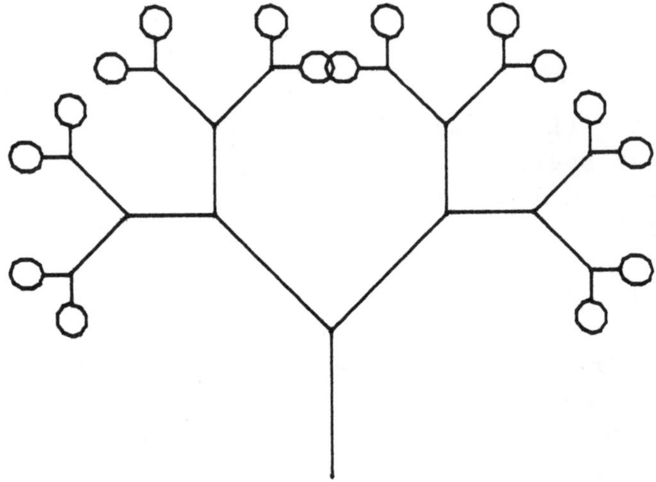

Figure 4-8

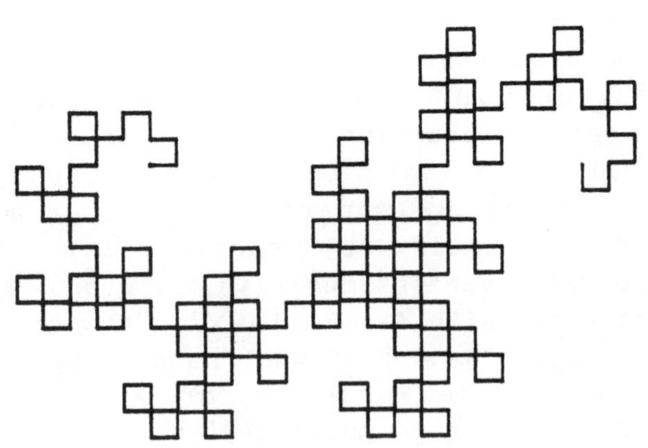

Figure 4-9

```
PROGRAM DRAGONS;
VAR SIZE:INTEGER;

PROCEDURE DRAGON(LENGTH:INTEGER);
BEGIN
  IF LENGTH=0 THEN MOVE(30)
  ELSE
    IF LENGTH>0 THEN
      BEGIN
        DRAGON(LENGTH-1);
        TURN(90);
        DRAGON(-(LENGTH-1));
      END
    ELSE
      BEGIN
        DRAGON(-(LENGTH+1));
        TURN(270);
        DRAGON(LENGTH+1);
      END;
END (*DRAGON*);

BEGIN (*MAIN PROGRAM*)
  WRITE('SIZE OF DRAGON:');
  READLN(SIZE);
  PENCOLOR(NONE);
  MOVETO(-200,0);
 (*USE ONE-FIFTH OF SCREEN WIDTH INSTEAD OF 200*)
  PENCOLOR(WHITE);
  DRAGON(SIZE);
END.
```

alteration on paper before you experiment with program changes. The change is very simple and you should get it right the first time you try. Next, try plotting the dragon upside down, but still pointing in the same direction shown in Figure 4-9.

If you find that the "power" revealed by this simple program is interesting, this might be a good point to experiment with additional alterations to the program of your own design. See if you can produce more interesting patterns than the dragon with equally simple programs. (The author would like to receive copies of any examples interesting enough for future publication.)

Example 4.13

If you are one of those who find the preceding two examples to be too simple a challenge for your taste, you might try experimenting with the patterns illustrated in Figure 4-10. The program to create this drawing follows a well known algorithm, and is similar to algorithms that can be used to create a wide variety of repeating complex patterns. Before referring to the sample program HILBERT, which drew all of the patterns in Figure 4-10, see if you can devise a recursive procedure to draw the same pattern.

Figure 4-10 part (a) shows the basic three sided figure which is repeated in various orientations to create all the others. Part (a) was drawn with ORDER initialized to 1 in the program. Part (b) was constructed by using the basic figure of part (a) four times, in three different orientations. It was necessary to draw three straight lines to connect the four basic figures together. Each of these straight lines is of the same length as each side of the basic figure.

```
PROGRAM HILBERT;
VAR SIZE,DELTA,N:INTEGER;
  ORDER:INTEGER;
  PROCEDURE HIL(I:INTEGER);
  VAR A,B:INTEGER;
    PROCEDURE HIL1;
    BEGIN
      TURN(A);  HIL(-B);  TURN(A);
    END (*HIL1*);
    PROCEDURE HIL2;
    BEGIN
      MOVE(SIZE);
      HIL(B);
      TURN(-A);  MOVE(SIZE);  TURN(-A);
      HIL(B);
      MOVE(SIZE);
    END (*HIL2*);
  BEGIN (*HIL*)
    IF I=0 THEN TURN(180)
    ELSE
    BEGIN
      IF I>0 THEN
      BEGIN
        A:=90;  B:=I-1;
      END
      ELSE
        BEGIN
          A:=-90;  B:=I+1;
        END;
      HIL1;  HIL2;  HIL1;
    END;
  END (*HIL*);
BEGIN (*MAIN PROGRAM*);
  WRITE('SIZE:');
  READLN(SIZE); (*ENTER SIZE FOR YOUR SCREEN*)
  WRITE('ORDER:');  READLN(ORDER);
  PENCOLOR(NONE);
  N:=ORDER-1;
  DELTA:=SIZE;
  WHILE N>0 DO
  BEGIN  (*COMPUTE STARTING (X,Y) POSITION *)
    DELTA:=DELTA*2;
    N:=N-1;
  END;
  MOVETO(-DELTA,-DELTA);
  PENCOLOR(WHITE);
  HIL(ORDER);
END.
```

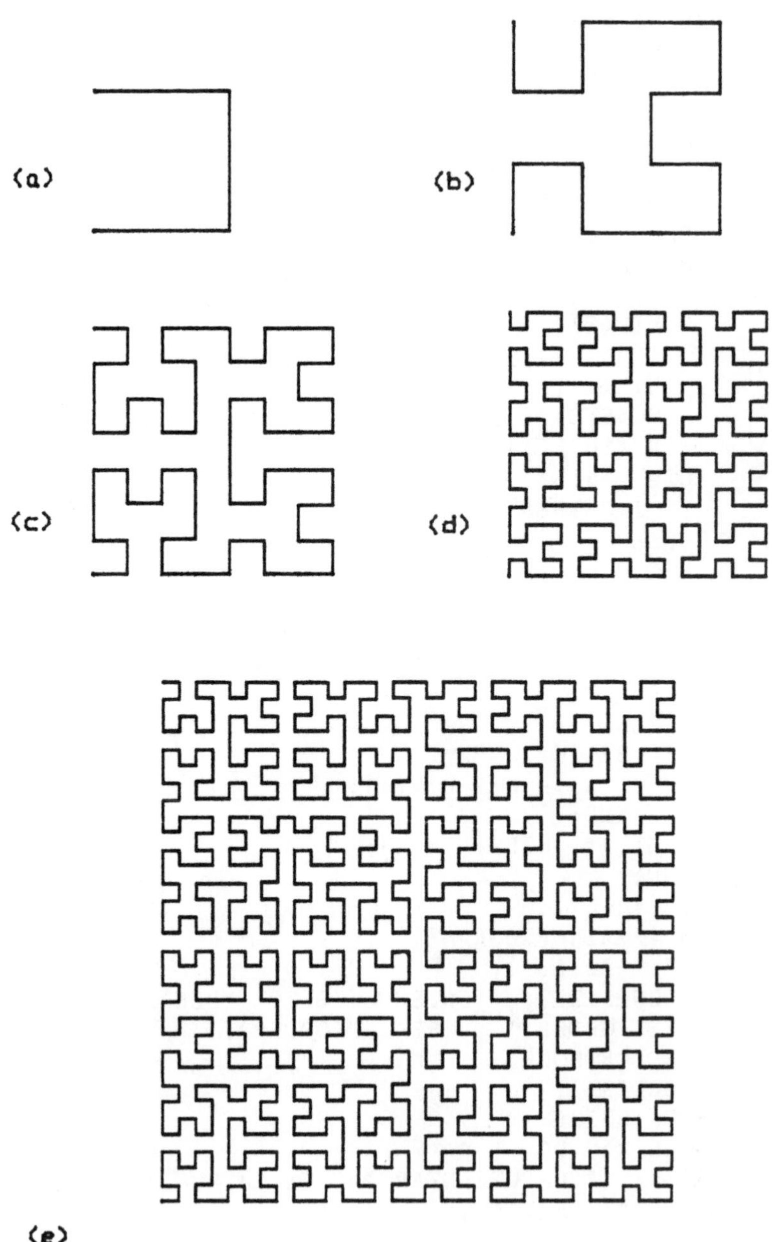

Figure 4-10

Figure 4-10 part (c) is obtained (ORDER=3) by connecting together four figures like the one in part (b). Again, three straight lines were used to connect the three part (b) figures together. Similarly, part (d) was produced from four repetitions of part (c) connected together, and part (e) was produced from part (d) in the same way.

If the effort to create the program to draw these figures yourself defeats you, don't be too disappointed. It would be helpful to study the operation of the HILBERT program by putting a READLN statement just before each MOVE statement in the program. Then you can watch the action develop on a line-by-line basis at a pace that allows you to keep track of the action as the program runs.

Problems

Problem 4.1:

In your own words, give answers to the following questions:

Under what conditions might you be led to use the same name for several different and distinct variables at different points within a program? Describe the rule that allows this to be done.

How does it simplify a program to have some procedures nested within others? Explain what this means.

In what way does it help you in designing a program to reduce as much as possible the number of variables that can be referred to in common by separate parts of the program? How would you design a program to accomplish this?

Describe the basic difference in operation of a variable parameter from the operation of a value parameter. For what purposes would each kind of parameter be used?

How does a function differ from a procedure. What are the main steps you would have to take to modify a procedure to make it a function?

What distinguishes a recursive procedure or function from an ordinary procedure or function?

Under what conditions might you think of using a recursive procedure or function to help simplify the solution of a problem?

What is a CASE statement and how does it operate? When would you consider using a CASE statement to simplify a program?

Chapter 5

WORKING WITH NUMBERS

1. Goals

The main objective of this chapter is to develop your ability to handle simple problems involving numbers on the computer. As in all the other chapters the emphasis is on problem solving and programming, not on mathematics.

1a. Develop a basic understanding of how computer hardware works, using many small steps to accomplish larger tasks.

1b. Study the binary representation of numbers in the computer, and its relation to the manner in which the computer handles numbers. Learn to use the equivalent representations of binary numbers and characters.

1c. Learn to work with arithmetic expressions in reasonable generality in the computer, and to convert these expressions from algebraic form to the computer form, and vice versa. Learn to use the rules of precedence.

1d. Use REAL variables.

1d. Learn how roundoff errors limit the accuracy of calculations performed by the computer, and how the order in which an expression is written affects the computed value of the expression.

1e. Study and understand all of the sample programs.

2. Background

Few people who use computers can avoid learning the basic principles of how to handle numbers in the computer, whether their interest is in the Arts and Humanities, Science and Engineering, Bookkeeping and Management for organizations, or whatever. Students of Natural Science and Engineering will be primarily concerned with numerical problems, and will have to pursue the field of "Numerical Analysis", which is a branch of mathematics. Students of the Social Sciences may use computers for non-numerical problems, but they are almost certain to use them for numerical work in statistics. Most others will only need to know enough about computations with numbers to be able to handle simple arithmetic problems.

This chapter is concerned with building a basis for numerical computations at the level needed by all students. A few of our sample programs are drawn from the mathematical side of computer applications. Students with a mathematics orientation will be interested in how these examples relate to other work they are doing. However, if you do not have a mathematics orientation, you should have no difficulty in understanding the problem statement given with each sample program. In both cases, our primary concern continues to be one of helping you to build a basis for solving future problems. At the level of this introductory textbook, the methods we use on the computer differ very little whether the examples are numerical or non-numerical.

Our first task will be to give a brief summary of the method used by virtually all "digital" computers for handling numbers. The term "digital" implies that the data handled by the computer consists of numbers. The term "analog computer" applies to a class of machines that use electrical signals, mechanical levers, pneumatic pressure, or other similar means to simulate the behavior of other systems. The vast majority of all computers in use today are of the digital variety discussed in this book. We will devote no further attention to analog computers.

You may be surprised to learn that all of the information handled by a digital computer is in the form of numbers. Usually the numbers consist of a sequence of binary digits. A binary digit, or "bit" in computer jargon, can only have a value of 0 or 1 (unlike the decimal system in which a digit can have any one of ten values 0, 1, 2, ..., 9). To handle items which are not fundamentally numbers in nature, it is necessary to agree on some scheme whereby non-numerical information is converted to a numerical "code" for processing by the computer. For handling the STRING variables we have been using, each character is converted to a numeric code from the American Standard Code for Information Interchange ("ASCII"), one of the most widely used coding schemes.

When we choose to regard the digits stored in the computer as numbers, rather than some code, we usually need the computer for doing arithmetic operations (add, subtract, multiply, or divide). The computer's hardware is only capable of performing one of these operations at a time, and always with just two numbers at a time. After performing one such operation, the result is stored back in the computer's memory, and another operation can begin. Frequently, one wants to perform a calculation that involves more than two numbers in some algebraic computation. All of the major programming languages provide a way for you to call for the complicated sequence of arithmetic steps to be performed by the computer by simply writing the algebraic expression directly in a special form. We have already made preliminary uses of this form in the earlier chapters.

Our second task in this Chapter will be to introduce in detail the use of the <arithmetic expression> in PASCAL, the means whereby an algebraic expression is converted into a series of instructions the computer itself can understand. As you will see, the computer does not perform arithmetic calculations with perfect accuracy, and some caution is needed to take this into account.

3. Basic Computer Logic

Virtually all of the computers in use today use stored programs which consist of sequences of very simple individual computational steps. On the earliest computers in general use, i.e about 20 years ago, everyone had to write programs in which each of these steps was individually spelled out in a program. It soon became clear that computers could be used to simplify, for human users, this process of generating programs in "machine language". Whereas the computing machines themselves directly understand only coded sequences of numbers, humans find it much easier to remember elements of a program identified by familiar words, or at least by sequences of letters and digits. Moreover, it was possible to lump together commonly used sequences of the simple machine steps into "higher level" operations more related to the problems people wanted to solve than to the design of the computer hardware. This led to the design of translator programs called "compilers", to which we have already referred, which convert programs written in higher-level languages (like PASCAL, FORTRAN, BASIC, ...) into sequences of machine code to run on the machines directly. One of the earliest tasks given to compilers was the translation of algebraic expressions into sequences of computer instructions to perform arithmetic operations.

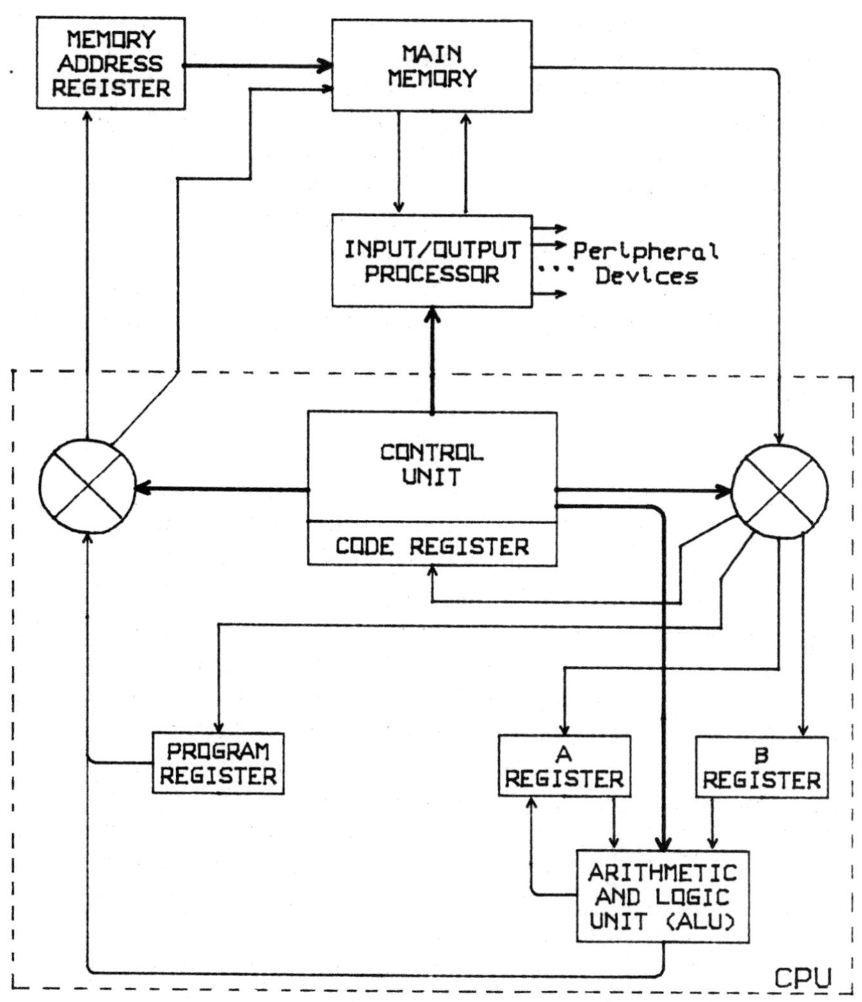
MEMORY
ADDRESS
REGISTER
MAIN
MEMORY
INPUT/OUTPUT
PROCESSOR
Peripheral
Devices
CONTROL
UNIT
CODE REGISTER
PROGRAM
REGISTER
A
REGISTER
B
REGISTER
ARITHMETIC
AND LOGIC
UNIT (ALU)
CPU

Figure 5-1

Figure 5-1 illustrates the principal "main frame" elements of a computing system. Most computers today are composed of a "central processing unit", often called a "CPU" for short, some kind of "Input/Output" processor (IOP), a reasonable amount of high speed data storage (called "memory"), cheaper low speed but high capacity storage, and a wide variety of "peripheral" devices. Whether the machine is large or small, these various independent "modules" can be plugged together to form a complete computer "system" according to the user's needs. The variety of such combinations is bewildering indeed. Moreover, the rate of progress in designing better modules for computer systems remains so high that we can predict with certainty that the inner workings of the modules produced ten years from now will differ markedly from those being produced today. Whereas computers of the future will probably have many CPU's, each serving a special function, it seems likely that the basic functioning of those CPU's will remain similar to those of today.

You can think of Figure 5-1 as representing a fairly crude level of abstraction in a diagram showing how any particular computer works. Quite often, even those programmers who still work in machine language (or the "assembler language" equivalent) are aware of only a higher level representation of the machine's actual inner structure.

4. Binary Logic

Virtually all modern digital computers use binary logic. The reason for this is that most of the fastest and cheapest electronic devices yet discovered for use in computers can function best in either of two stable "states". There have been many efforts to produce devices capable of more than two stable states. In most of these efforts, the results were either not as reliable or as cheap as comparable two-state (binary) devices. The most important binary devices are used:

a) To store binary digits (either 0 or 1)

b) To switch (provide alternate routing) information telling the state of various storage devices.

c) To provide logical combinations of "signals" which tell the state of various storage devices.

A "register" consists of a group of binary storage devices used together. A few registers on a computer are always made using very fast, but relatively expensive, electronic components. In Figure 5-1 these include the A-register, B-register, Program register, Code register, and the Memory Address register. Frequently a computer will contain many more fast registers than these for special purposes. A much larger number of registers are grouped together into the system's "main memory". These are always made with components that allow "stacking" large numbers of registers in a small volume, and that allow the use of a small number of switching devices to "address" (i.e. connect to) just one register in the stack at a time. Usually all of the registers in a memory stack contain the same number of binary digits (called "bits"). The content of a memory register is called a "word", and the number of bits in a word is known as the "word size". As far as the hardware is concerned, the address of a word in memory is the number of the register containing the word.

The speed of the various registers depends on the size and price of the computer, the faster the more expensive. The time needed to store or retrieve one word from a main memory register ranges from about 0.0000001 second (100 nanoseconds) to about 0.00001 second (10 microseconds = 10,000 nanoseconds). The fast registers of the CPU are typically at least 10 times faster than the main memory registers (10 nanoseconds to 1 microsecond). On most machines, signals can pass through about 10 switching or logical devices in the time taken to store or retrieve information in a fast CPU register. The speeds of the various devices used in a particular computer are chosen to provide a reasonable over-all balance. It would be of little value to have very fast CPU registers on a machine having only slow main memory. Likewise, there is little value in having main memory with 100 nanoseconds storage time if the CPU registers are no faster than 1000 nanoseconds (i.e. 1 microsecond).

The significance of the information stored in the various computer registers, i.e. the pattern of bits in each register, depends upon the use being made of the information. As a first approximation, the information can be either "operands", i.e. data, or "code". In the earliest digital "computers", only operands could be stored in memory registers. "Code" refers to the sequence of coded bit patterns used by the computer's control unit to determine switch settings which in turn determine how information flows from register to register. In the earliest machines, the code was all represented in "hard-wired" connections. The fantastic growth in use of the modern digital computer is traced to an observation of John Von Neumann, shortly after World War II, that both operands and code could be stored in the same main memory, and both could be manipulated by the logic of the computer.

An "operand" is an item of information which one wishes to have the computer manipulate in some way. The significance of a particular pattern of bits, stored in a register, will depend upon what use we wish to make of the stored word. The most familiar use of these bit patterns is to represent numbers. The simplest numbers one can store in a register are from the set of INTEGERs, viz:

..., -2, -1, 0, 1, 2, 3, 4, ...

Those of us from western cultures tend to represent the bits in a register, on paper, in the same way that we represent the digits of a decimal number, i.e. from left to right with the least significant digit at the right end. Thus a register containing the binary equivalent of the decimal number 10 might have the following bit pattern:

0 0 0 0 1 0 1 0

The word size of this register was assumed to be 8 bits. The position of each bit in the register has the place value of the corresponding digit in the binary numbering system. Thus the above number is equivalent to:

$$0*2^7 + 0*2^6 + 0*2^5 + 0*2^4 + 1*2^3 + 0*2^2 + 1*2^1 + 0*2^0$$

(Review for readers not familiar with this notation:

2^2 means: 2 raised to the power 2, i.e. 2*2 = 4

2^3 means: 2 raised to the power 3, i.e. 2*2*2 = 8

To understand the line above, make yourself a table of all the powers of 2 from 1 through 7. 2 raised to the power 0 has a value of 1.)

This 8-bit register could store all possible integers in the set:

0, 1, 2, 3, 4, ..., 255

Many of today's small computers have a memory word size of 16 bits, allowing storage of integers from the set:

0, 1, 2, 3, ..., 65535

This is true of almost any mini or micro computer you are likely to be using with this book. The IBM 360/370 line of computers uses a word size of 32 bits. The Burroughs B6700/7700 line of computers uses 48 bits. The Control Data Cyber computers use 60 bits. And so on. In all of these cases, provisions are made for representing negative numbers, as we will describe in Section 6.

Now to understand Von Neumann's observation, we can return to Figure 5-1. In proceeding from step to step of a calculation, the numbers we just mentioned proceed from memory to the A or B register via a switch (shown in the diagram as a cross hatched circle). If instead of representing a number, the information in the memory word represents "code", i.e. coded instructions for the computer, then the switch routes the code word to the Code Register instead. A typical control unit might allow as many as 255 different operations to take place. We will describe some of the kinds of operations that are possible in the next section. The designers of the computer assign 8 bits out of the word stored in the code register to designate which of the 255 possible operations will be followed on each computational step. You can think of each operation being assigned to an integer value in the range from 0 to 255.

For each computational step, the CONTROL first obtains another 8-bit control word. It then sets one or both of the switches shown in the diagram to some combination of registers. At the same time the ARITHMETIC & LOGIC unit (ALU) is instructed to carry out some particular operation in its repertoire (Add, Multiply, AND, Negate, etc. - See Section 5). The result of this arithmetic or logical operation is then stored back in memory, and also back in the

A-register. Finally, at the end of the computational step, the numerical value of the information in the Program Register is increased by 1, and the resulting value is placed in the Memory Address Register. The CPU is then ready for another computational step. You might notice that we have avoided mentioning how the Memory Address Register got set to allow the result of the ALU operation to be stored in the correct memory location. On the smaller machines, that address would have been set as the result of a separate computational step. In the larger machines, there may be additional logic built into the CPU, or additional information in the code word stored in the Code Register, to allow the address to be set within the time of one operational step (frequently called an operational "_cycle_").

Details of the Input/Output processor are beyond the scope of this book. The I/O processor is really a special purpose CPU designed to transmit data values _to_ an external device on "_output_", or to receive such values _from_ an external device on "_input_". Examples of such devices include the keyboard you are using, or a punched card reader for input, a display screen, electric typewriter, or line printer for output. Some devices, such as those which handle floppy disks, or tape cassettes, or standard size computer magnetic tape, can handle both input and output.

You may have noticed that the CONTROL can also route information from memory to the Program Register. Usually the code of a program is stored in a group of adjacent addresses in the memory. The Program Register points to one of those addresses on each computational step, and the computation proceeds in an orderly way from one address to the next on each step. However, it is sometimes necessary to alter the flow of control, diverting it out of this orderly sequence. For example, this might happen in the course of executing a WHILE, REPEAT or FOR statement. To do this, the CONTROL causes a completely new address value to be routed from memory to the Program

Register. The sequence of processing then jumps to the new location and proceeds from there again in an orderly way. In its simplest form, this jumping operation is represented by the GO TO construct of higher level programming languages. We discuss the GOTO statement of PASCAL in Chapter 11.

5. Arithmetic and Logical Operations

The Arithmetic and Logic Unit (ALU) shown in Figure 5-1 is designed to accept two operand words from registers A and B, and to combine these operands to produce a single result. The CONTROL unit determines which of many possible combinations will be the result, as indicated by the heavy line from CONTROL to the ALU. For example, the information content of the A-register (which we can designate by enclosing "A" in parentheses, as: (A)) may be added to the content of the B register (designated: (B)) yielding the numerical sum of the two quantities. If we use the general designator "(M)" to indicate a single memory register, without worrying about its address for the moment, then the ADD operation can be written:

```
(M) <-- (A) + (B)
(A) <-- (A) + (B)
```

where the left-pointing arrow indicates assignment of value. We use a left-pointing arrow here to avoid confusion in this book with the use of ":=" in PASCAL,since the operations described in this section cannot generally be accomplished directly using PASCAL statements. The above lines state that the addition operation of the ALU causes the content of memory location M, and of register A, to be replaced by the arithmetic sum of the contents of the A-register, and the B-register, as they were when the computational step began. At the end of the step, the former contents of M and A are destroyed, i.e. they are over-written with the new value.

On the next computational step, the new value of (A) could be used as one of the two input values for some other operation of the ALU. On many machines this would save time by avoiding the need to go to main memory for both operands before using the ALU. On many machines the result need not be stored in main memory, thus saving more time, if the program logic so allows.

On large computers, the ALU generally can handle ADD, SUBTRACT, MULTIPLY and DIVIDE operations on numeric operands of several types. On small computers, MULTIPLY and DIVIDE along with some other complex operations may be simulated using a program composed from the less complex operations. Usually the ALU can also perform bit by bit logical operations of several kinds. For example the operation:

```
(A) <-- (A) AND (B)
```

signifies that for each bit position in the word, the result contains a 1 bit if both (a) and (b) contained 1 bits in the same bit position at the start of the computational step. Otherwise the result is a 0 bit. Similarly, the OR operation causes a 1-bit result if the corresponding bit position in either (A) or (B) contains a 1-bit, and so on.

Another type of logical operation involves a comparison of the operands (A) and (B). For example:

```
(A) <-- 1 IF (A) = (B)
```

In other words, if at the start of the computational step the contents of the A and B registers are equal, then the resulting value in the A-register is set to 1 in the least significant bit position, and zeroes are put in the other bit positions. Most machines also have logical operations which have the effect of "shifting" the bit pattern in the A or B register by a designated number of positions in one operation. Finally there are operations whereby the CONTROL unit explicitly "fetches" information from memory to a register, for example:

(A) <-- (M)

and "store" operations which do the reverse:

(M) <-- (A)

While many machines also offer certain special purpose operations as functions of the ALU, the operations mentioned in this section constitute the main repertoire of most of today's computers. Since you know that computers handle large and very complex problems, you may wonder that so much can be accomplished by using only sequences of such simple operations. The ability to decompose large problems into such sequences is the main reason why computers can be used in the almost incredible variety of applications where they are found today.

6. Number Representations

You may already have perceived that the simple method, discussed in Section 4, for storing integer numbers in binary form would not be sufficient for many types of computations. Two other provisions are also made on all general purpose computers, viz:

a) Provision for storing negative numbers.

b) Provision for numbers of magnitude larger than the largest integer expressible within the memory word size, and for numbers of magnitude smaller than 1.

Unfortunately, there are three principal methods in use for representing negative numbers among the computers commonly in use today. Although many users never have to know about the method for representing negative numbers on the computer they use, there are many situations that do require this knowledge. The differences among the several manufacturers regarding negative number representations account for some of the messy problems of converting programs written on a "standard" language such as FORTRAN from one machine to another.

We have already shown how the decimal integer 10 would be represented in a computer with an 8-bit memory word size. For illustration, here is how negative 10 (i.e. -10) would appear in an 8-bit machine with each of the three methods of representing negative numbers:

a) Sign-magnitude 1 0 0 0 1 0 1 0
The left-most bit serves as the "sign" bit. Numbers ranging from -127 to +127 can be represented. -0 is distinguishable from +0, a point of interest in some mathematical applications.

b) Ones-complement 1 1 1 1 0 1 0 1
Each bit in the positive version of the number is reversed. 0's become 1's, and 1's become 0's. Numbers ranging from -127 to +127 can be represented. -0 is distinguishable from +0.

c) Two's-complement 1 1 1 1 0 1 1 0
This is formed logically by taking the ones complement, then adding the integer 1. Numbers ranging from -128 to +127 can be represented. -0 is not distinguishable from +0.

In all three methods, the "high order" bit, i.e. the one at the left end of the word, is set to 1 if the number is negative, and to 0 if positive. The choice of representation is a matter if engineering preference for the manufacturer. Burroughs chose sign magnitude for the B6700. Digital Equipment Corporation chose two's complement for the PDP-11. CDC uses ones-complement on its big machines.

Numbers of magnitude too large or too small to represent as integers can be represented in "floating point" form. This means that the position of the binary equivalent of the decimal point "floats" in relation to the bits stored in memory. A floating point number consists of two integer "fields" of bits, one called the "mantissa", the other the "exponent". If M is the integer value of the mantissa, and E is the integer value of the exponent, then the value represented by a floating point number is:

$$M * 2^{E}$$

on most machines, or sometimes:

$$M * 8^{E}$$

i.e. 2 or 8 raised to the power E. This means 2 or 8 multiplied by itself (E-1) times. Either the mantissa, or the exponent, or both may be negative using any of the methods mentioned above.

To be of much value in numerical work, a floating point number needs to occupy at least 32 bits including both mantissa and exponent. In most cases, if you are using a microcomputer system in connection with this book, the floating point numbers occupy 32 bits. The number of bits assigned to the mantissa determines the arithmetic precision with which a number can be represented (i.e. the number of binary or decimal "places" in a floating point number). The number of bits in the exponent portion of the number determines how large or how small the combined floating point number can be. On a machine which uses the exponent to represent a power of 8, the mantissa may have to include leading binary zeroes. The power of 8 system allows a wider range of magnitudes for floating point numbers using fewer bits of exponent, but it accomplishes this at the expense of roughly 2 bits of precision lost from the mantissa.

In PASCAL as well as in the FORTRAN, ALGOL, and PL/1 programming languages, floating point numbers are manipulated with variables of <type> "REAL". In PASCAL you can convert a REAL number R to an INTEGER I containing only the whole number portion of R using

```
I := TRUNC(R)
```

You could call for R to be converted to the nearest integer with

```
I := ROUND(R)
```

COBOL is oriented to the use of decimal numbers. Most implementations accomplish this through the use of integer values during the actual computation, and through routines which insert the decimal point appropriately when needed. APL and BASIC avoid worrying the user about distinctions between INTEGER and REAL variables.

As should already be apparent to you, we declare a REAL <variable> in PASCAL by means very similar to the syntax for declaring STRING, BOOLEAN, CHAR, and INTEGER variables that you have already been using. For example:

```
VAR X,Y,Z: REAL;
```

Here are some examples of REAL <constant>'s acceptable in PASCAL:

```
1.234
0.5
43210.5
1.5E-3 (*equivalent to 0.0015*)
-1.E+6 (*equivalent to negative one-million*)
```

Syntax for forming <signed number> constants in PASCAL is given in Figure 5-2. On the microcomputer you are probably using with this book, the mantissa portion of a REAL number may contain up to about 6 decimal digits.

Whereas the built-in functions ROUND and TRUNC (for truncate) are needed to convert a REAL value for assignment to an INTEGER variable, PASCAL allows you to assign an INTEGER value to a REAL variable, as it converts the INTEGER value to REAL form in this process. Otherwise, you can only assign REAL values to REAL variables, and INTEGER values to INTEGER variables.

7. Arithmetic Expressions - Assignment of Value

With the exception of APL, all of the other major programming languages use the technique of handling algebraic expressions that was originated with FORTRAN. There are fine points of difference among the languages, and you should be cautious about this when changing from PASCAL to another language at some later time. The main technique is described in this section.

Since the Central Processor Unit (Figure 5-1) has only two principal registers for operands, it is clearly necessary to decompose complicated algebraic expressions into a sequence of smaller operations. For example, to calculate the value of the expression:

$$\frac{X + Y}{C - D} \qquad (7\text{-}1)$$

the following sequence will probably be followed:

```
(T1) <-- (X) + (Y)
(T2) <-- (C) - (D)
(A-register) <-- (T1) + (T2)
```

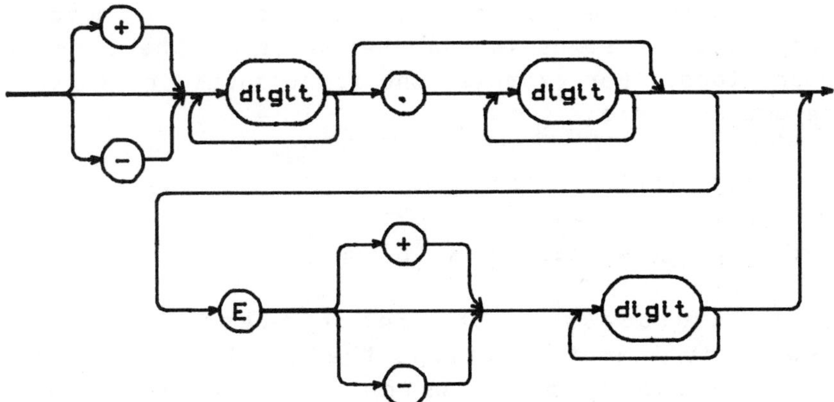

Figure 5-2

In words these three operations can be stated as follows:

Add content of the location labelled X to content of the location labelled Y and assign the result to the location labelled T1.

Subtract content of the location labelled D from the content of the location labelled C and assign the result to the location T2.

Divide content of T1 by content of T2 and place the result in the A-register.

Of course we have lumped together several computational steps in the statement of these three operations. For example, the first should be further decomposed into:

```
(A-register) <-- (X)
(B-register) <-- (Y)
(T1) <-- (A-register) + (B-register)
```

In this discussion the identifiers T1 and T2 represent memory locations that would normally be used by the compiler without the programmer's knowledge. In fact the compiler will not use "T1" or "T2" as an identifier, but will keep track of these locations using numbers so that no conflict will occur if you decide to use "T1" or "T2" for variables that you declare in a program. This discussion provides an example of the "bookkeeping" tasks that the compiler carries out to relieve the programmer of as much work as possible.

Though the sybols for ADD ('+'), SUBTRACT ('-'), MULTIPLY ('*'), and DIVIDE ('/') all produce the obvious operations, there is a complication regarding division. If you divide two integers, say 5/3, you should expect a REAL result of 1.66667 within the 6 digit accuracy of the computer. Since division generally produces a REAL result, i.e. there is a remainder, an <arithmetic expression> containing '/'

produces a result of <type> REAL. If you want either the closest INTEGER, or the remainder produced by the division, then two other division operators are provided in PASCAL for these purposes. Use "DIV" in place of '/' if you want just the INTEGER quotient from the division, with the remainder truncated. Use "MOD" in place of '/' if you want only the remainder.

In PASCAL, DIV and MOD can only be used for dividing one INTEGER valued expression by another, and both produce INTEGER valued results. An expression which includes '/' is automatically of <type> REAL, even if all of the components of the expression would otherwise be of <type> INTEGER. The syntax allows '/', DIV and MOD to be used wherever '*' would be appropriate in an <arithmetic expression>, and all three are of the same precedence as '*'.

Assuming that I is an INTEGER <variable>, and R is a REAL <variable>, here are some examples:

```
R := 10/4     (*value of R becomes 2.50000*)
I := 10 DIV 4 (*value of I becomes 2      *)
I := 11 MOD 4 (*value of I becomes 3      *)
I := 20 MOD 4 (*value of I becomes 0      *)
R := 20/4     (*value of R becomes 5.00000*)
```

In the last of these examples, had you displayed the result of the division with WRITELN(R), the displayed result might be either of the following:

```
5.00000
4.99999
```

depending upon which computer you are using, and on the features of the programming language. Obviously, the first of these is correct, while the second differs from the correct value by an amount equal to one bit in the position of lowest value in the register holding the REAL value. The error, if any, arises because it is necessary to represent the REAL number within a limited number of bits within the computer's registers. In some cases, the result of a division operation will require more bits than the computer provides if an accurate representation is to be achieved. It then is necessary either to "round" the result to the nearest value that can be expressed within the limited number of bits, or to simply regard all of the bits that cannot be represented as having a value of zero. The latter alternative is known as "truncation", to which we have already made a brief reference. In other words, the bits that cannot be stored in memory are simply chopped off. To assign the result of the calculation which evaluates expression (7-1) to a variable RESULT, we would use the following assignment statement:

```
RESULT := (X + Y) / (C - D)
```

Here we have included all terms of the expression in a single line, rather than using the more conventional multi-line representation of algebra as in expression (7-1). This is because most computer input devices are designed to handle a stream of characters, usually on a line by line basis, making it very awkward to associate information in the same columns on adjacent lines.

Convention dictates that the compiler should "scan" a line of input in an orderly way from left-to-right. It must also decide on the order in which the several arithmetic operations must be performed in computing the value of the expression. For example, the expression:

```
X + Y / C - D
```

might suggest ambiguous results if there were not an understanding on whether the division should be performed before or after either of the addition operations. To make this explicit, suppose that we have an expression composed of integer values:

    5 + 1 / 4 - 2

Is the value of this expression 3, or 3.25, or -0.5? The question is resolved by the convention that division and multiplication operations in an expression will be accomplished before addition and subtraction operations, in accord with the rules of precedence.

In the expression above, the division is accomplished first, yielding:

    5 + 0.25 - 2

Multiplication and division are said to have greater "precedence" than addition or subtraction. The operations are carried out in left to right order for operations of the same precedence. Thus

    5 + 0.25 - 2

becomes:

    5.25 - 2

and the final result is

    3.25

Now our original example from expression (7-1) showed the addition and subtraction occurring before the division. Provision is made for this by the convention that the value of an expression enclosed by parentheses will be computed completely before operations outside the parentheses are undertaken. In cases of a parenthetic expression enclosed within a parenthetic expression, the innermost parenthetic expression is evaluated first. This innermost expression is replaced by a simple value saved by the compiler temporarily, and the enclosing parentheses disappear. The evaluation process is then repeated for the resulting expression enclosed within the next pair of parentheses. The process continues until all pairs of parentheses have been removed in this manner. An example should make this clear:

```
((X + 5) * X + 8) * X + 7                    (7-2)

(T1) <-- (X) + 5
(T2) <-- (T1) * (X)
```

and so on. We have now reduced the expression to:

```
(T2 + 8) * X + 7

(T3) <-- (T2) + 8
(T4) <-- (T3) * X
(T5) <-- (T4) + 7
```

and the evaluation is completed.

The rules of precedence allow you to be sure of the order in which the compiler will evaluate an arithmetic expression. The rule about parenthesized sub-expressions allows you to change that order to get a different result. Often a programmer will find it a bother to check the order of processing of an expression lacking parentheses. It is sometimes simpler to force processing to take place in the order you want by inserting pairs of parentheses, even though doing so may seem redundant at times.

Another reason for using parentheses in expressions may be simply to make a program easier for humans to read and understand. Parentheses allow a complicated arithmetic expression to be regarded as composed of a number of smaller "<u>modules</u>", each of which is an expression itself within pairs of parentheses. Once again we find that humans can cope better with complicated structures if they are broken down into pieces of a modest size that a human can understand without making an effort of analysis. Thus the same concept of program structure applies both to arithmetic expressions, and to sequences of program statements broken down into modules by using compound statements and procedures.

8. Sample Program - Decimal to Binary Conversion

In this section, and in the next several, we give sample programs which make use of the principles discussed in the earlier parts of this chapter. You now know enough about PASCAL to be able to use it for some purposes as a medium of description for logical concepts that are awkward to express in straight English. Study these programs with that idea in mind, and try to understand what they do. If you run into problems, a good way to help sort them out would be to try running the sample program on the computer to obtain the same results claimed in this book. Then insert WRITE statements at strategic points to help clarify in detail what the processing does.

The program DECBIN illustrates the conversion of decimal numbers into binary notation. In response to the prompt, you type an integer constant no smaller than 0 and no larger than 1023, and terminate with <RET>. The program responds by displaying first the binary equivalent, and then the decimal number on the same line. For example:

```
DECBIN
TYPE AN INTEGER FROM 0 THRU 1023
0000001000 = 8
0000100000 = 32
0000111111 = 63
0010000011 = 131
```

The general approach taken in this program is to determine whether the value of DEC is greater than or equal to the "<u>place value</u>" of each binary digit, i.e. bit, in turn. If it is not smaller than the place value, then a '1' is displayed and the place value is subtracted from the remaining portion of DEC. Processing then continues to the next smaller place value by dividing BITVAL by 2 in line 24 of the program. By the time the last bit has been printed, the value of DEC will have been reduced to zero.

```
PROGRAM DECBIN;
VAR DEC: INTEGER;

  PROCEDURE PRINTBIN(DEC:INTEGER);
  VAR BITVAL,REMAINS:INTEGER;
  BEGIN
    IF DEC>=1024 THEN
      WRITELN('SORRY ', DEC, ' IS TOO BIG')
    ELSE
    BEGIN
      BITVAL:=512; (* 2 TO 9TH POWER = 512 *)
      REMAINS:=DEC;
      WHILE BITVAL>0 DO
      BEGIN
        IF REMAINS>=BITVAL THEN
        BEGIN
          WRITE('1');
          REMAINS:=REMAINS-BITVAL
        END ELSE
          WRITE('0');
        BITVAL:=BITVAL DIV 2;
          (* NEXT LOWER POWER OF 2*)
      END;
      WRITELN(' = ', DEC);
    END (*DEC IN ALLOWABLE RANGE*)
  END (*PRINTBIN*);

BEGIN (*MAIN PROGRAM*)
  WRITELN('DECBIN');
  WRITELN('TYPE AN INTEGER FROM 0 THRU 1023');
  READLN(DEC);
  WHILE DEC>=0 DO
  BEGIN
    PRINTBIN(DEC);
    WRITELN;
    WRITELN('TYPE ANOTHER');
    READLN(DEC);
  END;
END.
```

In order to avoid losing the original value of DEC, for display purposes, the original value is first copied into REMAINS, and REMAINS then serves in place of DEC for the rest of the computation. This program has been written to handle any non-negative number that can be expressed in 10 bits or less. The test in line 7 prevents processing if the value in DEC is too large. Checks of this kind should always be considered for a program likely to treat data values occasionally that are outside the "normal" range for which the program is designed. In this case we determined the maximum of 10 bits in order to make the displayed output more readable than would have been the case had all the bits in a memory word been displayed. PASCAL has some built in features to reduce the effort needed to make "validity" checks of this kind, a point that we will consider in more depth in Chapter 9.

Exercise 5.1:

Write and debug a program to display decimal integers in binary form using the following algorithm which differs from that used in DECBIN. Starting with the lowest place value, i.e. 2 raised to the 0 power, display a '1' if the remaining portion of the original value is odd, otherwise display a '0'. Next, divide the remaining portion by 2 using integer division (DIV). If the result of this division is not zero, then return to check whether the remaining value is odd. If the result of the division is zero, then the conversion is complete.

Note that this algorithm produces the lowest ordered binary digit first, which is opposite to the direction we normally read the digits of a number. Your program should save the digits generated by the loop just described until all have been generated. It should then display the digits in their proper order, with the most significant digit on the left.

Check to make sure that the binary numbers displayed by your program agree with those displayed by DECBIN for the following decimal numbers, and any others you think might be useful:

0, 1, 2, 3, 4, 8, 16, 31, 32, 33, 63, 64, 128, 131, 255, 256, 511, 512, 1023

Exercise 5.2:

Write and debug a program which does the reverse of the process carried out by the program DECBIN. Use a STRING variable to introduce a binary number consisting of a string of '0' and '1' characters. Suggested approach: Accumulate the decimal value in an INTEGER variable DEC. Scan the STRING variable from left to right. For each binary digit in the binary number, multiply DEC by 2, then add 1 to DEC if the binary digit equals '1'.

As a test for your program, use the following binary numbers:

0, 1, 10, 11, 100, 1000, 10000, 11111, 100000, 100001, 111111, 1000000, 10000000, 10000011, 11111111, 100000000, 111111111, 1000000000, 1111111111

which is the binary equivalent of the decimal sequence given in Exercise 5.1. Check to make sure that your program displays those decimal numbers for the binary numbers given in this list.

9. Sample Program - ALGEBRA

The program ALGEBRA is provided to illustrate two points:

```
PROGRAM ALGEBRA;
VAR R,W,X,Y,Z,EPS:REAL;
PROCEDURE ROUNDERR(EPS:REAL);
BEGIN
  R:=((1+EPS) * (1+EPS) - 1)/EPS;
  WRITELN('((1+EPS) * (1+EPS) -1)/EPS = ',R);
  R:=((1 + 2*EPS + EPS*EPS) -1)/EPS;
  WRITELN('((1 + 2*EPS + EPS*EPS) -1)/EPS = ',R);
  R:=(2*EPS + EPS*EPS)/EPS;
  WRITELN('(2*EPS + EPS*EPS)/EPS = ',R);
END (*ROUNDERR*);
BEGIN (*MAIN PROGRAM*)
  (*INITIALIZE VARIABLES*)
  W:=2; X:=5; Y:=4; Z:=10;
  EPS:=0.0006;
  R:=(X + Y*5)/(X - Y/0.2);
  WRITELN('(X + Y*5)/(X - Y/0.2)= ',R);
  R:=(((W+3)*W + 2) * W -10) * W + 4;
  WRITELN('(((W+3)*W + 2) *W -10) * W + 4 = ',R);
  R:=4*(X+Y)*(X+Y)/(X-Y);
  WRITELN('4*(X+Y)*(X+Y)/(X-Y) = ',R);
  R:=(1 + Z*Z/X*X)/(1 - Z*Z/X*X) + Y;
  WRITELN('(1 + Z*Z/X*X)/(1 - Z*Z/X*X) + Y = ',R);
  R:=(1 + Z*Z/(X*X))/(1 - Z*Z/(X*X)) + Y;
  WRITELN(
    '(1 + Z*Z/(X*X))/(1 - Z*Z/(X*X)) + Y = ', R);
  WRITELN('TYPE A SMALL REAL NUMBER FOR EPS');
  READLN(EPS);
  WHILE EPS>0.0 DO
  BEGIN
    ROUNDERR(EPS);
    WRITELN;
    WRITELN('TYPE ANOTHER');
    READLN(EPS);
  END;
END.
```

```
Display associated with ALGEBRA program
(X + Y*5)/(X - Y/0.2)= -1.666666
(((W+3)*W + 2) *W -10) * W + 4 = 32.0
4*(X+Y)*(X+Y)/(X-Y) = 324.0
(1 + Z*Z/X*X)/(1 - Z*Z/X*X) + Y = 2.979797
(1 + Z*Z/(X*X))/(1 - Z*Z/(X*X)) + Y = 2.333333
TYPE A SMALL NUMBER FOR EPS
0.000025
((1+EPS) * (1+EPS) -1)/EPS = 2.002716
((1 + 2*EPS + EPS*EPS) -1)/EPS = 1.997947
(2*EPS + EPS*EPS)/EPS = 2.000025
```

a) Conversion of complicated algebraic expressions into a form acceptable to PASCAL.

b) Accuracy problems that can arise because the representation of REAL numbers on the computer uses a limited number of bits.

The program first displays results from computing the five expressions in lines 21, 24, 27, 30, and 33 of the program listing. The associated display lines are shown on a separate page. You can easily verify the correctness of the first three results with hand computations. Line 21 computes the following algebraic expression:

$$\frac{X + 5Y}{X - \frac{Y}{0.2}}$$

Line 24 shows an efficent method for computing the following expression:

$$W^4 + 3W^3 + 2W^2 - 10W + 4$$

This expression is less efficient than the one in line 24, because it requires more multiplication operations, which often are relatively time consuming on small computers. As an exercise, multiply out the terms in line 24, and in this expression, to prove that you get the same result. PASCAL provides no explicit method for "exponentiation", i.e. raising a number to some power. (For example, the first term in this expression, in the algebraic form, is W raised to the 4-th power.) Don't worry if the mathematical significance of all this is unclear to you. Our focus here is only on the handling of algebraic expressions in PASCAL, not on their mathematical significance.

Line 27 computes the value of the following expression:

$$\frac{4(X + Y)^2}{X - Y}$$

Notice that the algebraic form of this expression does not require parentheses enclosing the denominator (the part of the fraction below the line, in this case X-Y), whereas PASCAL does require parentheses to get the same result. Carry out the computation of this expression by hand to make sure that you get the same result that the computer displays. What would the result have been if the denominator term in line 27 had not been enclosed in parentheses?

The two expressions in lines 30 and 33 illustrate one correct and one incorrect way of writing the following algebraic expression in PASCAL:

$$\frac{\left(1 + \frac{Z^2}{X^2}\right)}{\left(1 - \frac{Z^2}{X^2}\right)} + Y$$

As you can readily verify, the first of these two forms is not correct. Before reading on, see if you can determine what is wrong with the first form by comparing it with the second.

In line 30, the PASCAL sub-expression Z*Z/X*X appears twice. In both cases, it has the following effect expressed in algebraic form:

$$\left(\frac{Z^2}{X}\right)X$$

In other words, Z is squared, then the result is divided by X, then the combined result of that is multiplied by X. The net result is simply equivalent to the square of Z, with X having been "cancelled out". In line 33, the multiplication of X by itself to form the square of X is forced to take place before the division by enclosing X*X in parentheses. The computation of the value of the correct expression, with the values to which the variables were initialized in line 18, is fairly simple to carry out by hand. Do this computation by hand to verify that you get the same result as did the computer (0.333333 is the equivalent of one third).

All three expressions in the procedure ROUNDERR should calculate the value of the same algebraic expression, which when simplified as much as possible reads:

$$2 + EPS$$

Admittedly, the three examples shown have been contrived so as to illustrate the kinds of inaccuracy that often arise when computing with REAL numbers. The program has been arranged to allow one to experiment with different values of EPS. The identifier "EPS" is intended to suggest the use of "Epsilon", the Greek character often used in mathematics to estimate the magnitude of a small change in value. Obviously, only the third expression, in line 12 of the program, gives a result that is close to correct (in the case shown it is exact). The other two methods give results that are grossly inaccurate considering one's assumption that the computer does its calculations with six digits of "accuracy".

Exercise 5.3:

Experiment with the ALGEBRA program by running it and testing for the results you get by typing in different values for EPS. Notice the effect of small changes in EPS on the inaccuracy, and the fact that the errors are neither in the same direction nor associated with the same expressions for every value of EPS. Notice also that the large errors are only associated with a few "pathological" values of EPS. Programmers sometimes make the assumption, that they later live to regret, that the pathological cases are so unlikely that they do not need to take the precautions needed to avoid errors from those cases. As a minimum, test the program with the following values for EPS:

```
0.000025  (result should be same as in the book)
0.000024, 0.000026,
0.00003,  0.00002
0.000001, 0.00001, 0.0001, 0.001, 0.01, 0.1
1E-7  (i.e. 0.0000001)
```

The inaccuracy displayed by these expressions arises because the computer does not have enough bits in one word of memory to allow the sum (1 + EPS*EPS) to be stored with reasonable precision. For example, when the value of EPS is 0.00001, the addition looks like the following:

```
  1.000000¦
  0.000000¦0001
 ---------¦-----
  1.000000¦
```

where the vertical dotted line shows where truncation must start due to insufficient bits in the memory word. The truncation occurs when the computer attempts to align the two numbers to be added so that the decimal point occurs in the same column.

The number of columns from the decimal point itself is not a matter of concern. For example, if EPS = 0.00003, then EPS*EPS = 9.0E-10, (i.e. 0.0000000009). The reason for this is that the "leading zeroes", those to the left of the most significant non-zero digit, need not be retained in the memory in a floating point number. The amount stored in the memory following computation of EPS*EPS in this example would have a mantissa amounting to the binary equivalent of 900000, and an exponent amounting to the binary equivalent of 10 raised to the -15 power. In other words we would have the equivalent of:

$$\frac{900000}{10^{15}}$$

The process of aligning the columns of two numbers in a summation, to make the decimal point columns agree, is known as "normalizing". When a REAL number is stored in memory, it is normalized in such a way that there are no leading zeroes. This allows the number to be stored with as many bits of accuracy as are possible, but it cannot guarantee that all those bits will be used in a future addition.

Accuracy problems like those we have been describing comprise one of the principal obstacles in scientific calculations on the computer. Much of numerical analysis is devoted to the design of strategies to minimize the errors in computed results. These strategies take into account the roundoff and truncation errors that may arise, and attempt to order the various stages of the computation in such a way as to minimize these errors.

Accuracy problems with REAL numbers are also very important in administrative computations. One of the strategies used in most implementations of COBOL, the "Common Business Oriented Language", results in most computation being done with integers, even though the programmer thinks the numbers are really decimal fractions. COBOL provides ways for the programmer to specify how many decimal digits of precision must be carried. Unknown to the programmer, a <variable> intended to represent Dollars and Cents (2 decimal points of precision) would in fact be carried as an integer representation of Cents. Roundoff and truncation errors occur in business oriented programs in spite of such methods. Common examples arise when some Dollar amount needs to be multiplied by some percentage rate, perhaps as part of a computation of tax or interest payments.

Exercise 5.4:

Write and test a program which computes the total payments on a loan for an original amount called PRINCIPAL, using an interest rate IRATE. Arrange the program to loop, so that you can observe what happens using various amounts for PRINCIPAL and IRATE, both of which should be REAL variables. The basic calculation required is very simple:

```
TOTAL = PRINCIPAL * (1 + IRATE)
```

You should perform the calculation twice, once using REAL arithmetic, and once using integer arithmetic. You should then compare the results as measured by TOTAL. For working with integer arithmetic, carry all quantities in Cents. IRATE should be used as a REAL variable in both the floating point and integer computations. For the integer computation, compute the interest payment using

```
INTEREST := ROUND(IRATE*PRINCIPAL*100)
```

then add the principal as an integer in Cents. To test your program in such a way as to see the roundoff errors in action, try typing in 123.45 for the principal, and 0.11 for the interest. Try additional values for the principal and interest, both larger and smaller. Beware of the possibility that your program may "blow up" when it attempts to use an integer value larger than 32767. Add IF statements to the program to protect it from allowing this to happen.

10. <u>Sample Program Converge</u>

The program CONVERGE carries out a computation that the mathematically oriented will recognize as the series approximation to the quantity:

$$e^{x}$$

where "e" is the base of natural logarithms. You don't need a mathematics orientation to understand what this program does.The idea is to compute the value of the following summation:

$$1 + \frac{X}{1} + \frac{X^{2}}{2*1} + \frac{X^{3}}{3*2*1} + \frac{X^{4}}{4*3*2*1} + \ldots$$

The symbol "..." (called an "<u>ellipsis</u>") at the end of this summation signifies that additional "<u>terms</u>" are to be added to this "<u>series</u>" until the resulting sum is sufficiently accurate. Each sub-expression between "+" symbols in this sum is called a "term". Usually "sufficiently accurate" means that the computer on which one is working cannot represent the result with greater accuracy than possible within the bits contained in one memory word. Each successive term may be given a number, say N, that is one larger than the number designating the previous term. Thus a general way of describing each term would be as follows:

```
PROGRAM CONVERGE;
VAR R,EPS:REAL;
  COUNT:INTEGER;

FUNCTION SERIES(X:REAL; VAR CNT:INTEGER):REAL;
VAR TERM,SUM:REAL;
  N:INTEGER;
BEGIN
  N:=1;
  TERM:=1;
  SUM:=1;
  REPEAT
    TERM:=TERM*X/N;
    SUM:=SUM+TERM;
    N:=N+1;
  UNTIL ABS(TERM)<=EPS*SUM;
  SERIES:=SUM;
  CNT:=N;
END (*SERIES*);

BEGIN (*MAIN PROGRAM*)
  EPS:=0.0001;
  WRITELN('CONVERGE');
  WRITELN('TYPE A REAL NUMBER');
  READLN(R);
  WHILE ABS(R)<80.0 DO
  BEGIN
    WRITELN('SERIES(R)=',SERIES(R,COUNT),
                    ', EXP(R)=',EXP(R));
    WRITELN('COUNT WAS:', COUNT);
    WRITELN;
    WRITELN('TYPE ANOTHER');
    READLN(R);
  END;
END.
```

```
Display associated with CONVERGE program
CONVERGE
TYPE A REAL NUMBER
1.0
SERIES(R)=2.718254, EXP(R)=2.718281
COUNT WAS:9
TYPE ANOTHER
1E1
SERIES(R)=22025.43, EXP(R)=22026.46
COUNT WAS:35
TYPE ANOTHER
-1.0
SERIES(R)=3.678818E-1, EXP(R)=3.678793E-1
COUNT WAS 9
TYPE ANOTHER
100.0
```

$$\frac{X^N}{N*(N-1)*(N-2)* \ldots *1}$$

Another way would be the following:

$$t_{(n)} = t_{(n-1)} * \left(\frac{x}{n}\right)$$

In other words, to form a new term, take the old one and multiply by (x/n). Notice the similarity of this definition to the definitions used in the examples of recursive procedures in Chapter 4.

The computation continues, with each successive term eventually being smaller than the previous one, since the denominator (below the line) will end up growing much faster than the numerator (above the line). The program is told to stop looping when a term is found that is smaller than some small amount intended as an estimator of accuracy. In this sample program the estimator is the variable EPS, which is set in line 22. The value assigned to EPS has been chosen for this example to be large enough so that the inaccuracy of the result can be observed. PASCAL has a built-in function for computing this same series summation to the best accuracy available on the computer. This function, called EXP, is included in the WRITELN statement on line 29 so that you can see the difference in the results obtained by the two computations. The lines displayed by the CONVERGE program, for three representative values of R entered from the keyboard, are shown on a separate page.

The name of the program is chosen because the series is said to "converge" on the correct result as additional terms are added. Strictly speaking, the result can never reach the correct value with absolute accuracy, since doing so would imply a computer with an <u>infinite</u> number of bits per word.

Exercise 5.5:

Revise the program CONVERGE to make it compute the value of the following series:

$$X - \frac{X^3}{3!} + \frac{X^5}{5!} - \frac{X^7}{7!} + \frac{X^9}{9!} - \ldots$$

where the notation given for the denominator of each term is interpreted as follows:

```
3! = 3 * 2 * 1
5! = 5 * 4 * 3 * 2 * 1
7! = 7 * 6 * 5 * 4 * 3 * 2 * 1
```

and so on. Thus the method you use to compute the terms of this series will be very similar to the method used to compute the terms in CONVERGE as it is printed in the book. You can check to determine whether your results are correct by comparing with the value returned by the built-in function SIN(X). To get a more accurate value, experiment with the value of EPS, making it 1E-6 or smaller. Try the program using values of R, entered from the keyboard, ranging from -10 to +10 and including the following:

0.0, 3.14159, -3.14159, 0.78539, -1.57079

11. Random Numbers

In this section we present two programs intended to provide some amusement as well as some serious subject matter. Both programs employ a procedure whose job is to produce a new "random number" each time it is called. By "random" we mean a number effectively "picked out of a hat" containing a large quantity of numbers within a specified set of values. Thus each successive number generated by the procedure should have no relationship at all with the numbers previously picked. In practice, it is not possible to eliminate the relationship entirely, and so the numbers generated by a computer are sometimes known as "pseudo-random". Random number generator routines are used very commonly in computer simulations of all kinds of physical systems, in looking for possible (intentional) errors in bookkeeping systems, and in many other fields.

In both programs, the procedure RANDOM works by taking advantage of the loss of bits of information when a number is truncated to fit within the computer's memory. In this case, the built-in function TRUNC is used to obtain just the fractional content of the REAL variable SEED in line 9. This is accomplished by subtracting the INTEGER portion of the value of SEED obtained in line 8. The result of line 9 is a fraction whose value ranges from 0 to just below 1.000000, and may be anything in between these two limits. Line 10 then produces a nearly random integer ranging from 0 to 1 less than the constant by which SEED is multiplied. In the program RANDOMWALK, the product obtained in this way is reduced by 24.9 so that the <u>average</u> value of all the integers produced will be very close to zero.

The program RANDOMWALK produces the drawing shown in Figure 5-3. In each of many cycles of the loop in lines 25 thru 30, X and Y positions of the turtle are altered by the amounts returned in two calls to RANDOM. The result is the squiggly pattern that a random (or drunken) fly might make walking around on a piece of paper.

Figure 5-4 is the result of running RANDOMWALK slightly modified by changing the values of the constants used in lines 8 and 14 in the program to different values. In this case, the value used in line 14 was 7.5295141. The values used in line 8 were 3.1415917, and 2.7182813 respectively. The intent in using these complicated numbers is to create a complex bit pattern which is likely to lose bits each time a new value of SEED is computed. As

```
PROGRAM RANDOMWALK;
CONST XMAX=480; YMAX=350;
VAR SEED:REAL;
  X,Y,ANGLE:INTEGER;

FUNCTION RANDOM:INTEGER;
BEGIN
  SEED:=SEED*27.182813+31.415917;
  SEED:=SEED-TRUNC(SEED);
  RANDOM:=TRUNC(SEED*50-24.9);
END;

BEGIN (*MAIN PROGRAM*)
  SEED:=1.23456789; (*COMPLICATED BIT PATTERN*)
  PENCOLOR(WHITE);
  MOVETO(-XMAX,0);
  MOVETO(XMAX,0); (*X AXIS*)
  PENCOLOR(NONE);
  MOVETO(0,YMAX);
  PENCOLOR(WHITE);
  MOVETO(0,-YMAX); (*Y AXIS*)
  MOVETO(0,0);
  X:=0;
  Y:=0;
  WHILE (ABS(X)<XMAX) AND (ABS(Y)<YMAX) DO
    BEGIN
      MOVETO(X,Y);
      X:=X+RANDOM;
      Y:=Y+RANDOM;
    END;
END.
```

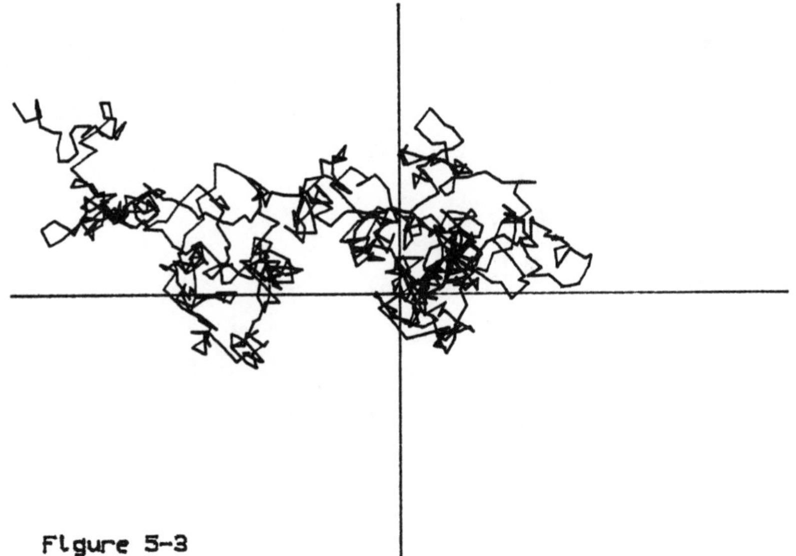

Figure 5-3

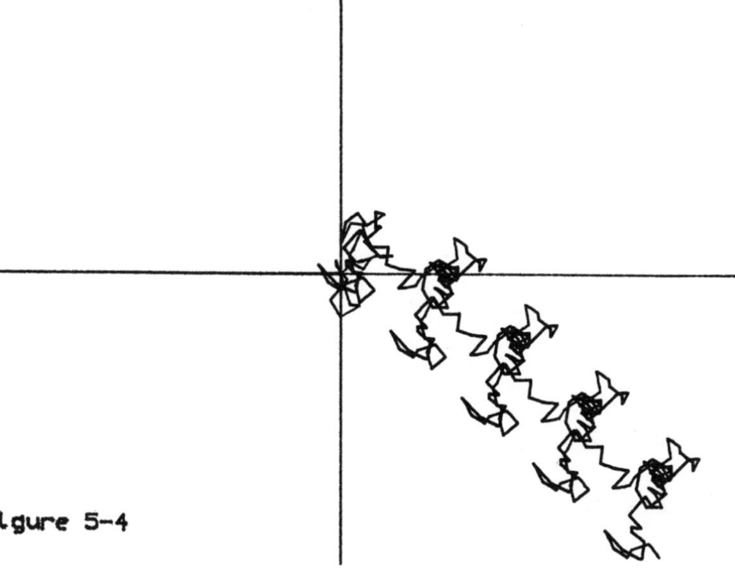

Figure 5-4

you can see, the pattern obtained with the constants used for Figure 5-4 had an obvious tendency to cause the numbers to repeat after a short time. The constants used for Figure 5-3 did not have nearly as obvious a tendency to cycle. You can use a function essentially identical to RANDOM on almost any computer, but the values of the constants will have to be changed to assure a nearly random sequence. The methods used to check on randomness are complicated, and beyond the scope of this book.

The program FOURLETTER displays a (nearly) random sequence of four letter words. When we ran the program on our computer, the following lines resulted:

```
ZXJF
KSYN
RXUF
PWTE
CKSY
ZEYF
TNQG
QIYX
GPQP
 ...
```

From this small sample, one might conclude that the familiar four letter words of the English language (not all of them polite!) may not be as randomly genererated as one would think at a glance. If you change the constants in the function RANDOM, a different sequence of "words" will result. How many words do you suppose would have to be generated before some recognizable English word resulted? If in doubt, try the program on your computer.

```
PROGRAM FOURLETTER;
VAR SEED:REAL;
  I,J:INTEGER;
  CH:CHAR;

FUNCTION RANDOM:INTEGER;
BEGIN
  SEED:=SEED*27.182813+31.415917;
  SEED:=SEED-TRUNC(SEED);
  RANDOM:=TRUNC(SEED*26);
END;

BEGIN (*MAIN PROGRAM*)
  SEED:=1.23456789; (*COMPLICATED BIT PATTERN*)
  WRITELN('FOURLETTER');
  REPEAT
    FOR I:=1 TO 20 DO
    BEGIN
      FOR J:=1 TO 4 DO
          WRITE(CHR(ORD('A')+RANDOM));
      WRITELN;
    END;
    WRITELN('TYPE <ESC> TO STOP,',
                      '<SPACE> FOR MORE');
    READ(CH);
  UNTIL CH=CHR(27(*ESC*));
END.
```

Exercise 5.6:

Write and test a program which generates random "headlines" by randomly selecting and displaying one word out of each of the following three lists.

PORTUGAL	GOVERNMENT	COLLAPSES
JAPAN	VOLCANO	ERUPTS
KISSINGER	MISSION	FAILS
BROWN	POLICY	SUCCEEDS
CALIFORNIA	ECONOMY	IMPROVES
STUDENT	LEADER	PROMOTED
BOSTON	AIRPLANE	CLOSED
AMERICAN	WEAPON	CRASHES
SECRET	EVIDENCE	DISAPPEARS
HOFFA	RAID	UNMASKED
ARAB	EMBARGO	NEGOTIATED

The easiest way to accomplish this is to use three CASE statements, each of which assigns a selected word from one of these lists to a corresponding STRING variable. If you call these variables S1, S2, and S3, then the following statement at the end of the loop will display the selected headline:

```
WRITELN(S1, ' ', S2, ' ', S3)
```

The selection from each list should involve calling the function RANDOM once. You will have to modify RANDOM to generate values ranging from 0 to 10 (or 1 to 11), corresponding to the 11 selections in each list.

Problems

Problem 5.1:

Convert each of the following expressions, given in algebraic form, into <arithmetic expression>'s of the form acceptable to PASCAL (NOTE: in these examples, each identifier contains only one letter):

$$\frac{L + \frac{R}{C}}{L - \frac{R}{C}}$$

$$AX^2 + BX + C$$

$$1 + \frac{AX + (B-A)X^2}{(1 - X)^2}$$

$$\frac{P + Q}{XN + A^2}$$

$$\frac{4(X + Y)^2}{2X - Y}$$

Problem 5.2:

Write out the value of I or R after execution of each of the following statements, if the statement is "legal", otherwise note what is wrong with the statement:

```
I := 10 DIV 2;

I := 11 DIV 2;

I := 25 MOD 10;

R := 1/(100000*100000);

I := 25 MOD 5;

I := 10 * 0.1;

R := TRUNC(10/3);

I := TRUNC(3.66667);

I := TRUNC(5/4);

R := 100 + 3*15;

R := 14/3 - ROUND(14/3);

R := 14/3 - TRUNC(14/3);
```

Problem 5.3:

Convert the following binary numbers into decimal form:

1010, 10011, 110110, 110111, 111000, 101010

Convert the following decimal numbers into binary form:

16, 15, 17, 35, 31, 128, 255, 510

Chapter 6

HANDLING COMPLEX PROGRAM STRUCTURE

1. Goals

In this chapter, we begin asking you to use an orderly approach to solving problems with the computer. This is the first chapter in which you will have to synthesize some of the program specifications based on a general description of the problem.

1a. Learn the distinct roles of an algorithm and the associated data items in combining to form a program.

1b. Learn to use Structure Diagrams to describe algorithms, and their close relationship to the action parts of a program.

1c. Learn to subdivide the solution of a problem into several distinct tasks to be taken roughly in sequence. These include:

- -conceptual description of the problem on paper
- -rough description of solution algorithm
- -definition of data representation
- -detailed design of algorithm by stages
- -write the program
- -enter program into computer & compile it
- -debug program operation

1d. Work out the solution(s) to one or more conceptually simple problems which lead to programs of moderate difficulty.

2. Background

As computer programs get larger, and are made to carry out more complex tasks, they become more complex and prone to errors in logic. One of our primary tasks in this chapter is to introduce a method for drawing diagrams of Structured Programs as an aid to visualizing how the various parts of the program inter-relate. Another task is to get you to begin breaking the job of solving a problem using the computer into a number of relatively distinct sub-tasks. You should begin to visualize what you do in solving a problem as if it were described by a diagram of the same type we introduce in this chapter.

Though you are already familiar with the flow chart as a medium for drawing diagrams that represent program logic, we make very little use of flow charts in this book. As a program gets larger and more complex, the flow charts that describe it can get equally large and complex. Even relatively simple flow charts can become so hard to comprehend that it is a waste of time to use them. Figure 6-1 displays an example of such a flow chart, without making the logic it is supposed to describe specific. Even for programs as simple as the one described in this diagram, it is all but impossible to prove whether the program functions correctly under all possible circumstances. For larger programs, the flow chart gets to look like a bowl full of spaghetti, and equally comprehensible as a logical description.

As a better alternative, we introduce the Structure Diagram in this chapter. Structure Diagrams help a programmer to visualize the branching "tree" structure of a well constructed program. Because there is only one path through which a program can arrive at each item in the diagram, the errors that arise from overlapping communication with other parts of the program are minimized. Once you appreciate the value of the tree structure for describing a program, you may end up finding that the PASCAL

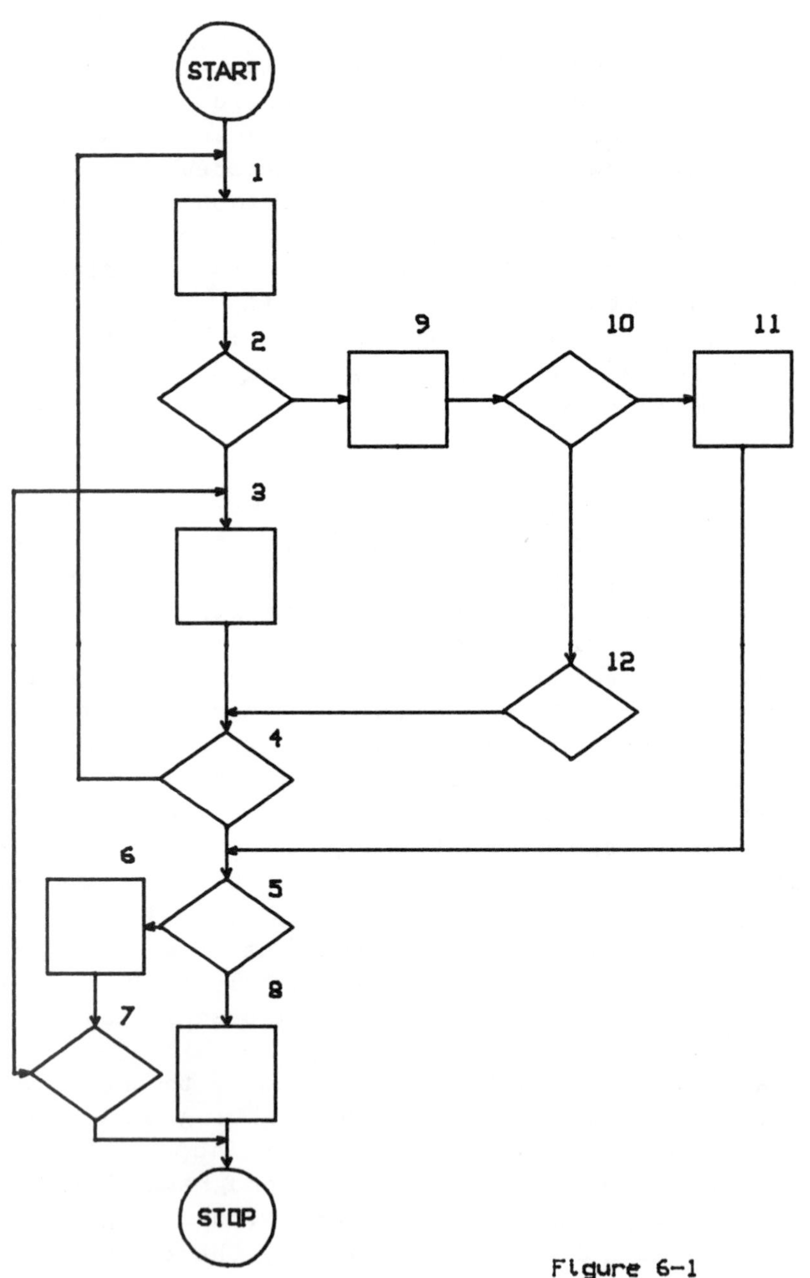

Figure 6-1

programs alone are sufficient for visualizing the program structure.

3. What is an Algorithm?

According to Webster's Dictionary, an "algorithm" is any special method for solving a certain kind of problem. The most familiar example of algorithms in everyday life is provided by cooking recipes, at least in the sense that the algorithms are recorded on paper. Actually you use an established algorithm for carrying out almost any familiar task, though you rarely stop to think of the various component steps of such algorithms. To be useful in the computing context, we'll have to narrow down the definition of an algorithm a bit further.

One recent textbook defines an "Algorithm" as "a list of instructions for carrying out some process step by step". This definition avoids specifying the level of detail to be used in the list. In fact we will find it useful to start with a list of very rough and informal instructions, and then to start refining these instructions in designing a final detailed version of the algorithm in the form of a program. Here is an algorithm you might use to make a long distance telephone call from a coin telephone:

1. Place dime in telephone
2. Call information operator for the number you want
3. Retrieve the dime returned to you
4. Place dime in telephone again
5. Dial the number you want
6. Give the intercept operator the number to which you want the call to be charged
7. Ask the answering person to get the party you want
8. Talk with your party
9. Hang up the telphone when done

Notice that this algorithm both specifies what things are to be done, and the order in which they are to be done.

You have already seen that the very nature of the digital computer leads to the specification of solutions to problems using algorithms, i.e. using "algorithmic" notation. Since the computer can perform only one small step at a time, people have generally been led to concentrate more on the order in which the steps are taken than on understanding how each step relates to the problem as a whole. Today we know that it is often better to reverse this process, leaving the order of processing to be determined after the various major steps of the task have been defined.

4. Level of Detail

When we express an algorithm such as the one above, each step embodies some level of aggregation or abstraction. For example, step #2 might well be expanded as follows:

2. Call information operator for the number you want
   - 2.1 Look up <area code> for city you want
   - 2.2 Dial (area code> 555 1212 (universal information operator's number)
   - 2.3 Wait for operator to ask "what city do you want?"
   - 2.4 Give the city
   - 2.5 Wait for the operator to respond "yes"
   - 2.6 Give name of the party you want
   - 2.7 Write down the number given by the operator

You can easily see how we might carry this detailed expansion to an additional level for several of these second level steps.

To see how a structure diagram fits into this scheme, let's start with a simpler problem. Here is a description of how one would take the "scenic route" to drive from La Jolla to Palm Springs. (Substitute places in your neighborhood if you wish.) You would go through the following places:

La Jolla - Miramar - Poway - Ramona - Santa Ysabel
Warner Springs - Aguanga - Anza - Idyllwild -
Banning - Cabezon - Palm Springs

Now flip the page and see how long you can remember all that! Suppose we now reduce the description, leaving only a few important bench marks on the route:

La Jolla - Ramona - Warner Springs - Idyllwild -
Palm Springs

You can probably remember this list without too much effort, even if you are not familiar with how all of these places fit on the map. Figure 6-2 shows a simplified version of the map. Figure 6-3 shows how we can regard the above list as a second level of detail relative to the original problem of following the route:

La Jolla - Palm Springs

Each second level box can be further broken down to a still greater level of detail, for example:

Warner Springs - Idyllwild

becomes:

Warner Springs - Aguanga - Anza - Idyllwild

And so on. When actually making the trip, you have little trouble remembering this short list of benchmarks after reaching Warner Springs. You might again look at your map, or perhaps consult a local resident upon reaching Idyllwild, before embarking on

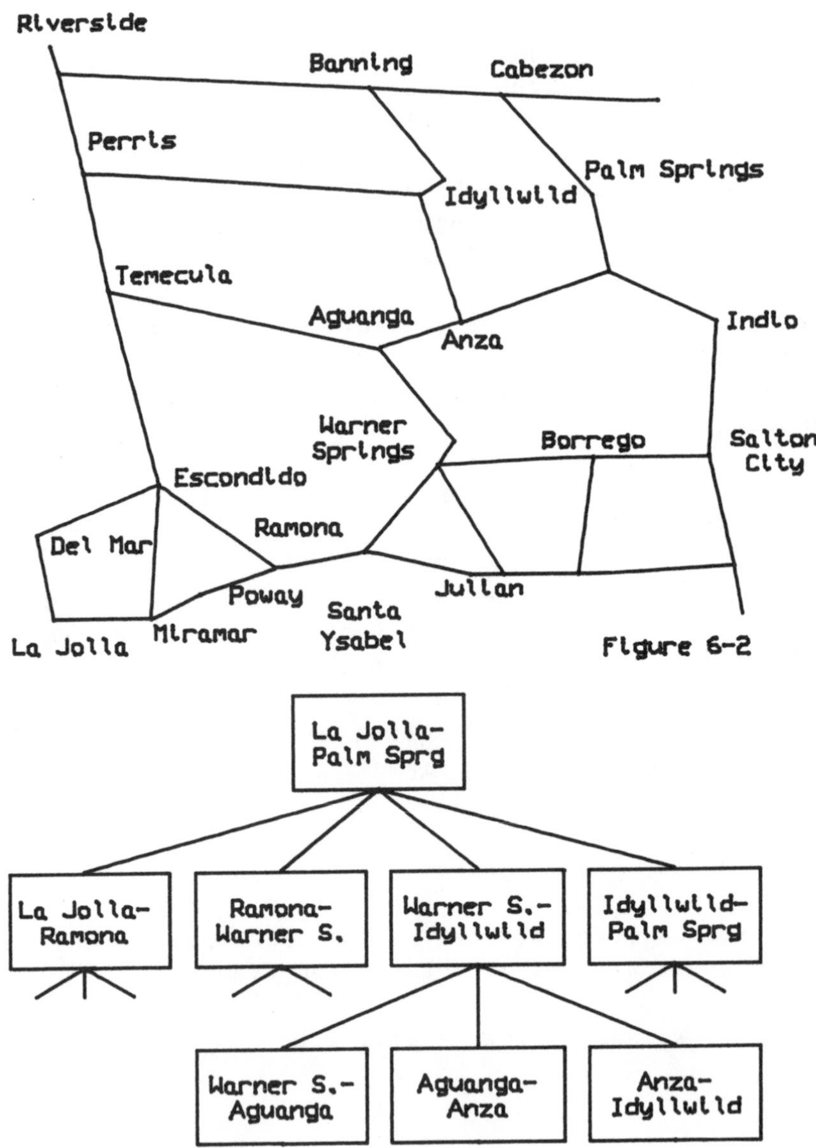

Figure 6-2

Figure 6-3

the last leg of the trip.

The point of all this is that our minds are not equipped to keep all levels of detail regarding some problem in sharp focus at the same time. However we are equipped to lump perhaps 5 to 7 detailed items together in forming a single item at a higher level of abstraction. Thus we have no trouble dealing with the concept of a single trip from La Jolla to Palm Springs, knowing full well that there are many details to consider in making that trip, but not having to cope with those details when just thinking of the trip itself as a single item. We introduced this concept when talking about the need for procedures in Chapter 2.

5. Structure Diagrams

With the foregoing ideas in mind, we can now re-express our algorithm for placing a telephone call. First let us reduce the number of detail items all at the same level:

1. Get telephone number
   - 1.1 Place dime in telephone
   - 1.2 Call informaton operator for wanted number
     - 1.2.1 Look up <area code> for wanted city
     - 1.2.2 Dial <area code> 555 1212
     - 1.2.3 Wait for operator
     - 1.2.4 Give the city
     - 1.2.5 Wait for operator
     - 1.2.6 Give name of party you want
     - 1.2.7 Write down the number
   - 1.3 Retrieve the dime returned to you
2. Establish connection with party desired
   - 2.1 Place dime in telephone
   - 2.2 Dial the number you want
   - 2.3 Give intercept operator the number to be charged
   - 2.4 Ask answering person for your party
3. Talk with your party
4. Hang up the phone when done

Figure 6-4 displays the same information in the form of a structure diagram. (I am indebted to Bob Doran & Graham Tate, Masey University, for a research publication "An Approach to Structured Programming", June 1972, in which they describe the idea of structure diagrams.) There are several things to notice:

a) The diagram is a branching structure, similar in many ways to a family "tree". In computer science such structures are in fact known as trees.

b) The tree has a single "<u>root</u>", it has branches some of which subdivide further into additional branches, and at the ends of the branches there are "<u>leaves</u>". Both the branching points and the leaves are often called "<u>nodes</u>". Leaves are "terminal" nodes in that they represent the end of a line of travel from the root node along a particular system of branches.

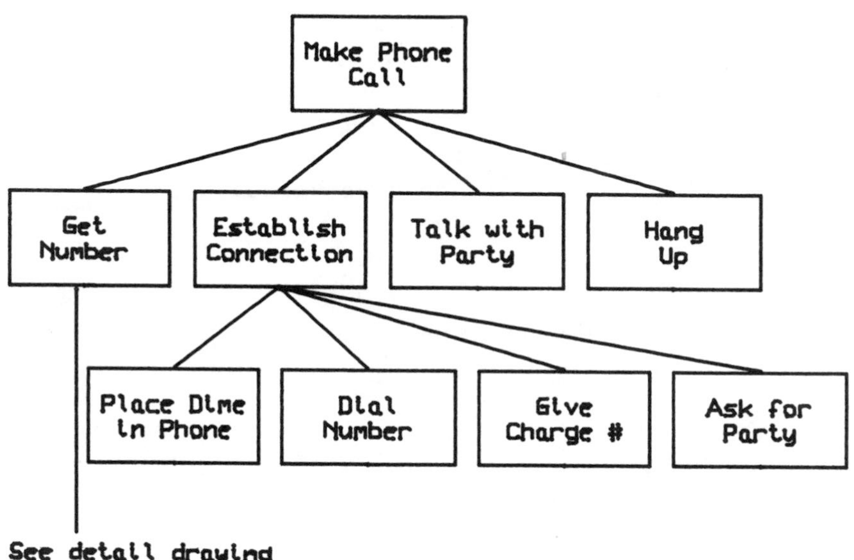
Make Phone Call
Get Number
Establish Connection
Talk with Party
Hang Up
Place Dime in Phone
Dial Number
Give Charge #
Ask for Party
See detail drawing

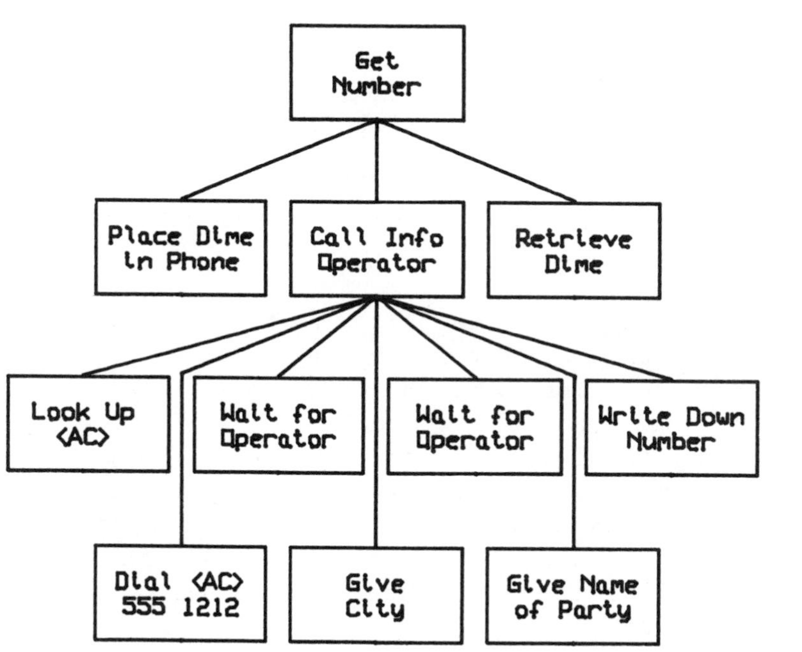
Get Number
Place Dime in Phone
Call Info Operator
Retrieve Dime
Look Up <AC>
Wait for Operator
Wait for Operator
Write Down Number
Dial <AC> 555 1212
Give City
Give Name of Party

Figure 6-4

c) In common with most trees drawn by computer scientists, the root of our tree is at the top of the diagram. This is not an important point, but one you may find confusing at first.

d) There is only one direct line of travel from any leaf node to the root, or vice versa. There are no short cuts to get directly from one leaf to another.

e) Leaf nodes may be found at a number of differing levels.

f) The order in which actions are processed in the algorithm is generally from left to right, passing via the leaf nodes.

You will be reading much more about tree structures like this in the rest of this book. Trees are also called "hierarchic" structures.

Thus far our structure diagram, and the algorithm it represents, contains only action nodes. To express the wide range of processes possible on a computer, we need also a way to express the following:

a) Choice among two or more alternative actions at the same node.

b) Repetition of some portion of the algorithm, usually changing one or more quantities related to the larger process on each repetition.

As an example of choice, consider adding a test in step 3 of our telephoning algorithm to determine whether the wanted party is at home. This can be represented in the structure diagram as shown in Figure 6-5, or it can be represented in structure table form as:

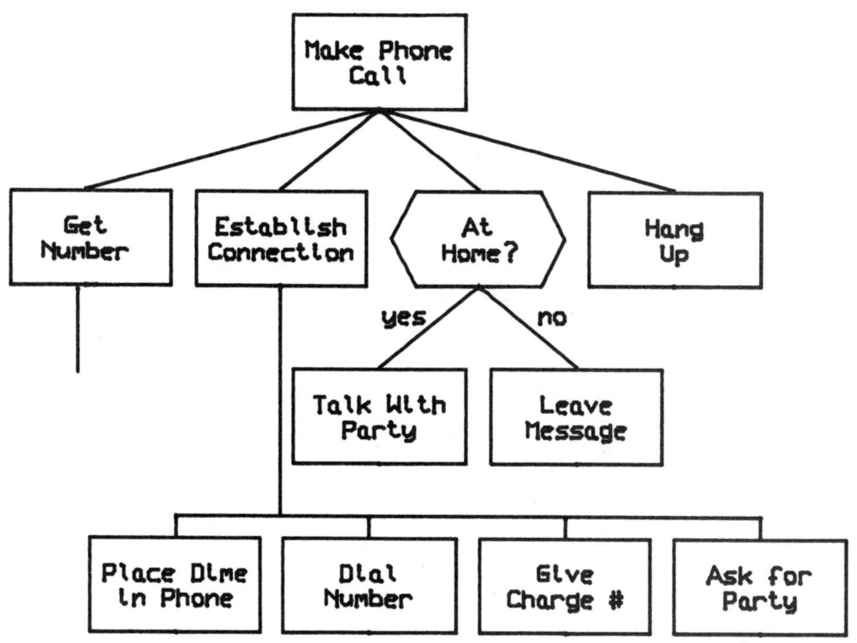
Make Phone Call
Get Number
Establish Connection
At Home?
Hang Up
yes
no
Talk With Party
Leave Message
Place Dime in Phone
Dial Number
Give Charge #
Ask for Party

Figure 6-5

3. Is wanted party at home ?
   3.1 (yes) Talk with your party
   3.2 (no) Leave message to call back

If the answer to "assertion" #3 had been NO, then you might also have specified that 3.2 signified no action to be taken. As shown in the figure, we will represent choice boxes in this book as a diamond shape.

To see the effect of a multiple-choice box, equivalent to a CASE statement, let's further change our telephoning algorithm in step 2.3. Now let's assume that we will have to plug coins into the telephone according to the amount of the charge requested by the intercept operator. A portion of the altered structure diagram is shown in Figure 6-6. In structure table form it would be:

2.3 Amount requested by operator ?
   2.3.1 ($0.10) Plug dime in phone
   2.3.2 ($0.15) Plug dime & nickel in phone
   2.3.3 ($0.20) Two dimes
   2.3.4 ($0.25) Quarter
   . . .
   and so on

Now to get the idea of a repetition node in the structure diagram, let us once again alter step 2.3. Let's assume that we have come to the telephone prepared to pay any charge up to $2.00 using dimes only. From our pocket(book) full of dimes, we plug as many as needed into the telephone after the operator tells how much is needed. This is shown in structure diagram form in Figure 6-7, and in structure table form as follows:

2.3 Repeat <amount requested> / ($0.10) times
   2.3.1 Plug dime in phone

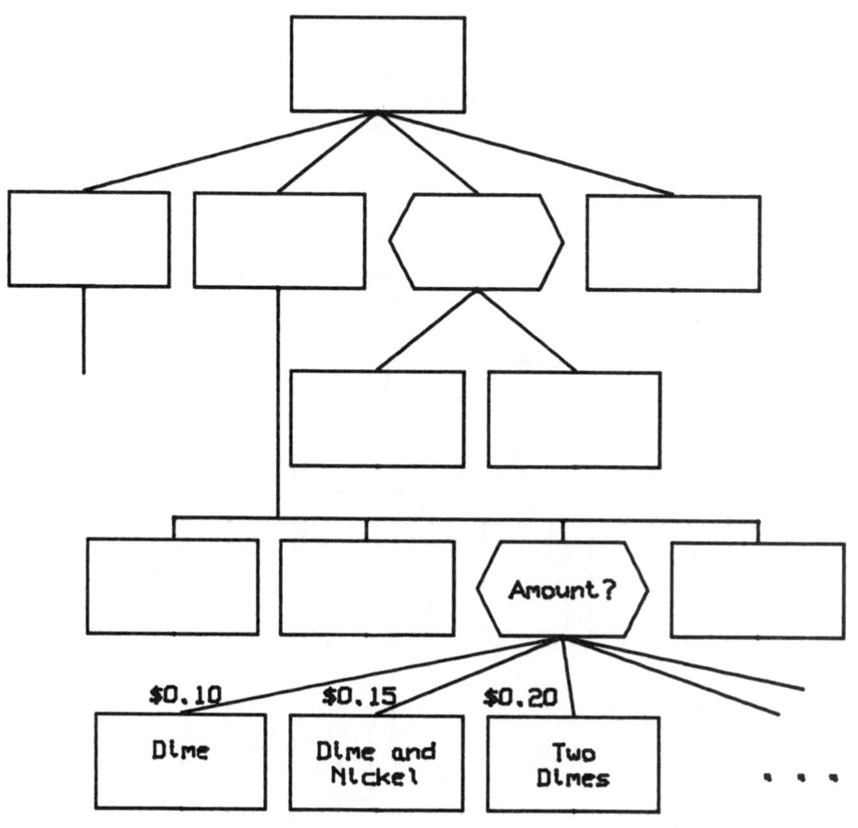

Figure 6-6

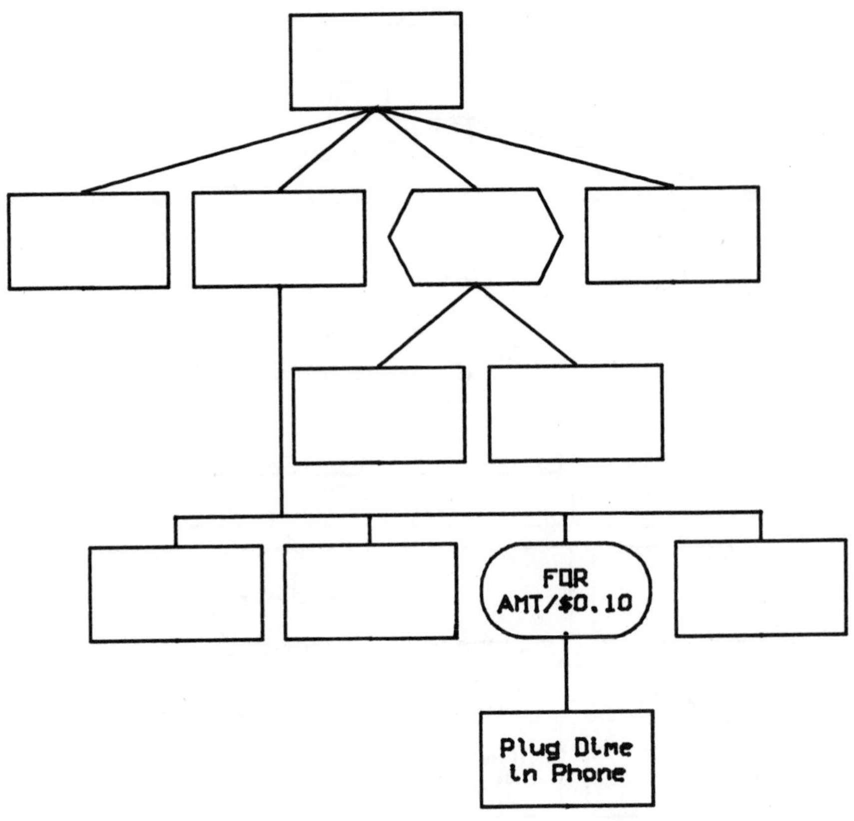

Figure 6-7

The portion of the structure repeated could be as complicated as you wish. We will use an oval shaped box to represent repetition action in structure diagrams. The repetition can continue a fixed number of times, as shown in this example, or it could continue as long as some assertion remains TRUE (or FALSE). For example:

2.3 Repeat UNTIL amount plugged into phone equals
    or exceeds amount requested.
  2.3.1 Plug dime in phone

Don't worry too much about the formalities of getting the content of structure diagram boxes exactly right at this point. The important point is to see how structure diagrams are constructed by decomposing a problem into separate steps, and showing how those steps are related. Generally the repetition box should contain one of the following:

a) The number of times the repetition is to be carried out, as in a PASCAL FOR statement.

b) The logical test to be used to determine how long the repetition should continue, as in the PASCAL REPEAT ... UNTIL and WHILE ... DO constructs.

6. Progressive Development of Algorithms

Development of algorithms for use on computers, and the programs to go with the algorithms, is almost always a process of making progressive refinements until a satisfactory solution is achieved. Only for the very smallest problems is it likely that you will be able to write down the algorithm, or the equivalent program, directly in its final form. The successive examples of the telephoning algorithm illustrate the process of progressive refinement. In this section we discuss a few of the tactics that have been found successful in developing programs which run correctly.

The issue of program correctness is one which is receiving a great deal of attention from computer scientists these days. Most large programs running today contain at least a few logical errors. You may well have fallen victim to such errors if a department store, motor vehicles bureau, or some credit card company has sent you an erroneous bill. Usually, if a computer program is used more than once, those responsible for it spend far more time trying to debug the errors than they spent in designing and implementing the program in the first place.

Most programs in use today have been designed without attention to the structure concepts discussed in this chapter. When diagrammed, these programs often look more like a bowl full of spaghetti than a tree. Computer scientists are trying to find ways of using computers to prove the correctness of algorithms and programs. The problem is sufficiently difficult that it seems unlikely that automatic proofs of correctness will be possible on any but carefully structured programs. Though it costs a little more effort to design algorithms and programs using the tree structure concepts, it seems quite clear that use of these concepts greatly reduces the total effort needed to develop and use programs of any but the smallest size.

The recommended procedure (see "Notes on Structured Programming" by E.W.Dijkstra in the book "Structured Programming", Academic Press, 1972) is to begin with a two-level structure diagram representing only a coarse description of the problem to be solved. The first level box represents the root node describing the whole problem. Each of the second level boxes should represent some sub-section of the problem, of complexity roughly equal to that of the other second level boxes. One should delay making decisions about things to be done in the third and higher levels as long as convenient. The point is to break down the over-all problem into 5 to 10 boxes at the second level in order to have no more detail in the description than a human can cope with in one lump. Each of the 5 to 10 second level boxes should be as independent of the others as possible, for the same reasons we discussed in connection with the communication between procedures.

Continuing the process, one then decomposes each second level box of the algorithm separately. If each second level box decomposes into 5 to 10 third level boxes, you will quickly reach the point where the whole structure diagram cannot fit conveniently on one page. The best way to cope with this situation is to limit the diagram on one page to no more than a few levels. Additional pages can be used to show the expanded tree portions connected to the higher level nodes. If you run out of space to put additional boxes in a structure diagram on one page, it is possible to waste large amounts of time by cramming smaller and smaller boxes into the corners and remaining open spaces. Having reached the point where you are tempted to do this, time will be saved by redrawing the diagram on another page, and arranging to use extra pages for the sub-algorithms.

Eventually you will reach a point where the level of detail in the structure diagram is sufficient to describe the algorithm for conceptual purposes, even though the exact details of the implementation may still be left as implied. Computer programs are composed of sequences of very small computational steps. In general it will not be necessary or desirable to decompose your algorithm to the point where each statement of the programming language is contained in its own box in the diagram. We will present a number of exercises later in this chapter, and later in the book, in which we call for converting structure diagrams to programs, and vice versa, at the statement level of detail. The main reason for doing this is to give you practice in relating program structure to the diagram structure, and not because we believe you will continue drawing structure diagrams to the same level of detail in your later problem solving efforts.

Having developed your algorithm to a reasonable level of detail, you may frequently find that you have reached a dead end, i.e. a point at which it is logically impossible to continue adding detail following the structure of the algorithm already in the structure diagram. Sometimes when this happens, you will be tempted to violate the structure rules of the tree representation in some way in order to make a "quick fix". This will almost always be a mistake in the long run. The recommended procedure is to back up to a level in the structure closer to the root, and to re-evaluate the problem from that point, keeping in mind the problem that caused you to back track. When we changed the definition of the telephoning problem slightly, we were engaging in this process of back tracking and re-definition of the problem.

If you have learned to speak a foreign language, you may already have experienced this backtracking and redefinition process in that context. Most natural languages follow rules that permit diagramming of sentences as tree structures. When you speak to someone in a language that is not your native language, you frequently come to a point where you don't know how to express a concept which you readily connect to a word in your native language. To get through this situation, you back up mentally and search for another way to express the thought you had in mind. You will find that the same approach often helps very much to avoid awkward problems in designing algorithms and computer programs.

In the jargon of computer science, the process of starting at the root of the tree, followed by progressive definition of more detailed levels, is known as "<u>top-down</u>" structured programming. The reasons for this terminology should now be obvious to you. The process of backtracking and re-definition until a satisfactory design is found is known as "<u>step-wise refinement</u>" of an algorithm.

7. Structure Diagrams of some Sample Programs

In this section we present structure diagrams that describe some of the sample PASCAL programs that were presented earlier in this book. You should refer back to the PASCAL program described by each diagram, and try to understand in detail how the structure diagram is related to the program. Here are some additional points to notice:

a) In Figure 6-8 we have added dotted lines to show how you can get from the tree form of the structure diagram to the sequential order of processing of the PASCAL program. The rule is that you start from the root node of the tree, and then proceed to the left most node on the next level down. If that node has branches, then regard the node you are in as the root, and repeat the process from there. Upon reaching a node that has no branches, that node should be executed, and then processing shifted to the next node to the right at the same level. If that node has branches, then regard it as the root, and repeat the process. And so on ... As you can see, the idea of repeating the logical process carried out when one reaches a root node, for each node that has branches, is recursive in nature.

b) In most algorithms it is necessary to initialize the values of various <variable>'s that are to be used. Often there are enough initializing steps that they alone would use up a full page of independent boxes in a structure diagram. The solution we have used for this is illustrated in Figure 6-9. In the box labelled 2., three simple variables are given initial values all in one box. There is no confusion in doing this, as regards the structure of the algorithm, because all of these simple steps are taken in strict sequential order. In fact it should be possible to rearrange the steps lumped together in a single box without altering the logic of the algorithm.

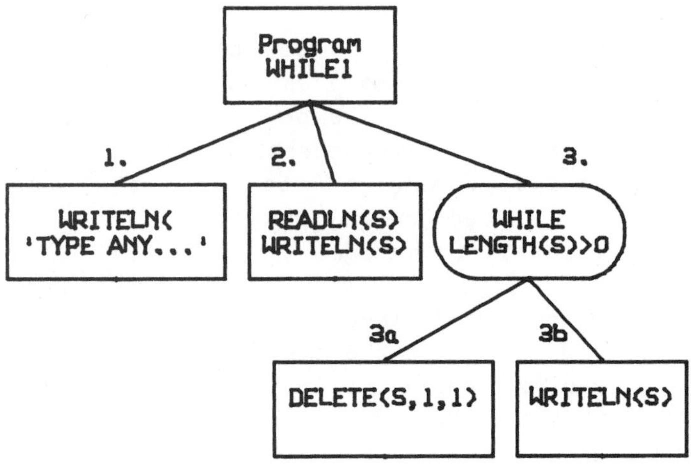

Figure 6-8

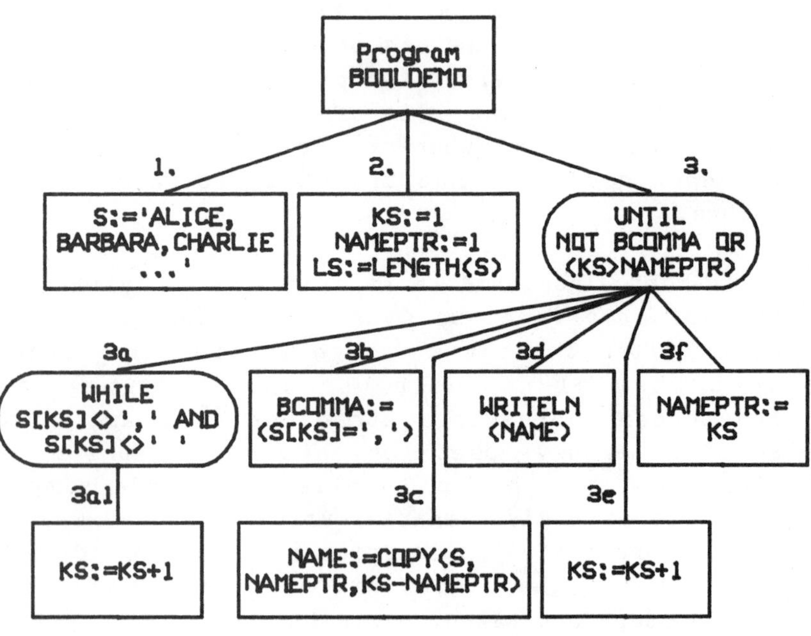

Figure 6-9

c) It is often helpful to label the boxes in a structure diagram in a way that conveys the tree structure within the labels. You can use the system we employed earlier in this chapter with the telephoning algorithm example. In this system, which is similar to the Dewey-Decimal system for organizing books in a library, an integer followed by period (".") indicates the position of the node within its level. For example, node 2. is the second node at the first level. Node 3.4. is the fourth node at the second level, in the group of nodes which all belong to the third node at the first level. The system used to label the nodes in Figure 6-9 is equivalent to the Dewey Decimal system, but uses integers and letters at alternating levels. It is a matter of personal preference whether you use one of these systems or the other. Once you understand the relationship among nodes embodied in the tree structure, and described in a structure diagram, it can also be a matter of personal preference whether you wish to use the diagram form or the structure table to describe an algorithm. We have used tables similar to structure tables for the Goals section in each chapter of this book. As you can see, the structure diagram and the structure table are equivalent forms to use in expressing the same relationships.

d) When one branch of a choice box leads to a group of nodes, we have the equivalent of the BEGIN ... END construction of the PASCAL <compound statement>. This is illustrated in Figure 6-10. The concept of the BEGIN ... END for enclosing a group of statements is equivalent to introducing an artificial level in the structure diagram where no action takes place. In Figure 6-10, nodes 1b and 1b3a1 are do-nothing nodes placed in the diagram to assist in showing the structure of the algorithm. In some cases it is useful to put a comment in or next to one of these group collecting nodes.

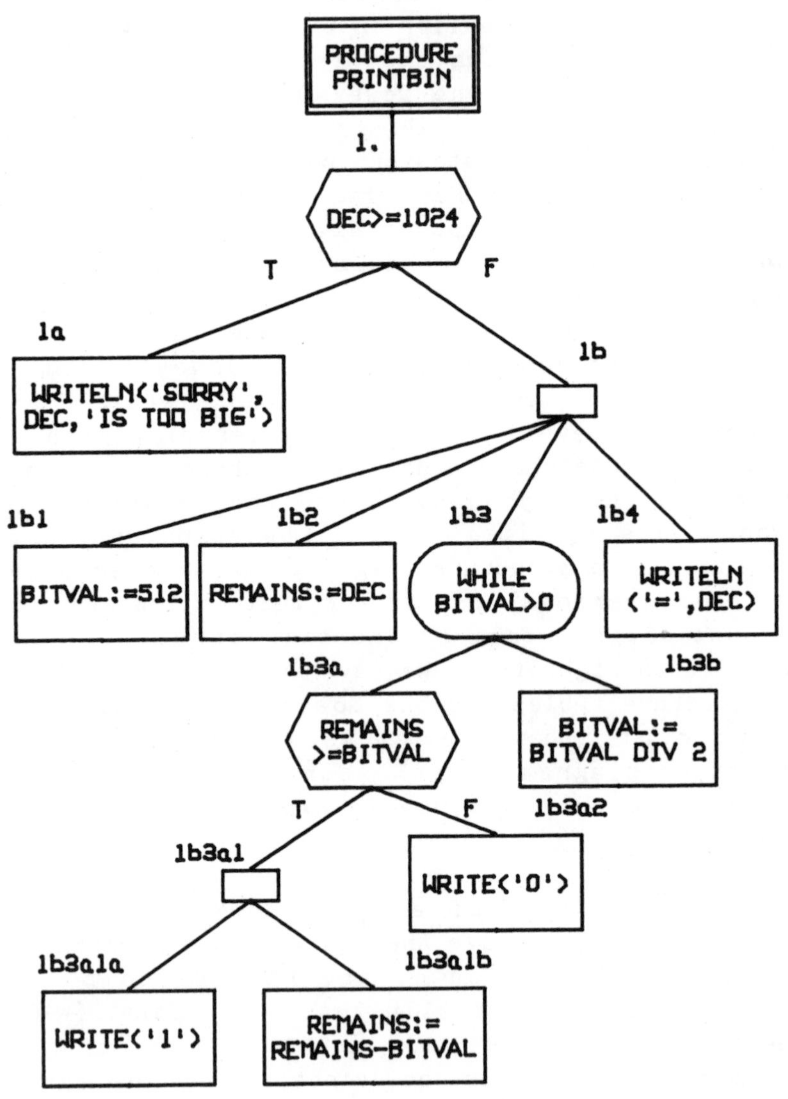
PROCEDURE
PRINTBIN
1.
DEC>=1024
T
F
1a
WRITELN('SORRY',
DEC,'IS TOO BIG')
1b
1b1
BITVAL:=512
1b2
REMAINS:=DEC
1b3
WHILE
BITVAL>0
1b4
WRITELN
('=',DEC)
1b3a
REMAINS
>=BITVAL
1b3b
BITVAL:=
BITVAL DIV 2
T
F
1b3a2
1b3a1
WRITE('0')
1b3a1a
WRITE('1')
1b3a1b
REMAINS:=
REMAINS-BITVAL

Figure 6-10

e) The concept of a procedure, and activations (i.e. calls to) a procedure, lend themselves well to expression in structure diagrams in some ways but not in others. When an algorithm is large enough to prevent complete description on one page, you can "carve off" a portion of the tree starting at any node that has branches. This node then serves as the root of a sub-tree that can be represented with a smaller structure diagram on another page. The same node remains in the "parent" diagram, and is given a name showing that the sub-tree is really attached at that point. Obviously this concept is very similar to the concept of breaking up a PASCAL program into procedures.

The idea of using boxes of different and distinct shapes to indicate distinct concepts in a structure diagram runs into trouble as the number of concepts increases. Since a procedure represents a special kind of <u>action</u>, we have chosen to show a procedure as a rectangle with a double border in the structure diagrams in this book. The procedure box is the root node of the structure diagram representing the procedure, as in Figures 6-10 and 6-12. The procedure box is a subsidiary node wherever the procedure is to be invoked as an action, as in node 2a1a of Figure 6-11. In that case the "procedure" is in fact a call to a function RANDOM, shown <u>underlined</u> in node 2a1a.

f) Notice that the indentation we have been using in programs and in structure tables bears a direct relationship to the concept of <u>level</u> in a structure diagram. The greater the level, the greater the number of columns of indentation. In fact, a properly indented program and a structure table are close cousins.

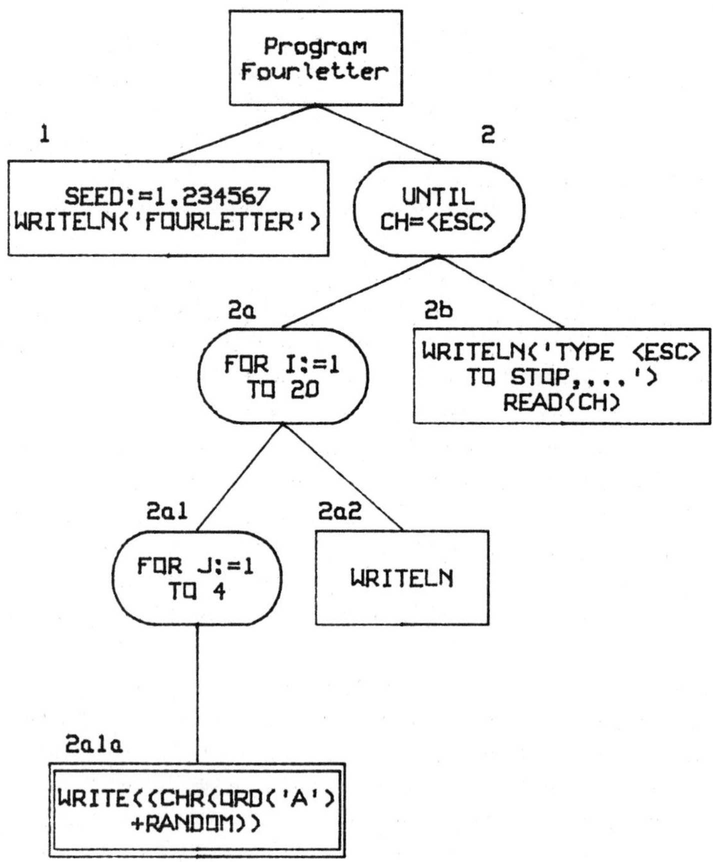

Figure 6-11

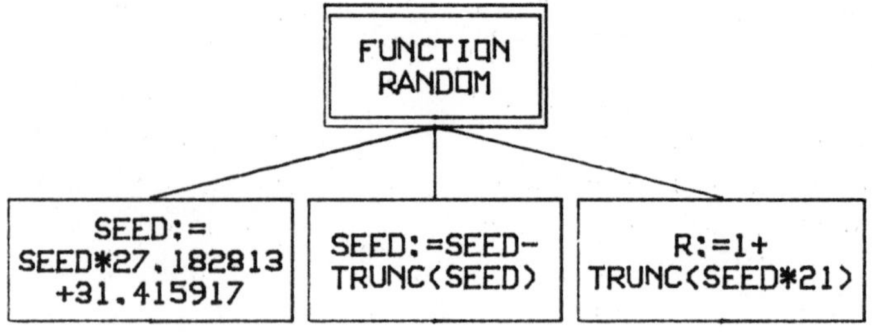

Figure 6-12

If you understand the principle of stepwise refinement, you should now be able to see the role played by comments in a program. When you design an algorithm at the first conceptual levels, you write brief descriptions of what should be done in each major section of your structure diagram. These descriptions can and should be placed in the program you write, as comments placed where the corresponding structure diagram node would be. With good indentation, and comments of this type, a PASCAL program can be made to double for the structure diagram it represents. Eventually you should be able to visualize such a program as if it were the equivalent structure diagram, and you can often dispense with the difficulty of actually drawing the diagram.

8. Solving a Problem based on Conceptual Description

You should now be able to tackle a problem of somewhat greater complexity than the problems presented earlier in the book. In this section, we will present a problem that seems conceptually simple, yet requires some careful thought to translate into an algorithm and eventually into a program. We will suggest a number of distinct steps you should take in solving this problem, but will leave as an exercise the final solution of the problem in form of a program.

The problem this time will be to write and test a PASCAL function which duplicates the action carried out by the POS built-in function for working with STRING variables. Your algorithm and program should not use any of the built-in string handling functions and procedures except for LENGTH. (i.e. do not use CONCAT, COPY, DELETE, INSERT or, of course, POS). You can use the built-in POS function to check your results.

Here is a rough description of how POS operates, referring to Figure 6-13 as an example. Given a subject string in a string variable SUBJ, and a pattern which is to be sought stored in PAT, we can use INTEGER variables IS and IP to point to locations in these two strings respectively. Starting with both pointers at 1, IS is increased one location at a time, and a check is made at each location to see if the character at SUBJ[IS] equals the first character of PAT. If not, then IS is increased again by one and the loop continues. If they are equal, then an inner loop commences in which IS remains fixed, and IP is advanced for reference to successive characters in both SUBJ and PAT. This inner loop continues until two characters which do not match are found, or until all of the characters in PAT have been checked against the corresponding characters in SUBJ. If the inner loop fails to find a match, then the outer loop should be resumed at the point where it left off, with another match being sought for the first character in PAT. If no match is found before IS becomes too large for a match to be possible, then the algorithm returns 0 as the value of POS. If a match is found, then the value returned is the value of IS at the point where the match is first seen.

Your first step in understanding how to solve this problem should be to form a mental image of what is happening using drawings that make sense to you, for example like those of the two strings SUBJ and PAT in Figure 6-13. Next, you should begin to define the variables you are likely to use eventually in a program. With assumed values for these variables, you should write down values for the variables which change through enough exemplary steps of the conceptual algorithm to begin to see some repetitive structure in what is going on. The table in Figure 6-13 is intended for this purpose. You should go through this table step by step to verify that it does indeed represent the action described for the POS function.

Figure 6-13

```
SUBJ                                        LS=25
-------------------------------------------------
| A | - | B | O | T | T | L | E | - | C | A | P |
-------------------------------------------------
  1   2   3   4   5   6   7   8   9  10  11  12

PAT                         LP=3
-------------
| T | L | E |
-------------
  1   2   3

IS   SUBJ[IS-1+IP]  PAT[IP]  IP           MATCH

 1        A            T      1    <>       F

 2        -            T      1    <>       F

 3        B            T      1    <>       F

 4        O            T      1    <>       F

 5        T            T      1     =       T
 5        T            L      2    <>       F

 6        T            T      1     =       T
 6        L            L      2     =       T
 6        E            E      3     =       T
                              4>LP          T
```

Note: The character '-' substitutes for a blank <space> in this figure.

Once you have a clear conceptual description of the algorithm, and a general idea of what variables to use in storing the data, it is time to form a rough description of the algorithm. Figure 6-14 is a partial solution to the problem in the form of a rough structure diagram. We drew the various boxes into this diagram in the order shown by the numbers in circles. You might see the problem in a different way and might draw in these boxes, or others, in a somewhat different order. The general idea, as we saw it, was to use the Boolean variable MATCH to control the looping. MATCH is assumed to be FALSE initially for the outer loop. When the initial character in PAT is found in SUBJ, MATCH is set TRUE tentatively while the inner loop is executing. The assignment in box (6) will set MATCH back to FALSE as soon as characters in corresponding locations of SUBJ and PAT do not match. It will leave MATCH TRUE if all of the characters are equal up until IP is greater than LP, the length of PAT. Both loops then terminate, and the condition which led to the outer loop terminating can be tested in box (7). Not shown yet are details on initialization, and on control of IS and IP.

Once the structure diagram of the algorithm has been brought to this rough design stage, it is time to fill in the details. The algorithm must generally be designed to cope with a variety of special cases and still return the correct result. As you add the details, you should go back to the tabular hand calculation stage to make sure that all of the steps in the conceptual "model" of the algorithm still operate as planned. You may find a problem at this point, and may have to backtrack and re-design some part of the algorithm to make it work correctly.

When you think that you have the algorithm constructed in enough detail to be sure that it will work correctly, it is time to start translating the structure diagram into the form of a PASCAL program. Notice that in the example shown here, you will have to use some identifier other than POS for the

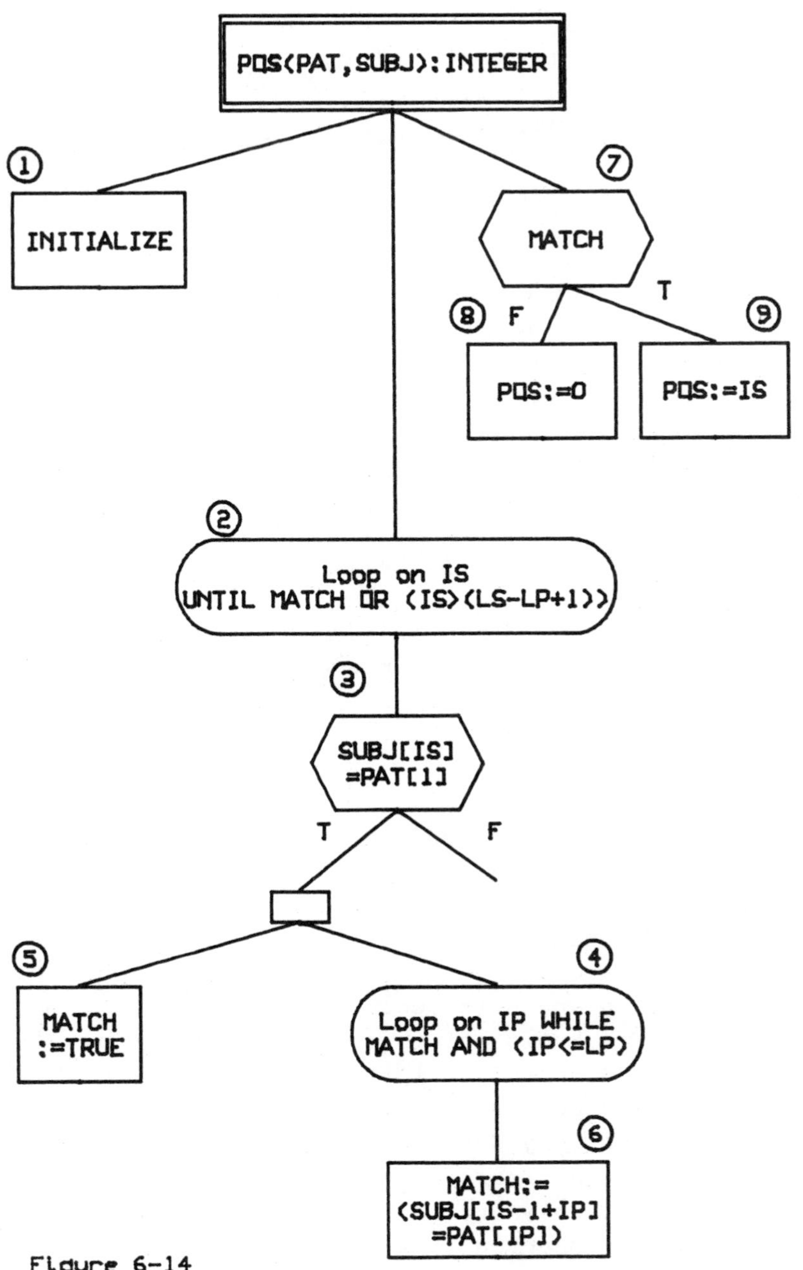
POS(PAT,SUBJ):INTEGER
1
INITIALIZE
7
MATCH
T
8
F
9
POS:=0
POS:=IS
2
Loop on IS
UNTIL MATCH OR (IS>(LS-LP+1))
3
SUBJ[IS]
=PAT[1]
T
F
5
4
MATCH
:=TRUE
Loop on IP WHILE
MATCH AND (IP<=LP)
6
MATCH:=
(SUBJ[IS-1+IP]
=PAT[IP])

Figure 6-14

function in order to be able to use the built-in POS to check your results. You can now type the program into the computer using the editor, and can attempt to compile the program. You will probably have to clean out a small number of syntax errors. If you find a large number of syntax errors when you get to this stage, you probably will save time by reviewing the program carefully on paper before proceeding.

Finally you reach the logical checkout and debugging stage. It is not enough to simply have the program operate and produce a correct result for one set of test data. You should add tracing display statements to the program temporarily, and make sure that the execution of the program agrees fairly closely with the tabulation you made when setting up the conceptual model, as in Figure 6-13. Then, if all is well so far, you should devise data to test the program involving all of the possible special cases that might arise. Only when correct operation is found for all of the possible test cases can you consider the program to be reasonably free of bugs.

Exercise 6.1:

Complete the design and checkout of the substitute POSition function as described in this section. As a minimum, you should check for correct operation under the following conditions:

a) Pattern known to occur in the subject
b) Pattern known not to occur in the subject
c) Pattern occurs at left-most position in subject
d) Pattern occurs at right-most position
e) Pattern only one character long at any position
f) Pattern at least three characters long
g) Subject only one character long
h) Subject shorter than the pattern (no match)
i) Subject or pattern empty (no match)

9. Two Challenging Problems

In this section we present two problems of sufficient difficulty that you may have to spend a significant amount of time in their solution. You have now encountered all of the PASCAL programming tools necessary to handle these problems. What distinguishes these problems from those we have seen so far is that they require a substantial amount of thought to create the necessary algorithm in a relatively simple way.

The Towers of Hanoi problem is classical in computer science. It can be solved in a program no longer than about 40 lines, without doubling up statements on a line. A reasonable solution would also include comment lines, and a tracing procedure to help in debugging. The Billiards problem is an example of a large number of "moving" pictures you should now be able to create on the computer. If the microcomputer you are using allows the Turtle to draw a BLACK line on top of WHITE lines, it is possible for you to erase each instance of the billiard ball before drawing the next, thus giving the appearance of a moving ball. This problem is not as difficult conceptually as the Towers of Hanoi problem, but the program to implement the Billiards moving picture will be over 100 lines long. If you find either of these problems to be too difficult for you at this stage, set them aside until you have progressed further in the book, and have had further experience in solving simpler problems. Then return to these problems. The experience gained in finishing them successfully will help you in later uses of computers.

Exercise 6.2: Towers of Hanoi

You may well have seen this problem in the form of a puzzle with blocks sold in a novelty store. The problem is illustrated in Figure 6-15. You are given three posts (the "towers") and a set of disks capable of being threaded onto any one of the posts from the top. Each of the disks is of a different diameter.

When the problem starts, all of the disks are on the left most post, which we might call post 'A'. The object of the exercise is to move all of the disks to the right most post, which we can call post 'C', in such a manner that no disk ever lies on top of another disk that is smaller. The problem can be solved for any number of disks initially on post 'A'. Figure 6-15 illustrates the problem solution in steps for 2, 3, and 4 disks separately.

For two disks, the middle post ('B') is used temporarily for saving the smaller disk. This allows the larger disk to be moved to post 'C'. The shift can then be completed by moving the smaller disk from B to C, thus placing it again on top of the larger disk.

For three disks, it is necessary to move the smaller two to the middle tower ('B') in order to allow the largest disk to be moved to C. To move the top two to B, use the same logic as used for the two disk problem, with B and C interchanged. After the largest disk has been moved to C, the two remaining on B can now be moved to C, using A for temporary storage of the smallest disk.

For four disks, one moves the top three to post B first. The largest is moved then to post C. Finally the smaller three are moved to C. This is accomplished by using the same algorithm as for three disks, but with the roles of posts A and B interchanged.

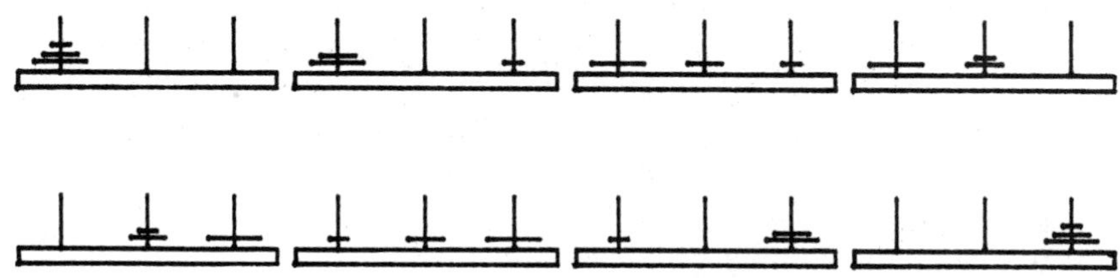

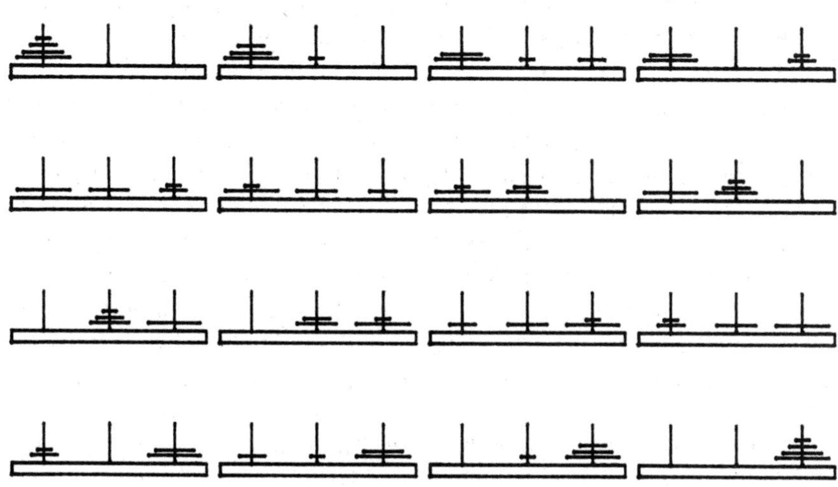

Figure 6-15

By now, you should have noticed that there is a <u>recursive</u> pattern in the manner of solution. To solve the problem for N disks, one simply solves for N-1 disks first using the alternate destination post. The largest disk can then be moved. Finally the N-1 disk solution is repeated with A and B changing roles.

Figure 6-16a suggests a conceptual model for a sub-algorithm HANOI which will be used eventually as the basis for a recursive procedure of the same name. In this case we refer to the Source (SRC), Destination (DEST), and Alternate (ALT) posts rather than A, B and C, since the latter change roles at successive levels in the recursion. CNT represents the Count of the disks to be moved when HANOI is called. Figure 6-16b makes the algorithm more explicit in terms of the sub-algorithm (procedure) calls.

To represent the towers we used three STRING variables A, B, and C. The disks were represented by the characters '1', '2', '3', and '4', each character standing for the size of disk it represents. Absence of a disk was represented by a blank space character. Towers B and C were initialized to have only blanks. Tower A was initialized to '4321' in the four disk problem. It proved convenient to use three count variables NA, NB and NC to represent the number of disks currently on each tower at any one time. It would also have been possible to use the LENGTH function for each tower instead.

With this introduction, you should be able to complete the solution of this problem. The TRACE procedure can be used to display, on one line each time TRACE is called, the content of each of the towers each time HANOI is entered, and also at the very end of the program. You don't need to plot the fancy picture of the towers on your screen except as an extra challenge.

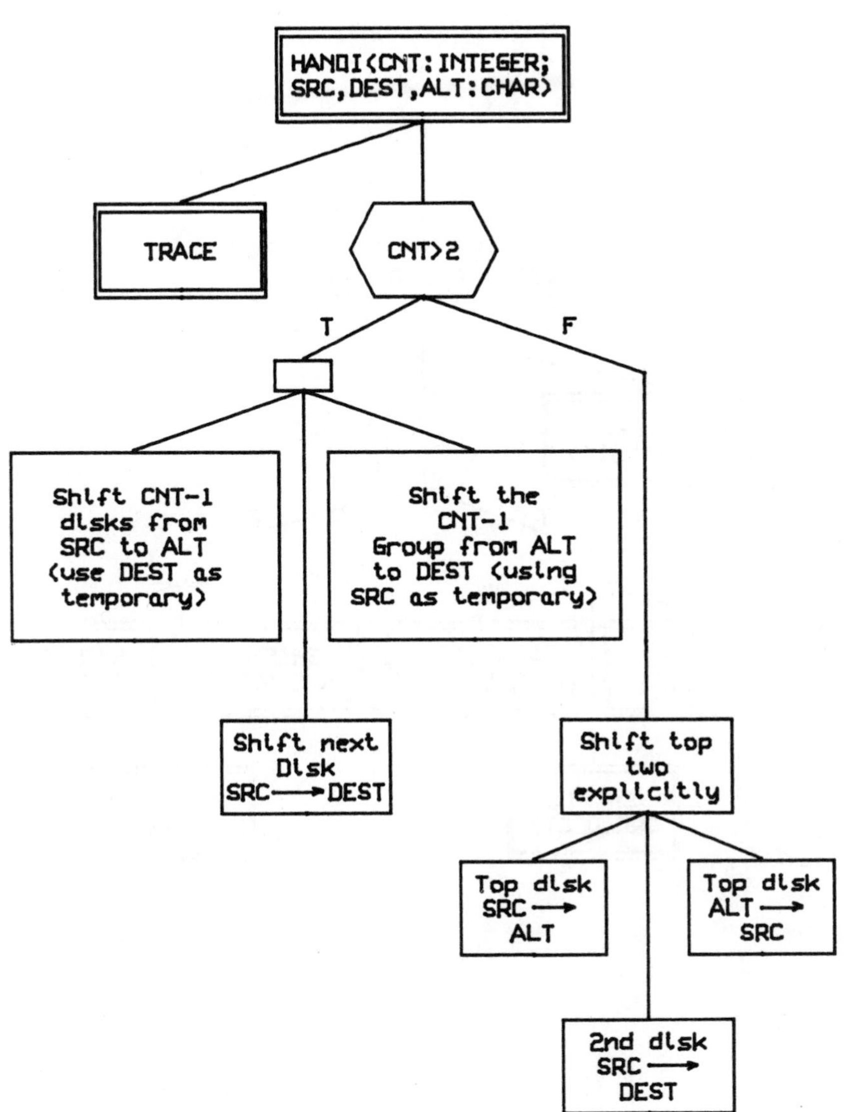
HANOI(CNT:INTEGER;
SRC,DEST,ALT:CHAR)
TRACE
CNT>2
T
F
Shift CNT-1
disks from
SRC to ALT
(use DEST as
temporary)
Shift the
CNT-1
Group from ALT
to DEST (using
SRC as temporary)
Shift next
Disk
SRC→DEST
Shift top
two
explicitly
Top disk
SRC→
ALT
Top disk
ALT→
SRC
2nd disk
SRC→
DEST

Figure 6-16a

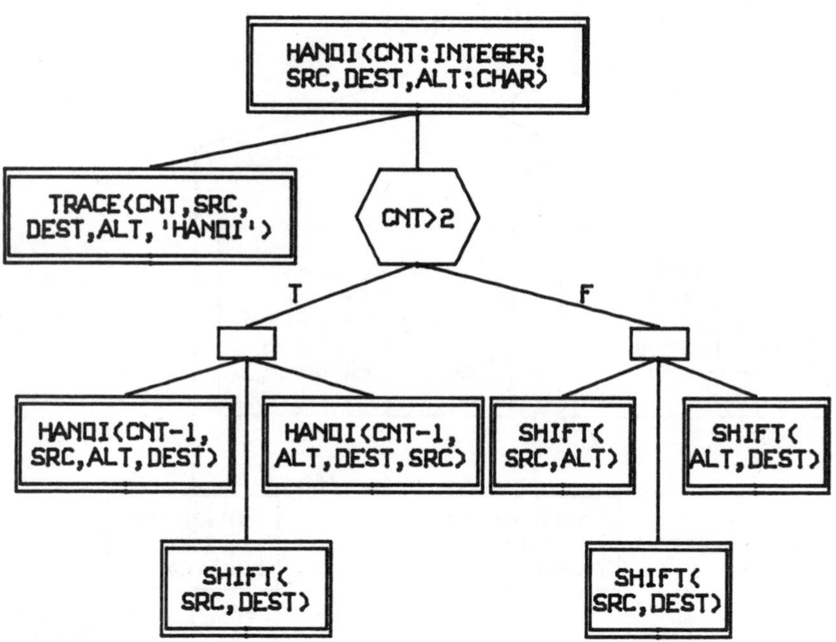
HANOI(CNT:INTEGER;
SRC,DEST,ALT:CHAR)
TRACE(CNT,SRC,
DEST,ALT,'HANOI')
CNT>2
T
F
HANOI(CNT-1,
SRC,ALT,DEST)
HANOI(CNT-1,
ALT,DEST,SRC)
SHIFT(
SRC,ALT)
SHIFT(
ALT,DEST)
SHIFT(
SRC,DEST)
SHIFT(
SRC,DEST)

Figure 6-16b

Exercise 6.3: Billiards Game

Small computers are now being used widely for simulating the "TV games" you probably have seen in public places. With a computer fitted with a graphics display that allows selectively plotting and erasing figures on the screen, the possibility for programming similar games is almost endless. This problem provides one illustration of such a game, the game of billiards.

Figure 6-17 illustrates the "moving" picture the program you write for this exercise should plot. It is shown on a display that does not have selective erase capability, and thus each successive position of the ball is shown. The program should be able to handle any initial direction of motion of the ball, where the direction can be typed in degrees from the keyboard. When the ball strikes a "wall" it "reflects". The angle enclosed between the original direction of motion and the wall is the same as the angle between the final reflected direction and the wall on the side opposite the reflection point. For example, if the ball strikes the top wall when moving at 45 degrees, it will point toward -45 degrees when it reflects. If it strikes the right end wall at 45 degrees, it will emerge from the reflection at 135 degrees.

The program should be able to detect when the ball falls into one of the six "pockets", and declare a "win". Otherwise the ball slows down on progressive steps, and finally stops at a new position. The program should then prompt for a new pointing direction for the next "play".

Figure 6-18 provides a rough structure diagram of the program we used to solve this problem. One possible complication is in computing NEWX and NEWY after each step in the loop that simulates motion of the ball. This can be done as follows: Assuming that the program has INTEGER variables

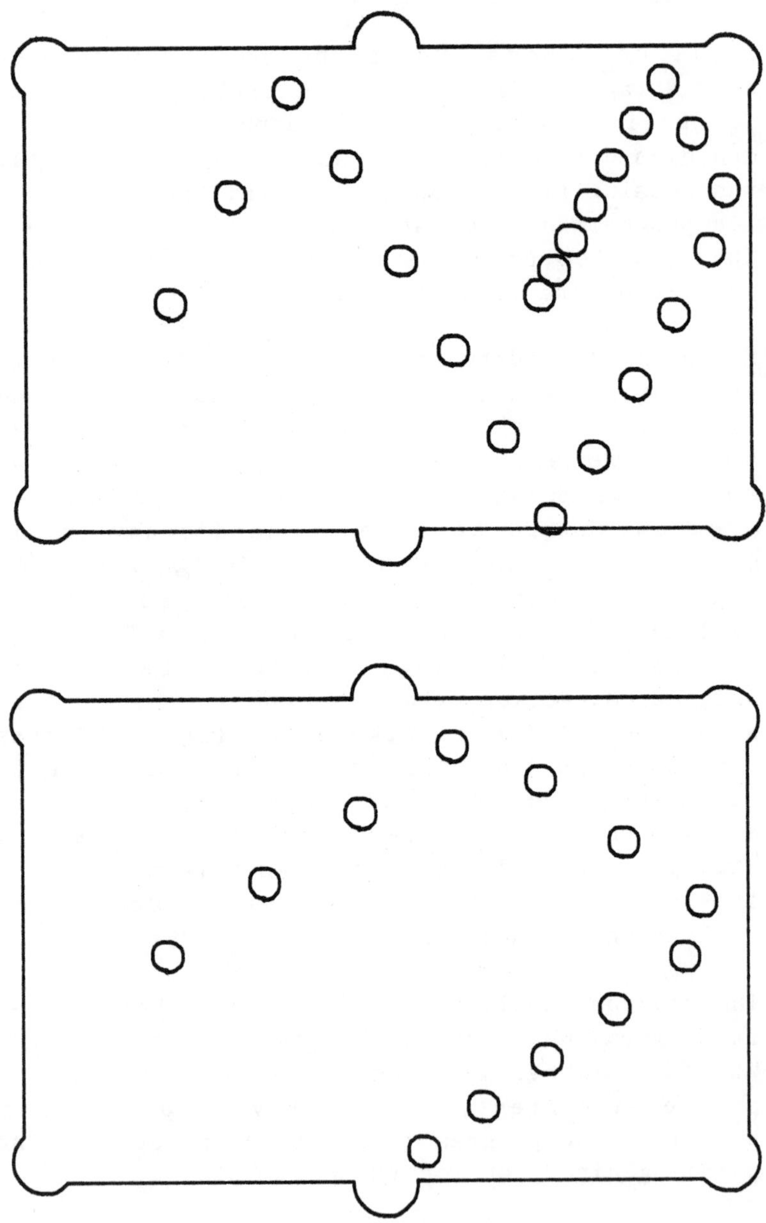

Figure 6-17

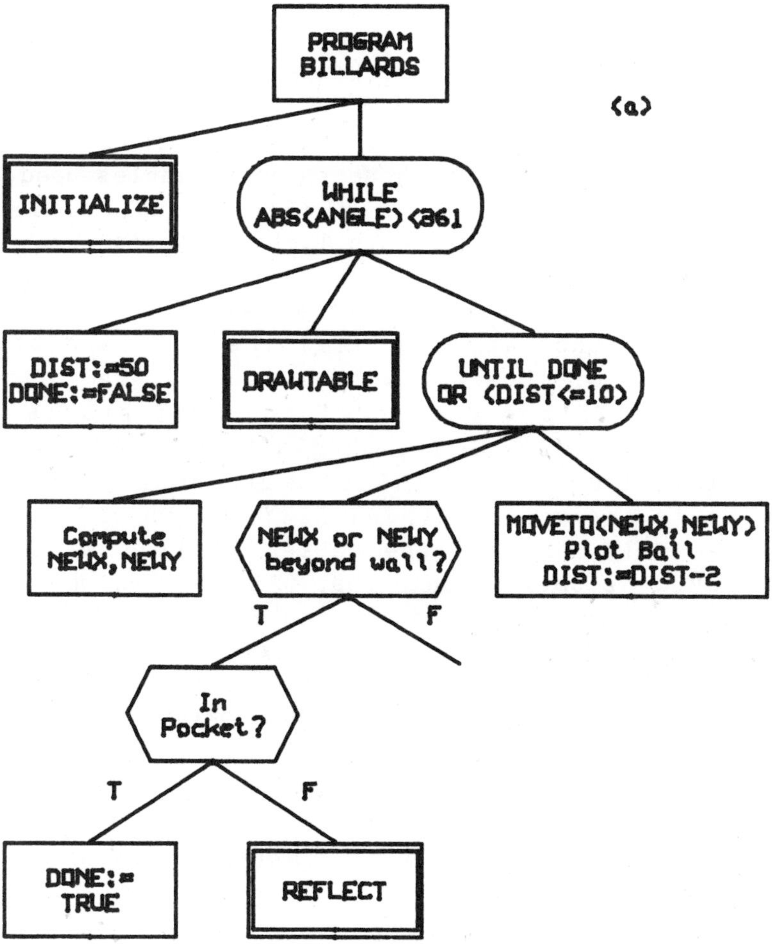

PROGRAM BILLARDS
(a)
INITIALIZE
WHILE ABS(ANGLE)<361
DIST:=50 DONE:=FALSE
DRAWTABLE
UNTIL DONE OR (DIST<=10)
Compute NEWX,NEWY
NEWX or NEWY beyond wall?
MOVETO(NEWX,NEWY) Plot Ball DIST:=DIST-2
T
F
In Pocket?
T
F
DONE:= TRUE
REFLECT

Figure 6-18

NEWX,NEWY
(b)
YWALL
ANGLE1
ANGLE2
OLDX,OLDY
NEWX,REFLY

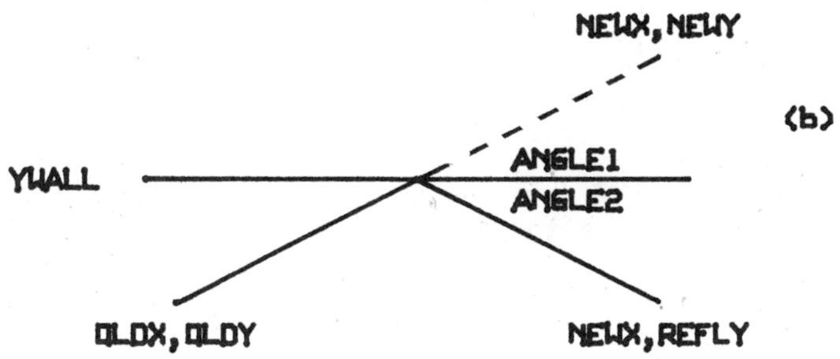

NEWX, NEWY, AND NEWANGLE, then

```
WHEREAMI(NEWX, NEWY, NEWANGLE)
```

will assign the current values describing the Turtle's position to these three variables used as variable parameters. WHEREAMI is a built-in procedure for working with Turtle graphics.

Refer to part (b) of Figure 6-18 for the basic geometry that applies when the billiard ball reflects off the top wall in the diagram of the table. If the center of the ball starts at location (OLDX,OLDY), then a MOVE(DIST) in the original direction ANGLE1 will result in the Turtle arriving at (NEWX,NEWY) which is outside the walls limiting the table. Note that DIST should be small enough that (NEWX,NEWY), were the turtle actually to draw a line ending there, would not be off screen. In the example shown, NEWX will be the same as calculated using WHEREAMI, after the MOVE(DIST), with PENCOLOR(NONE) being in force. But NEWY needs to be converted to REFLY, the value of Y resulting from the reflection at the wall. This can be obtained from the fact that REFLY is as far <u>below</u> the wall as NEWY is <u>above</u> the wall. Thus

```
REFLY := 2*YWALL - NEWY;
ANGLE2 := -ANGLE1
```

will produce the required new values of Y and the new angle. MOVETO and TURNTO will then be needed to establish the new position of the Turtle after reflection. Similar geometry applies when reflecting off each of the other three walls. Note that REFLECT does not have to draw in the lines shown in part (b) of Figure 6-18. It needs only to find the new location of the Turtle, so that the next position of the ball may be drawn.

Problems

Problem 6.1:

Write a complete PASCAL program to perform the algorithm shown in Figure 6-19. (SQRT(X) is a built-in function that returns, as its value, the square root of X). EXITSW is Boolean. Other identifiers are Integers. For the mathematically oriented: This algorithm computes the first 100 prime numbers. For the non-mathematically oriented: Solution of this problem does not require that you understand what this algorithm or equivalent program would be used for.

Problem 6.2:

Write a complete PASCAL program to perform the algorithm shown in Figure 6-20. All variables are Integers. You do not need to understand what this algorithm might be used for in order to write the program equivalent to the structure diagram.

Problem 6.3:

Draw structure diagrams to represent the programs COUNTWORDS (Chapter 4 section 6) and RCOUNT (Chapter 4, section 8).

Problem 6.4:

Draw a structure diagram to represent the program GROWTREE (Chapter 4, section 10).

Problem 6.5:

Draw a structure diagram to represent the program DECBIN (Chapter 5, section 8).

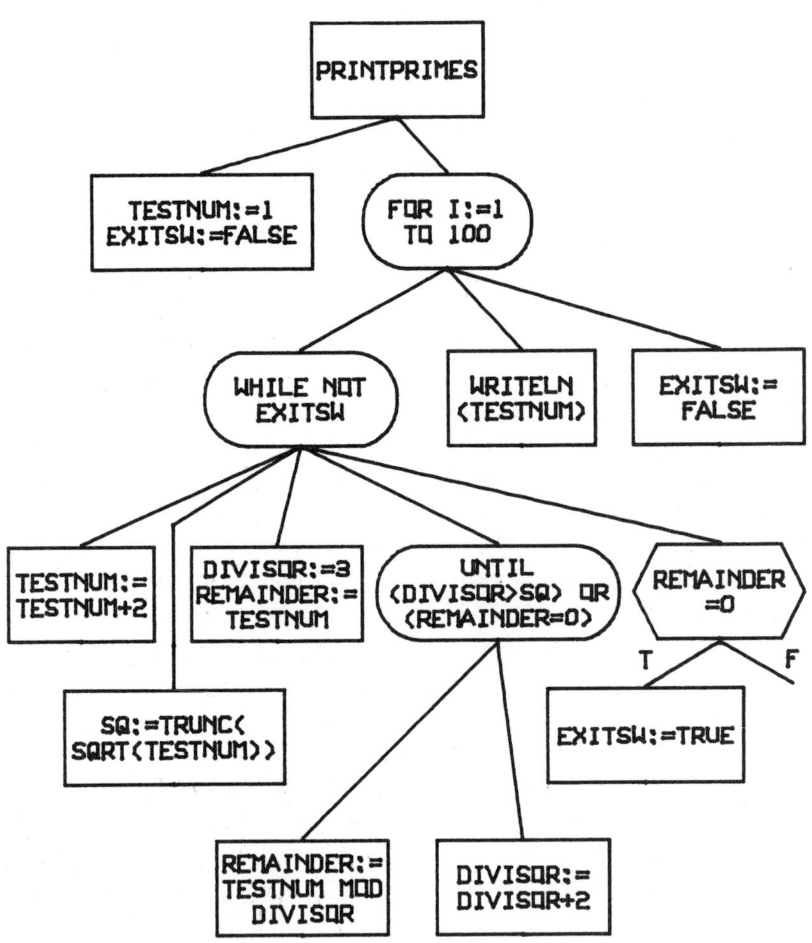

PRINTPRIMES
TESTNUM:=1
EXITSW:=FALSE
FOR I:=1
TO 100
WHILE NOT
EXITSW
WRITELN
(TESTNUM)
EXITSW:=
FALSE
TESTNUM:=
TESTNUM+2
DIVISOR:=3
REMAINDER:=
TESTNUM
UNTIL
(DIVISOR>SQ) OR
(REMAINDER=0)
REMAINDER
=0
T
F
SQ:=TRUNC(
SQRT(TESTNUM))
EXITSW:=TRUE
REMAINDER:=
TESTNUM MOD
DIVISOR
DIVISOR:=
DIVISOR+2

Figure 6-19

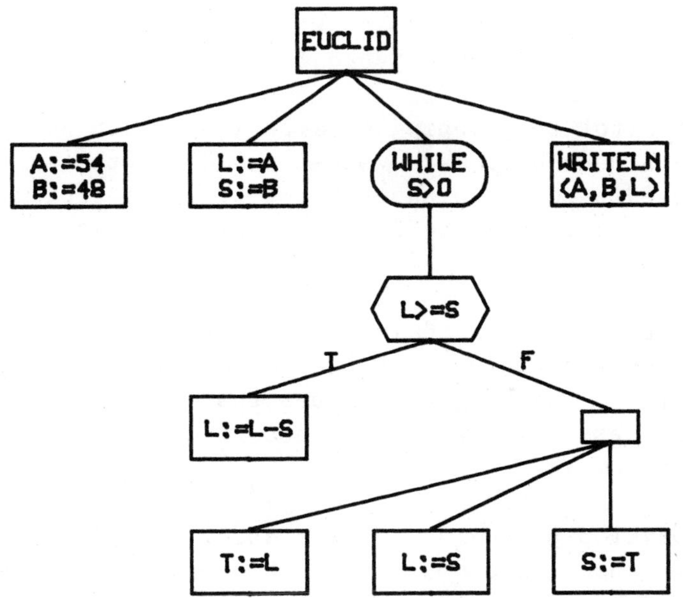

Figure 6-20

Chapter 7

DATA INPUT

1. Goals

This chapter concentrates on the input of data from external devices into a program, with principal attention being given to data from the keyboard connected to your computer.

1a. Learn to use the READ and READLN statements for handling numbers, single characters, and strings. Use READ both with and without automatic echoing of each character typed from the keyboard.

1b. Control the looping of a program which reads in a sequence of data values whose length cannot be predicted in advance at the time the program is written. Use the EOF and EOLN built-in functions.

1c. Learn to validate input data values to make sure that they are either correct, or at least within the range of values that your program can successfully handle without terminating abnormally.

1d. Develop programs to solve specified problems which require data values to be input from the keyboard.

2. Background

Up to this point we have avoided most of the complications associated with communicating information from some external device into a program you may write. Not all computer programs are designed to process external data, but a great many do so. Until fairly recently, the most common device used for the "input" of data into a program has been the punched card reader. In recent years, many users of large computers have switched to using magnetic tapes, tape cartridges, floppy disks or remote terminals for communicating data into large computers. On the microcomputer you are probably using in connection with this book, you will be using the keyboard on a CRT terminal, or perhaps one connected directly to the computer, for input of data.

Regardless of the nature of the device from which your program obtains input data, the standard method for communicating the data into your program uses the READ statement, or its close cousin the READLN statement. On some computers, and in some programming languages, the use of a READ statement is a command to the computer system to scan physically the data on a complete input "record". For example, all 80 columns on a standard computer punched card can contain data, usually several independent data items all on one card. The entire card is scanned physically when you execute a READ statement, and a separate "format" arrangement is then used to interpret each of the independent data items on the "card image". In PASCAL, each READ or READLN statement is instructed to interpret one or more data items from the input device, and the strict record orientation is not necessary.

The "format" arrangements used in some programming languages are really built-in procedures which provide for the translation of the characters handled by most "peripheral" (i.e. external) devices into the "internal" binary form in which Integer and

Real values are stored and manipulated in the computer. In PASCAL, the necessary translation is implied by the <type> of a variable named in a READ, or READLN statement. Similarly, on output using WRITE or WRITELN statements, the opposite translation is performed.

On some computing systems, the concept of separated records of data does not exist. Instead, the data is regarded simply as a continuous stream of characters. This concept may be difficult to visualize in the case of punched cards, but it is applied naturally to communications from a "conversational" computer "terminal", i.e. a device with which you can "converse" with the computer. Such terminals are also called "interactive" because the user interacts with the computer fairly directly, rather than through the more indirect medium of cards for input, and line printer listings for output. The arrangement embodied in the READ and WRITE statements of PASCAL works with both fixed length data records, and with variable length streams of data. This allows you to have considerable flexibility in handling a variety of data formats using simple program statements. The penalty for having this flexibility is that you may occasionally have to write a slightly longer program in PASCAL to accomplish things that can be done in a very terse, and arcane, shorthand using formats in some other languages.

Most programs that handle input data have to be arranged to cope with varying amounts of data from one processing run to another. This means that your program has to be designed to detect when the last item of data that may be available has been read in, i.e. when the end of the input "file" has been reached. The term "file" is computer jargon referring to the mechanism for transferring data to or from an external device. The jargon originated with the use of punched cards, in which the analogy with a conventional card file was quite obvious. The terminology has now been generalized, and refers to any external device, including a keyboard, a display unit, a communication line, and many others.

When a program has been reading data, and the last data item available has just been read, we say that the program has reached the "end of file" condition for the associated device. In the case of reading punched cards, the end of file or "EOF" condition arises when the last card in the deck has been read. In the case of input from a keyboard, it is necessary for some convention to be established whereby you can signal to the program that the EOF condition has been reached. Some computer systems do not provide an explicit built-in mechanism for recognizing when EOF has been reached. In those cases, it is necessary for the programmer to arrange that the occurrence of some special value within the input data stream will be interpreted as meaning that EOF has been reached. We will give examples of both techniques in this chapter.

3. Differences Among Input/Output Systems

Warning: Because of many differences in the physical characteristics among computer input devices, you should be prepared for some detailed differences between the methods described in this chapter and those you may encounter on other computers. This chapter represents a substantial revision of an equivalent chapter originally written to describe input via punched cards on a large computer. All of the sample programs required very substantial revision to make them appropriate for the use of a keyboard for input, and a display unit for corresponding output. These differences are part of the "real world" of computing that everyone who works regularly with computers must accept and deal with in whatever fashion may be required.

In this chapter we will give you a small taste of the kinds of differences that may arise. In this case we will show that READ can be used both in an arrangement that causes every character typed at the keyboard to "echo" immediately on the display screen, and in an arrangement in which no echo takes place. You may have noticed that the program editor, which you have been using to prepare PASCAL programs, employs the latter arrangement for most commands. The no-echo facility allows the programmer to control explicitly what will appear on the screen in response to every character typed. As you will see, both the echoing and no-echo arrangements introduce confusing complications that one must understand in order to design programs for sensible input actions.

One of the principal differences in working with "batches" of punched cards for input, compared with a keyboard, is the manner in which the programmer provides a way for the "user" of the program to be aware of what the program does at appropriate stages. In the punched card, or "batch" case, the cards are all submitted for processing at one time, and the printed output results are often not available until hours later. Even if the output is available within a minute or two after the deck of cards is submitted, the user has no opportunity to interact with the program while it is running. Therefore, any information needed so that the user can detect what the program did, after processing has been completed, must be provided in the printed listing while the program is running. For this reason, a good practice when debugging a program to be run in the batch environment is to provide WRITELN statements which cause copies of all data read into the program to appear on the printed listing.

In the interactive environment, with input from a keyboard and output via a display screen, the computer system will usually echo each character typed on the screen automatically, at least unless special steps are taken to suppress the echo. Thus a program written to echo characters to the standard output device with WRITE statements, as in the batch environment, will produce confusion on the screen, because each item typed will appear twice (once when echoed during typing, once when displayed by the WRITE statement).

Another point of difference is that the user of an interactive program should be kept informed when the program expects some input data to be typed on the keyboard. If the program reaches a READ statement without displaying any information on the screen at all, it will halt waiting for input as programmed, but the user will have no idea what is happening! This situation does not arise in the case of a batch oriented program, since the person who punches the input data cards must be aware in advance of the data that the program will expect, and how that data must be laid out on the cards. Some interactive systems intended for novice users automatically WRITE a colon (':'), or some other character to "prompt" the user, each time a READ statement is executed. This prevents the programmer from having complete control of what appears on the screen. In our PASCAL system, there is no automatic writing of prompt characters, and you will have to use WRITE statements when needed to cause a prompt character to appear.

4. READ and READLN Statements

To understand how data input works, one is more concerned with the "semantics" of the input statements than with syntax. In appearance, the syntax of the READ and READLN statements is very similar to the syntax of the WRITE and WRITELN statements. Unfortunately, there is no clear and concise method of describing the actions taken by READ and READLN, i.e their semantics, in the same sense that the syntax diagrams provide a reference description of the syntax rules. In this section, and the next two, we will give a variety of very short examples to show how the input facilities of PASCAL work. The remainder of the chapter is devoted to presentation and analysis of several sample programs which use data input.

In the discussion that follows, it will be assumed that these declarations apply:

```
VAR CH:CHAR;
    I,J,K,L:INTEGER;
    R,Q:REAL;
    S:STRING;
```

When execution of a program reaches a READ or READLN statement, the program halts temporarily and waits for data conforming to the variable named in the parameter list to be typed on the keyboard. For example:

```
READ(CH)
```

will cause the next character typed at the keyboard to be assigned as the value of the variable CH.

```
READ(S)
```

will append all characters typed to the end of S, up until the next <RET> is typed. If you try to type more characters into S than its declared size allows, usually 80 characters, the system will continue to accept and echo characters but they will not be appended to S. Only the first 80 characters will be assigned to locations in S in this case. If you make a mistake while typing characters into S, you can correct the error by using the "backspace" or <BS> key, or the <DEL> (<RUBOUT>) key. <BS> will erase one character from S each time it is pressed, and the corresponding character on the screen will disappear. <DEL> will erase the entire line, allowing you to begin typing the line once again. In both cases, the count of characters assigned to S is reduced by the number of characters erased.

```
READ(I)
```

will expect an <integer constant> to be typed. If, while the program is halted in the READ(I) statement, you type any character other than a digit ('0' thru '9') or a blank <space>, the program will terminate abnormally. After the first digit is typed, READ(I) will assume that the first non-digit typed will be the end of the intended integer. This applies to <BS> and <DEL> in the same way as it applies to any other non-digit. Thus you cannot correct a mistake in typing in an integer using those keys. (It is possible to arrange a program to accept integers as input, and to allow <BS> and <DEL> to be used for correcting mistakes, but this subject is beyond the scope of this book.) For example, if your program contains the following statements:

```
READ(I);
READ(J);
READ(K);
READ(L);
```

and you type:

```
  273   4 15<RET>
58
```

the result will be I=273, J=4, K=15, L=58 after all the statements have completed executing. The <RET> after the "15" is optional, and simply signifies using the Return key to start typing at the beginning of the next line. The READ(<integer>) statements interpret the use of <RET> as equivalent to typing a <space>. If you type any character <u>other than a <space> <RET> or digit</u> while these four statements are waiting for input, and before a digit has been typed, then the program will terminate abnormally. For example typing:

```
273, 4, 15, 58
```

will cause I to be assigned the value 273 correctly, but the program will terminate abnormally on the READ(J) because of the comma (',') typed immediately following the "273".

As we have already noted, the syntax for the READ statement is similar to the syntax for the WRITE statement. In particular, it is possible to have a list of parameters passed to READ. Thus:

```
READ(I, J, K, L)
```

is equivalent to the sequence of four READ statements shown above.

For reading REAL values,

```
READ(R)
```

will accept any REAL <constant> such as those illustrated in Chapter 5, Section 6, of this book. In addition to <space> and <RET> before any other characters are typed, the characters '+', '-', '.' and 'E' may appear at the places illustrated in the syntax diagram of Figure 5-2. Violation of the syntax rules described by this diagram will result in an abnormal termination of the program. At any point where the syntax allows an exit from the diagram, with no further characters needed, it will be legal to type any character other than those specified by the syntax to indicate the end of the number. Thus:

```
READ(R,Q)
```

will accept:

```
-1.0E3 0.123
```

assigning -1.0E+3 (-1000.0) to R, and +1.23E-1 to Q.

It is legal to <u>mix</u> READ requests for data of any of the <types> discussed in this section, but you must be careful in doing so. For example, suppose that your program contains the statement:

```
READ(I, CH, S)
```

and you type in the following:

```
5064Jones,Bill   123-22-6720<RET>
```

where, as usual, "<RET>" stands for pressing the Return key once. Then I will be assigned the Integer value 5064, CH will be assigned 'J', and S will be assigned the string 'ones,Bill   123-22-6720', where LENGTH(S) will return the value 23, including the 3 blank spaces after 'Bill'. If we had tried to re-order the different <type>'s of variables involved here, with S coming earlier than one of the other variables in the READ statement, it would have been necessary to finish typing the <string> on one line, terminating it with <RET>, and then continue with the other data on the next line.

The statement:

```
READLN
```

causes the program to ignore all input until <RET> is typed. This stands for "READ a Line". The actions associated with READ and READLN can be combined as in the following example:

```
READLN(I, J)
```

which is equivalent to:

```
READ(I);
READ(J);
READLN
```

In other words, the wait for the <RET> key to be pressed occurs <u>after</u> data has been assigned to all of the variables named as parameters. Thus:

```
READLN(I, J, K, L)
```

with input of:

```
12   34  5<RET>
678<RET>
```

will cause the READLN statement to complete when the <u>second</u> <RET> is typed, since the first <RET> will be ignored and interpreted as if it were <space> in scanning for the value of L (678).

5. <u>EOF and EOLN</u>

"<u>EOF</u>" stands for "End-Of-File". "<u>EOLN</u>" stands for "End-Of-Line". Both are the names of built-in Boolean functions that sometimes are convenient in writing interactive programs. Conceptually, both functions are somewhat better adapted to the batch environment of punched card input, or to the use of other input devices which really do store files of data broken into records.

EOF is initially FALSE when your program starts executing. It will remain FALSE until you terminate a READ or READLN statement by pressing <ETX> (or <ENTER>), or by typing 'C' <u>while holding down the <CTRL>, i.e. "control", key</u>. This feature can be used in either of the following ways:

```
WHILE NOT EOF DO              REPEAT
  BEGIN                          . . .
    . . .
    any statements               any statements
    . . .                        . . .
  END                         UNTIL EOF
```

<CTRL-C> is equivalent to the <ETX> (End of Text) key, which is sometimes called <ENTER>. Either loop will terminate on the first occasion after <ETX> is typed while a READ or READLN within the loop is executing. Notice that if the loop contains more than one READ statement, or other statements affected by the READ's, you may also have to include a statement beginning with

```
IF NOT EOF THEN ...
```

to prevent unwanted processing of statements inside the loop after <ETX> or <CTRL-C> is typed.

EOLN is similar in concept to EOF, except that EOLN is set to TRUE on termination of a READ by typing <RET>. The next READ will reset EOLN to FALSE again. Consider the following example:

```
READ(I);
IF EOLN THEN statement-1
        ELSE statement-2
```

If you then type:

```
123<RET>
```

then statement-1 will be executed. However, if you type:

```
123 <RET>
```

then statement-2 will be executed because the <space> typed before <RET> will terminate the READ. The operation of READ(<real variable>) will have similar properties.

READ(CH) will be satisfied by typing <RET> alone, and will set CH=' ', but it will also set EOLN to TRUE. The next READ(CH) will reset EOLN to FALSE again!

READ(S) allows typing <RET> at any time as illustrated earlier. EOLN should always be TRUE immediately following termination of READ(S).

6. The Files INPUT and OUTPUT

The PASCAL system provides ways of READing information from a device other than the keyboard, and of WRITEing information to a device other than the display screen. Thus far, we have avoided bothering you with the complications in the language associated with this possibility. For most purposes you can ignore these complications while working with the exercises in this book. There are two actions that you may well find very convenient, and these require a minimum of knowledge about the standard "*files*" INPUT and OUTPUT.

Our PASCAL system, as well as most others, assume that information to be brought into a program using a READ statement will come from the "standard" input device. Likewise, it is assumed that all WRITE statements refer to the standard output device. It is possible to change either READ or WRITE to refer to a different device by giving the name of its file, as in

```
READ(<filename>, I, J, K)
```

and

```
WRITE(<filename>, R, L, CH)
```

Thus far, we have left "<filename>," empty, with the result that the compiler has assumed that we want the standard input or output device respectively. However, the following two statements are exactly equivalent:

```
READ(INPUT, I, J, R);
READ(I, J, R)
```

similarly:

```
WRITE(OUTPUT, CH, S);
WRITE(CH, S)
```

also

```
EOF(INPUT) is equivalent to EOF
EOLN(INPUT) is equivalent to EOLN
```

The point of going into all this is that you may wish to use the built-in procedures "RESET" or "PAGE" which demand that the file name be mentioned explicitly. If, after having set EOF to TRUE by pressing the <ETX> or <CTRL-C> key, you wish to start reading again in a later part of your program, this can be done with:

```
RESET(INPUT)
```

If you wish to clear the entire display screen at once, in order to start displaying new information on a "clean sheet", you can do this with:

```
PAGE(OUTPUT)
```

Further discussion of files is beyond the scope of this book.

7. Sample Program AVERAGE

Starting with this section, we present several sample programs which illustrate the input of data. The written descriptions will be only partially effective in conveying to you what happens when these programs are run. We strongly suggest implementing each program on your computer. Then run the program and try to understand what it does, while comparing carefully with the printed PASCAL program statements.

The program AVERAGE is presented in two forms to allow comparison of two methods for terminating a loop which reads data values in a sequence of indefinite length. Both forms simply compute the average value corresponding to a column of integers. Most of the work is done in the repeated execution of lines 25 thru 34 in AVERAGE, and lines 25 thru 32 in EOLNAVG. At the beginning of each line of input, the program "prompts" for input by displaying the character '>'. The display listing then shows the result of typing a number immediately after the prompt character is displayed. The READ statement assigns the number typed to X, which is then added to SUM. The integer count variable N is increased by 1 to keep track of how many items are being averaged. The WRITELN then displays the value of N, and the current value of SUM. Notice the use of the function SIZE within the parameter list of the WRITELN. By displaying (6-SIZE(X)) blank spaces, the columns showing values of N and SUM are vertically aligned on the screen, regardless of the length (within reason) of the integer typed in.

Looping terminates in AVERAGE when a number is typed having an absolute value of 10,000 or more. The built-in function ABS returns a positive value having the magnitude of the Integer or Real expression used as its actual parameter. This illustrates one possible way of stopping the loop. It works if you can specify a data value that is outside the range of expected normal data to be processed by the program.

In EOLNAVG, looping terminates when a number is typed and immediately followed by <RET>. Without use of the file "KEYBOARD", and the associated WRITE statement for echoing, the display obtained would differ from that shown for AVERAGE in that the last line displaying values of N and SUM would be broken by the action of the <RET> key when it echoes. These values would then not be properly aligned with the columns. The file KEYBOARD has properties similar to INPUT, except that none of the characters typed in will be echoed to the screen. Remember that <RET> is

```
PROGRAM AVERAGE;
VAR N,X,SUM:INTEGER;
  AVG:REAL;

FUNCTION SIZE(X:INTEGER):INTEGER;
VAR SZ,AX:INTEGER;
BEGIN
  AX:=ABS(X);
  IF AX<10 THEN SZ:=1
  ELSE
    IF AX<100 THEN SZ:=2
    ELSE
      IF AX<1000 THEN SZ:=3
      ELSE
        SZ:=4;
  IF X<0 THEN SZ:=SZ+1; (*for minus sign*)
  SIZE:=SZ;
END (*SIZE*);

BEGIN (*MAIN PROGRAM*)
  WRITELN('AVERAGE');
  SUM:=0;
  X:=0;
  N:=0;
  REPEAT
    WRITE('>'); (*prompt for input*)
    READ(X);
    IF ABS(X)<10000 THEN
    BEGIN
      SUM:=SUM+X;
      N:=N+1;
      WRITELN(' ':6-SIZE(X),N:2,' ':2,'SUM=',SUM);
    END;
  UNTIL ABS(X)>=10000;
  AVG:=SUM/N;
  WRITELN; WRITELN;
  WRITELN('AVERAGE=',AVG, ' FOR ',N,' ITEMS');
END.
```

```
Display associated with AVERAGE program

AVERAGE
>6      1  SUM=6
>-8     2  SUM=-2
>15     3  SUM=13
>20     4  SUM=33
>19999

AVERAGE=8.25 FOR 4 ITEMS
```

```
PROGRAM EOLNAVG;
VAR N,X,SUM:INTEGER;
  AVG:REAL;

FUNCTION SIZE(X:INTEGER):INTEGER;
VAR SZ,AX:INTEGER;
BEGIN
  AX:=ABS(X);
  IF AX<10 THEN SZ:=1
  ELSE
    IF AX<100 THEN SZ:=2
    ELSE
      IF AX<1000 THEN SZ:=3
      ELSE
        SZ:=4;
  IF X<0 THEN SZ:=SZ+1; (*for minus sign*)
  SIZE:=SZ;
END (*SIZE*);

BEGIN (*MAIN PROGRAM*)
  WRITELN('AVERAGE');
  SUM:=0;
  X:=0;
  N:=0;
  REPEAT
    WRITE('>'); (*prompt for input*)
    READ(KEYBOARD,X);
    WRITE(X);
    SUM:=SUM+X;
    N:=N+1;
    WRITELN(' ':6-SIZE(X),N:2,' ':2,'SUM=',SUM);
  UNTIL EOLN;
  AVG:=SUM/N;
  WRITELN; WRITELN;
  WRITELN('AVERAGE=',AVG, ' FOR ',N,' ITEMS');
END.
```

interpreted as a <space> for reading into an INTEGER variable, thus avoiding any problem with abnormal termination of the program in line 27 when <RET> is typed. The READ in line 27 will not terminate until at least one digit is typed for this reason.

A third alternative might have been to use EOF instead of EOLN. Typing <ETX> or <CTRL-C> after '>' would have set EOF to TRUE, but it would also have assigned an undefined value to X in the READ statement. To avoid problems with trying to add an undefined value of X into SUM, it would be necessary to control lines 29 thru 31 in EOLNAVG (modified to use EOF instead of EOLN) within an IF NOT EOF THEN ... statement. Essentially the same technique is used in several of the later sample programs.

8. Sample Program MAKECHANGE

The main point of this program is to illustrate the use of several input data values on a single input line. The program simulates, in a simplified way, what happens at the checkout counter of a supermarket or at the cashier's desk in a store or restaurant. Typically you are presented with charges, amounting to several dollars, plus some fraction of a dollar expressed in cents. Often you offer payment in paper money only, handing the clerk one or more "bills" in one, five, or ten dollar denominations. This program accepts both the charges, expressed as an integer number of cents, and also the denomination of the bills you hand the clerk, expressed in dollars only.

The program first prompts for input of the charges, then for the currency payment as a series of integer constants separated by blank spaces, all on one line. See for example, lines 4, 7, and 10 of the separate page showing the lines displayed by this program. On those lines, the computer displays "CHARGES:", the interpreted dollar amount with dollar sign and period added, and the legend "CURRENCY:". The user types in the other numbers, terminating the line with <RET>

```
PROGRAM MAKECHANGE;
VAR CHARGES,CURRENCY,PAID,CHANGE:INTEGER;

PROCEDURE DISPLAY;
VAR DB,QTR,DIME,NICKEL,PENNY:INTEGER;
BEGIN
  DB:=0; QTR:=0; DIME:=0; PENNY:=0;
  WRITE('CHANGE:');
  CHANGE:=PAID-CHARGES;
  WHILE CHANGE>=100 DO
    BEGIN CHANGE:=CHANGE-100; DB:=DB+1; END;
  WHILE CHANGE>=25 DO
    BEGIN CHANGE:=CHANGE-25; QTR:=QTR+1; END;
  WHILE CHANGE>=10 DO
    BEGIN CHANGE:=CHANGE-10; DIME:=DIME+1; END;
  IF CHANGE>=5 THEN
    BEGIN CHANGE:=CHANGE-5; NICKEL:=1; END
    ELSE
      NICKEL:=0;
  WHILE CHANGE>=1 DO
    BEGIN CHANGE:=CHANGE-1; PENNY:=PENNY+1; END;
  WRITELN(' DOLLARS:',DB, ', QUARTERS:',QTR,
    ', DIMES:',DIME, ', NICKELS:', NICKEL,
    ', PENNIES:',PENNY);
  WRITELN;
END (*DISPLAY*);

BEGIN (*MAIN PROGRAM*)
  WRITELN('MAKECHANGE');
  REPEAT
    WRITE('CHARGES:');
    READ(CHARGES);
    IF NOT EOF THEN
    BEGIN
      WRITE('  $',(CHARGES DIV 100),'.',
                  (CHARGES MOD 100));
      PAID:=0;
      WRITE('  CURRENCY:');
      WHILE NOT EOLN DO
      BEGIN
        READ(CURRENCY); (*size of each bill*)
        PAID:=PAID+CURRENCY*100; (*in Cents*)
      END;
      DISPLAY;
    END;
  UNTIL EOF;
END.
```

```
Display associated with MAKECHANGE program

MAKECHANGE
CHARGES:237   $2.37  CURRENCY:5
CHANGE: DOLLARS:2, QUARTERS:2, DIMES:1, NICKELS:0, PENNIES:3

CHARGES:237   $2.37  CURRENCY:1 1 1
CHANGE: DOLLARS:0, QUARTERS:2, DIMES:1, NICKELS:0, PENNIES:3

CHARGES:571   $5.71  CURRENCY:10
CHANGE: DOLLARS:4, QUARTERS:1, DIMES:0, NICKELS:0, PENNIES:4

CHARGES:
```

after typing in the last dollar bill denomination. The program then displays a second line showing the numbers of dollar bills, quarters, dimes, nickels, and pennies owed by the clerk to the customer in change.

This program can be understood with the help of the structure diagrams in Figures 7-1a and 7-1b. After verifying that it is indeed the MAKECHANGE program that is running, in box 1, the main program loop is entered in box 2. First the prompt for "CHARGES:" is displayed, and the program waits for an integer to be typed in. Since it is planned that the loop will be terminated using the <ETX> mechanism to make EOF TRUE, it is necessary to make sure that the initial prompt message is not followed immediately with the change in EOF. If EOF is not yet set, then the dollar amount read in is interpreted in dollars and cents, and re-displayed in the more familiar format as a verification. The program then initializes PAID to zero, and prompts for input of the list of dollar bill denominations, both in box 2b2. Loop 2b3 then reads the currency amounts and adds them into PAID in cents. Loop 2b3 terminates when <RET> is typed immediately following the last integer in this list. Finally, the procedure DISPLAY is called to produce the line showing how many dollar bills and coins are to be returned in change.

Part (b) of the diagram illustrates one method for computing the number of each denomination of dollar bill and coins to be returned in change. The algorithm shown corresponds fairly closely to the algorithm a clerk would follow in counting out your change. The idea is to return as many bills or coins of the largest denomination available that is still smaller than the amount of the change still to be returned.

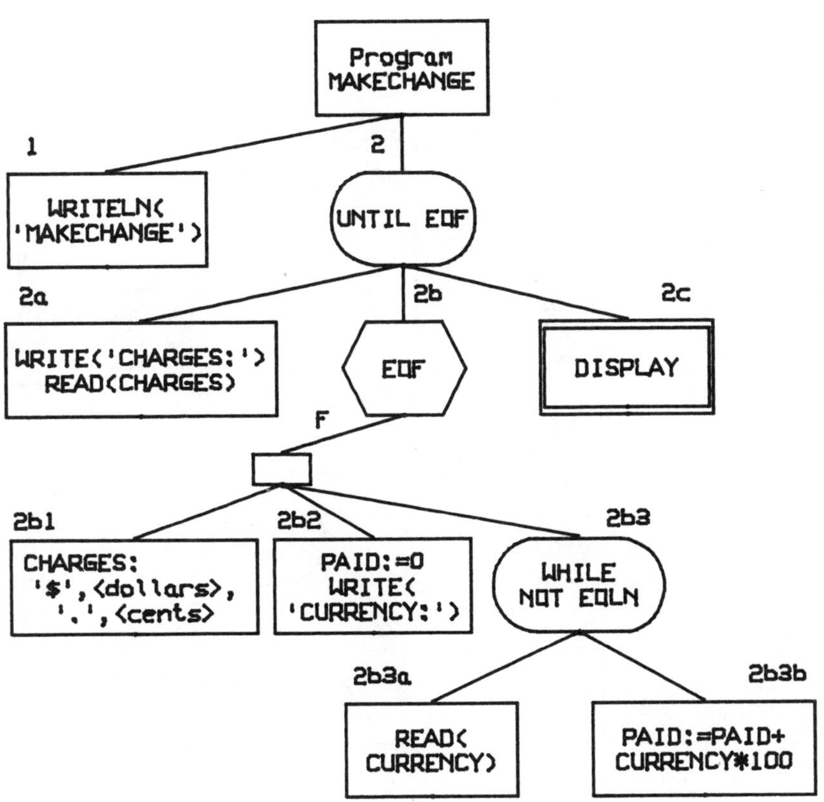

Program
MAKECHANGE
1
WRITELN(
'MAKECHANGE')
2
UNTIL EOF
2a
WRITE('CHARGES:')
READ(CHARGES)
2b
EOF
2c
DISPLAY
F
2b1
CHARGES:
'$',<dollars>,
'.',<cents>
2b2
PAID:=0
WRITE(
'CURRENCY:')
2b3
WHILE
NOT EOLN
2b3a
READ(
CURRENCY)
2b3b
PAID:=PAID+
CURRENCY*100

Figure 7-1a

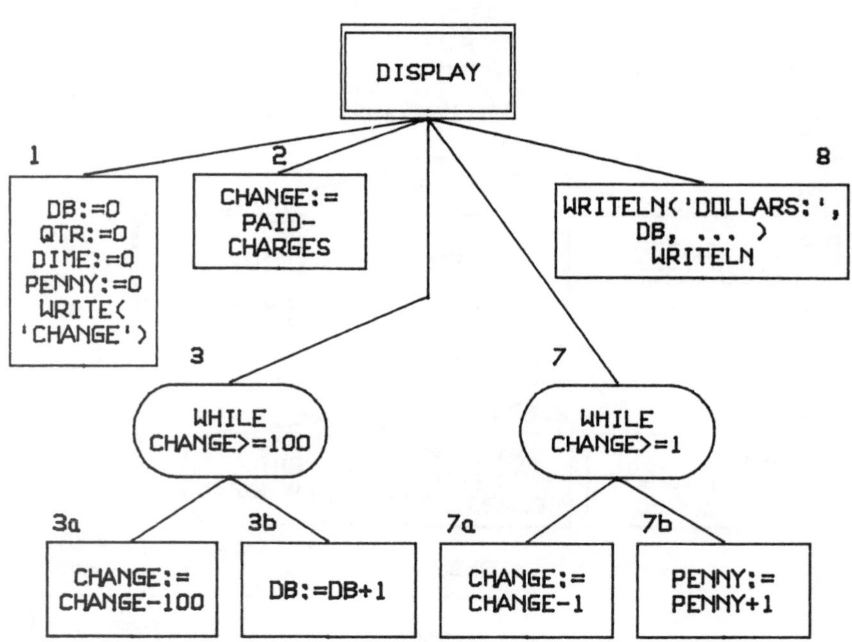
DISPLAY
1
DB:=0
QTR:=0
DIME:=0
PENNY:=0
WRITE(
'CHANGE')
2
CHANGE:=
PAID-
CHARGES
8
WRITELN('DOLLARS:',
DB, ...)
WRITELN
3
WHILE
CHANGE>=100
7
WHILE
CHANGE>=1
3a
CHANGE:=
CHANGE-100
3b
DB:=DB+1
7a
CHANGE:=
CHANGE-1
7b
PENNY:=
PENNY+1

Figure 7-1b

On large computers, the WHILE loops are not necessarily the best way to perform the computation, since it would be possible to substitute DIV and MOD operations to avoid looping. Some microcomputers and minicomputers, such as the one you may be using in connection with this book, have no hardware instructions for performing multiplication or division directly. Instead, multiplication and division on these machines requires the use of built-in procedures that use successive addition or subtraction operations to carry out the needed computation by a "long hand" method similar to the one you would use with pencil and paper. This particular program is short enough that you would probably not be able to detect the difference in speed of the large vs. the small machine using these two methods.

9. Sample Program DENOISE

This program shows part of the process often used to prepare indexes of the titles of articles published in the scientific literature. The same process, called indexing by "Key Word In Context" (KWIC), is also used by linguists and historians studying non scientific literature. The idea of the KWIC index is to print each title, shifted either to right or left, in such a way that the KEYWORD ends up aligned in the center of the page. Each title is printed once for each KEYWORD, each time shifted right or left by a different amount so that the KEYWORD selected shows up on the middle of the page. The shifted titles for many different documents are then sorted so that they may be printed out alphabetically ordered according to the selected KEYWORDS. This allows a reader to scan the list as an index, placing each KEYWORD in the context of the titles in which it occurs.

```
PROGRAM DENOISE;
VAR NOISE,S:STRING;
  P,I:INTEGER;
BEGIN
  WRITELN('DENOISE');
  REPEAT
    WRITE('>');
    READLN(S);
    IF NOT EOF THEN
    BEGIN
      FOR I:=1 TO 7 DO
      BEGIN
        CASE I OF
          1: NOISE:='THE ';
          2: NOISE:='A ';
          3: NOISE:='IN ';
          4: NOISE:='BY ';
          5: NOISE:='OF ';
          6: NOISE:='AS ';
          7: NOISE:='AND '
        END (*CASE*);
        P:=POS(NOISE,S);
        IF P>0 THEN DELETE(S,P,LENGTH(NOISE));
      END;
      WRITELN(S);
      WRITELN;
    END (*IF NOT EOF*);
  UNTIL EOF;
END.
```

If the KWIC index is to be useful, the program should not bother to index a title based on any "noise" word that contributes only readability, and no real information, to the title. For example, none of the short words shown in the right of the assignment statements in lines 14 thru 20 of the program would be of any real value in indexing. Therefore a program to prepare a KWIC index needs to be able to recognize the noise words and ignore them in the rest of its work.

Here is what a very short KWIC index might look like for some of the titles used as sample data with this program:

```
             CHROMOSOME  ANALYSIS BY COMPUTER
                SYSTEMS  ANALYSIS OF URBAN TRANSPORT
                         CHROMOSOME ANALYSIS BY COMPU
 CHROMOSOME ANALYSIS BY  COMPUTER
            THE FASTEST  COMPUTER
            THE USES OF  COMPUTERS IN EDUCATION
HE USES OF COMPUTERS IN  EDUCATION
```

In order to keep the listing compact, yet staying within prescribed limits for the width of a column of print, some of the titles are truncated at either the left end or the right end. Normally the listing would be wider than shown here, and it would include a reference code telling where detailed information could be found corresponding to each title.

After displaying its confirming line (line 5 of the program), the program prompts for input with the character '>' in column 1. It then waits for a string to be typed. The string appears on the screen as it is typed. Then the string appears again on the next line with the noise words removed. This program is only meant to illustrate the operation of removing the noise words, and it does none of the other work of building a KWIC index. If you were developing a KWIC indexing program, you might well design a procedure to do the noise removal. The program shown here might be used in the course of designing the procedure as a test vehicle for the algorithm involved. Once found to work correctly, the program could be converted to a procedure and added to the main KWIC program as it is being developed.

This program is an example of the use of <ETX> or <CTRL-C> being typed as the first character following the prompt character as a signal to stop looping. Here is an example of how the screen display might appear while using this program:

```
DENOISE
>SYSTEMS ANALYSIS OF URBAN TRANSPORT
SYSTEMS ANALYSIS URBAN TRANSPORT

>CHROMOSOME ANALYSIS BY COMPUTER
CHROMOSOME ANALYSIS COMPUTER

>MAN VIEWED AS A MACHINE
MAN VIEWED MACHINE

>THE FASTEST COMPUTER
FASTEST COMPUTER

>THE USES OF COMPUTERS IN EDUCATION
USES COMPUTERS EDUCATION
```

10. Sample Program DEVOWEL

The main purpose of this simple program is to illustrate the reading of one character at a time from the input data stream each time READ is called. A secondary purpose is to illustrate the kinds of alteration of text that a linguist might cause in order to discover how we humans extract information by reading text. In this case, the program takes out all of the vowels in the input data. Having read a line of input data in its normal English language form, you have no real difficulty in "reading" the text with all the vowels removed. Could you do that without having read the normal English version first?

```
PROGRAM DEVOWEL;
VAR CH:CHAR;
  S,TEMP:STRING;
BEGIN
  WRITELN('DEVOWEL');
  WRITE('>');
  READ(CH);
  WHILE NOT EOF DO
  BEGIN
    S:='';
    TEMP:=' '; (*one character*)
    WHILE NOT EOLN DO
      BEGIN
        IF (CH<>'A') AND (CH<>'E') AND (CH<>'I')
            AND (CH<>'O') AND (CH<>'U') THEN
          BEGIN
            TEMP[1]:=CH;
            S:=CONCAT(S,TEMP);
          END;
        READ(CH);
      END;
    WRITELN(S);
    WRITELN;
    WRITE('>');
    READ(CH); (*clear the EOLN*)
  END (*WHILE NOT EOF*);
END.
```

```
Display associated with DEVOWEL program

>HERE IS EDWARD BEAR, COMING DOWNSTAIRS NOW
HR S DWRD BR, CMNG DWNSTRS NW

>BUMP, BUMP, BUMP, ON THE BACK OF HIS HEAD,
BMP, BMP, BMP, N TH BCK F HS HD

>BEHIND CHRISTOPHER ROBIN. IT IS, AS FAR AS
BHND CHRSTPHR RBN. T S, S FR S

>HE KNOWS, THE ONLY WAY OF COMING DOWNSTAIRS.
H KNWS, TH NLY, WY F CMNG DWNSTRS.
```

The lines displayed by this program are printed (with apologies to A.A.Milne, "Winnie The Pooh", E. P. Dutton, 1926) on the same page as the program listing.

In this case, we read one character at a time within the loop controlled by the EOLN function starting in line 12. Consonant (non-vowel) characters are concatenated into the string variable S until <RET> is typed, causing EOLN to be TRUE until READ is again executed. The characters being typed appear on the screen as they are typed. In line 22 the content of S is then displayed on the next line of the screen. Eventually, <ETX> is typed causing EOF to become TRUE and the outer loop terminates.

11. Sample Program - DATECHECK

This program is presented to illustrate the technique of input data "validation". In administrative programs of more than minimal size, it is usually very desirable to have the program check input data values to make sure they appear to be valid. Such checks are generally necessary whenever the input data is prepared by people, either customers or full time clerks. Customers frequently make mistakes because they fail to read or understand the instructions for filling out forms. Even the best data entry clerks make errors in about one percent of the documents they prepare for the computer using a card punch or similar machine.

In many cases, the processing of erroneous data can lead to a variety of problems for the people affected by the computations for which data is submitted. You have probably heard of people being denied the right to buy something with "time" payments because the credit bureau had erroneous records on file. Similarly, department stores send out erroneous bills, universities reject qualified students, innocent people are charged with crimes, and so on. Often these errors occur because someone who wrote a

```
PROGRAM DATECHECK;
VAR CH:CHAR;
  MONTH,DAY,YEAR:INTEGER;

PROCEDURE SQUAWK(S:STRING; X:INTEGER);
BEGIN
  WRITELN(' *** ',S,' ERROR:',X,CHR(7(*BEL*)));
END;

FUNCTION GETSLASH:BOOLEAN;
BEGIN
  READ(CH);
  GETSLASH:=(CH='/');
  IF CH<>'/' THEN
    WRITELN(' *** SLASH EXPECTED:',CH,
                               CHR(7(*BEL*)));
END (*GETSLASH*);

PROCEDURE PUTMONTH(M:INTEGER);
VAR S:STRING;
BEGIN
  CASE M OF
    1: S:='JANUARY';
    2: S:='FEBRUARY';
    3: S:='MARCH';
    4: S:='APRIL';
    5: S:='MAY';
    6: S:='JUNE';
    7: S:='JULY';
    8: S:='AUGUST';
    9: S:='SEPTEMBER';
   10: S:='OCTOBER';
   11: S:='NOVEMBER';
   12: S:='DECEMBER'
  END (*CASE*);
  WRITE(S);
END (*PUTMONTH*);

BEGIN (*MAIN PROGRAM*)
  WRITELN('DATECHECK');
  CH:=' ';
  WHILE CH <> '#' DO
  BEGIN
    WRITE('MONTH/DAY/YEAR:');
    READ(MONTH);
    IF (MONTH<=0) OR (MONTH>=13) THEN
        SQUAWK('MONTH',MONTH) ELSE
      BEGIN
        IF GETSLASH THEN
        BEGIN
```

```
          READ(DAY);
          IF (DAY<=0) OR (DAY>=32) THEN
            SQUAWK('DAY',DAY) ELSE
            BEGIN
              IF GETSLASH THEN
              BEGIN
                READ(YEAR);
                IF (YEAR<=10) OR (YEAR>=65) THEN
                  SQUAWK('YEAR',YEAR) ELSE
                  BEGIN
                    PUTMONTH(MONTH);
                    WRITELN(' ',DAY,', ',YEAR+1900);
                  END (*YEAR*);
              END (*SECOND SLASH*)
          END (*DAY*)
        END (*FIRST SLASH*)
      END (*MONTH*);
    REPEAT
      WRITELN;
      WRITE('>');
      READ(CH); (*possible '#' indicating end file*)
      IF (CH<>' ') AND (CH<>'#') THEN
        WRITE(' --> BLANK OR "#" EXPECTED',
              CHR(7(*BEL*)));
    UNTIL (CH=' ') OR (CH='#');
  END (*CH<>'#'*);
END.
```

```
Display associated with DATECHECK program

DATECHECK
MONTH/DAY/YEAR:6/15/57 JUNE 15,1957

>MONTH/DAY/YEAR:6/15/1957 *** YEAR ERROR:1957

>MONTH/DAY/YEAR:15/ *** MONTH ERROR:15

>MONTH/DAY/YEAR:12/21/10 *** YEAR ERROR:10

>MONTH/DAY/YEAR:9/22/75 *** YEAR ERROR:75

>MONTH/DAY/YEAR:6/37 *** DAY ERROR:37

>MONTH/DAY/YEAR:6- *** SLASH EXPECTED:-

>6 --> BLANK OR "#" EXPECTED

> MONTH/DAY/YEAR:12/31/64#DECEMBER 31,1964
```

computer program failed to make the program clever enough to catch the obvious errors in the data prepared for input by data entry clerks.

This sample program is meant to show the typical validity checks one might want to make for input data consisting of dates. The general form of the expected data is:

<month>/<day>/<year>

where <month>, <day>, and <year> are all to be integers expressed in one or two digits. In the case shown, the checks are for reasonable dates of birth for students registering as freshmen at a university in the fall of 1977. We presume that a person born later than 1965 will be too young, and that a person born as early as 1910 is probably too old. Of course any date between these rather wide limits might be in error, but that error would have to be caught in some way other than a simple validity check on the reasonability of the year. The checks on the <month> and <day> are more obvious. The program does not take into account the fact that the number of days in each month vary, only because we wanted to keep the logic simple. Any variations from the specified format will also be judged to indicate erroneous data, even though a human might understand the variation with no difficulty.

11a. Detecting the End of File Without EOF

Just for the sake of illustration, we chose to assume that the EOF function was not available to control the repetition of the main loop of this program, lines 42 thru 76. Although PASCAL offers an EOF built-in function, some languages or systems do not. In such cases, the method shown with this program is employed in some form or another.

The idea is to place a "flag", consisting of some known data value that cannot logically occur within the series of data values the program is intended to process. In this case, we have chosen the pound sign character, ('#'), as an "escape character". We assume that the program will not be used in a case where no data at all is entered into the program. After reading each date, and checking it for validity, the program displays a prompt character '>', and then checks to see whether '#' is typed. If <RET> is typed to terminate the processing of one date, the READ in line 71 will assign a blank <space> to CH, since the system had to "look ahead" when READing the previous number to find a non-digit. Remember that the program receives the character ' ' when <RET> is typed.

In line 16 of the display, it is seen that a dash character '-' was typed instead of the slash '/' that was expected. The GETSLASH function rings the computer's "bell" to attract the operator's attention that an error has been committed. The attempt to type in a digit at the beginning of line 18 resulted in another error message from lines 73 and 74 of the program. The check for blank <space> or '#' at this point assures that the operator will not overlook the lack of the slash in the date, and will commence entering a new date from the beginning. On line 20 of the display, it is seen that a single blank <space> was typed, allowing the program to return to the main loop where the legend "MONTH/DAY/YEAR:" is again displayed. Finally, the pound sign '#' is used in line 20 of the display to terminate the program at the end of typing the last date. This date is validated before the program reaches the end of the main loop.

We suggest that you test this program on your computer. Not all of the possible validity checks have been made. Moreover, the program as written cannot cope with a number of errors that a typist will often make, resulting in abnormal termination errors. For example, if the first character typed

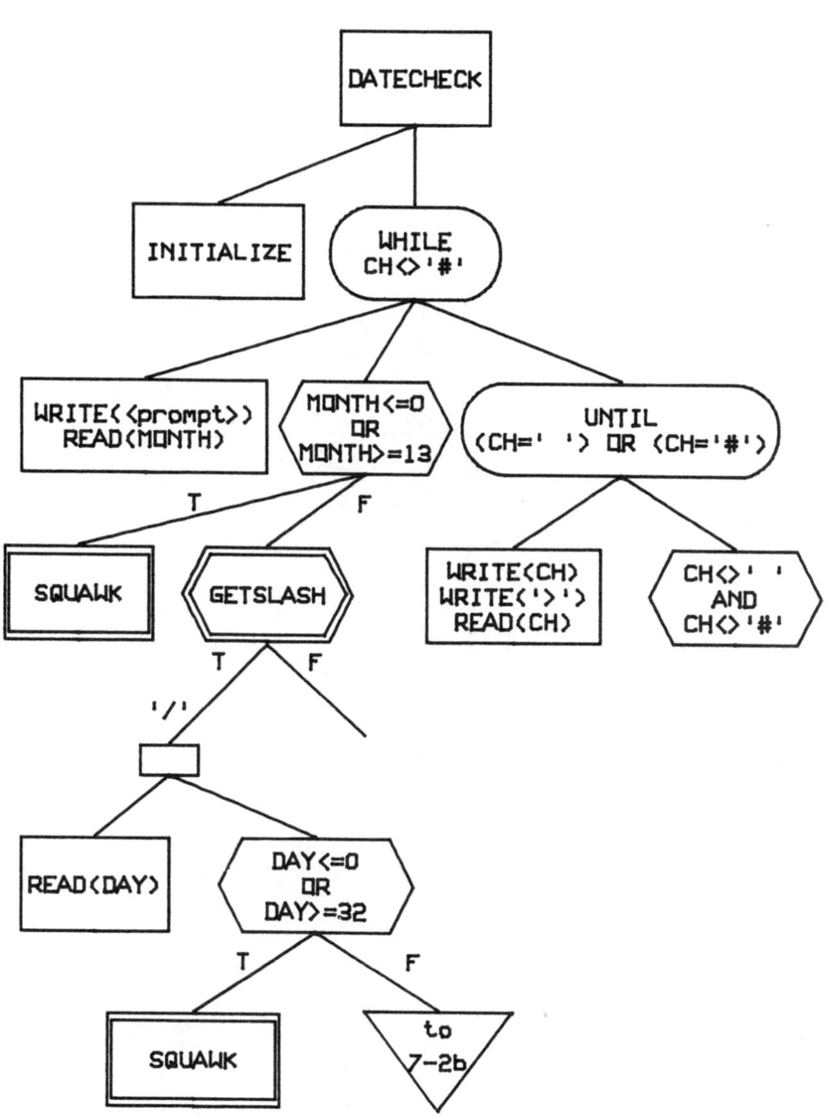
DATECHECK
INITIALIZE
WHILE CH<>'#'
WRITE(<prompt>) READ(MONTH)
MONTH<=0 OR MONTH>=13
UNTIL (CH=' ') OR (CH='#')
T
F
SQUAWK
GETSLASH
WRITE(CH) WRITE('>') READ(CH)
CH<>' ' AND CH<>'#'
T
F
'/'
READ(DAY)
DAY<=0 OR DAY>=32
T
F
SQUAWK
to 7-2b

Figure 7-2a

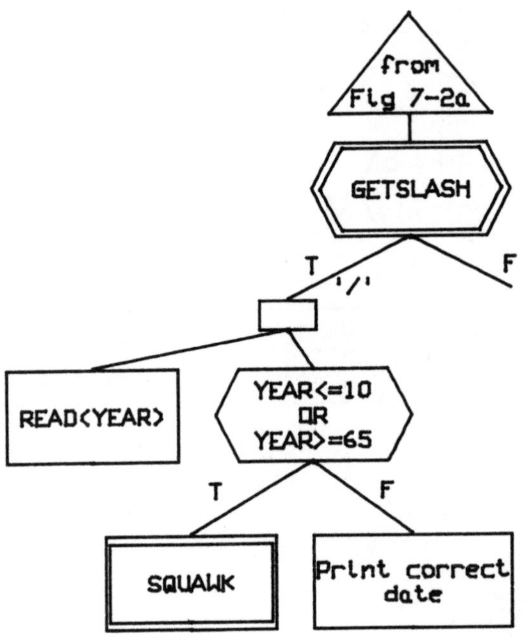
from
Fig 7-2a
GETSLASH
T
F
'/'
READ<YEAR>
YEAR<=10
OR
YEAR>=65
T
F
SQUAWK
Print correct
date

Figure 7-2b

when an integer is expected is not a digit, the program will terminate abnormally. If our PASCAL system were programmed to cope with this possibility, it would be less general and more bulky than desirable. However it is possible for you to write a more "intelligent" scanner for integers to allow additional errors to be made without killing the program.

11b. Program Structure

The general approach taken by this program is to check each portion of a data item for validity starting at the left. If the portion currently being scanned is not valid, then an error message is displayed, and the computer's alarm "bell" is sounded using the control character <BEL>. The decimal value of this character is 7. The WRITELN in line 7 of the program converts this decimal value to a character using the type conversion procedure CHR, since it is not possible to place the <BEL> character directly in a quoted <string constant>. Once an error is detected in a date, further scanning of that date is abandoned, and the operator prompted to start typing another date.

Figure 7-2 illustrates this program in the form of a structure diagram. As you can see the program is too complex for the structure diagram to fit on just one page. In this case we have allowed the main program to grow slightly larger than the maximum of about 25 lines that we normally try to use in any <block>. This allows the logic for checking validity of all parts of one data item to be handled in a single nested IF statement. It is debatable whether the program would be more understandable this way, or with the inner portion of the nested IF statement structure expressed separately in a procedure. As we have shown it, the program structure is much easier to see as long as we use indentation to express the levels of branching in the structure. The comments following each END also help considerably in avoiding errors.

Exercise 7.1:

Following is the specification of a program to calculate the average score earned by players in a sport such as bowling. Each player may have up to 10 scores earned for the season, but not all players will have scores earned for all games. (We'll bend the rules a little for this sport, so that the program might be used for any one of a number of sports.)

The program must accept the name of an individual player on each input line. Following the name, there will be given a sequence of up to 10 scores corresponding to individual games. The displayed output should contain one line for each input line, giving the player's name, the number of games reported, and the average score for those games. One reason for repeating some of the information on the displayed line is to provide a redundant check on correctness of the information received by the program.

Use 10 input lines with test data that you supply yourself. The format of these lines should be similar to the following:

```
Jones,Bill  150 115 175 140 112 145 160 148 203
Gonzalez,Maria 125 148 135 120 110 190 115 140
```

For this exercise, you should design the program to perform these actions, prepare a structure diagram to show to a reasonable level of detail how the program should work, and debug the program on the computer with test data.

Exercise 7.2:

Write a PASCAL program which reads data in a table like that shown below, on a line by line basis. After reading all lines in the table, the program should then display the number of the line containing the maximum sum of data values, the value of that sum, and the content of the line which was found in this way.

Sample data:

```
91  46  55
43  59  83
64  47  45
94  25  91
51  24  96
```

The program must be able to handle a variable number of input data lines. The output should appear roughly in the following format:

```
LARGEST SUM WAS: 210 ON LINE NUMBER: 4
CONTENT:94  25  91
```

Exercise 7.3:

Write and debug a PASCAL program which reads English text from the keyboard, counting the number of occurrences of each of the five vowels ('A', 'E', 'I', 'O', or 'U') as it goes. The program should be able to handle a variable number of input lines. Consider the text of this example to be the test data. You can simplify the problem by typing only upper case letters. After the text input terminates, the program should display separately the count accumulated for each vowel.

Exercise 7.4:

Write and debug a PASCAL program which reads a variable number of data lines, each line containing a student's name and a single grade on a scale of 0 to 100. The name information may fill up to 30 columns but not more. The program should then prompt, on the same displayed line, for the grade. The program should then check the grade, as might be done in a validation procedure, for students with grades of less than 65 or more than 100. If the grade is less than 65, the program should display a message "*** FAILING ***" on the input line, and should ring the computer's "bell". If the grade is more than 100, or less than zero, the program should display an error message, and also ring the bell.

While accepting the input data, the program should compute the average of all of the valid grades reported to it. After the last data has been entered, the program should display a message showing the average grade for all students reported. The program should be able to handle any number of students, including none at all, without terminating abnormally.

Exercise 7.5:

As part of its data processing activity, a credit card company must check each card number given on an input data document to make sure that it is a valid number. The card number consists of 10 decimal digits. Appended to this number are two additional digits obtained by summing the first 10 digits, and then taking the remainder from division of the sum by 11 (eleven). For example:

0123456789 01

The sum of the first ten digits is 45, and

(45 MOD 11) = 1

Write and debug a PASCAL program which reads credit card numbers encoded by this scheme (called a "check sum") and verifies in each case that the check sum is correct. If not correct, the program should display an error message and ring the computer's bell. The program should be able to handle any number of input lines.

Note: The binary value of a digit such as '2' is ORD('2'). Thus the integer V, corresponding to the character CH, assuming the value of CH is a digit, can be obtained from:

```
V := ORD(CH) - ORD('0')
```

where CH is a variable of <type> CHAR. Check the program with the line shown above, which is known to be correct, and with the following line, which is not correct:

0742267205 05

<u>Exercise 7.6:</u>

A task often performed by text editing programs, which prepare passages of text for publication in newspapers and books, is to "adjust" the length of a line so that it meets both right and left margins. This is accomplished by inserting extra blank spaces between words, for example:

THE QUICK FOX JUMPED OVER THE LAZY DOG

becomes:

```
                                              ¦
                                              ¦
THE  QUICK  FOX  JUMPED  OVER  THE  LAZY  DOG¦
```

where the character '¦' is intended to simulate the right margin.

Write a PASCAL program which reads text (containing no punctuation characters) from the keyboard, and performs the insertion of blanks to achieve right- left adjustment as shown. The number of blanks between pairs of words should not vary by more than 1 across the resulting line. For example, on the line above, either 2 or 3 blanks between words on the resulting line is correct. 1, 2, 3, 4, and 5 blanks all on the same line would not be correct. You may assume that the original input line contains exactly one blank space separating each pair of words.

Hint: Count the number of blank spaces between words, and the number of trailing blanks in the input line. Now copy characters one at a time to a new output line. Whenever a blank is found in the input line, insert one or more extra blanks in the output. The number of trailing blanks to be distributed in this way will not divide evenly among the words in the line. Use DIV to get the number of extra blanks to put between every pair of words. Use MOD to get the remainder which can be distributed one blank at a time until it has been exhausted.

Problems

Problem 7.1:

Draw structure diagrams for the sample programs AVERAGE, DENOISE, and DEVOWEL.

Chapter 8

BASIC DATA STRUCTURES - I. ARRAYS

1. Goals

This is the first of three chapters dealing with structured data types. This chapter introduces the "array" structure, which is used for referring to many items of data, all of the same <type>, under the same <identifier>.

1a. Learn to work with arrays of one dimension. Use them to save input data, as it is entered, for later use by your program.

1b. Work with arrays of two dimensions. Use them for working with tables of data.

1c. Learn how arrays of three and more dimensions are used.

1d. Write and debug several programs involving arrays.

2. Background

Just as is is useful to lump together many separate, but related, actions into a program or procedure under a single name, so it is useful to lump together many items of data into a single named "data structure". While many data structures can be regarded as hierarchic (i.e. they are "trees"), not all can. In this introductory book, we will consider only hierarchic data structures.

An "array" is a data structure which contains two or more items all of the same <type>. Each item in the array is reached by program statements using the <identifier> of the array, and the "index" number(s) which locate the item in the array. You have already been using arrays of a special <type>, namely STRING variables. The items (often called "elements") of a STRING variable are all of <type> CHAR, and their index numbers are pre-defined to run from 1 through 80. In this chapter, we show how to define an array containing elements of any of the <type>'s already introduced. In the next chapter you will see how to define more complicated <type>'s, and these can be combined in arrays if desired.

Arrays are used whenever it is convenient or necessary to let the program logic decide which item to select from a group of many.

3. Arrays Related to the Hardware

From chapter 5, you may recall that each <identifier> naming a <variable> of <type> REAL, INTEGER, CHAR, or BOOLEAN is really the name of a location in the computer's memory. An array uses one <identifier> to name a group of memory locations. In its simplest form, an array is a contiguous group of words in the main memory of the computer. Figure 8-1 illustrates a small portion of the main memory in the form of a "map".

Figure 8-1

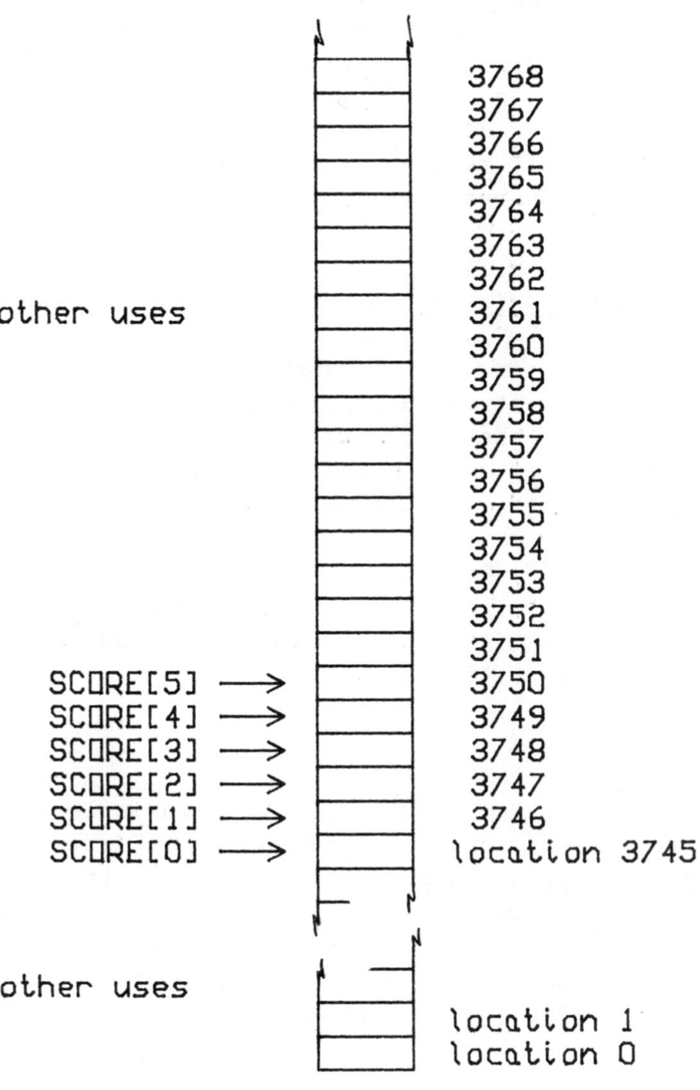
other uses
3768
3767
3766
3765
3764
3763
3762
3761
3760
3759
3758
3757
3756
3755
3754
3753
3752
3751
SCORE[5] → 3750
SCORE[4] → 3749
SCORE[3] → 3748
SCORE[2] → 3747
SCORE[1] → 3746
SCORE[0] → location 3745
other uses
location 1
location 0

The memory may be assumed to have capacity to hold at least 4000 words, numbered 0, 1, 2, 3, ... We have illustrated only the portion of these words starting at location number 3745 and continuing through location 3760. Within this small portion or "*range*" we show six words which are named by the single <identifier> SCORE. Each word within the six-word group is identified not only by the name "SCORE", but also by a number indicating its order of appearance in the group. The group is called an "*array*", and it must be declared before it is used, as are all non-reserved <identifier>'s in PASCAL.

4. Subscripted Variables

For most purposes, an array element may be used anywhere that it would be appropriate to use a simple <variable> of the same <type>. For example, we can assign to X (a simple integer variable) a value 1 greater than the third element of SCORE as follows:

```
X:=SCORE[2] + 1
```

Or we could assign a new value to the fourth location in the array SCORE by:

```
SCORE[3] := X + Y
```

assuming that Y is also an integer variable. In both of these uses, the <identifier> SCORE appears as a "*subscripted variable*". This term relates back to the usage in mathematics where variables may have "*subscripts*" to show their positions in a sequence. For example, we might use a variable T to designate the time of day. The successive values of T would be:

$$T_1 \quad T_2 \quad T_3 \quad T_4 \quad T_5 \quad T_6 \quad T_7 \quad \ldots$$

Since the subscripts (1,2,3,4,...) are difficult to handle on the keyboard of a computer input device (and even harder to represent on a single punched card), the sequence above would be represented as follows in PASCAL:

```
T[1]  T[2]  T[3]  T[4]  T[5]  T[6]  T[7]  ...
```

with successive values of the variable being stored in successive locations in the array T.

If all we could do with arrays would be with <integer constant>'s as subscripts, the usefulness of arrays would be very limited. Instead PASCAL allows you to use any <arithmetic expression> that evaluates to an integer in the role of subscript. For example, the following would be perfectly legal:

```
SCORE[X + (Y * Z) DIV 3]
```

The compiler deals with this situation by generating machine language instructions which first compute the value of the expression:

```
X + (Y * Z) DIV 3
```

and then uses this value as the index (i.e. subscript) with which to locate the correct array element. ALGOL and PL/1 also allow expressions as subscripts. FORTRAN, BASIC, and COBOL are more restricted.

5. Declaration of ARRAY Variables

Figure 8-2 shows syntax covering the declaration of ARRAY variables. Here are some examples of legal ARRAY declarations:

<simple type>

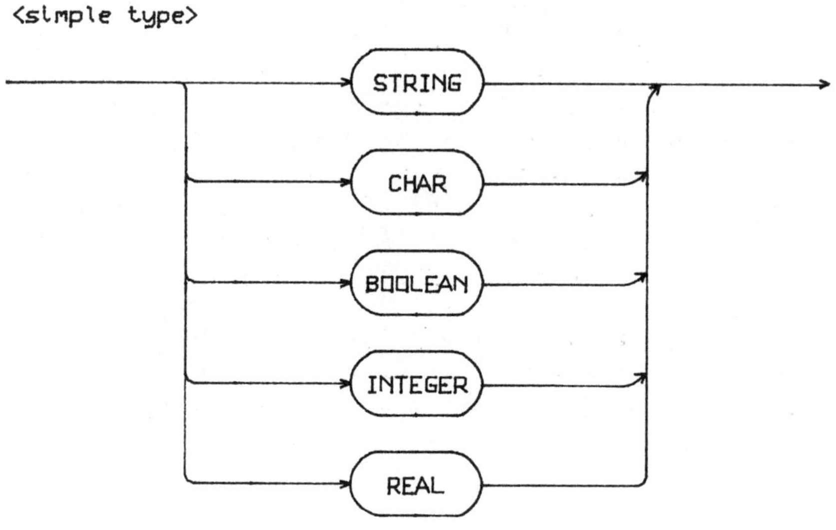

<type>

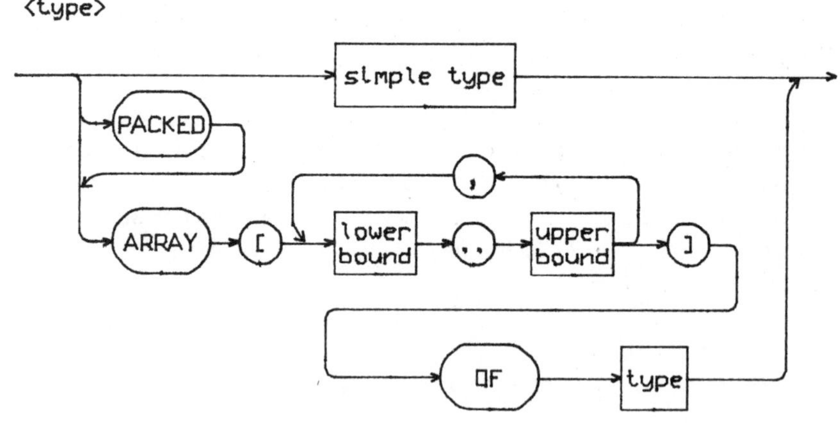

Figure 8-2

```
VAR TARA: ARRAY[1..10] OF STRING;
      (*array containing 10 STRING elements*)
      (*numbered 1 thru 10                  *)
    AC: ARRAY[0..79] OF CHAR;
      (* 80 elements of <type> CHAR, 0 thru 79*)
    ABOOL: ARRAY[-5..+4] OF BOOLEAN;
      (* 10 Boolean elements, -5 thru +4 *)
    ADOUBLE: ARRAY [1..10] OF
               ARRAY [0..4] OF INTEGER;
      (* 10 elements numbered 1 thru 10, each of
         which is itself an ARRAY of 5 integer
         elements*)
    ARDOUBLE: ARRAY [1..10] OF
                ARRAY[0..4] OF REAL;
      (*similar to ADOUBLE but contains REAL
         elements*)
```

The syntax shown in Figure 8-2 is slightly more explicit than the syntax shown in Appendix E. In Figure 8-2, both <lower bound> and <upper bound> are <integer constant>'s. The value of the index used to select an element of an array may be no less than the <lower bound> and not greater than the <upper bound>. As you will see in Chapter 9, there are several ways of defining the bounds of an array. Our purpose in using the <lower bound> and <upper bound> explicitly here is to avoid unnecessary confusion at this point.

6. Using Arrays of One Dimension

The program SPORTSCORE reads two items of data from each of a series of input lines. The first item is a three-digit number representing an earned score from some sport, the second is the last name of the player who earned the score. The object of the program is to select the player who earned the highest score, and to display that score with the player's name.

```
PROGRAM SPORTSCORE;
VAR SA: ARRAY[1..10] OF STRING;
    IA: ARRAY[1..10] OF INTEGER;
    K,LN,MAX,KMAX:INTEGER;
    CH:CHAR;
BEGIN
  K:=1;
  MAX:=0;
  REPEAT
    WRITE('SCORE:');
    READ(IA[K]);
    IF NOT EOF THEN
    BEGIN
      WRITE('NAME:');
      READ(SA[K]);
      LN:=LENGTH(SA[K]);
      IF IA[K]>MAX THEN
      BEGIN
        MAX:=IA[K];
        KMAX:=K;
      END;
      K:=K+1;
    END (*NOT EOF*);
  UNTIL EOF OR (K > 10);
  WRITELN;
  WRITELN('BEST SCORE:',IA[KMAX],'  ',SA[KMAX])
END.
```

With the following display during input:

```
SCORE:190 NAME:Gonzalez
SCORE:150 NAME:Jones
SCORE:135 NAME:Carlson
SCORE:160 NAME:Schultz
SCORE:203 NAME:Sanchez
SCORE:115 NAME:Peters
SCORE:148 NAME:Bergeron
SCORE:175 NAME:Douglas
SCORE:<ETX>
```

here is what the program should display before terminating:

```
BEST SCORE:203  Sanchez
```

The notation <ETX> is not actually displayed, but is shown above to indicate where the key(s) for End Of File is(are) pressed.

Since the identity of the player with the highest score is not known in advance, it is necessary to provide the program with a means of temporary storage. Only after all names and scores have been read (Line 13) will it be possible to determine which player has the highest score. We use the arrays SA and IA to save the names and scores temporarily while more data is being read. After it is known which player has the highest score, the desired output is displayed in line 26 of the program by selecting the data corresponding to that player from the arrays IA, for the score, and SA for the name.

Something to note about this program is that the amount of space for temporarily storing data values in main memory is usually fairly restricted on most computers. If the list processed by this example program were expanded to thousands of names, it would be impossible to store all of the names and scores in main memory at one time. When this happens, one typically has to use some auxiliary storage device, such as magnetic disk, to handle the overflow from main memory. Details on this subject are beyond the scope of this book.

Repetitive looping in this example ceases when either of two conditions becomes true. Because each array declaration has provided only 10 elements, looping must stop after the tenth pair of data values has been read into the program. In the example shown, there were fewer than 10 pairs of data values, and the program terminated because the End-Of-File condition was reached.

7. Packed Character Arrays - Two Dimensions

By now you must have recognized that a STRING variable is really a special kind of array. We have added STRING variables to the standard PASCAL language used internationally in order to provide a way to handle non-numerical data in the early stages of this book without unecessary complications. You can declare an array very similar to a STRING variable as follows:

```
VAR PCA: PACKED ARRAY[1..80] OF CHAR;
```

The reserved word "PACKED" designates the array as one in which the minimum possible amount of main memory should be used for storing the several characters in the array. The internal representation of a character uses only 8 bits of memory. If the word size of the computer memory is 16 bits, as is probably the case if you are using a microcomputer, then two characters can be "packed" into one word of memory. (Note: Although many microcomputers are based on 8 bit microprocessors, our PASCAL system operates on those microcomputers as if they had 16-bit memory words.) On larger computers, with more bits per memory word, it is sometimes possible to pack 6 or 8 characters in one word.

In the SPORTSCORE example discussed in the previous section, we sidestepped the difficulty presented by mixing integer and text information on the same input line. When the READ statement encounters a <variable> of <type> STRING, all of the remaining information on the line is assigned to that variable. This forced us to place the integer information to the left of the text information, so that the numbers in the data could be converted into the internal binary form for assignment to integer variables.

Now suppose that we have a good reason for wanting to place the text information on the displayed line first, followed by a series of numbers, for example:

```
  Gonzalez  190  150  178  135  163
```

If we were using punched cards for input, we might be forced to use a method similar to this. We could reserve a certain fixed number of columns on the card image to be used for names, say 15 spaces. The program SPORTSCORE2 might then be used to read this data, to calculate the average score of each player, and to identify the player with the highest <u>average</u> score. One of the principal differences between this program, and the one you probably wrote for Exercise 7.1 is the use of arrays for temporary storage in this program. Assuming the following display on input:

```
NAME:GONZALEZ,MARIA SCORES:125 148 135 120 110 190
  AVG:138.00
NAME:JONES,BILL SCORES:150 115 175 140 112 145 160
  AVG:142.43
NAME:CARLSON,CINDY SCORES:135 205 121 143 97 168
  AVG:144.83
NAME:SCHULTZ,TAD SCORES:126 149 115 162 157 188
  AVG:149.50
NAME:SANCHEZ,PETE SCORES:194 139 173 152 212 177<ETX>
  AVG:174.50
```

```
PROGRAM SPORTSCORE2;
VAR NAMES: ARRAY[1..10] OF
                PACKED ARRAY[1..15] OF CHAR;
  SCORES: ARRAY[1..10] OF
                ARRAY[0..9] OF INTEGER;
  SUM,IMAX,I,J,K:INTEGER;
  AVG,MAXAVG:REAL;
  CH:CHAR;
  CHOK:BOOLEAN;
BEGIN
  MAXAVG:=0;  I:=1;
  REPEAT
    WRITE('NAME:');
    J:=1;
    REPEAT
      READ(CH);
      CHOK:=((CH>='A') AND (CH<='Z')) OR (CH=',');
      IF CHOK THEN
        BEGIN  NAMES[I,J]:=CH;  J:=J+1;  END;
    UNTIL (NOT CHOK) OR (J > 15);
    WHILE J<=15 DO
    BEGIN
      NAMES[I,J]:=' ';
      J:=J+1;
    END;
    SUM:=0;  K:=0;
    WRITE('SCORES:');
    WHILE (NOT EOLN) AND (K < 9)  DO
    BEGIN (*read & save scores for this player*)
      K:=K+1;
      READ(SCORES[I,K]);
      SUM:=SUM+SCORES[I,K];
    END;
    IF EOLN THEN
      READ(CH); (*clear the blank left by <RET>*)
    SCORES[I,0]:=K;
    AVG:=SUM/K;
    WRITELN('  AVG:',AVG:6:2);
    IF AVG>MAXAVG THEN
      BEGIN  MAXAVG:=AVG;  IMAX:=I;  END;
    I:=I+1;
  UNTIL EOF OR (I > 10);
  WRITELN;  WRITELN('BEST PLAYER:');
  WRITE(NAMES[IMAX]);
  FOR J:=1 TO SCORES[IMAX,0] DO
      WRITE(SCORES[IMAX,J]:5);
  WRITELN('  AVG:', MAXAVG:6:2);
END.
```

the following is then displayed when the program terminates:

```
SANCHEZ,PETE  194  139  173  152  212  177 AVG:174.50
```

Once again, <ETX> is not actually displayed, but shows where the End Of File key(s) might be employed.

The main loop of this program runs from line 12 to line 42. As each line of data is entered, up to 15 characters of the name are stored in one of the packed arrays of characters in the array NAMES. The list of up to 9 scores is then read and saved in the array SCORES.

This program illustrates the use of arrays with two dimensions. Heretofore, we have been working with one dimensional arrays in which a single integer valued <expression> is used as the index. A two dimensional array can be thought of as an array of one dimensional arrays, as is suggested by the declarations of NAMES and SCORES in lines 2 and 4.

Lines 31 and 32 illustrate how explicit references are made to individual items in the array SCORES. The second index "K" refers to individual items within the subsidiary array SCORES[I] in the usual manner. Simplified syntax covering these references is shown in Figure 8-3. The order of appearance of the indexes in a subscripted variable with two subscripts, such as I and J in this instance, is the same as the order of appearance of the declarations of the constituent arrays, as in lines 2 thru 5.

In this program example, our main purpose for using arrays is to provide temporary storage space for saving data on each of the players. Only after all of the data on all of the players has been read into the program can it be determined which of the players has the highest average score. Only then can we select the appropriate rows of the NAME and SCORE arrays for use in printing the data on the highest scoring player.

<variable> (simplified)

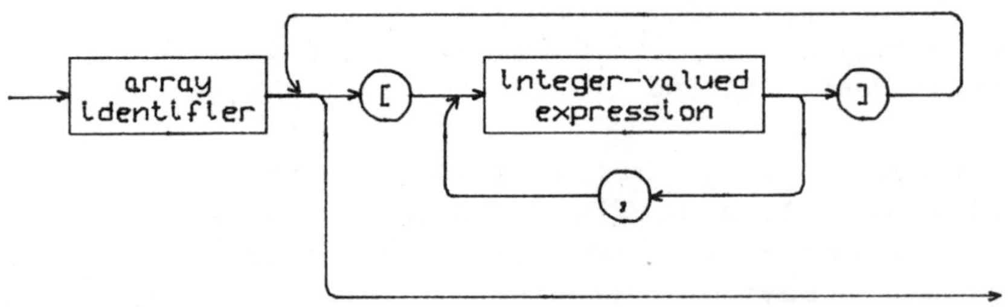

Figure 8-3

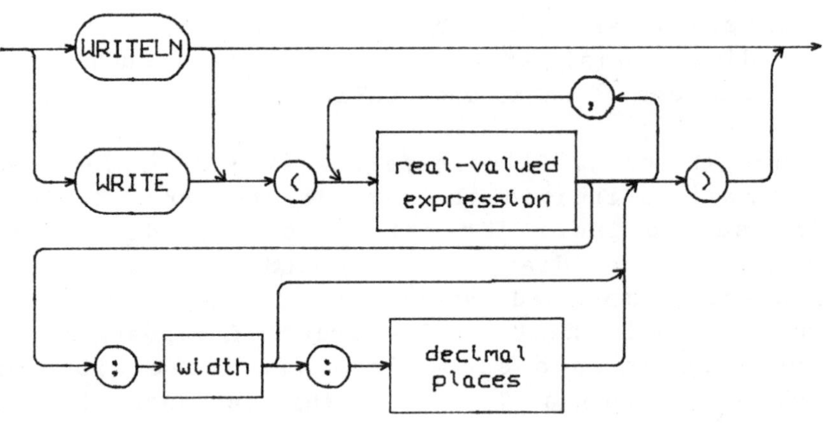

<width, decimal places>

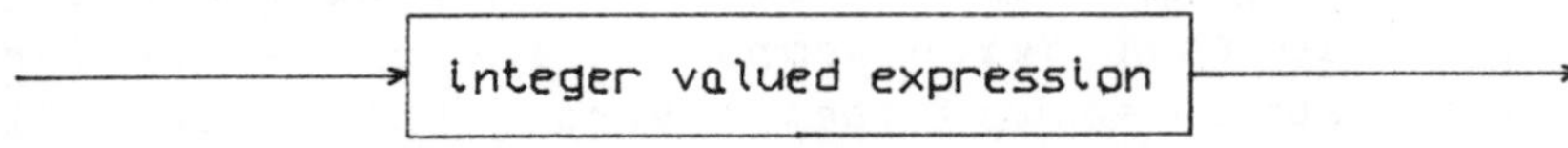

Figure 8-4

In lines 38 and 47, the field width notation ":6:2" appears, where the 6 determines the full desired width of the characters to be displayed by the WRITE statement. Applicable syntax is shown in figure 8-4. The notation ":2" here determines how many digits are to be displayed following the decimal point. If the real number to be displayed requires more than 6 columns, including decimal point and the two fractional digits, then the larger number of columns will apply. If the number can be displayed in fewer than 6 columns, then blank spaces will be inserted on the left so as to make the full width of the displayed field conform to the first of the two specifications.

8. Row and Column Sums - Crossfooting

When processing data entered into the computer by humans, it is generally advisable to provide ways to check for errors, and if possible to correct them. As an example, situations often occur in which several items of data associated with a single individual are entered into the computer as separate "transactions" at different times. One result of the processing is that the various data items covering one individual are eventually brought together for storage. In the course of the processing, a number of changes are typically made in the data, and these changes offer possibilities of errors being committed.

Let's suppose that the data consists of payments made by students to distinct offices of a university, for example the housing office, the medical clinic, the cafeteria, the library (for overdue books), the bookstore, and so on. When all of the records are brought together, it is possible to calculate the total paid individually by each student. It is also possible to calculate the sum of all payments to each of these distinct offices of the university. Clearly the sum of payments made by individual students should equal the sum of payments received by the separate offices. Checking to make sure that both summations yield the same total helps to uncover possible errors in the processing of the data. If the sums differ, the fact of the difference does not tell <u>where</u> in the processing the error occurred, but it does serve as a notice that something is wrong in the processing and that a correction is needed. The program CROSSFOOT illustrates this situation.

Each input line processed by this program contains three items of information. First a letter code designates which of the five university offices is to receive the payment. Next, the dollar amount is given. Finally a number is entered to stand for the student's identifying code. In the illustration below, these numbers are very small simply to avoid cluttering the illustration. Had we used the student's name, or perhaps the student's full identification card number, it would have been necessary to search a table containing this identifying information in order to associate a student with the number of his/her entry in the payments table. We will examine algorithms for searching in Chapter 13. For purposes of the CROSSFOOT example, you will have to assume that the simple identifying number shown represents the number that would have been obtained from a search strategy by another program.

Here is an example of the lines displayed during input to the CROSSFOOT program:

```
PROGRAM CROSSFOOT;
VAR TRANS: ARRAY[1..10]
             OF ARRAY[1..5] OF REAL;
  CH:CHAR;
  COL,ROW,SNUM:INTEGER;
  PAID,ROWTOTAL,COLTOTAL:REAL;
  COLSUMS: ARRAY[1..5] OF REAL;
  ROWSUMS: ARRAY[1..10] OF REAL;

PROCEDURE SUMS;
BEGIN
  FOR ROW:=1 TO 10 DO
  BEGIN
    FOR COL:=1 TO 5 DO
      ROWSUMS[ROW]:=ROWSUMS[ROW]+TRANS[ROW,COL];
    ROWTOTAL:=ROWTOTAL+ROWSUMS[ROW];
  END;
  FOR COL:=1 TO 5 DO
    COLTOTAL:=COLTOTAL+COLSUMS[COL];
END (*SUMS*);

PROCEDURE SAVE(SNUM,COL:INTEGER);
BEGIN
  TRANS[SNUM,COL]:=PAID;
  COLSUMS[COL]:=COLSUMS[COL]+PAID;
END (*SAVE*);

PROCEDURE GETDATA;
BEGIN
  WHILE NOT EOF DO
  BEGIN
    WRITE('SERVICE CODE:');
    READ(CH);
    WRITE('  AMT:');
    READ(PAID);
    WRITE('  IDENT:');
    READ(SNUM);
    WRITELN;
    CASE CH OF
      'B': SAVE(SNUM,1);
      'C': SAVE(SNUM,2);
      'H': SAVE(SNUM,3);
      'L': SAVE(SNUM,4);
      'M': SAVE(SNUM,5)
    END (*CASE*);
    READ(CH); (*discard blank after SNUM*)
  END (*READING*);
END (*GETDATA*);
```

```
PROCEDURE INIT;
BEGIN
  FOR COL:=1 TO 5 DO COLSUMS[COL]:=0;
  FOR ROW:=1 TO 10 DO ROWSUMS[ROW]:=0;
  FOR ROW:=1 TO 10 DO
    FOR COL:=1 TO 5 DO
      TRANS[ROW,COL]:=0;
  ROWTOTAL:=0;  COLTOTAL:=0;
  WRITELN('CROSSFOOT');
END (*INIT*);

PROCEDURE DISPLAY;
  PROCEDURE PUTREAL(R:REAL);
  VAR I:INTEGER;
  BEGIN
    IF R>=1.0 THEN WRITE(R:7:2) ELSE
      BEGIN
        I:=ROUND(R*100); WRITE(' ':4);
        IF I=0 THEN WRITE('  0') ELSE
          BEGIN
            WRITE('.');
            IF I<10 THEN WRITE('0',I)
                    ELSE WRITE(I);
          END;
      END (*R < 1.0*);
  END (*PUTREAL*);
BEGIN (*DISPLAY*)
  WRITELN('BOOKS':7,'CAF':7,'HOUS':7,'LIB':7,
           'MED':7,'TOTAL':7);
  FOR ROW:=1 TO 10 DO
  BEGIN
    FOR COL:=1 TO 5 DO
      PUTREAL(TRANS[ROW,COL]);
    PUTREAL(ROWSUMS[ROW]); WRITELN;
  END;
  WRITELN;
  FOR COL:=1 TO 5 DO  PUTREAL(COLSUMS[COL]);
  PUTREAL(COLTOTAL); WRITELN;
  IF COLTOTAL<>ROWTOTAL THEN
    BEGIN
      WRITELN('*** ERROR: ROWTOTAL=');
      PUTREAL( ROWTOTAL);
    END;
END (*DISPLAY*);

BEGIN (*MAIN PROGRAM*)
  INIT;
  GETDATA;
  SUMS;
  DISPLAY;
END.
```

```
SERVICE CODE:B  AMT:7.95  IDENT:2
SERVICE CODE:H  AMT:150.00  IDENT:1
SERVICE CODE:H  AMT:150.00  IDENT:3
SERVICE CODE:L  AMT:4.00  IDENT:2
SERVICE CODE:C  AMT:2.25  IDENT:4
SERVICE CODE:M  AMT:55.60  IDENT:9
SERVICE CODE:M  AMT:10.00  IDENT:7
SERVICE CODE:B  AMT:15.80  IDENT:6
SERVICE CODE:B  AMT:14.25  IDENT:8
SERVICE CODE:C  AMT:75.00  IDENT:10
SERVICE CODE:H  AMT:300.00  IDENT:5
SERVICE CODE:L  AMT:0.50  IDENT:6
SERVICE CODE:M  AMT:40.00  IDENT:1<ETX>
```

After termination of input data, the program should display the following table:

```
 BOOKS    CAF   HOUS    LIB    MED  TOTAL
     0      0 150.00      0  40.00 190.00
  7.95      0      0   4.00      0  11.95
     0      0 150.00      0      0 150.00
     0   2.25      0      0      0   2.25
     0      0 300.00      0      0 300.00
 15.80      0      0    .50      0  16.30
     0      0      0      0  10.00  10.00
 14.25      0      0      0      0  14.25
     0      0      0      0  55.60  55.60
     0  75.00      0      0      0  75.00

 38.00  77.25 600.00   4.50 105.60 825.35
```

We have illustrated this program using only a small amount of data on transactions so that you would be able to check the addition by eye. The line across the bottom of the printed table contains sums of the several columns of data. The number in the lower right hand corner should be both the sum of all entries across the bottom line, and also the sum of all entries in the right hand column. This number is computed as COLTOTAL, and printed as such in line 63. Since the error message in the WRITELN statement in line 92 is not actually displayed, the computation has apparently correctly computed ROWTOTAL to be equal to COLTOTAL. The horizontal lines of numbers in a table like this are commonly called "rows" while the vertically grouped numbers are called "columns". The method of checking for equality of the sum of the column totals with the sum of the row totals has often been called "crossfooting". This is a term that dates back to the terminology used with some of the early punched card computing machines.

The procedure PUTREAL is used in this program to avoid having Real numbers less than 1.00 displayed in scientific notation, for example to avoid having $0.50 display as 5.0E-1. If the amount is less than one dollar, then the equivalent integer number of cents is computed, and that is displayed in the appropriate format by PUTREAL.

9. Three and More Dimensions

Quite often one has occasion to perform computations on tables of numbers with more than two dimensions. In this section we discuss a typical application for such computations, but leave it to you to write programs. The principles involved are simple extensions of the principles just discussed for two dimensional arrays. However illustrations become progressively more difficult to make, with diagrams and simple programs, as the number of dimensions increase.

Suppose that you are a staff member of a public interest lobbying organization like Common Cause, the Sierra Club, the Environmental Defense Fund, etc. The organization needs to sample the opinions of its membership on a regular basis in order to determine what priorities should be assigned to each of several topics currently considered to be important. The following table illustrates the kind of data collected from sampling approximately 1000 members.

	Increase 1.	No Change 2.	Reduce 3.	No Opinion 4.
1.Environment	243	527	149	53
2.Energy	185	617	195	78
3.Inflation	318	442	83	27
4.Unemployment	306	499	117	62
5.Defense	97	377	270	141

Each number in this table represents the number of members in the sample who indicated that the organization should devote the attention shown in the column headings to the topics shown in the 5 rows. Clearly this data can easily be stored in a two dimensional array. But the organization must sample its membership on these opinions about once every three months in order to detect whether a significant shift is taking place. For example, one might expect that the opinions on the importance of energy would have increased dramatically after the sudden embargo of petroleum shipments was imposed by the oil exporting nations. Thus it is desirable to have several versions of this table representing data collected at different times. A program designed to analyze trends in the data would then need to have all versions present in the computer's memory at the same time.

This can be arranged by using an array of two dimensional arrays. Such an array is usually described more simply as a three dimensional array. Here is how such an array might be declared in PASCAL:

```
VAR OPINION: ARRAY[1..12] OF (*quarterly samples*)
               ARRAY[1..5] OF(*5 topics per sample*)
                 ARRAY[1..4] OF INTEGER;
                      (*four opinion codes*)
```

To refer to any single location in this array one would use a subsripted variable with three indexes, one for each dimension, such as:

```
  OPINION[QTR, TOPIC, CODE]
```

where QTR, TOPIC, and CODE are all integer variables.

Carrying this one step further, you might also wish to have a way to determine something about the age groups among the organization's membership regarding the analysis of preferences. You might then add yet another dimension to the array OPINION, giving something like the following:

```
VAR OPINION: ARRAY[1..4] OF (*four age groups*)
               ARRAY[1..12] OF (*quarterly samples*)
                 ARRAY[1..5] OF (*five topics*)
                   ARRAY[1..4] OF INTEGER;
                         (*four opinion codes*)
```

References to this array as a subscripted <variable> require you to use four indexes.

<u>Exercise 8.1:</u>

Write and debug a PASCAL program to solve the following problem. Draw a structure diagram to describe the algorithm you use.

Computers are often used to eliminate duplicate entries from lists of items. Examples include processing of lists of signatures submitted for a petition, lists of names and addresses maintained by a company that sells address lists, lists of identifying numbers (such as Social Security) in which mistakes may have been made or false numbers may have been submitted, and so on. In this problem we will use small integers for illustration purposes, although the data to be checked would typically involve strings of alphanumeric characters, or perhaps numbers containing many more than two digits. The list we present here will be short enough that there is no need to consider efficient searching and sorting techniques like those presented Chapters 13, 14 and 15.

Given a list of input numbers, the problem is to eliminate duplicate numbers from the list, displaying at the end only the first occurring instance of each number. Arrange your program to handle a list of up to 100 input numbers. Use the following short list to test your program:

2 3 2 2 6 4 9 7 4 5 3

The result should read: 2 3 6 4 9 7 5

Now run the program with the following list:

```
74  74  92  72  29  34  65  34  43  23
91  81  61  43  74  83  83  77  79  83
64  24  22  20  49  65  88  60  43  63
99  84  23  48  27  43  83  74  83  91
```

The program should display the list with the duplicates removed, and with the remaining numbers still in the order in which they were added to the list originally. Then as a check on the results, it should also display the numbers that were found to be duplicated and the number of times each occurred. Go through the original list and check it by hand, making sure that the results from the program are correct.

The program should be designed so that the numbers in the list of data may be up to 5 digits long. This would be more like the kind of data one would encounter in a realistic application of this problem.

Suggested method: Store each successive input number in one array, but without entering duplicates into this array. In a second array, store the number of occurrences of each input number. On reading each number, scan through the entries already made in the first array looking for a duplicate. If one is found, then simply increase the corresponding count by 1 in the second array. If no duplicate is found, then a new entry is required in the first array, and the corresponding count should be set to 1. After all the data has been read, the resulting list can be displayed directly from the first array, since the numbers contained there are in the same order as those originally read by the program. The list of duplicated numbers can be produced by scanning through the second array of counts, looking for entries greater than one. Use a separate integer variable to keep track of the count of the numbers already entered, and to point to the next available empty position in the first array.

Exercise 8.2:

Modify the program SPORTSCORE2 so that it displays the player names, their scores and averages, all in the order of decreasing average value (i.e. the player with the highest average should be displayed first). Hint: Use an auxiliary array AVERAGES to use as the basis for keeping track of the averages, and controlling the order of display. When all input lines have been read, scan AVERAGES for the largest value, display the corresponding name and scores list, then set the corresponding location in AVERAGES to zero since it need not be used again. Repeat this process until all of the values in AVERAGES equal zero.

Exercise 8.3:

Programmers are often asked to reorganize a set of data along lines similar to those illustrated by this problem. The "before" side of the table below shows an array DATA containing 101 rows of five elements per row, and a companion array SELECT containing Boolean elements. The content of DATA is to be rearranged so as to contain only the data rows corresponding to a value of TRUE in SELECT (with all other data rows replaced by FALSE), and so that the order of appearance of the selected rows is reversed. The non-selected rows, which are to be filled with zeroes, are to be placed at the end of the reorganized DATA array.

First draw a structure diagram describing an algorithm to carry out this reorganization. Then write and debug the corresponding program in PASCAL. Note: You may find it convenient to declare a second array of the same <type> as DATA for temporary storage while the reorganization is going on.

As test data, fill the DATA array initially with random numbers generated by a procedure similar to the procedure RANDOM used with the FOURLETTER and RANDOMWALK programs in Chapter 5 Section 11. Arrange the random number generator to produce numbers ranging from 1 to 99. Set SELECT to TRUE for a row in DATA only if the first random number in the row ends in the digit "3".

		BEFORE	AFTER
ROW	SELECT	DATA	DATA
0	F	27 54 32 68 13	93 32 04 53 67
1	T	93 74 08 16 56	83 33 09 54 14
2	T	73 61 01 91 76	
3	F	16 55 27 36 79	etc. etc.
4	T	53 90 52 82 58	
			53 90 52 82 58
			73 61 01 91 76
			93 74 08 16 56
		etc. etc.	0 0 0 0 0
97	T	83 33 09 54 14	etc. etc.
98	F	95 98 44 33 86	
99	T	93 32 04 53 67	0 0 0 0 0

Exercise 8.4:

Write and debug a PASCAL program which scans English text, from a variable number of input lines, and counts the number of occurrences of each letter. You can ignore blanks and special punctuation characters. Assume that all letters are upper case. After reading all cards, display a table summarizing the counts and the corresponding letters. Hint: It is legal to declare an array to have a lower bound of 'A' and an upper bound of 'Z', and to refer to an array location ARA[CH] where CH is a variable of <type> CHAR.

Exercise 8.5:

Draw a logically rough, but easily readable, structure diagram describing how you would solve the following problem. Then write and debug the corresponding PASCAL program.

Read 6 integer data values from each of 12 input lines (72 values in all). Place the data values in a two dimensional array with 12 rows of 6 columns each, each row corresponding to the data from one input line. Reorder the data in each column so that the smallest value will appear in the first row, and successively larger values will appear in succeeding rows. Finally, display the total of the values appearing in each row of the reordered data.

Exercise 8.6:

Suppose that you are a linguist interested in studying how often different words are used in the English language. Assume that the Enlish text that you read into your program contains no more than 200 distinct words from a variable number of input lines. Draw a conceptual (approximate) structure diagram describing how you would solve the following problem. Then develop and debug a PASCAL program to carry out the actions of the algorithm described by the diagram.

Count the number of times each distinct word appears in the input text. You may assume that each word is no longer than 15 characters, and that no words are split between lines by hyphenation. At the end, display each word and its associated count, starting with the word having the highest count, and proceeding in the order of decreasing counts. You may use the text of this Exercise as test data. Simplify the problem by using only upper case letters. If S1 and S2 are STRING variables, note that it is legal to use:

```
IF S1 = S2 THEN ...
```

Exercise 8.7:

All three of the sample programs analyzed in this chapter have the annoying property of being rather "unforgiving" about typing errors on input. We presented them in this form mainly to avoid complications about display formats, which would have distracted us from the main points of the analysis. If you implemented and tried any of these programs, you may have discovered that you could not use the <backspace> key or <rubout> to erase a typing error in the manner that was possible in many of the earlier sample programs.

One simple way to avoid this problem is to use STRING variables for input. For input to a STRING variable, our PASCAL system accepts all characters typed up until <RET> is pressed, and <backspace> and <rubout> (i.e. <DEL>) serve to erase individual characters or the whole line typed so far. Not until <RET> is typed does your program get to examine the typed characters. This allows simple correction of errors on the screen before the program runs into problems that would be complex to correct. One difficulty with this method is that you have to accept each new item of data on a new line, if a prompt for each item is to be used, or you have to type the data "blind" without separate prompts for each item.

For this exercise, modify the SPORTSCORE2 and CROSSFOOT programs to use the method of input just described. You will have to change the manner in which numbers are converted from characters to internal binary form by using your own function to do the conversion. Remember that the integer value of a digit, say D, can be obtained from:

```
D := ORD(CH) - ORD('0')
```

where CH is of <type> CHAR, and the built-in function ORD converts a character to integer form.

Chapter 9

BASIC DATA STRUCTURES - II. SETS

1. Goals

This chapter is primarily concerned with methods for handling information that needs to be broken into categories for processing. PASCAL's SET <type> and several related concepts are introduced.

1a. Learn to define scalar variables for handling non-numeric data that can be categorized.

1b. Learn to use subrange variables to prevent a program from attempting to process data values that should not occur.

1c. Learn to define your own <type>'s for variables and to declare and use variables of those <type>'s.

1d. Learn to use sets to simplify testing for complex combinations of data values.

1e. Modify a program of moderate complexity using the new concepts introduced in this chapter.

2. Background

Whereas the concept of an array allows you to keep many associated data items of the same <type> together under one name, it is often necessary to perform the same processing actions on many data items which are associated only by their *values*. For example, in a university, one set of data processing actions might apply only to students registered for science majors, another for students majoring in arts and humanities, and so on. Typically, the records on students would contain a "*coded*" item representing the declared major. In the course of processing, one might then have to use a complex sequence of IF statements to determine whether a student is a science major. For example:

```
IF (MAJOR=2) (*biology*)
  OR (MAJOR=4) (*chemistry*)
  OR (MAJOR=15) (*physics*)
  OR (MAJOR=16) (*applied physics*)
    THEN HANDLESCIENCE;
```

In this example, assume that HANDLESCIENCE is a procedure written to handle processing for the science students. The "codes" are numeric values assigned arbitrarily to represent each major. Codes like this have often been used in business data processing because they save storage space, and they allow some kinds of processing in the computer to be more efficient than would be the case if the strings humans recognize most easily were used instead.

Of course it is possible to make a test such as this once at the time the data is first entered into the computer, and to place a separate coded value in each record denoting whether the student belongs to a science major, or to arts or humanities, or whatever. However, one cannot always predict in advance just which categories of this kind may be important. So the likelihood remains that one may have to write a sequence of complicated IF statements to separate the data into the relevant categories.

PASCAL provides several facilities which greatly simplify the handling of related data values, viz:

a) A "SET" <variable> is similar to an array containing only Boolean data items. Each item in a SET corresponds to a specific data value. It is possible for any of the Boolean items within a SET to be TRUE simultaneously. For example, in a SET representing all undergraduate students, the items representing Freshman, Sophomore, Junior and Senior would all be TRUE, but those representing Graduate and Extension students would not be FALSE. The items corresponding to TRUE values are said to be "members" of the SET.

b) A "SCALAR" <variable> allows you to associate a name with each possible code value for data which must be categorized. This makes it unnecessary for you to remember the code value in writing programs, since the PASCAL compiler remembers for you. As an example, the IF statement above could then be changed to the following:

```
IF (MAJOR=BIOLOGY) OR (MAJOR=CHEMISTRY)
  OR (MAJOR=PHYSICS) OR (MAJOR=APPLPHYS) THEN
    HANDLESCIENCE
```

As you will see in this chapter, even this complexity can be avoided by associating a SET <variable> with the named codes, so that this IF statement can be made very simple indeed.

c) A "SUBRANGE" <variable> can be defined to include all of the Integer or Scalar values between specified limits. Thus a <variable> called UNDERGRAD might be allowed to take on any value ranging from FRESHMAN to SENIOR. A <variable> called HOUR might be allowed to take on any value from 0 thru 24. If you try to assign a value outside the specified range to a SUBRANGE variable, the PASCAL system will terminate your program abnormally. Because the PASCAL system checks to make sure that only values that make sense are assigned to SUBRANGE <variable>'s, you are protected against running programs that contain hard-to-find logical errors.

To illustrate these concepts in this chapter and the next, we will examine the kinds of processing that might be used by a professor interested in determining how well various students are progressing in her/his class. Detailed aspects of this example will be studied as we progress from section to section.

3. Scalar Types

Whenever data processing problems make it convenient to subdivide the items of data into several distinct categories it proves convenient to attach a simple numeric code to each distinct category. For example one might use the following numeric codes to separate students into one category associated with each class level.

LEVEL	CODE
freshman	1
sophomore	2
junior	3
senior	4
graduate	5
extension	6

Such a code is economical of computer memory or storage space, compared with the spelled-out name of the level, since the code can be stored in no more space than needed for a single character (or in some cases for an integer).

Codes of this kind have long been used in data processing both to save space on punched cards, or in computer memory, and also to reduce the amount of processing required. For example it is much simpler to perform a test such as:

```
IF LEVEL = 2 THEN <statement>
```

than to program the loop which compares a <string> containing the word 'SOPHOMORE' with an array containing the same using character by character tests. Unfortunately the simplification of the programs resulting from use of number codes rather than words has also had the effect of making the same programs more prone to errors due to mistakes made in confusion by the programmer. In a large program, where several distinct data items are categorized into numeric codes, it becomes very easy for the programmer to forget the several different meanings that might be associated with the same code value. Another problem is that it is all too easy to write a program in such a way that attempts are made to use non existent code values.

PASCAL has been designed to avoid these problems, which are characteristic of virtually all of the popular programming languages. You can declare a new <type> which will be associated with <variable>'s which can take on only the allowed code values. For example:

```
VAR L1, L2: (FRESHMAN, SOPHOMORE, JUNIOR, SENIOR,
             GRADUATE, EXTENSION);
```

This allows the test shown above to be written as follows:

```
IF L1 = SOPHOMORE THEN <statement>
```

Each of the identifiers in the <type> portion of the declaration for L1 and L2 may be considered to be a <constant> of one type associated with that declaration. Thus it is legal to use a statement such as:

```
  L2 := JUNIOR
```

or

```
  IF L2 >= GRADUATE THEN <statement>
```

The codes that equate to the <identifier>'s in the declaration of L1 and L2 have numeric values for internal processing of your program. The first named identifier in the declaration has an internal code value of 0, the second a value of 1, and so on. Thus SOPHOMORE is greater than FRESHMAN, and all of the values from FRESHMAN thru SENIOR are less than the value of GRADUATE.

It is also possible to use a CASE statement such as the following:

```
  CASE L1 OF
    FRESHMAN: P1;
    SOPHOMORE: P2;
    JUNIOR, SENIOR: P3;
    GRADUATE: P4;
    EXTENSION: P5
  END (*CASES*);
```

where P1 thru P5 are all presumed to be procedures declared earlier in the program.

The <type> of the variables L1 and L2, as established by the declaration above, is <u>SCALAR</u>. The PASCAL compiler will protect you against assigning an improper value to a <variable> such as L1, since there are only six possible values associated with L1. Similarly, you can regard a Boolean <variable> as being equivalent to one appearing in a declaration such as

```
  VAR BOOL: (TRUE, FALSE)
```

Note however that you cannot use the reserved identifiers "TRUE" and "FALSE" in this kind of declaration. Such declarations have the effect of associating a constant value with each identifier in the list between parentheses, and TRUE and FALSE are predeclared by the system in association with the <type> BOOLEAN. If an attempt is made to assign anything but one of the declared constant identifiers, or the value of an expression associated with the same <type>, then the compiler should generate a syntax error message.

4. Declaring Your Own Types

Another way of declaring the variables L1 and L2 used in the previous section would be as follows:

```
TYPE LEVEL =(FRESHMAN, SOPHOMORE, JUNIOR, SENIOR,
             GRADUATE, EXTENSION);

VAR L1,L2: LEVEL;
```

The reserved identifier "TYPE" is used in a manner similar to the use of the identifier "VAR" in that it introduces a sequence of declarations in the heading of a <block>. The relevant syntax is shown in Figures 9-1 and 8-2. The declaration above associates the <identifier> LEVEL with the SCALAR <type> shown on the right of the equal sign ('='). Thereafter, appearance of the identifier LEVEL in variable and parameter declarations satisfies the requirement of the syntax for a <type> to be given. Notice that the syntax for <block> requires that all declarations of new <type>'s must come before the VAR announcing variable declarations in that block. The scope of <type> identifiers follows the same rules as the scope of <variable> identifiers.

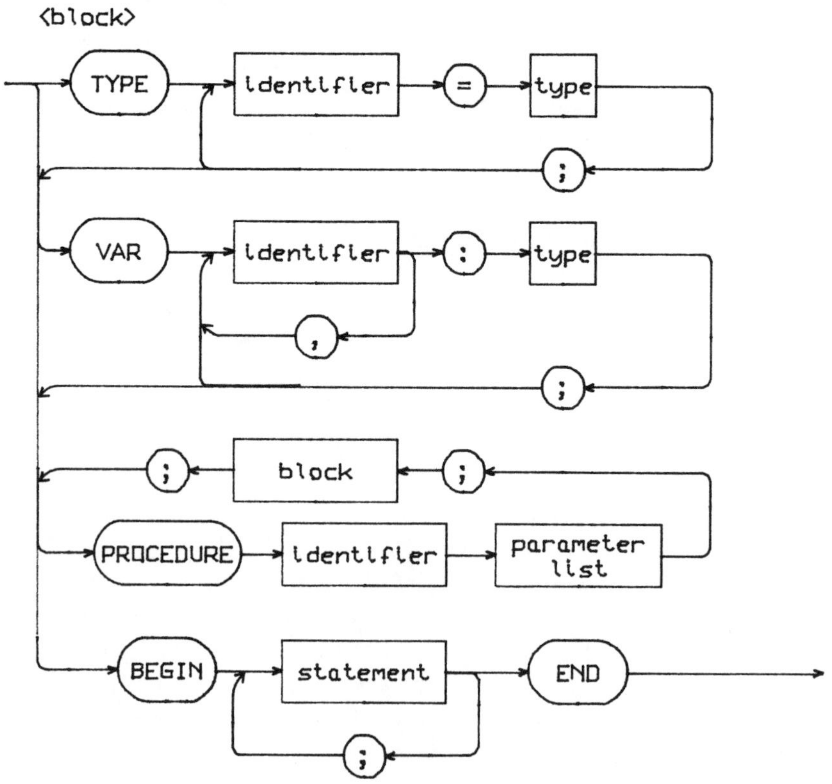
<block>
TYPE
identifier
=
type
;
VAR
identifier
:
type
,
;
;
block
;
PROCEDURE
identifier
parameter list
BEGIN
statement
END
;

Figure 9-1

As you will see in later sections of this chapter, and in the next chapter, you can declare identifiers to be associated with a wide variety of new <type>'s. One of the benefits of using your own declared <type> for variables used for a particular purpose, is that the compiler can then assist you to avoid making errors. Whenever a new value is assigned to a variable, the compiler checks to make sure that the <type> of the expression on the right of the assignment operator (':=') is compatible with the <type> of the variable. If they are not compatible, then a syntax error message is generated. The simplest interpretation of "compatible" in the case of Scalar variables would be a requirement that the <type>'s be identical.

The compiler also does <type> checking of the expressions in a logical comparison, as in the heading of an IF statement. Once again both expressions must be compatible, or a syntax error message will be generated.

As programs get more complex, you find that it is hard to keep in mind the associations of different variables and constants with specific tasks. The compiler is able to assist you to avoid mixing variables intended for different purposes through the mechanism of <type> checking. In order to take advantage of this checking, of course it is necessary to use special variable <type>'s whenever appropriate.

5. Subrange Types

In some cases, the logic of an algorithm may call for a program variable to be restricted to take on values only between specified limits within the full range of values variables of the associated <type> are allowed to take. The "range" of a variable extends from the minimum value that the variable can assume up to the maximum value. A "subrange" is some portion of the range of a variable in which all of the values between a specified minimum and a specified maximum are included.

Assuming that the <type> LEVEL has been declared as in the previous section, then:

```
TYPE
     etc.   etc.
   UNDERGRAD = FRESHMAN .. SENIOR;
     etc.   etc.
VAR
  SL: UNDERGRAD;
```

declares the variable SL to be of <type> UNDERGRAD. Then the assignment:

```
SL := JUNIOR
```

is legal, but

```
SL := GRADUATE
```

will cause the program to terminate abnormally.

At first it may seem to you an annoyance to have the PASCAL system provide yet another way for your programs to terminate abnormally. In fact the reason for causing abnormal termination when an attempt is made to assign an illegal value to a subrange variable is to make it easier for you to find logical errors. Quite often a programmer will realize, at the time when the program is being written, that a certain variable can logically take on only certain values. This limitation is easy to forget when assigning a value to the variable at a later time. Failure to add a check on the value explicitly in the program can then lead quite often to obscure errors that are very hard to find during debugging. Use of a subrange variable is a request to the compiler to insert checks on values automatically. When the program terminates abnormally, the error message from the system will point you directly to the place in the program where the infraction takes place, and you then can take corrective steps with minimal effort.

In addition to allowing declaration of a subrange of a SCALAR <type> PASCAL allows you to declare subranges of INTEGER and CHAR <type>'s. For example:

```
TYPE SUBI = 1..10;
     SUBCH = 'I' .. 'N';
VAR
  IRV: SUBI;
  SV: 0..9;
  I: INTEGER;
  CHRV: SUBCH;
  CH: CHAR;
```

Then:

```
I := 11;
IRV := I;
```

will cause an abnormal termination when thesystem tries to assign the value of I to IRV, since 11 falls outside the subrange SUBI with which IRV has been declared to be associated.

Refer to the syntax diagrams for <type> and <simple type> in Appendix E with particular attention to the syntax for an ARRAY declaration. The expression of a <simple type> used as an index (selector value) for an array may now be seen to be of either a Scalar or a Subrange <type>. Moreover, the <constant>'s defining the lower and upper bounds of an ARRAY declaration may be seen to define the bounds of a SUBRANGE <type>. Thus in:

```
TYPE BOUNDS = -5 .. +5;

VAR
  A1 : ARRAY[-5 .. +5];
  A2 : ARRAY[BOUNDS];
```

the arrays A1 and A2 are of equivalent size, and have the same lower and upper bounds. An "invalid index" program termination occurs when an attempt is made to:

a) refer to a non-existent array location, i.e. one outside the declared bounds of the array

b) assign a value to a subrange variable outside the bounds associated with its <type>.

6. Sets

Imagine now that our hypothetical professor is interested in comparing the grades earned in his course by students in the Arts, Humanities, Natural Sciences and Social Sciences areas. But the files available from the university registrar show only the major, and not the area of study. To make the desired comparison, the professor's computer program must first associate each student with an AREA. This could be done with a CASE statement such as:

```
CASE MAJOR OF
  ANTHROPOLOGY: AREA:=SOCSCI;
  APPLPHYS, BIOLOGY, CHEMISTRY: AREA:=NATSCI;
  COMMUNICATIONS: AREA:=SOCSCI;
  DRAMA: AREA:=ARTS;
  ECONOMICS: AREA:=SOCSCI;
  HISTORY, LINGUISTICS, LITERATURE: AREA:=HUMAN;
  MATHEMATICS: AREA:=NATSCI;
  MUSIC: AREA:=ARTS;
  PHILOSOPHY: AREA:=HUMAN;
  PHYSICS: AREA:=NATSCI;
  POLITSCI, PSYCHOLOGY, SOCIOLOGY: AREA:=SOCSCI;
  VISARTS: AREA:=ARTS
END (*CASES*);
```

Further processing could then depend upon the value of the <variable> AREA.

There is an easier way to do this using Sets. First we have to define a Scalar <type> that we can call MAJORS.

```
TYPE MAJORS = (ANTHROPOLOGY, APPLPHYS, BIOLOGY,
    CHEMISTRY, COMMUNICATIONS, DRAMA, ECONOMICS,
    HISTORY, LINGUISTICS, LITERATURE, MATHEMATICS,
    MUSIC, PHILOSOPHY, PHYSICS, POLITSCI,
    PSYCHOLOGY, SOCIOLOGY, VISARTS);

VAR ARTSET, HUMANSET, SOCSCISET, NATSCISET:
                              SET OF MAJORS;
```

At this point we now have four <variables> that are of <type> SET OF MAJORS. Each contains one Boolean element corresponding to each constant declared in the Scalar <type> MAJORS. Before the program starts running, all of the elements in these Sets are undefined. It is necessary to initialize the Set variables before they can be used, just as it is necessary to initialize any other variable by assigning a value to it. This is done with statements like the following:

```
ARTSET := [DRAMA, MUSIC, VISARTS]
```

where the brackets on the right side enclose a special kind of <expression> known as a Set "<u>constructor</u>". Syntax for this is included in the definition of <factor> in the diagrams of Appendix E. This assignment statement assigns a value equivalent to Boolean TRUE to the three elements of ARTSET which correspond to the MAJORS included in the constructor. All other elements in ARTSET are assigned a value equivalent to Boolean FALSE. Now, if we have a variable declared to be of <type> MAJORS, for example:

```
VAR MAJ: MAJORS
```

the value of that <variable> can equal any one of the constants shown in the TYPE declaration of MAJORS. We can then use a test such as:

```
IF MAJ IN ARTSET THEN <statement>
```

rather than having to write out the equivalent test, which is:

```
IF (MAJ=DRAMA) OR (MAJ=MUSIC)
   OR (MAJ=VISARTS) THEN <statement>
```

The operator "IN" tests whether the <scalar variable> on the left is a "member" of the value contained in the <set variable> on the right. Operations are also available to allow you to combine two or more <set variables> declared to be attached to the same <type> in a <set expression>. Here are some examples:

```
VAR S1,S2,S3,S4: SET OF MAJORS;

S1 := [LITERATURE] + ARTSET;

S2 := [COMMUNICATIONS,DRAMA,ECONOMICS];

S3 := S1 * S2;

S4 := S2 - S1;
```

S1 is assigned as its value the SET

```
[DRAMA,LITERATURE,MUSIC,VISARTS]
```

When dealing with Sets, the "+" operator yields a new SET containing a TRUE element for every element that is TRUE in either the SET on its left OR the one on the right. The result is called the "union" of the two Sets.

S3 is assigned as its value the SET

[DRAMA]

because the "*" operator, when referring to Sets, yields a new SET containing only TRUE elements corresponding to elements that were TRUE in both the set expression on the left AND the one on the right. The result is called the "intersection" of the two sets combined by the "*" operator.

S4 contains TRUE corresponding to all elements that were TRUE in S2 and FALSE in S1. Thus S4 is assigned the value

[COMMUNICATIONS, ECONOMICS]

The result yielded by the "-" operator is called the set "difference". For syntax relating to SET declarations, see <type> and <simple type> in Appendix E. The syntax for <expression>, <simple expression>, <term> and <factor> covers the operations just described.

7. Sample Program FOODSETS

The program FOODSETS provides a simple illustration of the use of both Scalar variables and of SET variables attached to such a Scalar. Following is what this program should display:

FOODSETS

ITEM	S1	S2	S3	+	*	-
APPLE	T	T	F	T	F	T
BANANA	F	F	F	F	F	F
CARROT	F	F	T	T	F	F
BEAN	F	F	T	T	F	F
GRAPE	F	F	F	F	F	F
HOTDOG	F	F	F	F	F	F
POTATO	F	F	T	T	F	F
TOMATO	F	T	T	T	T	F
PEAR	T	T	F	T	F	T
ORANGE	T	T	F	T	F	T

The program first initializes the Sets S1, S2, and S3 in lines 33, 34 and 35. It then displays the elements stored in each of these Sets along with the union, intersection, and difference of S2 and S3 as passed to the display procedure TORF ("T OR F"). We suggest that you check each line in this table to make sure you understand how each entry acquires the value that is shown.

Note the use of the constant values declared in lines 2 and 3 as steering constants for the CASE statement in the procedure PUTNAME. Note also the use of the declared <type>'s FOOD and FS in the declarations of the parameters for PUTNAME and TORF.

```
PROGRAM FOODSETS;
TYPE FOOD=(APPLE, BANANA, CARROT, BEAN, GRAPE,
           HOTDOG, POTATO, TOMATO, PEAR, ORANGE);
  FS=SET OF FOOD;
VAR
  S1,S2,S3: FS;
  F: FOOD;
  U,I,D: CHAR;
PROCEDURE PUTNAME(N:FOOD);
BEGIN
  CASE N OF
    APPLE: WRITE('APPLE ');
    BANANA: WRITE('BANANA');
    CARROT: WRITE('CARROT');
    BEAN: WRITE('BEAN  ');
    GRAPE: WRITE('GRAPE ');
    HOTDOG: WRITE('HOTDOG');
    POTATO: WRITE('POTATO');
    TOMATO: WRITE('TOMATO');
    PEAR: WRITE('PEAR  ');
    ORANGE: WRITE('ORANGE')
  END (*CASES*);
END (*PUTNAME*);

PROCEDURE TORF(F:FOOD; S:FS);
BEGIN
  IF F IN S THEN WRITE(' T  ')
            ELSE WRITE(' F  ');
END (*T OR F*);

BEGIN  (*MAIN PROGRAM*)
  WRITELN('FOODSETS');  WRITELN;
  S1:=[APPLE,PEAR,ORANGE];
  S2:=S1 + [TOMATO];
  S3:=[CARROT,BEAN,POTATO,TOMATO];
  WRITELN('ITEM    ', ' S1 ', ' S2 ', ' S3 ',
          ' +  ', ' *  ', ' -  ');
  FOR F:=APPLE TO ORANGE DO
    BEGIN
      WRITELN;  PUTNAME(F);  WRITE('  ');
      TORF(F,S1);  TORF(F,S2);  TORF(F,S3);
      TORF(F, S2+S3);  (*union*)
      TORF(F, S2*S3);  (*intersection*)
      TORF(F, S2-S3);  (*difference*)
      WRITELN;
    END;
END.
```

8. Sample Program SETDEMO

This program reads a student name, an abbreviation for a major, and a grade. The display associated with test input for 7 students is shown on a separate page. After the input phase is terminated, with EOF being set by typing <ETX> (line 35 of the display), the program displays the average grade reported for each area of studies.

Notice that the arrays GRADES, COUNT, MT and AREANAME all are indexed with subranges of scalar variables. This may be seen in the declarations (lines 12, 13, and 20 of the program), and also in the use of those arrays as subscripted variables (e.g. lines 55 thru 71 of INIT).

In line 89, we use the built-in "<u>successor</u>" function SUCC to increment the <variable> M which is of <type> MAJORS. To make this usage explicit,

```
M := SUCC(BIOLOGY)
```

assigns the value CHEMISTRY to M. Since VISARTS has no successor, looping on lines 88 and 89 must stop when M=VISARTS, i.e. the last constant declared in MAJORS. Otherwise the program would terminate abnormally for trying to assign a non-existent successor of VISARTS to M. A companion "<u>predecessor</u>" function works in the reverse direction, for example:

```
M := PRED(CHEMISTRY)
```

assigns the value BIOLOGY to M. Since ANTHROPOLOGY has no predecessor, an attempt to use PRED(ANTRHOPOLOGY) will result in abnormal termination.

```
PROGRAM SETDEMO;
TYPE
  MAJORS=(ANTHROPOLOGY, APPLPHYS, BIOLOGY,
    CHEMISTRY, COMMUNICATIONS, DRAMA, ECONOMICS,
    HISTORY, LINGUISTICS, LITERATURE,
    MATHEMATICS, MUSIC, PHILOSOPHY, PHYSICS,
    POLITSCI, PSYCHOLOGY, SOCIOLOGY, VISARTS);
  MAJSET=SET OF MAJORS;
  AREAS=(ARTS, HUMAN, SOCSCI, NATSCI);
VAR
  ARTSET, HUMANSET, SOCSCISET, NATSCISET:MAJSET;
  GRADES,COUNT: ARRAY[ARTS..NATSCI] OF INTEGER;
  MT: ARRAY[ANTHROPOLOGY..VISARTS] OF
                            PACKED ARRAY[1..4] OF CHAR;
  ABUF: PACKED ARRAY[1..4] OF CHAR;
  G,I,MAXI: INTEGER;
  CH: CHAR;
  M: MAJORS;
  A: AREAS;
  AREANAME: ARRAY[ARTS..NATSCI] OF STRING;
  NAME,S: STRING;

PROCEDURE CONFIRM;
BEGIN
  WRITELN;
  WRITELN(NAME, ' ':3, G, ' ':3, AREANAME[A]);
  WRITELN;
END (*CONFIRM*);

PROCEDURE WRAPUP;
VAR G:INTEGER;
BEGIN
  WRITELN;  WRITELN('AVERAGES:');
  FOR A:=ARTS TO NATSCI DO
    BEGIN
      WRITE('  ',AREANAME[A],'   ');
      IF COUNT[A]>0 THEN
        G:=10*GRADES[A] DIV COUNT[A]
      ELSE
        G:=0;
      WRITELN(G DIV 10,'.', G MOD 10);
    END;
END (*WRAPUP*);

PROCEDURE INIT;
BEGIN
  ARTSET:=[DRAMA,MUSIC,VISARTS];
  HUMANSET:=[LINGUISTICS,LITERATURE,PHILOSOPHY];
  SOCSCISET:=[ANTHROPOLOGY,COMMUNICATIONS,
              ECONOMICS,PSYCHOLOLGY,SOCIOLOGY];
  NATSCISET:=[APPLPHYS,BIOLOGY,CHEMISTRY,
              MATHEMATICS,PHYSICS];
```

```

  (*now initialize MT with abbreviations*)
  MT[ANTHROPOLOGY]:='ANTH'; MT[APPLPHYS]:='APHY';
  MT[BIOLOGY]:='BIOL';      MT[CHEMISTRY]:='CHEM';
  MT[COMMUNICATIONS]:='COMM';  MT[DRAMA]:='DRMA';
  MT[ECONOMICS]:='ECON';      MT[HISTORY]:='HIST';
  MT[LINGUISTICS]:='LING';MT[LITERATURE]:='LIT ';
  MT[MATHEMATICS]:='MATH';      MT[MUSIC]:='MUSI';
  MT[PHILOSOPHY]:='PHIL';     MT[PHYSICS]:='PHYS';
  MT[POLITSCI]:='POLI';   MT[PSYCHOLOGY]:='PSYC';
  MT[SOCIOLOGY]:='SOCI';      MT[VISARTS]:='VISA';

  (*initialize area names*)
  AREANAME[ARTS]:='ARTS';
  AREANAME[HUMAN]:='HUMANITIES';
  AREANAME[SOCSCI]:='SOC SCIENCE';
  AREANAME[NATSCI]:='NAT SCIENCE';
  FOR A:=ARTS TO NATSCI DO
    BEGIN  GRADES[A]:=0; COUNT[A]:=0; END;
END (*INIT*);

BEGIN (*MAIN PROGRAM*)
  INIT;
  WHILE NOT EOF DO
  BEGIN
    WRITE('NAME:');
    READ(NAME);
    WRITE('MAJOR:');
    READ(S);
    ABUF:='    ';
    IF LENGTH(S)>4 THEN MAXI:=4
                   ELSE MAXI:=LENGTH(S);
    FOR I:=1 TO MAXI DO ABUF[I]:=S[I];
    (*look for match of abbrev with major*)
    M:=ANTHROPOLOGY;
    WHILE (MT[M]<>ABUF) AND (M < VISARTS) DO
      M:=SUCC(M); (*M to successor of M*)
    IF M IN (SOCSCISET + NATSCISET) THEN
      BEGIN
        IF M IN SOCSCISET THEN A:=SOCSCI
                          ELSE A:=NATSCI;
      END ELSE
        IF M IN ARTSET THEN A:=ARTS
                       ELSE A:=HUMAN;
    WRITE('GRADE:');  READ(G);  READ(CH);
    GRADES[A]:=GRADES[A]+G;
    COUNT[A]:=COUNT[A]+1;
    CONFIRM;
  END (*WHILE*);
  WRAPUP;
END.
```

```
Display associated with SETDEMO program

NAME:Brown,Bill W.
MAJOR:ECON
GRADE:85
Brown,Bill W.  85   SOC SCIENCE

NAME:Green,John L.
MAJOR:PSYC
GRADE:80
Green,John L.  80   SOC SCIENCE

NAME:Jones,Jenny T.
MAJOR:PHYS
GRADE:88
Jones,Jenny T.  88   NAT SCIENCE

NAME:Mitchell,Martha Q.
MAJOR:VISA
GRADE:92
Mitchell,Martha Q.  92   ARTS

NAME:Peters,Sally F.
MAJOR:LIT
GRADE:75
Peters,Sally F.  75   HUMANITIES

NAME:Public,John Q.
MAJOR:POLI
GRADE:95
Public,John Q.  95   HUMANITIES

NAME:Smith,Eleazar A.
MAJOR:CHEM
GRADE:77<ETX>
Smith,Eleazar A.  77   NAT SCIENCE

AVERAGES:
ARTS  92.0
HUMANITIES  85.0
SOC SCIENCE  82.5
NAT SCIENCE  82.5
```

The effect of the nested IF statement in lines 90 through 96 is similar to the effect of the CASE statement shown at the beginning of Section 6. We first determine whether M falls in one of the two science Sets. If so, then it is determined which science Set is appropriate. If not, then it is presumed that M falls in either the arts or humanities, and which of the two is determined by the test in line 95. This method of partitioning the IF statements is slightly more efficient in processing time than the following would be:

```
IF M IN ARTSET THEN A:=ARTS
  ELSE IF M IN HUMANSET THEN A:=HUMAN
    ELSE IF M IN NATSCISET THEN A:=NATSCI
      ELSE A:=SOCSCI;
```

Notice the use of the <variable> A of Scalar <type> AREAS to control the FOR statements in lines 34 and 70.

9. Using Sets with Characters

Sets provide an especially useful device for working with strings of characters in many applications. For example, consider again the sample program DEVOWEL of Chapter 7 Section 10. The complicated test in lines 14 and 15 of that program, i.e.

```
IF (CH<>'A') AND (CH<>'E') AND (CH<>'I')
    AND (CH<>'O') AND (CH<>'U') THEN
```

can be replaced by:

```
IF NOT (CH IN ['A','E','I','O','U']) THEN
```

Similarly, we could have

```
VAR VOWELS,CONSONANTS,LETTERS: SET OF CHAR;
```

and

```
VOWELS := ['A','E','I','O','U'];
CONSONANTS := ['A' .. 'Z'] - VOWELS;
```

in which the set constructor in the second assignment statement makes all of the characters from 'A' thru 'Z' members of a set. The vowels are then taken away to leave only the consonants. We could also construct a set of all the letters, including both upper case and lower case:

```
LETTERS := ['A'..'Z', 'a'..'z']
```

One can also test whether two sets are equal or not equal, as in

```
IF S1 = S2 THEN ...
IF S2 <> S3 THEN ...
```

Finally, one can test whether one set is <u>included</u> in another. This test can be made clearer by referring to the sample program CHARSETS. In line 21, the phrase

```
IF VOWELS <= LETTERS
```

tests whether the set of vowels is included in the set of letters. Line 3 of the display shows that this test evaluated TRUE. However, in line 23, the test was expressed in reverse, i.e.

```
IF VOWELS >= LETTERS
```

which tests whether LETTERS is included in VOWELS. As shown in line 4 of the display, this test was evaluated as FALSE. Thus the two tests for set inclusion are symmetric, i.e. we could have used

```
IF LETTERS >= VOWELS
```

```
PROGRAM CHARSETS;
TYPE SOFCH = SET OF CHAR;
VAR LETTERS, DIGITS, VOWELS, CONSONANTS,
                ALPHA, SPECIAL:SOFCH;

PROCEDURE SHOWSET(S:SOFCH);
VAR CH:CHAR;
BEGIN
  FOR CH:='0' TO '_' DO
    IF CH IN S THEN WRITE(CH) ELSE WRITE(' ');
  WRITELN;
END (*SHOWSET*);

BEGIN
  LETTERS:=['A'..'Z'];
  VOWELS:=['A','E','I','O','U'];
  CONSONANTS:=LETTERS - VOWELS;
  DIGITS:=['0'..'9'];
  ALPHA:=LETTERS + DIGITS;
  SPECIAL:=[' '..'_'] - LETTERS - DIGITS;
  IF VOWELS <= LETTERS THEN
    WRITELN('VOWELS <= LETTERS');
  IF NOT (VOWELS >= LETTERS) THEN
    WRITELN('NOT (VOWELS >= LETTERS)');
  WRITELN;
  SHOWSET(LETTERS);
  SHOWSET(VOWELS);
  SHOWSET(CONSONANTS);
  SHOWSET(DIGITS);
  SHOWSET(ALPHA);
  SHOWSET(SPECIAL);
END.
```

```
Display associated with CHARSETS program

VOWELS <= LETTERS
NOT (VOWELS >= LETTERS)

                 ABCDEFGHIJKLMNOPQRSTUVWXYZ
                 A   E   I     O     U
                  BCD FGH JKLMN PQRST VWXYZ
0123456789
0123456789       ABCDEFGHIJKLMNOPQRSTUVWXYZ
          :;<=>?@                          [\]^_
```

with the comparison evaluated as TRUE.

The remaining lines displayed by the program CHARSETS show the values of the various sets initialized in lines 15 thru 20 of the program. Only a few of the special characters are shown due to column width limitations for publishing this book. You could display all of the special characters in the first 64 of the 95 displayable characters in the ASCII (American Standard Code for Information Interchange) set by changing '0' to ' ' in line 9 of the program. The remaining 31 characters could be displayed separately using

```
FOR CH:=CHR(96) TO CHR(126) DO . . .
```

Here we use the integer to character transfer function CHR because of character set problems related to our printing process for this book.

Exercise 9.1:

If you were to use the program SETDEMO as printed in this chapter, you would find that it is not very well protected against certain possible errors in the typed input. As presented, the program would either terminate abnormally, or incorrect results would be obtained, on any of the following errors:

a) MAJOR abbreviation incorrect or not contained in the array MT (majors table)

b) GRADE incorrectly typed, and hence outside the range of acceptable data, i.e. 0..100

c) Characters other than the alphabetic characters plus ',' and '.' in the input for NAME

Modify the program so that it can recover "gracefully" from any and all of these errors. In general, if an error is detected, the program should display an error message, ring the computer's bell, and then return to request the same data item to be typed again. You should alter the program to cope, among other things, with any character other than ['0'..'9',' '] (including the <space> resulting from <RET>) on reading GRADE. Test and debug the program with your changes installed, using input data designed to test all of the error conditions noted above.

Exercise 9.2:

The sample program CROSSFOOT of Chapter 8 Section 8 does not check for validity of the service code needed to identify the column into which the transaction amount should be entered. Modify the program to make it display an error message if an incorrect code is entered from the keyboard, and to request keyboard input to commence again. Test and debug the modified program to verify that your changes work correctly.

Exercise 9.3:

Suppose that you are employed by your state energy resources agency to write programs for keeping track of all contracts and planned contracts for delivery of energy within your state. It is necessary to keep records on the following resources and mechanisms for generating consumable energy:

oil, natural gas, coal, hydroelectric power,
geothermal power, solar electric power, wind,
wood, urban waste, nuclear fission, nuclear fusion,
special crops, other

The job is complicated because the first three of these are also used as resources for the petrochemical and plastics industries, because the nuclear resources are controversial and considered dangerous by some people, because the hydroelectric, solar and wind resources are strongly dependent on the weather, and so on.

Write and debug a program which accepts as data, a 20 character identifying name for the source of an energy contract, an abbreviation for the type of energy, the number of BTU's (in Billions) promised for delivery per year, and the price (in Millions of dollars), for an indefinite number of sources. The program should keep a summary total of the number of BTU's from all sources in each of several groupings:

fossil fuel (oil, natural gas, coal)
nuclear (fission and fusion)
replenishable (hydro, solar, wind, wood, urban waste, crops)
depletable fuel (oil, natural gas, coal, geothermal,fission)

After accepting a sequence of data entries containing the specified information, the program should display a summary of the BTU's and dollar amounts for each of these categories. It should also summarize the contracts in each category for each separate contractor listed by name. For test data, create your own entries, making sure that you use values that represent each of the different energy sources, and that at least 5 different contractor names are used. Check the output of the program by hand calculation to be sure that the correct results are achieved

Note: This exercise and the next one refer to data processing that normally would make use of some permanent data storage medium such as magnetic disks for storing files of data to be processed long after it is collected. Unfortunately, the details of using such a medium are beyond the scope of this book. For this reason, it will only be practical to test the programs you develop with very small data samples to represent the data that would be acquired in a realistic situation.

Exercise 9.4:

Most large urban communities now have regional planning agencies similar to the San Diego Comprehensive Planning Organization (CPO). One of the main functions of the CPO is to maintain records on the many different ways in which each section of the community occupies and uses its land area. This information is needed each time approval is requested for some new building or industrial development, when changes in the schools or transportation are planned, when attempting to improve police and fire protection organizations, when coping with air and water pollution, when preparing to cope with natural disasters like earthquakes and floods, when establishing plans for future parks and recreation areas, and so on... One of the bigger tasks confronting San Diego's CPO in recent years has been the requirement to recommend a location for a new international airport. The present airport is near the center of the city and is becoming overloaded.

To carry out its mission, the CPO maintains computer based records amounting to maps of the region broken into small sections. The borders of these sections are defined by natural boundaries such as creek beds, rocky bluffs, the Pacific Ocean shoreline, and by man-made boundaries such as housing subdivisions, major shopping centers, industrial parks, farming areas, and so on. The record kept on each section includes a characterization of that section (effectively) expressed as a Set. The members of the set classify the section according to categories such as:

population density (rural, suburb, dense)
industry(none, farming, light, heavy)
air pollution(light, moderate, heavy, excessive)
crime rate(low, moderate, high, excessive)

Assume that the sections of the region are identified on the maps simply by arbitrary integers in the range 1..<number of sections>. Write and debug a program which will accumulate records on up to 20 sections of the region (a small number for testing purposes). The records should be kept as an array of Sets whose members include, as a minimum, all of the possible categories mentioned above. In the input phase of the program, the user should be prompted to indicate which section applies to each new data entry, and then to indicate which categories of the selected record should be altered. Before termination, the program should display a summary of the data accumulated for all sections. To simulate the kind of analysis for which such data is often used, the program should also identify those sections where there is:

a) suburban population density AND excessive air pollution

b) light industry OR dense population both being combined with a high crime rate

Create your own test data, putting representative characteristics in each of the 20 sections used in testing the program. Arrange your data to test both TRUE and FALSE conditions for the combined categories (a) and (b).

Chapter 10

BASIC DATA STRUCTURES - III. RECORDS

1. Goals

This chapter introduces the concept that various related data items of differing <type> can be handled together as a single unit called a "record". This concept is fundamental in business data processing, in software engineering, and in related computing fields.

1a. Learn to declare record <variable>'s and record <type>'s.

1b. Handle constituent data items within individual records.

1c. Use record variables as complete units, without concern for their constituent items, where appropriate.

1d. Use arrays of record variables, and records as constituents of other records.

1e. Modify a program of moderate complexity using records.

2. Background

Frequently we have occasion to handle several closely related data items of differing <type>'s. For example, the input data for the program CROSSFOOT of Chapter 8 was contained in groups of three items, each group being contained as a "message" regarding a single transaction. In the SPORTSCORE2 example, each group consisted of the name of a person followed by 1 to 10 integer values representing earned scores associated with the same person. We stored the names in one array, called NAMES, and the scores in another called SCORES. After this data had been stored in memory in these arrays, the only way of associating a name with the corresponding scores was to use the fact that both array rows had the same value for the row index. In other words, the name in NAMES[ROW] corresponded to the scores in SCORES[ROW]. If the size of the arrays is large, and if there are more than two items with a correspondence, it is easy to make errors in writing programs which preserve relationships of this type.

To avoid this confusion, PASCAL allows you to declare a composite <variable> called a "record" which is made up of two or more entries whose <type>'s may be mixed. You can think of a RECORD <variable> as similar to the data contained on a punched card, or perhaps on a library catalog card. Usually each card contains several related specific values of certain data items. For example, one card might contain the value of a Scalar encoding the student's class level, plus the student's name in the form of a string, and also a grade in the form of an integer constant. When you hold a card in your hand, it is clear that all of the data punched into that card is associated mutually. A RECORD <variable> provides a way to store data values together in the computer's memory in such a way as to preserve the inter relationships of the several items contained in the record.

For some purposes, you find it desirable to refer to the specific data items within a record. For other purposes, it is convenient to be able to refer to the entire record as a unit. PASCAL provides features that allow you to make references by either method. COBOL and PL/1 provide similar features. The other popular languages we have mentioned do not provide facilities for handling records. Records for structuring of data items are now considered to be essential in business data processing and in the design of large "system programs" such as compilers for programming languages. Records might also be used more widely in numerical applications for science and mathematics if suitable facilities were more readily available.

3. Sample Program CLASSDATA

With the background already given, the most effective way for us to introduce the use of Records is to refer directly to the sample program CLASSDATA. Relevant syntax is given in Figures 10-1, and 10-2. The initial version of this program is constructed to show the use of a simple RECORD <variable> called STUDENT, and declared in lines 5 thru 10 of the program. The program could have been written without using a RECORD <variable> without much difficulty. Writing it with the record structure will allow us to add the record features in easy stages.

The syntax for declaration of a <record type> shown in Figure 10-1 is simplified relative to the complete PASCAL syntax shown in Appendix E. The more complete syntax allows a CASE clause which provides for several "variants" to be declared for the same record. This is a useful concept in connection with applications which require external storage devices such as magnetic disks. Use of the record variant concept is beyond the scope of this book.

```
PROGRAM CLASSDATA;
VAR I,FCNT,MCNT: INTEGER;
  FSUM,MSUM:REAL;
  CH:CHAR;
  STUDENT:
    RECORD
      NAME: STRING[20];
      GRADE: REAL;
      SEX: (FEMALE,MALE)
    END (*STUDENT*);

PROCEDURE ACCUMULATE;
BEGIN
  IF STUDENT.SEX=FEMALE THEN
  BEGIN
    FSUM:=FSUM+STUDENT.GRADE;
    FCNT:=FCNT+1;
  END ELSE
  BEGIN
    MSUM:=MSUM+STUDENT.GRADE;
    MCNT:=MCNT+1;
  END;
  WRITELN;
  WRITE(STUDENT.NAME,' ':20-LENGTH(STUDENT.NAME),
        ' ',STUDENT.GRADE:3:1,'  ');
  IF STUDENT.SEX=FEMALE THEN WRITELN('F')
                        ELSE WRITELN('M');
  WRITELN;
END (*ACCUMULATE*);

PROCEDURE PUTRESULTS;

  PROCEDURE DETAIL(S:STRING; R:REAL; I:INTEGER);
  VAR DIVISOR:INTEGER;
  BEGIN
    IF I>0 THEN DIVISOR:=I ELSE DIVISOR:=1;
    WRITELN(S,' ':13-LENGTH(S),
            R/DIVISOR:3:1,' ':15,I);
  END (*DETAIL*);

BEGIN
  WRITELN(' ':10,'AVG GRADE',' ':5,
                 'STUDENT COUNT');
  WRITELN;
  DETAIL('FEMALE', FSUM, FCNT);
  WRITELN;
  DETAIL('MALE', MSUM, MCNT);
END (*PUTRESULTS*);
```

```
BEGIN (*MAIN PROGRAM*)
  FSUM:=0; MSUM:=0;
  FCNT:=0; MCNT:=0;
  WHILE NOT EOF DO
  BEGIN
    WRITE('NAME:');
    READ(STUDENT.NAME);
    IF NOT EOF THEN
    BEGIN
      WRITE(' GRADE:');
      READ(STUDENT.GRADE);
      READ(CH); (*discard <space> or <RET>*)
      WRITE(' M/F:');
      READ(CH);
      IF CH IN ['F','f'] THEN
        STUDENT.SEX:=FEMALE
      ELSE
        STUDENT.SEX:=MALE;
      ACCUMULATE;
    END;
  END (*WHILE NOT EOF*);
  WRITELN;
  PUTRESULTS;
END.
```

```
Display associated with CLASSDATA program

NAME:Anderson,Pat
 GRADE:3.8
 M/F:f
Anderson,Pat        3.8  F

NAME:Brown,Ed
 GRADE:2.4
 M/F:m
Brown,Ed            2.4  M

NAME:Carlson,Elizabeth
  GRADE:2.9
  M/F:f
Carlson,Elizabeth   2.9  F

NAME:Daniels,Sharon
 GRADE:3.3
 M/F:f
Daniels,Sharon      3.3  F

NAME:Edwards,Bill
 GRADE:2.7
 M/F:m
Edwards,Bill        2.7  M

NAME:Franklin,Gene
 GRADE:3.5
 M/F:m
Franklin,Gene       3.5  M

NAME:Granger,John
 GRADE:3.2
 M/F:m
Granger,John        3.2  M

NAME:<ETX>

           AVG GRADE     STUDENT COUNT

FEMALE:       3.3                 3

MALE:         3.0                 4
```

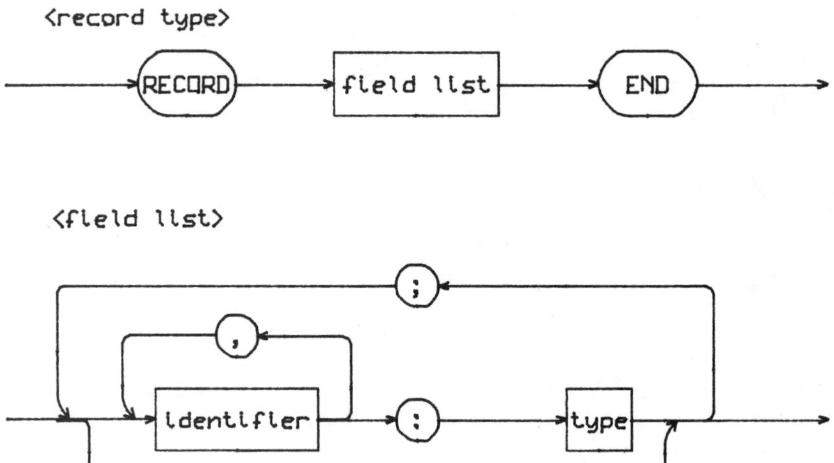

Figure 10-1

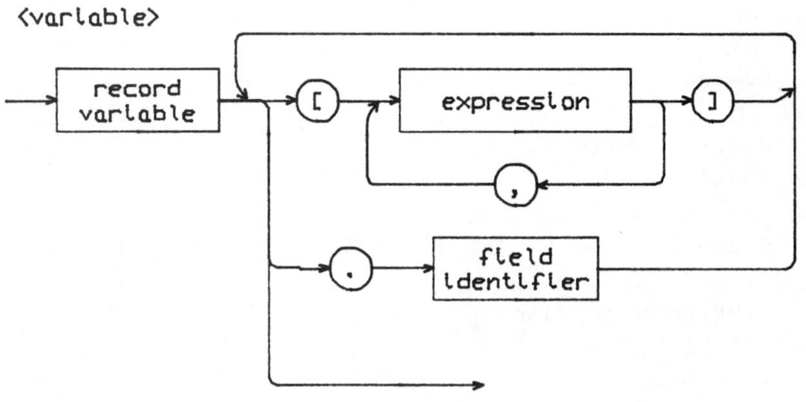

Figure 10-2

The RECORD <variable> STUDENT is declared to be composed of three "<u>fields</u>", called NAME, GRADE, and SEX. The three items of information will be stored in adjacent locations in the computer's memory. If you draw a diagram of this area of memory, it will appear to be a map containing several "fields", hence the terminology. Each of the fields is a <variable> in its own right, with the <type> being declared on the corresponding line of the record declaration. The field NAME is a string like any that we have been using throughout the book, except that in this case the declaration restricts the length of the STRING to 20 characters. The variable SEX is a Scalar with two possible values, FEMALE and MALE.

The most direct way to refer to a variable which is a field of a RECORD <variable> is to join the name of the record with the name of the field, separating the two with a period. For example:

```
STUDENT.GRADE
```

is used in lines 16, 20, 25 and 60 of the program. Since you can re-use the same field name within several different record variables in the same program, the compiler requires that you designate which record name is associated with a field <variable> name.

Figure 10-2 shows the syntax for <variable> expanded to include references to fields within a record. Note that NAME in the example shown here is an array (STRING <variable>), thus allowing one to refer to the N-th character in NAME by a reference such as:

```
STUDENT.NAME[N]
```

Since the syntax shown in Figure 10-1 shows that a field may be associated with any <type>, which includes now <record type>, it is apparent that you can:

a) declare a record containing another record as a field

b) declare an array, each of whose elements is a record

c) declare a record, containing a field which is an array of records

and so on. Data relationships in large programs can sometimes get quite complex. This syntax for record declarations is quite general, and allows for a very large variety of data relationships within record structures. As the declaration of the record STUDENT shows, the relationships are <u>tree</u> structured, i.e. <u>hierarchic</u>, just as are the relationships in a structure diagram for a program, or in the equivalent structure table.

The CLASSDATA program accepts three items of data, prompting for each, as shown in the upper part of the page illustrating the display associated with this program. After accumulating the three items of data in the associated fields of the record STUDENT, the procedure ACCUMULATE confirms the input with a single line containing all three data items. Once again, we have avoided cluttering the program with logical steps to make the program less prone to abnormal termination caused by errors in typing the GRADE or M/F code. At the end of input, signalled by the <ETX> in line 38 of the display, the procedure PUTRESULTS prints a summary table showing the average grades for the two sexes, and the number of students in each sex.

4. The WITH Statement

The work of writing out a program containing RECORD <variable>'s can be simplified considerably by the use of the WITH statement of PASCAL. Associated syntax is shown in Figure 10-3 in a form slightly more explicit than the form shown in Appendix E.

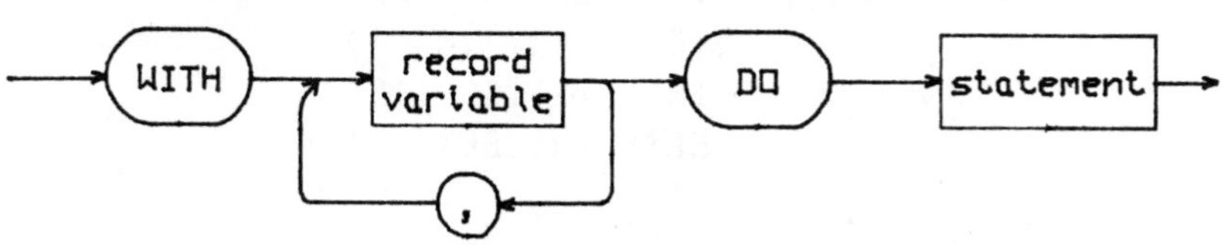

Figure 10-3

Here is how the procedure ACCUMULATE can appear, making use of the WITH statement:

```
PROCEDURE ACCUMULATE;
BEGIN
  WITH STUDENT DO
    BEGIN
      IF SEX=FEMALE THEN
      BEGIN
        FSUM:=FSUM+GRADE;
        FCNT:=FCNT+1;
      END ELSE
      BEGIN
        MSUM:=MSUM+GRADE;
        MCNT:=MCNT+1;
      END;
      WRITELN;
      WRITE(NAME,' ':20-LENGTH(NAME),
                 ' ',GRADE:3:1,'  ');
      IF SEX=FEMALE THEN WRITELN('F')
                    ELSE WRITELN('M');
    END (*WITH*);
  WRITELN;
END (*ACCUMULATE*);
```

Compare this version of the procedure with the original version included in the program CLASSDATA. Notice that references to the three fields NAME, GRADE and SEX of the STUDENT record no longer need to include the explicit reference to STUDENT as a prefix. Instead, the phrase "WITH STUDENT DO" serves as a prefix including all of the subsequent statement, which in this case is compound (BEGIN ... END). The effect is logically equivalent to placing 'STUDENT.' in front of every occurrence of a field identifier associated with STUDENT within the statement controlled by the WITH clause. Variable references not declared to be associated with STUDENT are not affected in this way.

5. Sample Program STURECORD

This program is provided mainly to illustrate the use of TYPE declarations in connection with RECORD <type>'s. The program, as printed, performs the very simple actions involved in reading, repeatedly, the names of people in last name first order, then confirming the complete name in normal order. The declared <type> ADDRESS is not actively used in the program as shown. It has been provided in preparation for one of the exercises in this chapter.

Notice that you can use a previously defined <type> as part of the definition of another <type>. For example the new <type> ALFA is used in defining the <type>'s NAME, and ADDRESS. Both ADDRESS and NAME are used in defining STUREC. You could continue to declare additional new <type>'s, using earlier declared <type>'s in this manner. However recursive <type> declarations are not allowed.

The nested record declarations shown in this sample program have the advantage that they simplify the writing of complex data structures. They also allow the compiler to perform more effective <type> checking as described in Chapter 9. A disadvantage is that references to the fields within a nested record structure get more complex. For example:

```
STUTABLE[I].STUNAME.FIRSTNAME[3]
```

is a reference to the 3rd character in the FIRSTNAME field of the STUNAME field within the I-th element of the array STUTABLE. Clearly, you would get very tired having to refer to this long sequence of identifiers every time you wanted to use a character in FIRSTNAME. The best way out of this problem is to use the WITH statement, as illustrated in lines 49 thru 51 of the sample program.

```
PROGRAM STURECORD;
CONST ARRAYROWS=10;

TYPE ALFA=STRING[20];
  NAME=
    RECORD
      LASTNAME: ALFA;
      FIRSTNAME: ALFA;
      MIDDLEINIT:CHAR
    END;
  ADDRESS=
    RECORD
      STREETADDR: ALFA;
      CITY: ALFA;
      STATECODE: PACKED ARRAY[1..2] OF CHAR;
      ZIPCODE: INTEGER
    END (*ADDRESS*);
  STUREC=
    RECORD
      STUNAME: NAME;
      STUADDR: ADDRESS;
      GRADE: INTEGER;
      SEX: (FEMALE, MALE)
    END;

VAR STUTABLE: ARRAY[1..ARRAYROWS] OF STUREC;
  I: INTEGER;

PROCEDURE GETDATA;
VAR NAMEREC: NAME;
BEGIN
  WITH NAMEREC DO
  BEGIN
    WRITE('LASTNAME:');
    READ(LASTNAME);
    WRITE('FIRSTNAME:');
    READ(FIRSTNAME);
    WRITE('MIDDLE INITIAL:');
    READLN(MIDDLEINIT);
  END (*WITH*);
  STUTABLE[I].STUNAME:=NAMEREC;
END (*GETDATA*);
```

```
BEGIN (*MAIN PROGRAM*)
  I:=1;
  WHILE NOT EOF AND (I<=ARRAYROWS) DO
  BEGIN
    GETDATA;
    WITH STUTABLE[I].STUNAME DO
      WRITELN(FIRSTNAME,' ',MIDDLEINIT,'. ',
                   LASTNAME);
    I:=I+1;
    WRITELN;
  END;
END.
```

```
Display associated with STURECORD program

LASTNAME:Brown
FIRSTNAME:Bill
MIDDLE INITIAL:W
Bill W. Brown

LASTNAME:Green
FIRSTNAME:John
MIDDLE INITIAL:L
John L. Green

LASTNAME:Jones
FIRSTNAME:Jenny
MIDDLE INITIAL:T
Jenny T. Jones

LASTNAME:<ETX>
```

By this time, you may also have recognized that copying the values stored in one record into another record of the same <type> could get complicated, at least if you had to make explicit reference to every field in each of the two records. PASCAL provides a simple way to carry out this conceptually simple task, as illustrated in line 41 of the sample program. In this case, both STUTABLE[I].STUNAME and NAMEREC have been declared to be of <type> NAME. Thus they are <u>compatible</u>, and the compiler arranges for the content of the entire record NAMEREC to be assigned to the I-th element of STUTABLE. The same kind of assignment operation is possible between any two <variables> of identical structured <type>. For example given the declaration:

```
VAR A,B: ARRAY [1..10] OF
           ARRAY [0..99] OF
             RECORD
               R: REAL;
               I: INTEGER;
               S: STRING[10]
             END;
```

it is legal to use the simple assignments:

```
A := B
```

or

```
B[6] := A[3]
```

Assignments are sometimes possible also between structured variables which are not of the same <type> but are nevertheless <u>compatible</u>. Details on what constitutes compatibility are more complex than bears description here. You might experiment in case of need, and allow the compiler to decide whether your structured variables are compatible.

Finally, notice the declaration

```
CONST ARRAYROWS = 10
```

in line 2 of the program. This is a "constant" declaration. Related syntax may be found in the complete syntax for <block> in Appendix E. A constant declaration associates an identifier with the constant value on the right side of the equal sign ('='). Thereafter, any appearance of the identifier within the text of the program will result in substitution of that value for the identifier. Since the same constant value appears in several places in the program, in this case referring to the index range of an array, it is possible to change all occurrences of that constant by simply changing the "CONST" declaration and re-compiling.

When working with large programs, or programs in which the same dimensional constant appears many times, one can save much debugging time by using the declared constant identifiers rather than explicit constants within the program. If a change needs to be made, it can be done very quickly by changing the CONST declaration. Also you can then use the editor's F(ind) command to locate all places in the program where the same constant is used with relative ease. Note that the syntax requires the CONST declarations to appear before TYPE declarations within a <block>. It is legal to declare a <constant> identifier to have an value which is an Integer, Real or String constant. Additional examples are given in sample programs later in this book.

Exercise 10.1:

One of the main occupations of people who work full time as programmers is the modification of programs that have already been written and used for some time. This exercise requires that you modify the program STURECORD in the following ways:

a) Add a facility to read the student's address, including values for all four fields in the declaration of ADDRESS.

b) Add a facility to "capture" values of a GRADE and the student's SEX.

c) Add a facility allowing a record previously entered into a particular element of STUTABLE to be modified by changing any selected field. This requires allowing the user to indicate which element needs to be changed by giving the (index) number of that element.

d) Add a procedure to substitute for lines 50 and 51 in the printed version of the program, adding neatly formatted display output for all fields in a record of <type> STUREC. Use this procedure to echo confirmation of the new value of a record, as in lines 6, 11, and 16 of the simpler display from STURECORD as printed. The procedure should also be used to allow verification of the current status of a record before it is modified, as in step (c).

Records of this type would normally be stored on a disk for later processing any number of times desired. Unfortunately, the complications associated with saving files on disks are slightly beyond the scope of this book.

Exercise 10.2:

Like most (perverse) supervisors, we now want you to modify the program STURECORD in a different way. Change it so that the procedure GETDATA will store the State abbreviation and Zipcode of the student's address in the same record in STUTABLE as the name. Alter the declarations so that Zipcode values greater than 32767 can be stored without terminating the program abnormally on a microcomputer with 16-bit words.

Exercise 10.3:

Use STURECORD as the starting basis for a program which will be used to compute the final term grade of a student for a course involving 8 quizzes, a midterm exam, and a final exam. For simplicity, all ten exams should be given equal weight in the final term grade. Thus it will be necessary only to add all of the quiz and exam grades, then divide by 10. Eliminate all references in the printed STURECORD program to address information and sex. Arrange the program to store all grade values in the array STUTABLE, as modified, to allow possible modifications to erroneous input. Compute the term average grade, and display with the student's name, when the program terminates.

Chapter 11

THE GOTO STATEMENT

1. Goals

The GOTO statement is available to cause program control to jump explicitly from one place in a program to another labelled location. In general, it should be used only as a way to alter program flow in unusual circumstances, and then only within a <block> when the regular PASCAL control constructs are awkward to use.

1a. Learn the mechanics of using the GOTO statement, including declarations of labels, and placement of labels among the executable statements.

1b. Learn to use the EXIT built-in procedure, which provides a means of executing a restricted GOTO out of a <block> back to a calling <block>.

1c. Learn to use GOTO constructs to imitate the main control statements of PASCAL, as preparation for working with a programming language which lacks those constructs.

2. Background

In its normal sequence of processing, a digital computer performs one instruction and then moves to the next following instruction stored in memory. All digital computers also provide a means whereby the program control can "jump" from one location to another in the sequence of machine language instructions. Each of the major programming languages has a "GO TO" statement (sometimes called simply "GO" or, as in PASCAL, "GOTO") whereby you can cause the compiler to generate a jump instruction explicitly.

After many thousands of people had been writing programs in the earlier programming languages (particularly FORTRAN and COBOL), computer scientists began to appreciate that undisciplined use of the GOTO statement leads to program errors that are difficult to uncover. PASCAL was designed with the idea in mind to avoid the sources of program errors that have commonly arisen from use of the earlier languages. Use of the GOTO statement is de-emphasized in PASCAL, but not totally eliminated. Situations do arise in which a program written completely without the GOTO can be awkward and inefficient compared with a similar program containing only one or two GOTO statements. Hence PASCAL has a GOTO statement, though it is in a form that discourages more than occasional use.

While the general principles of structured programming are now widely accepted in computer science, certain issues are still considered to be controversial. The degree to which one should be allowed to use the GOTO statement is one of the most controversial topics in this field. The version of PASCAL implemented in our software system allows you to jump from one location to another within the same <block> using the GOTO statement. The GOTO cannot be used to jump from one <block> to another in this version of PASCAL.

In larger programs, containing many procedures, we have found it particularly awkward not to have the ability to jump out of a procedure when handling certain exceptional conditions. The need to do this is frequently encountered when writing executive programs or large interactive programs. To cope with those problems, we have implemented the built-in procedure EXIT, which is a very specific and limited form of the GOTO statement. As we will show in more detail in the following sections, the EXIT procedure allows you to terminate the execution of any procedure that is currently active. This has the effect of terminating all of the procedures that were *called* by that procedure, including the one containing the EXIT statement.

The control statements of PASCAL (REPEAT, WHILE, FOR, IF, CASE) can be understood as carefully limited uses of the jump operation of the computer hardware. In effect, they are "safe" uses of the GOTO. Once one understands the uses of the control statements of PASCAL, it is possible to achieve very similar effects in any of the popular programming languages. Since these languages do not generally have the same control statements as PASCAL, it is necessary to use the GOTO in those languages to imitate PASCAL. Various people find it most effective to design their algorithms using "program" statements written in PASCAL or in a similar language. Then they translate the PASCAL into the popular language that is most convenient on the computer they use to do their work. Though this scheme seems awkward and round-about, it has proven to be very effective in helping these people to reduce the errors in their programs, and hence to reduce debugging time.

3. Mechanics of the GOTO

To use a GOTO statement, three separate items must be included in your PASCAL program. In addition, a pseudo-comment must be included as a control message to the compiler telling it that it should allow use of the GOTO statement. The items involved are as follows:

a) Declaration of a label

A "label", if present, must be the first thing declared in a <block>. See the syntax for <block> in Appendix E. In PASCAL, a label is an <unsigned integer> containing no more than 4 decimal digits. More than one label may be declared in the LABEL declaration portion of a <block>, but this should rarely be necessary.

b) Labelled statements

Once an <unsigned integer> has been declared to represent a label, it may be used to mark any single <statement> in a <block>. The same label may not be used in this way more than once in a <block>. Otherwise the meaning of any GOTO statement referring to that label would be ambiguous. Syntax for this usage of a label is given at the top of the syntax for <statement> in Appendix E. The label is mentioned there as <unsigned integer>. One marks a <statement> in this way if it is intended to use a GOTO statement elsewhere in the <block> to jump to the beginning of the marked statement. Though the syntax does not require it, we believe it important to place all labels at the left hand margin of a program, thereby making them clearly visible at a glance.

c) The GOTO statement itself

Syntax for the GOTO statement is given in the syntax diagram for <statement> in Appendix E. For example:

```
GOTO 5
```

means that program control should jump to the beginning of the <statement> marked with the label "5:". Note carefully, that though there is a superficial similarity between a label used in this way, and the selectors or markers used in a CASE statement, the two are quite different.

d) Compiler directive G+

By default our PASCAL compiler disallows the use of GOTO statements. This control can be over-ridden by using a comment line reading:

```
(*$G+*)
```

at the beginning of the program. The dollar sign as the first character after "(*" tells the compiler that the content of the comment is a directive to the compiler itself, not part of the PASCAL program proper. Copy this "pseudo-comment" exactly as shown here to turn on the ability to use GOTO statements. Most compilers have some means for you to give instructions on how they should do their work. The "dollar sign comment" convention used with our PASCAL compiler is similar to the conventions used on some other compilers, but there are no industry wide standards for such instructions.

4. Sample Program GOTODEMO

The output displayed by this program should be the same as the output of the program BOOLDEMO of Chapter 3 Section 9.

This program is illustrated in the form of a structure diagram in Figure 11-1. We have added two new box shapes to the structure diagram to express what is happening in the use of the GOTO statements. The octagonal box (like a highway STOP sign) is for the GOTO (and for EXIT). The small circle will be used for a label.

The basic algorithm followed by this program is the same as the algorithm used in the program BOOLDEMO of Chapter 3. We have modified that program, not so much to make it better, but simply to illustrate the use of the GOTO statement. If the example seems a little strained, then perhaps you now appreciate why the GOTO statement is of limited use in PASCAL.

In using the GOTO statement, you should refer back to the structure diagram representation of your algorithm. A "safe" use of the GOTO is one having the effect that you terminate processing of some node of the structure diagram which is located along the direct path from the root node to the node where the GOTO is located. In the program GOTODEMO, the GOTO in node 2b1a results in termination of node 2b, and all of the nodes branching from 2b (if there were any others). Since processing continues at the same level as 2b (the next node on the right), the label (1:) is located effectively between nodes 2b and 2c.

The GOTO in node 2a1 (line 12) has the effect of jumping out of node 2, which is the entire REPEAT statement starting on line 11. In this case there is no <statement> following the REPEAT statement. Hence, the label must be shown on the structure diagram as if it were on a phantom node of the structure.

```
(*$G+*)
PROGRAM GOTODEMO;
LABEL 1,2;
VAR NAME,S:STRING;
  LN,LS,KS:INTEGER;
BEGIN
  S:='ALICE,BARBARA,CHARLIE,DORIS,ED,FRANK  ';
  LS:=LENGTH(S);
  KS:=1;
  LN:=1;
  REPEAT
    IF S[KS]=' ' THEN GOTO 2;
    FOR KS:=KS TO LS DO (*node 2b*)
      IF S[KS] IN [',',' '] THEN GOTO 1;
1:  NAME:=COPY(S,LN,KS-LN); (*node 2c*)
    WRITELN(NAME);
    KS:=KS+1;
    LN:=KS;
  UNTIL KS>LS;
2:
END.
```

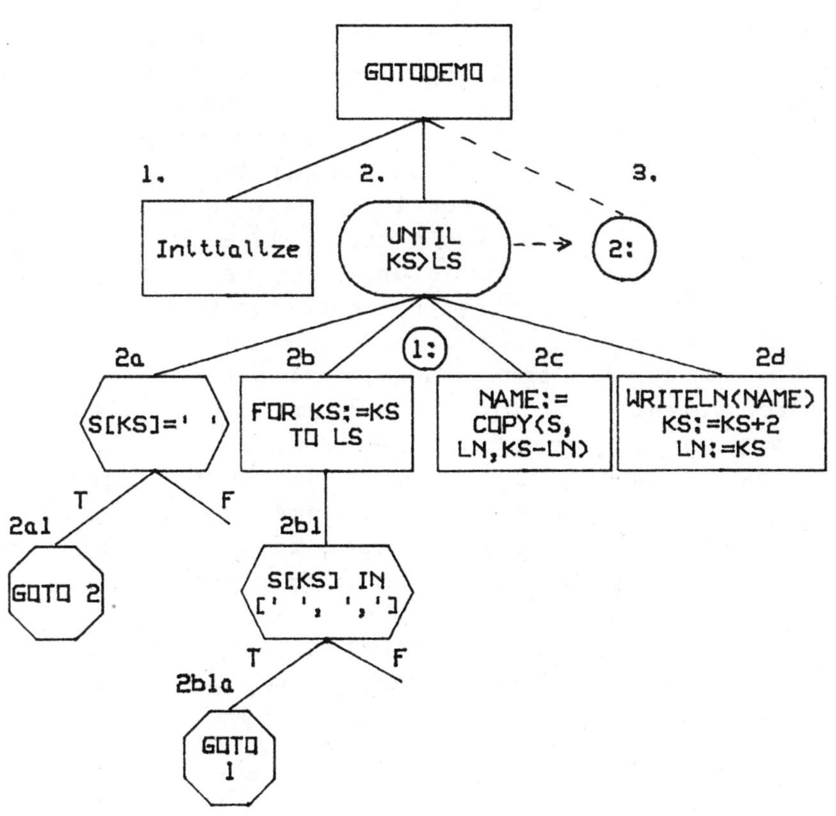
GOTODEMO
1.
2.
3.
Initialize
UNTIL
KS>LS
2:
1:
2a
2b
2c
2d
S[KS]=' '
FOR KS:=KS
TO LS
NAME:=
COPY(S,
LN,KS-LN)
WRITELN(NAME)
KS:=KS+2
LN:=KS
T
F
2a1
GOTO 2
2b1
S[KS] IN
[' ', ',']
T
F
2b1a
GOTO
1

Figure 11-1

5. EXIT

Our version of the EXIT built-in procedure extends the GOTO statement of PASCAL in a specially controlled and limited way. The one parameter of the EXIT procedure is the <identifier> of a procedure that is currently activated. To explain what we mean by "activated", it is necessary again to refer to the structure diagram representation of an algorithm. For purposes of making the diagram useful as a way to describe algorithms, we have chosen to separate the portion of a structure diagram representing a procedure or function from the portion representing the main program. However it is easy to imagine how the structure diagram would appear if each invocation of a procedure (or function) were replaced by the entire structure diagram representing that procedure at the place of invocation. Of course this would make the actual diagram large and unwieldy. The EXIT is equivalent to a GOTO which terminates processing of any one of the procedure invocation nodes along the path from the root node to the point where the GOTO occurs. Since the procedure is known by its <identifier>, there is no need to use a label to inform the compiler where the program should jump.

To explain this concept further, we refer to the sample program EXITDEMO. Here is what this program should display:

```
INPUT TO P:First line
LEAVE P
LEAVE Q
LEAVE R

INPUT TO P:# Ringer
LEAVE R

INPUT TO P:Second line<ETX>
LEAVE P
LEAVE Q
LEAVE R
```

```
PROGRAM EXITDEMO;
VAR S:STRING;
  CN: INTEGER;

PROCEDURE Q; FORWARD;

PROCEDURE P;
BEGIN
  WRITE('INPUT TO P:');
  READ(S);
  IF S[1]='#' THEN EXIT(Q);
  WRITELN('LEAVE P');
END (*P*);

PROCEDURE Q;
BEGIN
  P;
  WRITELN('LEAVE Q');
END (*Q*);

PROCEDURE R;
BEGIN
  IF CN <= 10 THEN Q;
  WRITELN('LEAVE R');
END (*R*);

BEGIN (*MAIN PROGRAM*)
  CN:=0;
  WHILE NOT EOF DO
  BEGIN
    CN:=CN+1;
    R;
    WRITELN;
  END;
END.
```

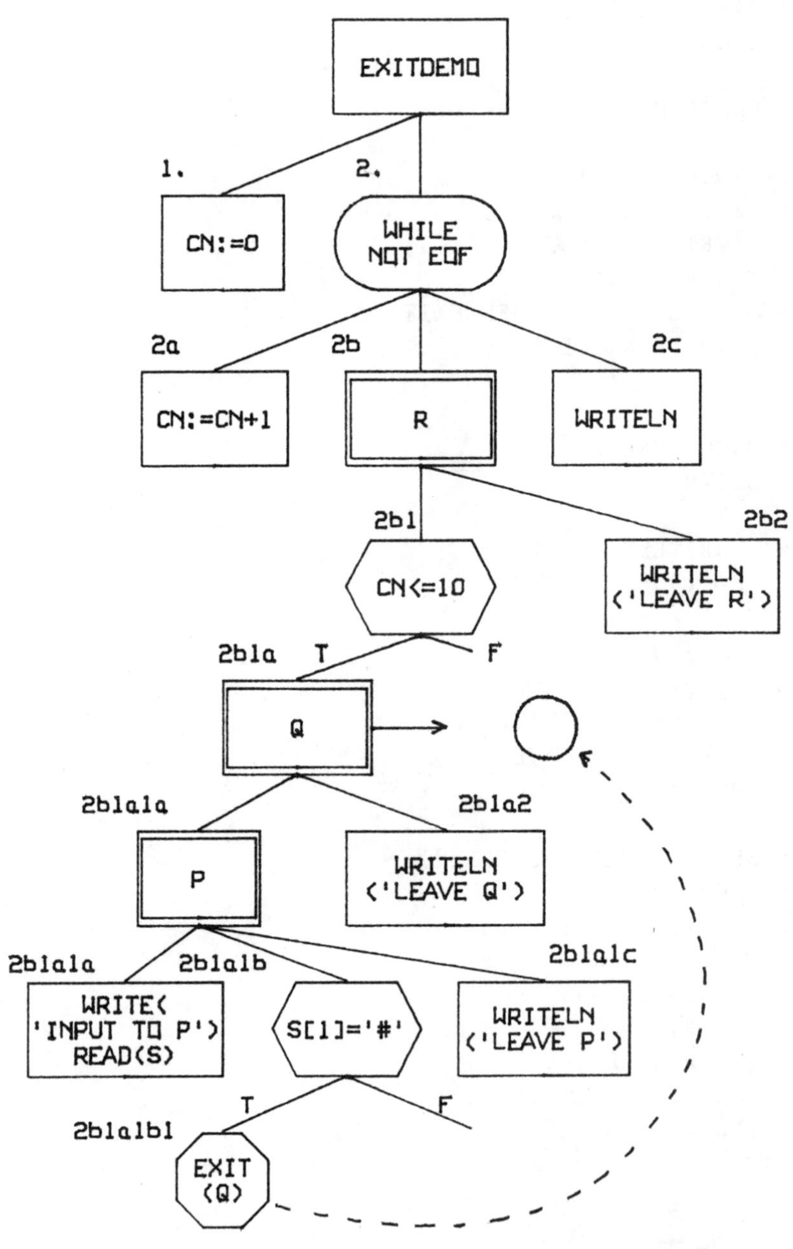
EXITDEMO
1.
2.
CN:=0
WHILE
NOT EOF
2a
2b
2c
CN:=CN+1
R
WRITELN
2b1
2b2
CN<=10
WRITELN
('LEAVE R')
2b1a
T
F
Q
2b1a1a
2b1a2
P
WRITELN
('LEAVE Q')
2b1a1a
2b1a1b
2b1a1c
WRITE(
'INPUT TO P')
READ(S)
S[1]='#'
WRITELN
('LEAVE P')
T
F
2b1a1b1
EXIT
(Q)

Figure 11-2

This program is meant to suggest the kind of action that might be taken by a program which processes input data in the case where an invalid data value is detected. The structure diagram is given in modified form in Figure 11-2. This diagram shows the separate procedures as if they had been written into the main program in the order they are called. The EXIT(Q) in line 11 causes the procedure P to be terminated, followed by the termination of Q. Processing continues normally on the line following the call to Q, i.e. on line 24. Thus the only line of output following the input "# Ringer" is "LEAVE R" at the end of the procedure R. In the two cases where EXIT is not called, processing proceeds normally through the terminations of procedures P and Q.

Notice that the action of the EXIT(Q) statement is equivalent to having a GOTO statement in node 2b1a1b1 which is capable of jumping to a label placed immediately to the right of node 2b1a. This is suggested by the dotted line in Figure 11-2.

Notice also that we found it necessary to declare the procedure Q FORWARD in order that the EXIT could operate properly inside procedure P. Had this not been done, the reference to Q as a parameter of EXIT would have resulted in a syntax error message for an undeclared identifier. Q is allowed as a parameter of EXIT, in spite of the general limitation that our version of PASCAL cannot handle procedure names as parameters, because EXIT is a built-in procedure which is not subject to that limitation.

6. Using GOTO to Imitate PASCAL Control Statements

If, after finishing this book, you end up having to use one of the older programming languages that does not have PASCAL's control statements, you can obtain a very similar effect using GOTO statements. Here are examples for all four of the principal control statements of PASCAL:

```
  IF BOOL
    THEN S1
    ELSE S2;
```

becomes:

```
      IF NOT BOOL THEN GOTO 1;
        S1;
      GOTO 2;
  1:    S2;
  2:      etc. etc.
```

or:

```
      IF BOOL THEN GOTO 1;
        S2;
      GOTO 2;
  1:    S1;
  2:      etc. etc.
```

where S1 and S2 represent any statement or <u>group</u> of statements that you might wish to use. Note the use of indentation to preserve a visual effect of program structure relationships equivalent to our use of indentation in conventional PASCAL programs. The indentation can be used to give the visual effect that we have used with compound statements, since most languages that would require the use of GOTO to simulate control statements do not have any equivalent of the PASCAL compound statement. Continuing with the examples:

```
  WHILE I <= 10 DO
  BEGIN
    PROCA;
    I := I+1;
  END;
```

becomes:

```
1:  IF I > 10 THEN GOTO 2;
      PROCA;
      I := I+1;
    GOTO 1;
2:    etc. etc.
```

similarly:

```
REPEAT
  PROCB;
  I := I+1;
UNTIL I > 10;
```

becomes:

```
1:  (*a comment would show structure here*)
      PROCB;
      I := I+1;
    IF I <= 10 THEN GOTO 1;
      etc. etc.
```

Many people who use this method to write structured programs in FORTRAN find it helpful to add comments to the program stating explicitly the PASCAL control construct that is being simulated. Finally:

```
FOR CV := SV TO LV DO
BEGIN
  PROCA;
  X := Y*Z;
END;
```

becomes:

```
    CV := SV;
1:  IF CV > LV THEN GOTO 2;
      PROCA;
      X := Y*Z;
      CV := CV+1;
    GOTO 1;
2:    etc. etc.
```

If any of these conversions are not obvious to you, we suggest that you review the flow charts shown in Chapter 3 for each of the four control constructs IF, WHILE, REPEAT and FOR. In the last three examples, PROCA and PROCB are assumed to be procedures declared elsewhere in the program.

Exercise 11.1:

Because of the need to use many nested IF statements, the program DATECHECK of Chapter 7 Section 11 is somewhat awkward to read and hence subject to possible programming errors. Rewrite DATECHECK, and debug your resulting program, using GOTO statements to terminate the processing of a date that is found to be in error, allowing the program to continue again in the main loop. The program should otherwise operate in exactly the same way as DATECHECK, given identical input data.

For this conversion, you need only to use forward pointing GOTO statements, i.e. ones pointing to labels located later on in the program. Whenever possible, if you have to use GOTO statements at all, you should at least try to make them point forward in the program. This is equivalent to the structure diagram rule described earlier in this chapter.

Exercise 11.2:

Though EXIT is used properly in the sample program EXITTWO, it is really not necessary. Implement the program on your computer, and test it with the following input data lines:

```
PROGRAM TEST; VAR X,Y: INTEGER; BEGIN X:=1;
Y:=2; WRITELN(X+Y); END.
```

```
PROGRAM EXITTWO;
VAR CH: CHAR;
  LN: INTEGER;
  S: STRING;

PROCEDURE SCAN;
VAR C: CHAR;
  I:INTEGER;
BEGIN
  I:=1;
  WHILE I<=LENGTH(S) DO
    BEGIN
      C:=S[I];
      I:=I+1;
      IF C IN [';','.'] THEN
        BEGIN
          WRITELN(C);
          IF (C='.') OR (I>LENGTH(S)) THEN
            EXIT(SCAN);
          LN:=LN+1;
          WRITE(LN:3,': ');
        END ELSE
          WRITE(C);
    END (*WHILE*);
END (*SCAN*);

BEGIN (*MAIN PROGRAM*)
  LN:=1;
  WHILE NOT EOF DO
    BEGIN
      WRITELN('INPUT LINE:');
      READ(S);
      WRITE(LN:3,': ');
      SCAN;
      LN:=LN+1;
      WRITELN;
    END;
END.
```

noting the displayed output that the program generates. Having done this, modify the program to remove the reference to EXIT, yet leaving the program logic otherwise unchanged. Note: You can do this by changing two program lines, and adding no more than four program lines!

Exercise 11.3:

Some programming languages have no equivalent of the CASE statement, and no equivalent of the two-way IF ... THEN ... ELSE ... statement of PASCAL. Rewrite the program CASEDEMO to produce the same effect using the GOTO and one-way IF statements. Test the program in both the original and the rewritten forms using the following lines for input data, making sure that you get the same results:

```
+ 100 200
*  32  64
-  10  20
/  50 150
```

Exercise 11.4:

Rewrite the program DENOISE of Chapter 7 Section 9 to eliminate the use of REPEAT, FOR and CASE statements. The modified program should not use a WHILE statement either. Test the rewritten program to make sure that it produces the same results as printed in the book for DENOISE.

Exercise 11.5:

Rewrite the program DEVOWEL of Chapter 7 Section 10 to eliminate the use of WHILE statements. The modified program should not include REPEAT or FOR statements. Test the rewritten program to make sure that it produces the same output as printed in the book for DEVOWEL.

```
PROGRAM CASEDEMO;
VAR CH:CHAR;
  X,Y:INTEGER;
  R:REAL;
BEGIN
  WRITELN('CASEDEMO');
  WHILE NOT EOF DO
  BEGIN
    WRITE('+ - * or / :');
    READ(CH);
    WRITE('  X:');
    READ(X);
    WRITE('  Y:');
    READ(Y);
    CASE CH OF
      '+': R:=X+Y;
      '-': R:=X-Y;
      '*': R:=X*Y;
      '/': R:=X/Y
    END (*CASE*);
    READ(CH); (*discard blank after READ(Y)*)
    WRITELN;
    WRITELN(X,' ',CH,' ',Y,' = ',R);
    WRITELN;
  END (*WHILE*);
END.
```

Chapter 12

FORMATTED OUTPUT

1. Goals

Gain problem solving experience by studying and understanding the sample programs given in this chapter, and by working out the exercises.

1a. Learn to place characters where you want them on a display screen or printed page using program logic.

1b. If you are using a bit-map display screen, revise the examples given in this chapter to "plot" with higher resolution.

2. Background

Up to this point each chapter has presented either basic programming tools, or concepts about applying program structure to problem solving. In this chapter, and all of the remaining chapters, we present examples of programs worked out to solve simple but typical problems. If you have had to struggle to reach this point, you now have a reasonably complete understanding about how problems are solved using computers, but you are likely to find it difficult to use computers for solving problems of more than simple complexity. If you reached this point with relatively little difficulty, you should press on through the remaining chapters. If these too come easily, you would be well advised to pursue some aspect of computers and/or computer programming in greater depth.

In this chapter, we give several examples of the formatting of program output. For most programmers, the formatting of output is a mundane but necessary activity. The methods used for presenting images on a graphic display device based on the "bit-map" principle (see Figure 0-1) are very similar to those used for placing characters on a display or printed page for many other purposes. We concentrate more on formatting characters in this chapter because your later programming activities are more likely to involve the display or printing of characters than of graphics.

Several of the major programming languages use an output editing mechanism known as a "format". Formats have traditionally provided one of the major sources of confusion for students in beginning programming courses. A format is basically a program for converting items of data stored internally in the computer into strings of characters for output to a device such as a printer or CRT (or for handling the reverse operation on reading). The language used to write formats amounts to a way to call special built-in procedures which perform the data conversion. Unfortunately, the syntax used in the major programming languages for formats is entirely different from the syntax used for other parts of the programs. In effect, the student is forced to learn two languages at once in order to have any reasonable control of the way output information appears on a display screen or printed page.

The output format mechanisms of PASCAL are very simple, and you are already familiar with most of them. One detriment of this is that PASCAL does not have the wide variety of output formats that are available in the other languages. For example, PASCAL has no built-in mechanism for printing numbers in the Octal (base 8) or Hexadecimal (base 16) numbering systems, although these are frequently needed in computing work. Nor does our version of PASCAL give you complete control over the printing format of a REAL number. In spite of the simplcity, the ideas embodied in program steps to WRITE out to the printer or display device can be translated easily into the special formats required by the other languages.

You have already seen how one can display several independent items of data on the same line of output, merely by calling WRITE with appropriate parameters a number of times. The principal new idea presented in this chapter revolves around the use of an array containing one cell for each character position on the display screen or printed page. This allows data to be positioned for output whenever tne flow of the program makes this convenient. It avoids the problem created by the fact that printers typically accept data only in a strict left-to-right, top-to-bottom order on a line by line basis.

3. Sample Program FORMATDEMO

This program expands on the demonstrations given in Chapter 8 on use of the field-width specification in WRITE statements as a means of controlling the number of columns to be output. In general, one has to keep track of the number of columns of information displayed on each line if lines displayed by different statements are to be mixed together in a way that pleases the eye. To accomplish this, one can control the number of blank spaces displayed to the left of an operand, and one can control the number of columns occupied by the information itself if that makes sense.

Lines 11 through 14 of this program illustrate this point for displaying Real numbers. If no field width at all is specified, then the default format uses as many columns as are needed to display the number in its full accuracy. In line 3 of the display listing, one column to the left of "14" has been left blank, since that column would be used for the minus sign ('-') if the number were negative. If a single field width is given, as in lines 12 and 13 of the program, then one of two possible actions occurs. If the stated field width is less than needed to represent the number with full accuracy, then the larger number of columns needed for that purpose will be used, thus over-riding the field width specification. If the specification calls for more columns than needed for full accuracy, then the additional columns are left blank to the left of the displayed number (line 5 of the display listing).

One can specify that fewer digits to the right of the decimal point will be displayed. This is shown in line 14 of the program. Line 6 of the display shows that the second field width specification of 3 has limited the number of decimal places displayed.

```
PROGRAM FORMATDEMO;
VAR R:REAL;
    I:INTEGER;
    CH:CHAR;
    A:PACKED ARRAY[1..10] OF CHAR;
BEGIN
  R:=100/7;
  I:=16384;
  CH:='*';
  A:='FORMATDEMO';
  WRITELN('(REAL DEFAULT)',R);
  WRITELN('(R:6)',R:6);
  WRITELN('(R:16)',R:16);
  WRITELN('(R:10:3)',R:10:3);
  WRITELN;
  (*integers now*)
  WRITELN('(INTEGER DEFAULT)',I);
  WRITELN('(I:3)',I:3);
  WRITELN('(I:5)',I:5);
  WRITELN('(I:7)',I:7);
  WRITELN;
  (*single character*)
  WRITELN('(CHAR DEFAULT)',CH);
  WRITELN('(CH:5)',CH:5);
  WRITELN;
  (*packed array of characters*)
  WRITELN('(DEFAULT FOR CHAR ARRAY)',A);
  WRITELN('(A:5)',A:5);
  WRITELN('(A:15)',A:15);
END.
```

```
Display associated with FORMATDEMO program

(REAL DEFAULT) 14.28571
(R:6) 14.28571
(R:16)        14.28571
(R:10:3)    14.286

(INTEGER DEFAULT)16384
(I:3)16384
(I:5)16384
(I:7)  16384

(CHAR DEFAULT)*
(CH:5)    *

(DEFAULT FOR CHAR ARRAY)FORMATDEMO
(A:5)FORMA
(A:15)     FORMATDEMO
```

For integer operands, the rules are similar to those for real operands. Unless needed, no column is reserved for a minus sign. The number of columns used is either the minimum needed to display the integer value, or a larger number of columns. A field width specification too small to handle all the digits in the integer will result in the field width specification being ignored. A larger field width than the minimum needed will result in additional blanks being displayed on the left of the number itself.

For character operands, the default is to display just one column. If the specified field width is greater than 1, then extra blanks are inserted on the left.

For strings, i.e. packed arrays of CHAR operands, the default is to display the number of characters declared to be in the array. This is to be distinguished from the default for displaying the value contained in a STRING variable. If a STRING variable S is displayed with no field width specification, then the default is to display LENGTH(S) characters. As the display listing for FORMATDEMO shows, a field width specification of fewer columns than the number of characters contained in the array will result in the smaller number of columns being displayed. A field width greater than the content of the array will insert blanks on the left as with the other operand <type>'s.

4. <u>Sample Program CHARPLOT</u>

The displayed output associated with CHARPLOT is shown in Figure 12-1. This program is presented mainly to illustrate the use of the two-dimensional array PAGE as a temporary holding place for characters that will eventually be displayed line by line. This allows the program to "write" characters anywhere on the page in whatever order makes the program run most easily. Without this temporary

```
PROGRAM CHARPLOT;
CONST
  WIDTH=25;
  HEIGHT=11;
TYPE
  DX=-WIDTH .. +WIDTH;
  DY=-HEIGHT .. +HEIGHT;VAR
  PAGE:ARRAY[DY] OF
         PACKED ARRAY[DX] OF CHAR;
  X: DX;
  Y: DY;

PROCEDURE RECT(H,W:INTEGER; CH:CHAR);
VAR I,XMIN,XMAX:DX;
    J,YMIN,YMAX:DY;
BEGIN
  XMAX:=W; YMAX:=H;
  XMIN:=-W; YMIN:=-H;
  (*mark top and bottom of rectangle*)
  FOR I:=XMIN TO XMAX DO
  BEGIN
    PAGE[YMAX,I]:=CH;
    PAGE[YMIN,I]:=CH;
  END;
  (*mark sides*)
  FOR J:=YMIN TO YMAX DO
  BEGIN
    PAGE[J,XMAX]:=CH;
    PAGE[J,XMIN]:=CH;
  END;
END (*RECT*);

PROCEDURE BLANKPAGE;
VAR I:DX;
    J:DY;
BEGIN
  FOR J:=-HEIGHT TO HEIGHT DO
    FOR I:=-WIDTH TO WIDTH DO PAGE[J,I]:=' ';
END (*BLANKPAGE*);

BEGIN (*MAIN PROGRAM*)
  BLANKPAGE;
  RECT(11,10,'*');
  RECT(5,25,'#');
  RECT(8,15,'&');
  FOR Y:=HEIGHT DOWNTO -HEIGHT DO
  BEGIN
    FOR X:=-WIDTH TO WIDTH DO WRITE(PAGE[Y,X]);
    IF Y > -HEIGHT THEN WRITELN;
  END;
END.
```

```
               *********************
               *                   *
(a)            *                   *
          &&&&&&&&&&&&&&&&&&&&&&&&&&&&&&&
          &    *                   *    &
          &    *                   *    &
##########&#############################&##########
#         &    *                   *    &         #
#         &    *                   *    &         #
#         &    *                   *    &         #
#         &    *                   *    &         #
#         &    *                   *    &         #
#         &    *                   *    &         #
#         &    *                   *    &         #
#         &    *                   *    &         #
#         &    *                   *    &         #
##########&#############################&##########
          &    *                   *    &
          &    *                   *    &
          &&&&&&&&&&&&&&&&&&&&&&&&&&&&&&&
               *                   *
               *                   *
               *********************
```

Fig 12-1. Display associated with CHARPLOT program

```
      ***************         ###############
(b)   *             *         #             #
      *             *         #             #
      *             *         #             #
      *             *         #             #
      *             *         #             #
      *             *         #             #
      *             *         #             #
      ***************         ###############

      @@@@@@@@@@@@@@@         &&&&&&&&&&&&&&&
      @             @         &             &
      @             @         &             &
      @             @         &             &
      @             @         &             &
      @             @         &             &
      @             @         &             &
      @             @         &             &
      @@@@@@@@@@@@@@@         &&&&&&&&&&&&&&&
```

storage, even as simple a pattern as the one shown would be very awkward to display on a line by line basis.

The program first deposits blank characters in all locations of the PAGE array. Thereafter, characters representing the figures to be displayed can be placed at any location in the array. Notice that the character '*' is replaced by both '#' and '&' which come later, while '#' is replaced by '&' where they coincide. As a last step, the content of the array PAGE is then displayed on a row by row basis.

In line 46, note that the first row displayed is at the top of the figure, and that displaying then proceeds downward, i.e. through PAGE in reverse order. Otherwise the figure displayed would be inverted. This is of no consequence for the symmetric figure displayed by this program, but could be of importance for displaying figures that do not have vertical symmetry.

Notice that the spacing between the displayed characters is wider vertically than it is horizontally. If the spacing were the same in both directions, then the figure plotted with the asterisks ('*') would appear to be nearly square. If the figure you want to "plot" with a conventional display screen or computer line printer should have equal horizontal and vertical scale factors, then you will have to multiply the horizontal displacements, or divide the vertical displacements, by an equalizing factor.

5. Sample Program CURVEPLOT

This program illustrates the use of the computer alphanumeric display screen, or of a line printer, for plotting crude graphs of computed functions. The function plotted by this program, as illustrated in Figure 12-2, will be recognized by mathematically inclined readers as the function Sin(x)/x. However,

```
PROGRAM CURVEPLOT;
CONST
  WIDTH=25; HEIGHT=22;
TYPE
  DX= -WIDTH..+WIDTH;
  DY= 0 .. HEIGHT;
  DATAVECT= ARRAY[DX] OF REAL;
VAR
  PAGE: ARRAY[DY] OF PACKED ARRAY[DX] OF CHAR;
  X:DX;
  Y:DY;
  F: DATAVECT;
  RX: REAL;
  YZERO: INTEGER;
PROCEDURE SCALE(VAR A:DATAVECT);
(*adjust data to fit within vertical scale of plot*)
VAR SFACTOR,DMIN,DMAX: REAL;
  I:DX;
BEGIN
  DMIN:=1.0E+30;
  DMAX:=-1.0E+30;
  FOR I:=-WIDTH TO WIDTH DO
  BEGIN
    IF A[I] < DMIN THEN DMIN:=A[I];
    IF A[I] > DMAX THEN DMAX:=A[I];
  END;
  IF DMAX<>DMIN THEN
    SFACTOR:=HEIGHT/(DMAX-DMIN);
  FOR I:= -WIDTH TO WIDTH DO
    A[I]:=(A[I] - DMIN)*SFACTOR;
  YZERO:=ROUND( -DMIN*SFACTOR);
END (*SCALE*);
PROCEDURE INIT;
BEGIN
  FOR Y:=0 TO HEIGHT DO
    FOR X:= -WIDTH TO WIDTH DO PAGE[Y,X]:=' ';
  (*vertical axis*)  FOR Y:=0 TO HEIGHT DO PAGE[Y,0]:='.';
END (*INIT*);
```

```
PROCEDURE XAXIS;
BEGIN
  IF YZERO IN [0..HEIGHT] THEN
    FOR X:= -WIDTH TO WIDTH DO
      PAGE[YZERO,X]:='.';
END (*XAXIS*);

PROCEDURE PLOT(VAR A:DATAVECT; CH:CHAR);
VAR J:DX;
BEGIN
  SCALE(A);
  FOR J:= -WIDTH TO WIDTH DO
    PAGE[ROUND(A[J]),J]:=CH;
END (*PLOT*);

BEGIN (*MAIN PROGRAM*)
  INIT;
  FOR X:= -WIDTH TO WIDTH DO
  BEGIN
    (*RX is X multiplied by arbitrary horiz scale*)
    RX:=X * 0.25;
    IF RX=0.0 THEN F[X]:=1.0 ELSE
      F[X]:=SIN(RX)/RX; (* function to plot into F*)
  END;
  PLOT(F,'*');
  XAXIS;
  (*print out results*)
  FOR Y:=HEIGHT DOWNTO 0 DO
  BEGIN
    FOR X:= -WIDTH TO WIDTH DO WRITE(PAGE[Y,X]);
    IF Y>0 THEN WRITELN;
  END;
END.
```

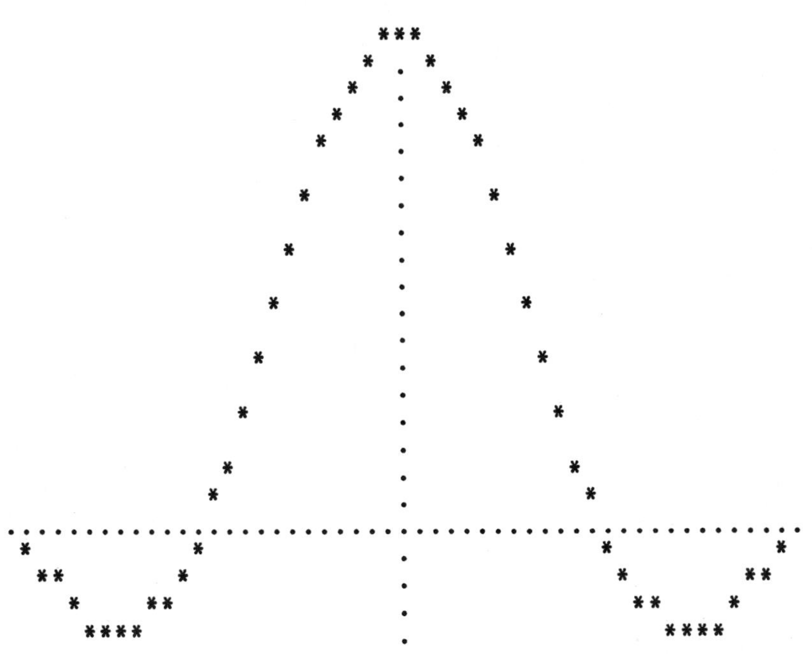

Figure 12-2. Display associated with CURVEPLOT program

knowledge of the built-in SIN function is not necessary to understand this program. The illustration has been obtained using the SIN function, but you could equally well have substituted any function of your own in line 64. In fact you could superimpose many such graphs on the same page or display, as long as the result was not too hard to read from the displayed graph.

The strategy followed here is similar to the strategy used in plotting geometric figures as in the previous section. It is necessary to round the Real number values of the function, which represent vertical displacement, in order to select a specific character position. In the horizontal direction, one is usually free to establish the value of the independent variable X before calling the function to compute the corresponding value of Y. As may be seen in the main program, it may be necessary to multiply the Integer value of X by some "scale" factor (in this case 0.25) in order to have the function fill the desired total distance horizontally.

Because there are relatively few rows of characters to work with, it is desirable to make the graph fill the screen vertically in order to obtain as smooth a curve as is possible. Since we generally will not have a function whose values just happen to cover the right number of rows to fill the screen, it will be necessary to multiply all Y values by a "_scale factor_".

This program first computes a value of the function to be plotted for each planned value of X, placing the values in the array F in lines 63 and 64. The IF statement takes care of one awkward characteristic of the Sin(x)/x function when x=0, for which the function value is known to be 1.0. Without this IF test, the program would terminate abnormally upon trying to divide Sin(0) by 0. After all of the function values have been computed, PLOT is called with F being passed as a parameter. PLOT calls SCALE to adjust the values in F (referred to as A within

SCALE and PLOT) so that they cover exactly the range of rows 0..HEIGHT. At the end of SCALE, the global variable YZERO is set to the number of the row in which Y=0. This row number may or may not be on the screen, depending upon the range of values of the function, a fact which is tested when XAXIS is called to plot the horizontal row of dots representing the X axis.

Notice that the "graph" plotted by this program has a number of flattened places and stair steps where an accurate plot would show gentle curves. This flattening results from the fact that we cannot plot points between the fixed locations where characters are allowed to appear on the screen or printed page. Devices made for plotting graphs would do a much better job at this, possibly at the expense of a more complex plotting algorithm.

6. Note on Bit-Map Graphics

If you are using a microcomputer fitted with a screen device which plots lines by the method illustrated in Figure 0-1, then the methods described in this chapter can be used for drawing figures of much better quality than shown here. The UCSD PASCAL software system provides a method whereby you can exercise direct program control over every dot position within the display screen. This section is a brief description of that method. We encourage you to experiment with more complex drawings than those we have been able to show in this book.

We describe the figure plotted by the method illustrated in Figure 0-1 as a "_bit-map_" because each dot on the screen corresponds uniquely to a bit in the computer's memory. If, instead of the array PAGE used in the sample programs in this chapter, you were to use an array SCREEN for the same purpose, the declaration might look like this:

```
VAR SCREEN: ARRAY[0..HEIGHT] OF
                PACKED ARRAY[0..ROWSIZE] OF BOOLEAN;
```

Here ROWSIZE is the number of bits (minus 1) from left to right on the screen, and HEIGHT is one less than the number of rows of bits that fit along a vertical line. For example, on the Terak 8510A microcomputer, the value of HEIGHT should be 239 and the value of ROWSIZE should be 319, corresponding to a screen of 240 by 320 dots. This compares with 24 rows by 80 character positions available on most alphanumeric display screens. In our sample programs in this chapter, which are designed specifically for an alphanumeric display, we used a line width of only 51 characters in order to conform with limits for publishing this book. If you have a bit-map display screen, it may have a characteristic HEIGHT and ROWSIZE different from the values applying to the Terak unit, but those values will generally be substantially larger than apply to the PAGE array shown in this chapter.

In addition to the dimensions, our SCREEN array differs from the PAGE arrays used in this chapter in another respect. Whereas PAGE stored characters for later display in the form of characters, SCREEN simply stores a Boolean value signifying whether the bit position on the screen will be shown as a bright spot or dark. When TRUE, the spot is bright, when FALSE it is dark.

The exact arrangements needed to communicate the values of the bits in the SCREEN array to the display screen will probably vary from one machine to another depending upon the characteristics of the hardware. On the Terak 8510A unit, the mechanics are very simple. During initialization of the program, you should include the following statement:

```
UNITWRITE(3, SCREEN, 63)
```

where UNITWRITE is a built-in procedure normally reserved for use only by "system programmers" who work on compilers, editors, and other large system programs. The first parameter "3" refers to the display screen. The second, SCREEN, should be the name of the two-dimensional array of Boolean values such as we have been discussing. When this UNITWRITE statement is executed, it tells the graphics unit to display the bits stored in memory in the array called SCREEN. The third parameter, represented here by the integer constant 63, is an expression used to control the display unit. The value of 63 applies specifically to the Terak 8510A unit, and will probably be quite different for other makes and models of equipment. Once the UNITWRITE has been executed, all changes in the bits within the SCREEN array will be visible on the display unit up until your program terminates.

For further information on the use of a bit-map display, you should refer to the reference manual for the equipment you are using, and to a supplement that describes how the PASCAL software system communicates to that equipment.

<u>Exercise 12.1:</u>

Modify the program CHARPLOT to make it display the four small rectangles shown in part b of Figure 12-1. Note: If you understand how the program works, this should be a very simple exercise. We made the change by declaring two new identifiers (we won't tell you where, for that would reveal the solution), by adding those identifiers to four statements, and by replacing three other statements.

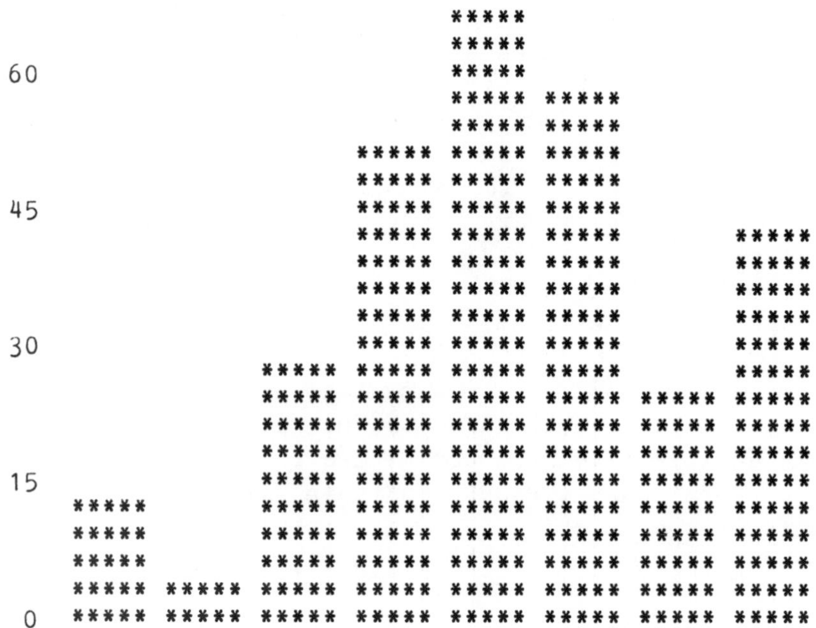

Figure 12-3. Histogram associated with Exercise 12.3

Many students attack this problem by a "let's see what happens if we do this" approach, without really understanding the program. This is a good way to waste time. If you are having trouble understanding CHARPLOT, you will save time by eliminating the plots of two of the three rectangles, then experimenting with what remains. In effect, the final display of the entire content of the PAGE array amounts to one large debugging statement. You could move the output loop (lines 46 thru 50) into a new procedure, then call that procedure at strategic places within RECT to see how the sides and top of the rectangle are getting plotted.

Once you understand how the program as given works, then it may help to think of the required modification in the following way. Each rectangle is drawn symmetrically about its own center point. All three of the rectangles plotted by the original program are centered at X=0, Y=0. To plot the new rectangles, new values of X and Y need to be used.

Exercise 12.2:

Revise the program CURVEPLOT to make it plot both the built-in function SIN and the built-in function COS, using different plotting characters for the two curves to identify them visually on the display. Try changing the constant 0.25, as shown on line 62 in the sample program, to values of 0.20 and 0.33, and explain the changes in the plotted figure that result from doing this.

Exercise 12.3:

For statistical studies, it is often useful to have a "histogram" showing the relative sizes of several similar items, for example energy consumption in each of several years. Write and debug a PASCAL program designed to plot the histogram shown in Figure 12-3, using as data the following list of percentages:

12 5 29 51 66 59 25 43

Before charging ahead to solve this problem, think about how your algorithm should be designed. It is true that one can create the display shown in Figure 12-3, including the numbers in the left margin to indicate scale, using a PAGE array similar to the arrays used in the sample programs in this chapter. This is not the easiest way to solve the problem! Consider how you would have solved the problem after finishing no more than Chapter 3 of this book. Then proceed with your solution. (Moral: Real life is rarely like a textbook in which you are led by the hand to the obvious method for solving a problem. Before committing much time to specifics of an algorithm, consider the repertoire of methods available to you that might be relevant to the problem.)

Exercise 12.4:

If you have a bit-map display unit, revise the sample programs CHARPLOT and CURVEPLOT to make them plot using a bit-map. Make your revisions in such a way as to be able to repeat the changes requested in Exercises 12.1 and 12.2. Try plotting the histogram of Exercise 12.3 with the vertical bars "shaded in" using evenly spaced sloping lines. If your display unit is capable of displaying a bit-map in color, try shading in each of the bars with a different color!

Exercise 12.5:

Computers are used extensively for performing many of the tasks in working with maps that humans find tedious. One of those tasks is the "shading-in" of irregular areas in a map to mark them as having some common characteristic. For example the entire area of a state or county might be shaded one color, while adjacent political subdivisions might be shaded using other colors. On a computer display or printer that cannot handle colors, equivalent shading is possible by controlling the density or angle of crosshatch lines drawn across the area to be shaded. If the map is shown on a crude plot using a character display unit or printer, the shading can be indicated by using different characters.

As a first step for this exercise, use turtle graphics to display the irregular map bounded by lines joining points at the following (x,y) coordinate positions. You will have to multiply each number by an appropriate scale factor, probably ranging from 5 to 25, in order to get this map to fill a reasonable part of your display screen. The figure has been given a squared-off boxey look intentionally, to allow you to simulate the turtle graphics lines with simple FOR or WHILE loops in a bit-map or character display. When properly drawn, the figure will be completely enclosed. In other words, the boundary line will be like a fence having no gate. Here are the coordinates:

(1,2) (4,2) (4,6) (-1,6) (-1,3) (-3,3)
(-3,5) (-6,5) (-6,1) (-2,1) (-2,-3) (3,-3)
(3,-1) (1,-1) and back to (1,2)

Write and debug a program to plot this map as a bit-map, or an equivalent character plot, and then to shade in the figure leaving no positions inside its boundary blank. Assume that this figure is just one subdivision of a larger map, with many adjacent subdivisions. Thus the program logic for shading cannot simply start at the left edge of the picture on each displayed row, going to the right until it finds a boundary, then shading in positions until the next boundary is found. The boundary of this figure has been made very irregular to simulate the real world of map making. The procedure which does the shading should be written to handle any map drawn in roughly the same manner, and it should not be specific to this particular map!

Hint: This problem can be solved with a simple recursive procedure once any position on the boundary has been located from a point inside the closed figure. From the current boundary position, the procedure checks to see whether there is an unshaded row above the present position. If there is, the procedure notes its current position in local variables or parameters, and then calls itself again giving the next location to be checked. If there is no unshaded position in the next row higher, then attention shifts counterclockwise along the boundary. If this results in moving down a row, then the procedure returns to its caller. The caller then "knows" the row number (Y position), and both the left and right horizontal positions of the boundary. This allows shading of the row before the procedure returns to its caller.

When the first instance of the procedure terminates, the problem has been logically completed half-way. Now the procedure should be called to proceed to rows below the present row rather than above. When the positions checked by the procedure instances finally return to the original starting position, the map is completely shaded.

Chapter 13

SEARCHING

1. Goals

This chapter, and the next two, use algorithms for searching through long lists of data, and for sorting unordered data, as problem examples. We have broken the topic into three chapters as a way to focus on the problem solution aspects rather than on specific details of searching and sorting techniques. You should gain problem solving and programming experience by studying and understanding the sample algorithms and programs given in this chapter, and by working out the exercises.

2. Background

Searching and sorting activities probably account for more running time on medium and large computers than any other single group of computing problems. Since the time of such machines is expensive, a great deal of ingenuity has been expended in devising better and faster ways to design searching and sorting algorithms. This has led to a rich variety of algorithms in this field for us to study as examples.

Usually in searching or sorting problems one is concerned with long sequences of data records such as we discussed in Chapter 10. Familiar examples of data that might be stored as a series of records would be:

a) Reference cards in the card catalog of a library

b) One line entries in the telephone book, identifying subscribers and their addresses

c) The index that you find at the back of any textbook

In each of these cases, one record contains several elementary data items. For example, one record in the telephone book contains these data items: Last name, first name, middle initial, telephone number, street number, street name, town name.

When you go to the telephone book to find the number belonging to someone you want to call, you "search" through the book for the record corresponding to the person you want. The number desired is located next to the name. The telephone company makes it relatively easy for you to find the name you want by listing all of the names in alphabetical order. Can you imagine the problem you would have in locating a name if the numbers were in some other order, say in the order of increasing telephone number?? Since the telephone company does not receive applications for new telephone numbers from people in the alphabetic order of their names, it is necessary for the company to sort the file of records in order to produce a telephone book in alphabetic sequence.

If you go to the telephone business office to ask for a correction in the records on file about your telephone, the clerk there may use a computer program to search for, and retrieve, the computer's record of your account. Thus we see typical applications of the searching and sorting techniques to everyday problems for which computer solutions are very useful. Sorting algorithms are discussed in Chapters 14 and 15. In this chapter we concentrate on algorithms for searching through data that has already been sorted into some logical sequence.

3. Review of Problem Solving Approach

As you go through the algorithms described in this chapter, keep in mind the general method used here for application to problems of your own. To review, here are the steps we have been discussing:

a) If the whole problem is too large to comprehend in your mind all at one time, then break the problem into sub-algorithms.

b) For each sub-algorithm, develop a mental picture of what needs to be done on a step by step basis. In doing this, it often helps to consider a small amount of test data items written down on paper or shown in a diagram. Go through the step by step mental process of converting the test data from its original form into a new form which you want your sub-algorithm to produce. Once you understand <u>what</u> the sub-algorithm is supposed to do, proceed to the next step to decide <u>how</u> it will be done.

c) Now draw a structure diagram which tells, in an orderly but approximate way, how you performed the mental data conversion in step (b). Be on the lookout for steps that are repeated two or more times, for places where you had to decide which of two or more actions to take (choice boxes), and for sequences of the same actions that appear in several different places in your diagram (sub-algorithms). You can start with a rough diagram to get a general picture in mind of how the algorithm should go. Then you can add details, and correct the fuzzy aspects of your logic.

d) Having developed a structure diagram, you can now convert it into statements in whatever programming language you are using. This will be a straight forward conversion problem if you are programming in PASCAL. If not, you may find it useful to convert the structure diagram first to PASCAL. Then, with a simple set of conversion rules, you can convert the PASCAL into some other programming language.

e) Now you need to debug the program written in step (d). The first step in debugging consists of correcting the syntax errors flagged by the compiler. The second, and more difficult step of debugging is the effort to discover "run-time" logical errors in the program. This requires the use of test data for which the correct results for running the program or sub-program should be known. For this purpose, it will often be a good idea to use the data for testing that you used in step (b) above in arriving at a mental picture of what needed to be done. Until each procedure or function works correctly with a small amount of test data, they should not be tried together in the complete program, nor should any part of the program be tried with a larger amount of data. Not until a reasonably thorough test has been made with test data should the program be used for "production" calculations.

4. Linear Search

In this and the subsequent chapters we will be concerned with searching through, or sorting, lists of numbers. In real life applications it is more usual to search or sort a sequence of names or other words of text. The use of numbers here is simply a short cut to make the programming easier, and to allow us to concentrate on the structure of the algorithms being considered.

To get a mental picture of a linear search, we start with a short sequence of test data:

```
8687,3831,5138,1064,0730,4308,4687,8540,3667,9430
 0    1    2    3    4    5    6    7    8    9
```

If this looks like a series of numbers lifted out of the local telephone directory, it was. The telephone directory often can provide a good source of random numbers for checking algorithms. Below each data item in this sequence is shown the index number of the item, i.e. the number giving the order in which the data item appears. Clearly we are looking ahead to the possible use of this index number if the data sequence is to be stored in an array in the computer.

In a "linear" or "sequential" search, we look up a data item in a list by looking at each item in order starting at the beginning (or end if that is more convenient). When we reach the item we are looking for we stop. For example, we might be looking for the number 4308 in the list above. (If it troubles you to be looking for a specific number, try to remember an occasion when you jotted down a telephone number for later use, but forgot to write down the name of the person who gave the number to you. Then, at a later time, you find you need to recall who that person was.) We start at location "0" with the data item 8687. Since this is not the item we want, we go on to the next, finding 3831. We continue this process, rejecting records containing numbers other than the one for which we are searching.

By repeating this process over and over, we hope eventually to reach the data item for which we are searching. Of course, it is possible, in the typical case, that the data item for which we are searching is not present in the list. So our mental image of the algorithm has to contain some provision for stopping with a "fail" indication if the end of the list is reached without the desired item being found.

The mental image of this process is pretty simple, and we can proceed directly to the structure diagram describing the process. Clearly the structure diagram needs a repetition box. For each repetition, we need to advance an index variable by 1 to keep track of where we are located in the list. The repetition has to continue until either one of two conditions is met, viz:

a) We reach the data item for which we were searching

b) We reach the end of the list

Condition (a) specifies that the search will terminate if the wanted item is found. Of course it would be possible for the algorithm to be slightly simpler if we allowed it to look at <u>every</u> data item in the entire list regardless of whether the wanted item is actually found. In that case we would set a "flag" variable to TRUE if the wanted item is found. However, this is obviously not what you would do if you were visually scanning a list upon reaching the desired item. At that point, you would stop searching further if you knew that there could be only one instance of the value being sought within the list. After finding that value, it would be a waste of your time to continue scanning the list. The same concept applies to the searching algorithm for the computer, since it is expensive to waste computer time needlessly (at least on the larger machines).

Having thought of the data as stored in an array, it will be instructive to plan on stopping the repetition action based on reaching a special "stopper" data item rather than using an EOF condition. Such a stopper would typically be placed at the end of the data list when it is first brought into memory by the main program. All this leads to the (Boolean function) algorithm shown in Figure 13-1. The figure is shown as a sub-algorithm having one parameter ITEM, giving the value of the item for which we are to search. The value of the function will be set to a value of FALSE if the search fails, otherwise to TRUE. The value of the stopper item must be some value that cannot logically turn up in the actual list of data items. In the case of the 4-digit positive integers shown in the list above, a suitable stopper might be -1 (since there are no negative telephone numbers), 0 (since we might be able to assume that the number 0000 is never used as a telephone number), or 10000 or a larger integer (since these integers cannot be expressed in 4 digits).

Study Figure 13-1., noting the following points:

a) Having decided to use the

REPEAT action UNTIL condition

form of repetition box, the array location LST[mentioned in the condition is checked at the end of execution of the repeated action. Since the action must include a statement which increases the value of the index variable I on each repetition, I must be initialized to -1 before the REPEAT box starts. Otherwise the first location checked would be LST[1].

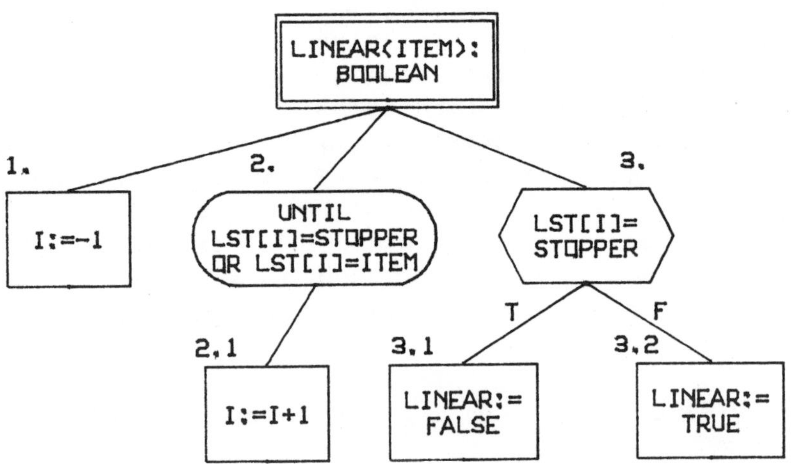

LINEAR(ITEM):
BOOLEAN
1.
I:=-1
2.
UNTIL
LST[I]=STOPPER
OR LST[I]=ITEM
2.1
I:=I+1
3.
LST[I]=
STOPPER
T
F
3.1
LINEAR:=
FALSE
3.2
LINEAR:=
TRUE

Figure 13-1

b) The choice in box 3 is needed to determine whether the REPEAT box terminated because the wanted item was found, or whether the search failed.

Figure 13-2 shows a second way to express the linear search. Study this version, and compare it with Figure 13-1, noting the following points:

a) The price of the simpler condition in the REPEAT box is that we must use an EXIT box, or the equivalent GOTO, to bail out of the loop if the second condition is found to be true.

b) It is slightly simpler to set LINEAR to FALSE as part of the initialization action, instead of performing a check on how the REPEAT box terminated. LINEAR remains set to FALSE unless the wanted item is found, in which case box 2.2.1 is executed.

c) Had we used a box #3 to set LINEAR to FALSE, we would have had to arrange the EXIT to go out of the root node of the sub-algorithm in order to avoid box #3 if the wanted item were found.

To check your computer program for either form of the linear search algorithm, use the short list of data items given in the text above. Use the function to search for the following numbers:

a) 4308 (in middle part of the list)

b) 8687 (first value in the list)

c) 9430 (last value in the list)

d) 7777 (legal value but not in the list)

e) -123 (illegal value relative to the assumed legal range)

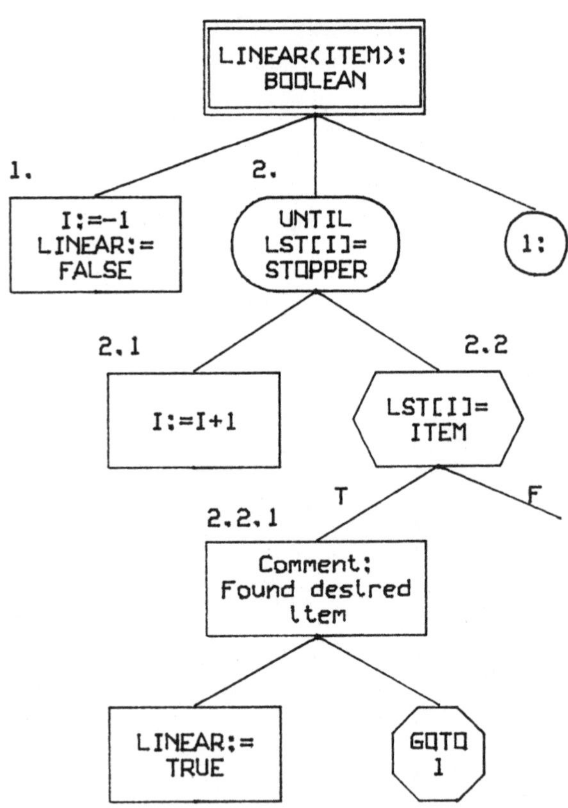

LINEAR(ITEM):
BOOLEAN
1.
I:=-1
LINEAR:=
FALSE
2.
UNTIL
LST[I]=
STOPPER
1:
2.1
I:=I+1
2.2
LST[I]=
ITEM
T
F
2.2.1
Comment:
Found desired
item
LINEAR:=
TRUE
GOTO
1

Figure 13-2

Set up your main program for the test to display the value of the variable I after the function LINEAR terminates. In each of the cases above, check to see whether the value of I reported by your program agrees with the test data.

Now let's suppose that your program runs, but it gives incorrect results and you cannot see why in studying your program statements. When this problem arises, it is often useful to "monitor" the values of the several variables used by the function. To do this, you add temporary WRITE statements to your program at strategic points. You can then study the values in the output on a step by step basis to see if the computer results are like those you expected. Usually this step by step analysis will help you to discover an error quickly.

5. Binary Search

Though simple, the linear search process discussed in the previous section is too time consuming except for lists containing no more than a few dozen values. You would never consider performing a linear search of the telephone book, or of a dictionary, yourself. Obviously, it takes too long to look at every data value (a name in the telephone book, a word in the dictionary) starting at the beginning and extending until you find the value for which you are searching. Instead you take another approach which you know from experience works faster. For the same kind of reasons, we generally do not program a computer to do a linear search of long lists. The method used instead is similar to the logic *you* use in searching for an item in the telephone book or dictionary. In its simplest form, this method is called a "*binary search*".

For a mental picture of the binary search, consider how you go about finding the page of the telephone directory containing a name for which you are searching. Suppose the name is "Smythe". You search for the "S" portion of the book by first opening it to a page near the middle. You check that page to determine whether the letter "S" occurs later or earlier in the book. If it occurs later, as would probably be the case with "S", you then narrow the search by dividing the second half of the book into two sections of roughly equal size. In this way, you reach a new page, and check to see if this page is within the "S" part of the book. If instead you have turned to a page of names starting with "P", you repeat the subdivision process by looking somewhat later in the book. You look approximately as far later as one-half of the quarter of the book resulting from the previous subdivision. If instead you arrived in the "T" section of the book, you would look a little earlier.

Continuing this process of subdivision, you eventually arrive in a portion of the book where the names start with "S". Now you have to narrow the search further by looking for names starting with "SM", then "SMY", in each step subdividing a smaller portion of the book either earlier or later than the point just reached. Upon reaching the page containing names starting with "SMYTH", you are probably close enough to make it worthwhile to use a linear search within that page for the name you desire.

Whereas a linear search requires no assumptions to be made about the order in which the items in the list are kept, a binary search requires that the items be sorted into an increasing or decreasing sequence. In the case of the telephone book, or the dictionary, the sequence is the familiar alphabetic sequence. To sharpen our mental image, let us instead use an ordered sequence of 3-digit numbers, each number being equal to or greater than its predecessor in the list. Following is the list we will use to explain the algorithm, again with location index numbers given with each data item:

Figure 13-3.

```
105,172,221,279,324,324,331,392,426,439,541,615,684
 0   1   2   3   4   5   6   7   8   9  10  11  12
```

Now we go through the binary searching process just described using this list. Assume that we are searching for the value 392.

Figure 13-4.

```
step 1:
105,172,221,279,324,324,331,392,426,439,541,615,684
 0   1   2   3   4   5   6   7   8   9  10  11  12
                         :
step 2:
                            392,426,439,541,615,684
                             7   8   9  10  11  12
                                     :
step 3:
                            392,426
                             7   8
                             :
```

In the first step, we split the list at item 6, and found that the value of 331 located there was smaller than the value for which we were searching. Eliminating 331, since it was already examined and rejected, we now search the upper half of the list in step 2. We locate the "middle" of this half as being item 9. The exact middle is at 9.5, but we have no split items. Accordingly we made the arbitrary decision to take the next lower integer, i.e. 9 as the location of the new "middle". The value found there is 439, which is larger than the value being sought. Eliminating the value at location 9, we are left with items 7 and 8 as all that remains on the list. We take the "middle" of this new smaller sequence, by the same rule as in step 2, getting 7.5

which reduces to 7. Since we find that the value at location 7 is 392, the value we wanted, the search thus terminates after step 3.

Now let's go through the same process for another search item, say 279, as in Figure 13-5.

Figure 13-5.

```
step 1:
105,172,221,279,324,324,331,392,426,439,541,615,684
 0   1   2   3   4   5   6   7   8   9  10  11  12
                         :
step 2:
105,172,221,279,324,324
 0   1   2   3   4   6
         :
step 3:
            279,324,324
             3   4   5
                 :
step 4:
            279
             3
             :
```

By now you should be getting a good idea of how to draw the structure diagram for the algorithm to perform this kind of search. However, before we proceed to the algorithm, it will be instructive to see what happens if we search for a value that happens not to be present in the list, say 329. This is shown in Figure 13-6.

Figure 13-6.

```
step 1:
105,172,221,279,324,324,331,392,426,439,541,615,684
 0   1   2   3   4   5   6   7   8   9   10  11  12
                                                            :
step 2:
105,172,221,279,324,324
 0   1   2   3   4   5
             :
step 3:
            279,324,324
             3   4   5
                 :
step 4:
                    324
                     5
                       :
```

6. <u>Recursive Binary Search Algorithm</u>

Now let's go on to design the sub-algorithm to solve the binary search problem on the computer. Assume that the data list is in an array called LST, and that we know in advance what index values are associated with the first and last items in the list for use in parameters passed to the sub-algorithm. These values would be 0 and 12 in our example.

You can see an obvious possibility for using a repetition box to control the number of steps to be taken, from a casual study of Figures 13-4 thru 13-6. However, it is simpler to think of the sub-algorithm as recursive. Thus at step 1 we split the list into three parts (the lower "half", the "middle", and the upper "half") and, in most cases, decide to examine just one of those three parts. If the new part to be examined is either the lower half or the upper half, that part can be regarded as a new list to be searched using the same sub-algorithm. For example, in Figure 13-6 the result of doing a binary search on the list LST[0], ...,LST[12] is that we need to do a binary search on the list LST[0], ...,LST[5]. But the result of doing a search on LST[0], ...,LST[5] is that we decide to do a binary search on the list LST[3], ...,LST[5]. Finally as a result of step 3, we decide to do a binary search on a list that has, at most, just one element. Having reached that point, no further use of the sub-algorithm is needed. Figure 13-7 illustrates the recursive form of the sub-algorithm.

Here are some points to notice about Figure 13-7:

a) The term "key"

In Figure 13-7, the identifier "KEY" is the value for which a search is required. The term "Key" is often used in searching and sorting problems to identify the data element being sought or being used to determine the final order of the list. The key used to order a telephone directory consists of the concatenation of:

Last-name First-name Middle-initial

If the key used in preparing the telephone directory were the telephone number instead, then the directory would come out ordered according to the telephone numbers in numerically increasing sequence. Similarly, the key used in ordering the entries in the dictionary is the word being defined. All of the other data in a dictionary entry "goes along for the ride" when the word-definitions list is sorted to produce a dictionary.

b) Termination of the algorithm

The sequence of calls to the sub-algorithm BINSEARCH stops when the last box executed is not another call to BINSEARCH. This means that execution of box 2.2, or failure to execute box 2.1.1.1 or 2.1.2.1 will cause the algorithm to

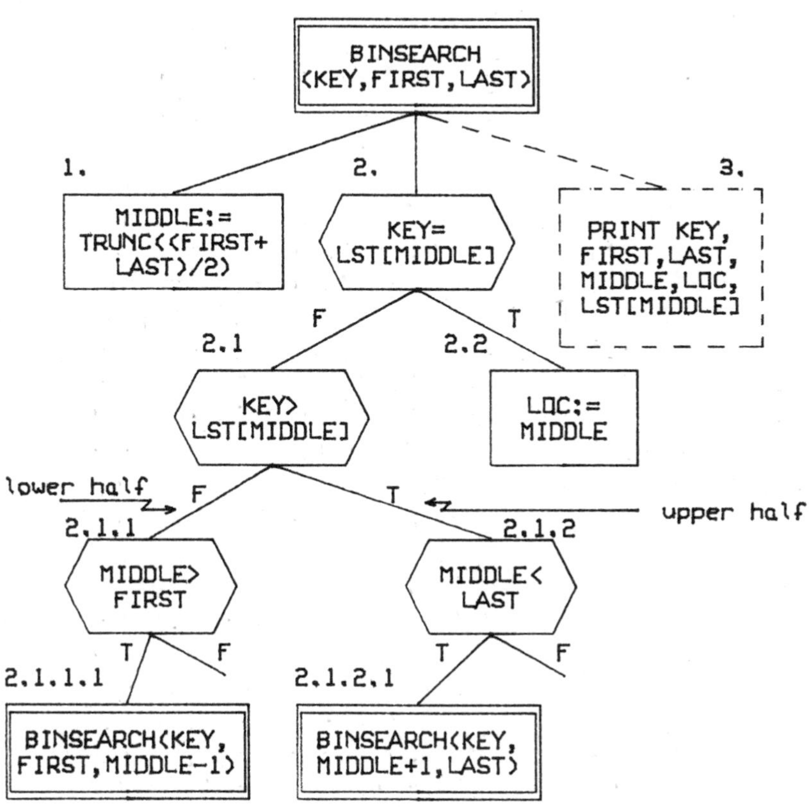
BINSEARCH
(KEY,FIRST,LAST)
1.
2.
3.
MIDDLE:=
TRUNC((FIRST+
LAST)/2)
KEY=
LST[MIDDLE]
PRINT KEY,
FIRST,LAST,
MIDDLE,LOC,
LST[MIDDLE]
F
T
2.1
2.2
KEY>
LST[MIDDLE]
LOC:=
MIDDLE
lower half
F
T
upper half
2.1.1
2.1.2
MIDDLE>
FIRST
MIDDLE<
LAST
T
F
T
F
2.1.1.1
2.1.2.1
BINSEARCH(KEY,
FIRST,MIDDLE-1)
BINSEARCH(KEY,
MIDDLE+1,LAST)

Figure 13-7

complete, leaving the variable LOC (for location) set to some value. LOC is assumed to be a global variable declared in the <block> which called BINSEARCH in the first place. LOC is set to -1 before BINSEARCH is called. If the value being sought is found, then LOC is the index number of the location of that value in the array LST. If the value is not found anywhere in the list, then LOC is still set to -1, a value that cannot correspond to any location in the array.

Exercise 13.1:

The technique of recursion has proven useful in explaining how the binary search operates, but virtually the same algorithm can be written without recursion. Write and debug a program including an Integer function BINSEARCH which returns the location of the key as its value. The function should be non-recursive.

Test your program with the same list of data we have used in this chapter for illustration purposes. After reading in the list of data from the keyboard, test your program with the following values of the key:

a) 105 (smallest value in the list)
b) 684 (largest value in the list)
c) 331 (value of the middle location)
d) 426 (value somewhere in midst of list, but not the middle)
e) 200 (value not in the list, but would be in the midst of the list if present)
f) 0 (value smaller than smallest in the list)
g) 999 (value larger than largest in list)
h) 324 (value which appears duplicated)

Now modify the data list on a second run by removing one of the 324 values, and repeat the list of tests again. (Binary search programs tend to be fussy about odd/even length difficulties.) Make sure that the program delivers correct results for all of these cases. Unless all of them are correct, the program is not likely to work correctly for much longer lists.

Now generate a list of all the numbers from 1 thru 1000, and try the search function on this list again. Try the search for this list with key values of 497, 498, 499, 500, 501, 502, and 503. In this case, the location of each key should be equal to the key, or one less, depending on how you have declared the array LST. For this latter trial, add logic to count the number of times the procedure compares the key with LST[MIDDLE], and to report the value of the count when the function terminates. None of the keys given in the short list above should result in more than 10 comparisons being made, in spite of the length of the list. In general, the binary search should complete its work in less than

$$\log_2(N)$$

comparison steps (rounded up to the next higher integer), if N is the number of items in the list being searched. The linear search will require an average of about N/2 comparisons, which is much larger.

Chapter 14

SORTING - I. SIMPLE ALGORITHMS

1. Goals

In this chapter we present two simple sorting algorithms, and the closely related subject of merging. Your main goal should be to gain additional problem solving experience by writing and debugging computer programs which carry out these algorithms.

2. Background

Searching is one of the main reasons why it is desirable to sort lists of data into some orderly sequence. Another reason is associated with the problem we face when trying to put a few "changes" into data entries that are already in a long list. If both the main list, and the list of changes, are in the same sorted sequence (such as alphabetical, or numerical), then it is only necessary to go through the two lists exactly one time in order to put the changes together with the original entries in the main list. This latter application is called "merging", a topic that we also treat briefly.

Partly because efficient sort algorithms save on computing costs, and partly because sort algorithms present an interesting intellectual challenge to computer buffs, there are many popular sort algorithms in regular use. Which algorithm to use may depend upon the type of computer you are using, the expected partial ordering of the data to be sorted, the kind of data to be sorted, the length of the list to be sorted, and many other factors, not to mention the esthetic preferences of the programmer.

In this chapter, we will give brief analyses of two sort algorithms to give you some idea of the variety that is possible. Study these algorithms carefully, as they will give you some idea of how to design algorithms of increasing complexity.

3. Insertion Sort

The simple Insertion Sort algorithm is sometimes called the "Sinking Sort", sometimes the "Sifting Sort", with only minor changes. The algorithm is very much like the algorithm you use to organize a "hand" of playing cards into their order of increasing importance. In that case, you start with the first card dealt to you. When you get the second card, you put it either in front of, or back of, the first card. When you get the third, you may put it between the first two, ahead of both, or back of both depending on its value. When you get the fourth, you compare the new card with each of those already in the deck starting at the front of the deck. When you find two cards, one larger and one smaller than the new one, you <u>insert</u> the new card between these two. For each new card, you repeat this process until all cards in the hand have been received. At that point the hand of cards is in sorted sequence.

Once again we will use numbers to illustrate the algorithm, even though it works in basically the same way if the data consists of names or other non-numerical information. Figure 14-1 shows the insertion sort in action.

Notice that the new item inserted at each step is mareked with an asterisk ('*'). Notice also that the larger numbers (the heavier ones) sink further toward the "bottom" of the list. In this case, we have chosen to represent the bottom as the highest value of the location index LOC.

If done as shown, the insertion sort can be performed in the array locations occupied by the original list of data. We need to have one simple variable, call it HOLD, in which to hold the value being inserted temporarily. We then start at the top (lowest index value in this example) of the list assembled so far, and compare the value in HOLD with the value in the list. If the value in the list is smaller, then that value is popped up one location. HOLD is then compared with the next value in the list. The process continues, with all smaller values being popped up just one location. When a larger value than HOLD is found in the list, the value of HOLD is stored in the location immediately above that larger value.

Figure 14-1.

LOC	ORIGINAL LIST											
0	43											12
1	87										12	23
2	29									12	23	29
3	38								12	23	29	34
4	34							12	23	29*	34	38
5	46						12	23	34	34	38	39
6	12					12*	23	34*	38*	38	39	43*
7	68				23	23	39	39	39	39	46	46
8	23			23*	39	39	46*	46	46	46	55	55
9	75		39	39	55	55	55	55	55	55	68	68
10	55	39	55	55	68*	68	68	68	68	68	75	75
11	39*	55*	75*	75	75	75	75	75	75	75	87*	87
STEP	1	2	3	4	5	6	7	8	9	10	11	12

Figure 14-2 illustrates the structure diagram of the Insertion Sort. When the sub-algorithm starts, the unsorted data elements are in the array LST running from LST[0], ...,LST[N]. The variables HOLD, I, and J can be local variables in the sub-algorithm as they are only needed for the duration of the sorting process.

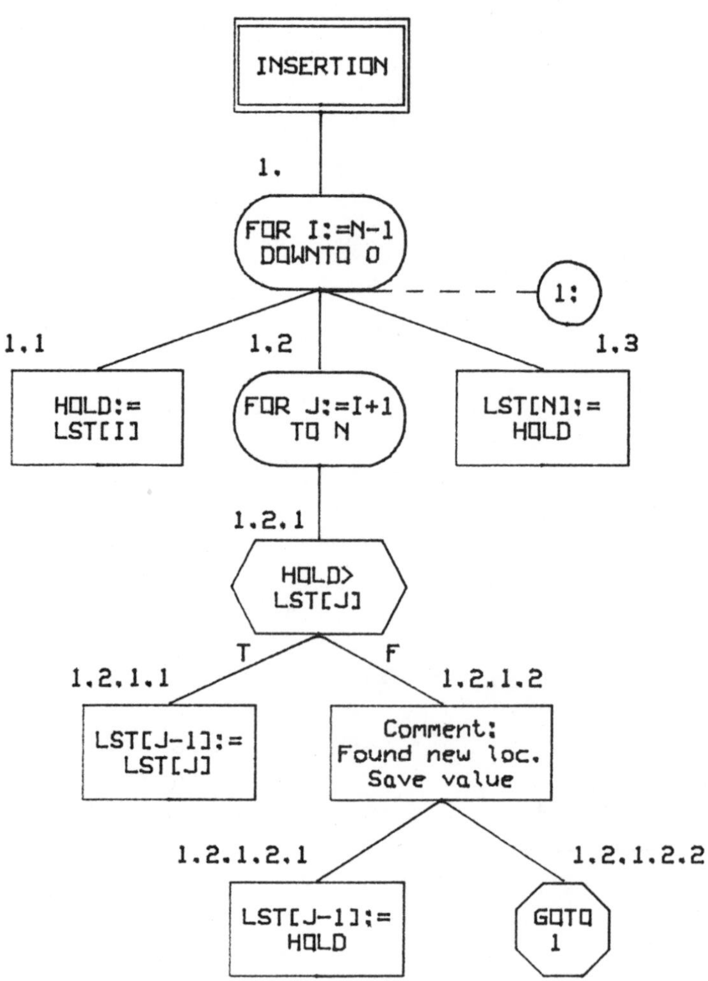
INSERTION
1.
FOR I:=N-1
DOWNTO 0
1:
1.1
1.2
1.3
HOLD:=
LST[I]
FOR J:=I+1
TO N
LST[N]:=
HOLD
1.2.1
HOLD>
LST[J]
T
F
1.2.1.1
1.2.1.2
LST[J-1]:=
LST[J]
Comment:
Found new loc.
Save value
1.2.1.2.1
1.2.1.2.2
LST[J-1]:=
HOLD
GOTO
1

Figure 14-2

For purposes of comparing this algorithm with the other sort algorithms we will be studying, we should estimate the number of repeated calculations needed to perform the insertion sort. Box 1 in Figure 14-2 calls for N repetitions, where there are N+1 data elements to be sorted.At the beginning, step 1.2 calls for just one repetition. At the end, step 1.2 calls for N repetitions at the most. Step 1.2 is terminated if the proper location for a new data value is found before the end of the list by the GOTO box 1.2.1.2.2. This is an example of a use of the GOTO which we did not discuss in Chapter 11. In this case, the GOTO is used to Exit from one _cycle_ of repetition within the portion of the algorithm controlled by box 1. Thus the processing will start again at Box 1.1, provided that another repetition is called for by Box 1.

At most, the number of repetitions called for by Box 1.2 (which is repeated under control of Box 1.) will be N*(N/2) times, i.e. half the square of N. This would only occur if the original list were in exactly the reverse of the desired order. If that were true, then every new data item would have to "sink" to the bottom of the list. In the more typical case, each new data item will have to sink about half way down the portion of the list which has been sorted so far. Therefore the algorithm requires approximately N*(N/4) repetitions of Box 1.2.1. If the original list is already in the correct sorted sequence when the sub-algorithm starts, there will still need to be N repetitions of Box 1.2.1 for the sub-algorithm to terminate.

To complete your mental image of what is going on in this algorithm, you should go through the first five or more steps of Figure 14-1, noting what happens in the structure diagram of Figure 14-2 on a box by box basis. Do you see the need for Box 1.3??

For debugging a program written to perform the insertion sort, it is very desirable to add temporary display statements to boxes 1.2.1.1, 1.2.1.2.1, and 1.3. Each display statement should include identification of its location with the box number. It should also give the values of LST[J-1], LST[J] and HOLD. You can add READLN statements to stop the action temporarily while you study the results of recent loops. Typing <RET> will allow the action to continue.

Caution: The value of J following termination of the FOR ... construct in Box 1.2 is not well defined even in PASCAL. Depending on the implementation of the language, the value of the control variable after a FOR statement terminates may or may not be usable. Even if usable, the value may be equal to the limit value of the FOR statement, it may be one more or less than the limit value, or even some other value. Thus you should not depend upon J after the FOR statement terminates until a new value is assigned to J.

If the above debugging approach is not sufficient for you to visualize what is happening in this algorithm, then it may be time to add more debugging statements, so that you can observe the results of the sorting process after each step. To do this, add a statement as Box 1.4 which displays the set of data items from location I to location N in the list. You can run the list of items horizontally on a single output line, rather than vertically as we have done in preparing Figure 14-1. Obviously, you would only do debugging at this level of detail with a relatively short list of data values.

4. Bubble Sort

The Bubble sort algorithm is a member of the family of algorithms which "exchange" neighboring data values to implement the rearrangement of data. The "bubble" description implies that lighter (smaller) values will "float" to the top of the list. For partially ordered data, the bubble sort is relatively fast as it provides a way to recognize when no more exchanges are required. In other respects, it is quite similar to the simple insertion sort described in Section 3. To get a mental image of how the bubble sort works, see Figure 14-3.

At each step in this figure, the "bubbles" are marked with asterisks ('*'). For example, consider step 1. In the original list, 39 is smaller than 55, so the two are exchanged. Then 39 is exchanged with 75. On the next comparison, 39 proves to be larger than 23 so no exchange takes place. Since 23 is smaller than 68, 23 becomes the next bubble. Finally, 12 is smaller than any other data item, so the 12 rises all the way to the top.

Figure 14-3.

LOC	ORIGINAL LIST										
0	43	12*	12	12	12	12	12	12	12	12	12
1	87	43	23*	23	23	23	23	23	23	23	23
2	29	87	43	29*	29	29	29	29	29	29	29
3	38	29	87	43	34*	34	34	34	34	34	34
4	34	38	29	87	43	38*	38	38	38	38	38
5	46	34	38	34*	87	43	39*	39	39	39	39
6	12	46	34	38	38	87	43	43	43	43	43
7	68	23*	46	39*	39	39	87	46*	46	46	46
8	23	68	39*	46	46	46	46	87	55*	55	55
9	75	39*	68	55*	55	55	55	55	87	68*	68
10	55	75	55*	68	68	68	68	68	68	87	75*
11	39	55	75	75	75	75	75	75	75	75	87
STEP:		1	2	3	4	5	6	7	8	9	10

In preparing for step 2, we know that the smallest value in the list has now been moved to location 0. There is no purpose in making any further comparisons with the value at that location. Therefore, for step 2, the last value to be compared at the top of the list can be at location 1, having an initial value of 43 for step 2. As the process proceeds, the next smallest value in the list rises to location 1. For step 3, we need only do comparisons as high as location 2. In each step, the dashed horizontal line shows where the last comparison that results in an exchange of values is made. In step 7, the last exchange could have been made between items 6 and 7 (43 and 46). Since they were already in the correct sequence, no exchange was needed. This allowed the remaining list to be shortened by two locations in one step.

You can keep track of where the last exchange occurs in each pass over the list with a simple variable EXCH. Initialize EXCH to N-1 at the beginning of a pass. At the end of a pass, set a variable BOUND to the value of EXCH+1. The next pass needs only to go from the Nth item down to BOUND.

You can see that the Bubble Sort might require relatively few operations if the original list of data were nearly in correct sorted sequence at the start. As an example, consider the list in Step 10 of Figure 14-3, but imaging that a new value 10 were added to the list between the values 55 and 68. It would take just one pass over the list for the value 10 to float to the top of the list. On the second pass, there would be no exchanges. At the end of that pass, the variable EXCH would still be set to N-1, BOUND would therefore be set to N and the repetition would terminate.

It could also happen that a large value might occur near the top of a nearly sorted list. As an example counter to the one just discussed, suppose that the value 90 were inserted just below the 12 in the sorted list of Step 10 (Figure 14-3). Now the number of passes over the list to move the 90 to its correct place at the bottom of the list would be N-1. This suggests that the Bubble Sort works better for small values rising to the top of the list than it does for large values that have to fall to the bottom.

A remedy for this would be to make a pass first going upward, followed by a pass going downward. This procedure could be followed in pairs with both upper and lower BOUND values becoming progressively closer to each other. In odd numbered steps the exchanging would start at the lower BOUND and work toward the top as in Figure 14-3. In even numbered steps, the exchanging would start at the upper BOUND (in the diagram) and work toward the bottom. When the lower bound becomes equal to the upper, the algorithm terminates. This back and forth version of the Bubble Sort is sometimes called a "Cocktail Shaker Sort". It has the advantage of finishing relatively quickly if the original data is nerly sorted correctly, regardless of the placement of the few keys that are out of order.

5. Merging

In sorting and/or searching problems, one often has occasion to combine two or more lists of data in sorted sequence. If the lists are already in sorted sequence, before they are combined, then the most efficient and direct method for combining them is to "merge" the lists. Suppose that you wish to combine two lists that are already sorted in "ascending" sequence (smallest item first), say List-A and List-B, by merging them to yield a new List-M. You compare the first items in List-A and List-B, selecting the smaller of the two and moving it to List-M. You also delete the item moved from the list it came from. Now you return for another comparison of the earliest items still left in the two lists, adding the smaller item to the growing List-M. Eventually all items will be moved by this process to List-M, and List-A and List-B will both be empty. Figure 14-4 gives an example of this process. Notice that the two lists do not have to be of the same length.

Here are some things to notice about this process:

a) You need some rule to resolve what happens when the earliest values are equal in List-A and List-B. In this example we picked up the item from List-A first when this happened.

Figure 14-4.

START									
9	15	16	18	25	37	44			List-A
3	6	9	17	25	34	45	47	48	List-B
Step 1									
3									List-M
9	15	16	18	25	37	44			List-A
	6	9	17	25	34	45	47	48	List-B
Step 2									
3	6								List-M
9	15	16	18	25	37	44			List-A
		9	17	25	34	45	47	48	List-B
Step 3									
3	6	9							List-M
	15	16	18	25	37	44			List-A
		9	17	25	34	45	47	48	List-B
Step 4									
3	6	9	9						List-M
	15	16	18	25	37	44			List-A
			17	25	34	45	47	48	List-B
Step 5									
3	6	9	9	15					List-M
		16	18	25	37	44			List-A
			17	25	34	45	47	48	List-B
Step 6									
3	6	9	9	15	16				List-M
			18	25	37	44			List-A
			17	25	34	45	47	48	List-B

etc. etc. etc.

b) Sooner or later you will exhaust all of the entries in one of the two lists, while the other will still have entries remaining. Your algorithm has to be able to recognize this condition and continue extracting values from the other list until it too is empty.

c) This algorithm requires that there be enough temporary memory space available to store at least twice the total number of items that have to be merged. The algorithm runs relatively quickly because each item needs to be picked up only once.

Merging is generally used as a strategy in the later stages of sorting when the list to be sorted cannot be stored completely at one time in the main memory of the computer. Instead, it becomes necessary to use a secondary storage medium such as a magnetic disk or magnetic tape. In this case the sort proceeds in stages. In the first stages, sequences of items from the unsorted list are brought into main memory until there is no space to spare. The short sequence introduced into memory in that way is then sorted by one of the faster "internal" sorting algorithms. "Internal" in this case implies that the sorting can be done internally in the main memory of the computer, without recourse to any auxiliary storage device. When a short sequence has been sorted in this way, it is then saved on disk or tape, and another similar sequence is introduced into main memory.

Eventually, all of the original list will have been separated into short sequences, and these sequences internally sorted and saved. In the next stages of sorting, the short sequences are merged in pairs yielding longer sequences which are still in sorted order. The merging does not require that all of the information in each short sequence has to be in main memory at one time. The result of the merging is a set of longer sub-sequences that are again saved on disk or tape. These sub-sequences are merged to produce still longer sub-sequences. The process continues until the entire set of data from the original list has been merged into the final list, which is now in correct sorted sequence.

A strategy similar to merging is used very commonly for processing administrative data. Usually an organization will keep a "master" list of information on individuals on whom records are kept (e.g. students in a university, customers of a utility company, employees in any organization, ...). Each month, a set of new "transactions" will be collected, and the object of the computer data processing will be to "update" the records on file for the individual, using the data from the transactions. The master list is kept in sorted sequence from one month to the next. The transaction list is sorted in one of the first stages of the processing. When both a master record, and a transaction record, are found for the same individual, the master record is corrected, i.e. "updated", taking the new transaction information into account.

In the case of a department store's records on charge account customers, a transaction might be on a new purchase, or it might be data on a payment received from the customer. Having "merged" together the information from the old master record, with the information on the transaction, the corrected record can now be saved in a new copy of the master list. If a master record appears with no corresponding transaction record, the old master record is simply copied into the new list. If there is a transaction which fails to be matched with a record in the master list, then some kind of error has occurred. the merge-update program therefore should provide a way to display or print out a listing of cases in which peculiar results are found. This allows humans to go through these "exception" cases to correct erroneous input data, to add new master records, and so on.

Exercise 14.1:

Draw a structure diagram showing approximately how the Bubble sort operates. Write and debug a program including the Bubble Sort as a procedure. After testing the program with the data used for illustrating the algorithm in figure 14-3, try a longer sequence of data generated by a random number generator such as the one used in the programs FOURLETTER and RANDOMWALK of Chapter 5 Section 11. If you have problems making the program work properly, add debugging WRITE statements to assist you to find the problems.

Exercise 14.2:

Write and debug a program to merge two sorted sequences of numbers in the manner shown in Figure 14-4. Start your design work with an approximate structure diagram describing what the algorithm is supposed to do. Test your program with the data sequence used for the illustration in Figure 14-4. After doing this, test with two longer sequences generated by a random number generator, which have been sorted using the Bubble sort. Each sequence should be approximately 100 items long, but one list should be at least 10 items longer than the other. Check the entire merged list carefully to make sure all items have been merged. In particular, check to make sure that all the expected items from the beginning and the end of the original lists have found their way into the merged list.

Chapter 15

SORTING - II. QUICKSORT

1. Goals

In this chapter we present an important sorting algorithm of moderate complexity called "QUICKSORT". Once again, your main goal should be to gain additional problem solving experience by converting the conceptual description of this algorithm into a functioning computer program.

2. Background

Though the two sorting algorithms described in Chapter 14 have the advantage of simplicity, they are much slower than is necessary when dealing with randomly ordered data. "Quicksort", which is described in this chapter, is one of several algorithms which require roughly

$$N * Log_2 (N)$$

operations, rather than roughly

$$\frac{N^2}{2}$$

as was true of the Bubble Sort and the Insertion Sort. Once again we will see the "divide and conquer" approach paying off as it did in the case of the Binary Search. Once again, the general structure of the faster algorithms is found to be similar to a tree structure. Once again, a recursive approach allows a major conceptual simplification of the algorithm.

To get a tangible idea of the relative speed advantage of Quicksort, consider a sequence containing 1000 items to be sorted. This would be quite small compared with the length of typical sequences encountered in data processing programs for administration. The larger the sequence, the greater will be the advantage for using Quicksort. The simple algorithms require roughly (N*N/2) or about 500,000 operations. Quicksort requires roughly 1000*Log(N), or about 10,000 operations. So the simple algorithms consume about 50 times as much processing time as does Quicksort for N = 1000.!

Quicksort has been used as the basis for development of several important advanced sorting algorithms which are widely used.

3. Description of Quicksort

To get a mental image of how the Quicksort algorithm operates, study Figure 15-1 which shows the sorting of our test list of numbers by this algorithm. The general idea of the algorithm is to subdivide or partition the data list into two parts, one containing only values larger than a comparison item, the other containing only smaller values. Each of these two parts is then regarded as a separate subsequence to be sorted itself. The algorithm is invoked recursively to partition each of these two parts separately. This process continues until the partitions are so small that they can each be sorted using a simple sort algorithm such as Bubble Sort.

Referring to Figure 15-1, the purpose of steps 1 through 5 is to partition the original list into three parts, of which the comparison value is one. To do this, we first have to guess or estimate that some value from the original list will end up near the middle of the final sorted list when the algorithm has terminated. In this illustration, we hve made the guess that the value 43, which is originally in the top location of the list, will be acceptably close to the middle. In steps 1 thru 5, we are progressively moving values smaller than the guess value of 43 to locations higher in the list (smaller index values) than the location occupied by the guess value. This is done in step 1 (going to step 2), in step 3 and in step 5, i.e. in all of the steps with the arrow pointing downward. In the alternate steps, i.e. those with even numbers, we are moving values larger than the guess value to positions below (at higher index numbers) the position occupied by the guess value. To avoid cluttering the figure, positions shown blank in this figure are positions which have not changed from the last values held at

Figure 15-1.

LOC	ORIGINAL LIST														
0	43	43#	39	39	39	39	39	39	39	39#	12#	12	12	12	12
1	87		87*	43#	23	23	23			23		23#	23	23	23
2	29				29	29	29			29			29#	29	29
3	38				38	38	38			38				38#	34
4	34				34	34	34			34				34*	38
5	46				46*	43#	12			12*	39	39	39	39	39
6	12					12*	43	43	43	43	43	43	43	43	43
7	68					68	68#	55	55#	46	46	46	46	46	46
8	23			23*	43#	46	46	46	46*	55	55	55	55	55	55
9	75			75	75	75	75	75*	68	68	68	68	68	68	68
10	55			55	55	55	55*	68#	75*	75	75	75	75	75	75
11	39	39*	43#	87	87	87	87	87	87	87	87	87	87	87	87
STEP		1	2	3	4	5	6	7	8	9	10	11	12	13	14

those positions.

Positions marked by a crosshatch ('#') in the figure are the positions containing the guess value at each step. Positions marked by an asterisk ('*') are positions satisfying the condition for an exchange in each step. For example, consider step 3 in which we search for a value smaller than the guess value. Scanning starts in location 10, since the result of step 2 had been to leave a value larger than the guess value at location 11. The first value encountered that is smaller than the guess value is 23. That value is then exchanged with the guess value to complete step 3. Next, scanning starts downward from location 2 in a search for a value larger than the guess value. There is no need to scan starting at location 0 since the values now in locations 0 and 1 are known to be smaller than the guess value. The first value found in step 4 to be larger than the guess value is 46, and this is then exchanged with the guess value to terminate step 4.

The process of dividing the list into partitions completes in step 5 because both the upward scan and downward scan locations in the list have changed to become equal to the location of the guess value itself. Thus the list which starts step 6 (completes action of step 5, as shown in the figure above the Step 6 marker) now is partitioned into three parts, viz:

a) The part running from locations 0 to 5 containing values that are all smaller than the guess value.

b) The part containing the guess value itself.

c) The part running from locations 7 thru 11 containing values that are all larger than the guess value.

One point we have avoided by selecting a list for our example which contains no duplicated data values. Before reading on, you might give some thought to how you would handle the problem of duplicated data values if the guess value happens to be a value that appears more than once in the original list.

Having completed the first partitioning process as a result of step 5, we start in step 6 to partition one of the two partitions created in the first process. We have arbitrarily picked the part running from locations 7 through 11 for the second partitioning process. This is done in steps 6 and 7, giving the list shown adjacent to the step 8 marker. Once again, we have used the value at the top of the starting list as the guess value (68 in this case). The result is another triplet of partitions. The larger part and the smaller part are each small enough now that two simple exchanges in step 8 are all that are required to complete the process for all data values that are larger than the original guess value of 43. The result so-far is shown next to the step 9 marker, with the part of the list that is smaller than the original guess value still as it was at the end of step 5, i.e. as shown next to the step 6 marker.

Our attention now shifts in step 9 to the part of the list smaller than the original guess value of 43. Steps 9 through 13 show the successive partitioning of this part of the list. Compare this partitioning process with the part running from step 6 to step 8. You can see that things haven't gone as well for the part containing the smaller values. The reason for this is that the guess value chosen in each step now happens to be a very bad estimate of the "middle" of the list (statisticians call it the "median"). In effect, steps 9 thru 13 have degenerated into the equivalent of the "cocktail shaker" sort algorithm which we mentioned just briefly at the end of the discussion on Bubble Sort in Chapter 14. Unless we take some kind of counter measure, this problem of bad estimates can destroy the speed advantage of the partitioning algorithms compared to the Bubble Sort.

4. Improving on Bad Median Guesses

As a general rule, the Quicksort algorithm will not fall into the trap of repeated bad guesses unless the original list of data is nearly sorted at the beginning. In cases where you can be fairly sure that a long list of data is in nearly random order before sorting, no countermeasure needs to be added to the Quicksort to cure this problem. Since this problem of bad estimates was discovered, a number of authors have published suggested ways of making better guesses of the middle or median value. The simplest method seems to be the following:

> At each step in which a new partitioning process is to start, identify three data items to use in making the required guess. Use the first and last items in the original list, and also the item located physically closest to the middle of the original list. If there is an even number of data items, choose the smaller index of the two "middle" items. In the example shown in Figure 15-1, the three values would be:
>
> FIRST = 43, MIDDLE = 46, LAST = 39
>
> Now sort these three values to identify the one which is neither largest nor smallest. This intermediary value should be used as the "guess" for the next stage of partitioning. If necessary, the intermediary value should be exchanged with the first value, in order to place the correct guess value at the beginning of the partition before the process begins.

Figure 15-2 shows how this refinement in the algorithm would operate starting in step 9. Notice that the guess, made in the first partitioning process on the complete original list, was the same as the guess that would have been made had this refinement been in effect from the beginning.

Figure 15-2.

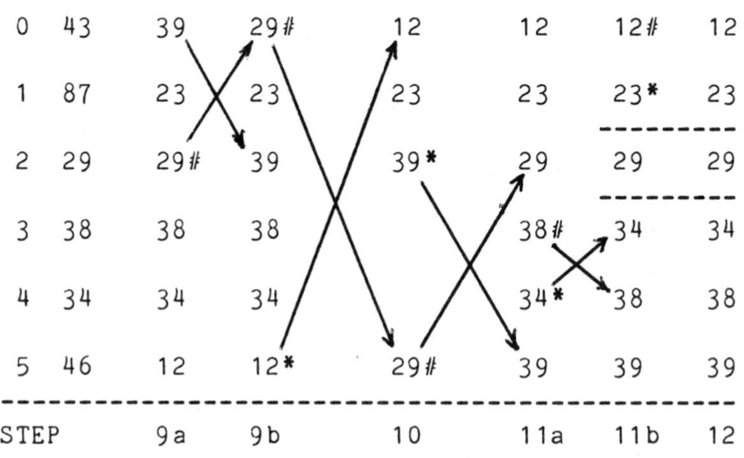

LOC	ORIGINAL LIST						
0	43	39	29#	12	12	12#	12
1	87	23	23	23	23	23*	23
2	29	29#	39	39*	29	29	29
3	38	38	38		38#	34	34
4	34	34	34		34*	38	38
5	46	12	12*	29#	39	39	39
STEP		9a	9b	10	11a	11b	12

In this figure, step 9 is split to show formation of the improved guess for the median value. Step 11 is also split for the same reason. However, the partition considered in step 11 only contains three values. Hence there is no reason to continue the partitioning process after those three values have been sorted as a preliminary to the next stage.

Don't expect the Quicksort (in either form) to cost much less computing time than the Bubble Sort for a list of test values as short as the one used here. If you use a list of 100 randomly ordered test values, the Bubble Sort will require about 5000 comparisons of pairs of data items, whereas the Quicksort should require only about 700. The advantage of Quicksort over the Bubble Sort should become much better for lists longer than this.

Before proceeding to consider the structure diagram for this algorithm, let's dispense with the problem created by having more than one instance of a guess value in the list to be sorted. In the example given here, what would you have done if there had been more than one instance of the value 43?? In the first stage of partitioning, steps 1 thru 5, the best solution to this problem would be to allow additional instances of the value 43 to fall in either the high partition or the low one. Doing this simply delays the decision on where those extra instances of the guess value should be placed. As you can quickly verify, the next stage of partitioning will have the effect of moving thse extra instances to positions immediately adjoining the final position of the guess value itself.

5. Recursive Structure Diagram

Now we begin setting up the structure diagram for the algorithm. It is clearly complicated enough that we would be wise to consider the use of one or more sub-algorithms. An obvious application of a sub-algorithm would be to the process of going through one stage of partitioning. A sub-algorithm PARTITION(FIRST,LAST) would be called once to cover steps 1 thru 5 in Figure 15-1, once for steps 6 and 7, once for steps 9 thru 11 (revised). The sub-algorithm should be able to cope with the problem of small partitions containing only two or three items.

In fact the sub-algorithm has to be written in such a way as to indicate whether additional stages of partitioning will be required, or whether the "end of the line" has been reached in a particular area of the list. This suggests that a recursive definition of the algorithm might be the easiest to understand for a first try. Figure 15-3 illustrates such a recursive definition. Study this algorithm carefully and verify that the action it takes is the same as illustrated in Figure 15-1. For a first try, ignore

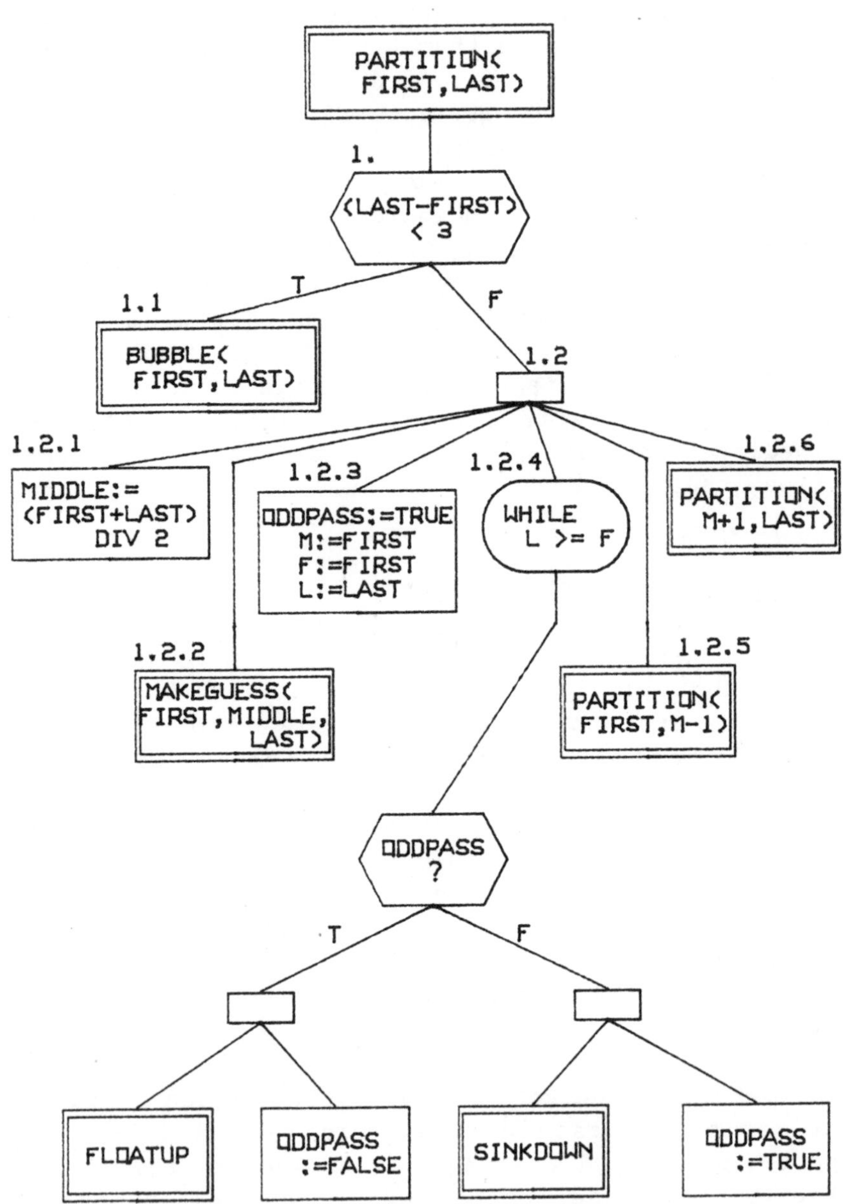
PARTITION(
FIRST,LAST)
1.
(LAST-FIRST)
< 3
T
F
1.1
BUBBLE(
FIRST,LAST)
1.2
1.2.1
MIDDLE:=
(FIRST+LAST)
DIV 2
1.2.2
MAKEGUESS(
FIRST,MIDDLE,
LAST)
1.2.3
ODDPASS:=TRUE
M:=FIRST
F:=FIRST
L:=LAST
1.2.4
WHILE
L >= F
1.2.5
PARTITION(
FIRST,M-1)
1.2.6
PARTITION(
M+1,LAST)
ODDPASS
?
T
F
FLOATUP
ODDPASS
:=FALSE
SINKDOWN
ODDPASS
:=TRUE

Figure 15-3

the operation of Box 1.1 (calls Bubble Sort) and Box 1.2.2 (calls MAKEGUESS sub-algorithm). LAST is the largest index value (location number) of an item in the partition to be sorted. FIRST is the smallest index value for the same partition. In the example of Figure 15-1, PARTITION starts at step 1 with FIRST=0, LAST=11.

Notice the following points about this algorithm:

a) The sub-algorithms FLOATUP and SINKDOWN do most of the work of the PARTITION sub-algorithm. FLOATUP applies to the odd numbered steps, 1, 3, 5,... SINKDOWN operates in the even numbered steps. In a program, these two sub-algorithms are simple enough that they might not be implemented as procedures.

b) M points to the guess value, F to the value closest to FIRST which is next to be compared to the guess value. Similarly L points to the value closest to LAST which is next to be compared to the guess value and possibly exchanged.

c) A single partitioning stage (such as steps 1 thru 5 in the example) is complete when L is no longer greater than F. In fact when FLOATUP completes, L should equal M. When SINKDOWN completes, F should equal M.

d) In general, the result of completing a partitioning stage will be to leave two new partitions which still need to be sorted. The one with the smaller values is sorted by calling PARTITION(FIRST, M-1) in Box 1.2.5. The other is sorted by calling PARTITION(M+1, LAST) in Box 1.2.6.

e) The BUBBLE sub-algorithm is borrowed from Chapter 14. It is only invoked when the size of a partition is only 3 items or fewer, at least as illustrated in Figure 15-3. Because of the extra computing needed to make guess values, the entire sort algorithm will probably run more efficiently for long lists if the BUBBLE sub-algorithm is invoked for partitions containing ten or fewer items, rather than 3 as shown.

f) The entire Quicksort process is carried out by calling this recursive form of PARTITION with FIRST set to the smallest index, LAST to the largest index referring the the list to be sorted. It is assumed that the array LST contains the original data when PARTITION is first called.

Exercise 15.1:

Program and debug the Quicksort algorithm, testing first with the sequence of test data used in Figure 15-1, and then with a list of test data at least 100 items long generated by a random number generator.

This program will be complex enough that you will waste large amounts of time unless you use the step by step program development and testing process that we have been recommending. When working with the short sequence of test data given in this book, you should arrange a debugging display showing the results of each step in the sorting process. Check each step, and make sure that it duplicates the results shown in Figures 15-1 and 15-2.

To get all of the data for a step on your display screen at once, you can cause the items to be output along a horizontal line, rather than in a vertical column as in our figures. Your debugging display probably should also include a second line for each step, showing the values of the relevant variables such as F, L, M, ODDPASS, and so on. If at all possible, you should conduct your debugging using a copy of your program printed on paper, while referring to the successive lines displayed by the debugging statements. As in several earlier instances, we suggest that you place

READLN statements just after a group of debugging WRITE statements to allow you to study the results of each step of processing before continuing to the next (by typing <RET>).

Appendix A

DIFFERENCES BETWEEN UCSD'S PASCAL AND STANDARD PASCAL

The PASCAL language used in this book contains most of the features described by K. Jensen and N. Wirth in PASCAL User Manual and Report, Springer Verlag, 1975. We refer to the PASCAL defined by Jensen and Wirth as "Standard" PASCAL, because of its widespread acceptance even though no international standard for the language has yet been established. The PASCAL used in this book has been implemented at University of California San Diego (UCSD) in a complete software system for use on a variety of small stand-alone microcomputers. This will be referred to as "UCSD PASCAL", which differs from the standard by a small number of omissions, a very small number of alterations, and several extensions. This appendix provides a very brief summary of these differences. Only the PASCAL constructs used within this book will be mentioned herein. Documents are available from the author's group at UCSD describing UCSD PASCAL in detail.

1. CASE Statements

   Jensen & Wirth state that if there is no label equal to the value of the case statement selector, then the result of the case statement is undefined. UCSD PASCAL treats this situation by leaving the case statement normally with no action being taken.

2. Comments

   In UCSD PASCAL, a comment appears between the delimiting symbols "(*" and "*)". If the opening delimiter is followed immediately by a dollar sign, as in "(*$", then the remainder of the comment is treated as a directive to the compiler. The only compiler directive mentioned in this book is (*$G+*), which tells the compiler to allow the use of GOTO statements. The UCSD compiler does not handle nested comments correctly.

3. EOF(F)
To set EOF to TRUE for a textfile F, including the standard INPUT file, the user must press the <ETX> or <ENTER> key (CONTROL-C on a keyboard lacking an explicit key for that purpose). The specific code used for this purpose may be altered from <ETX> if desired.

If the file F is closed, then EOF returns TRUE. If EOF is TRUE, and the file is of <type> TEXT, then EOLN is also true for the same file. Following RESET(F), EOF will return FALSE if the file is present. The system automatically performs a RESET on the files INPUT, OUTPUT, and KEYBOARD when a program is initialized.

4. EOLN(F)
EOLN(F) is defined only if F is a file of <type> TEXT. EOLN becomes TRUE only following a READ during which the end-of-line character (<RET> by default) is received, and before the next READ.

5. GOTO and EXIT(P) statements
UCSD PASCAL only allows a GOTO within the same <block> that contains the declaration of the target label. EXIT provides a limited capability equivalent to GOTO with a target label immediately following the point where the procedure P was called most recently. See Appendix C for further discussion of EXIT. GOTO is disabled by default in UCSD PASCAL when the system is initialized for student use. It can be enabled using the compiler directive (*$G+*).

6. Packed Variables

UCSD PASCAL supports packed arrays of characters, and packed RECORD <type>'s. Characters are packed two to a 16-bit word. Within a record, packing and unpacking are performed automatically within groups of fields that are at most 16-bits wide. UCSD PASCAL has no equivalent of the built-in procedures PACK and UNPACK described by Jensen & Wirth.

7. Procedures and Functions as Formal Parameters

UCSD PASCAL does not support the use of Procedure or Function identifiers as parameters. One exception is the EXIT built-in procedure.

8. Program Headings

In the early releases of UCSD PASCAL, the list of standard file names in the PROGRAM line must not be included as pseudo parameters. Later releases will include this mechanism on an optional basis for use with the X(ecute) command of the operating system.

9. READ and READLN

Jensen & Wirth define READ(F, CH) to be equivalent to the sequence

```
CH := F^;
GET(F);
```

In UCSD PASCAL this sequence is <u>reversed</u> when F is either of the standard console input files INPUT or KEYBOARD. Without this change, it would be extremely awkward to write programs which interact closely with the user.

10. RESET(F)
In UCSD PASCAL, RESET(F) points the file window to the start of a file, but does not load the window variable F^. Thus the UCSD equivalent to the standard definition is:

```
RESET(F);
GET(F);
```

11. REWRITE(F)
UCSD PASCAL does not support the standard procedure REWRITE. OPENNEW provides similar facilities.

12. Sets
In UCSD PASCAL a set may have a maximum of 255*16 elements, i.e. a set may be up to 255 16-bit words in size. All of the set operations described by Jensen & Wirth are supported.

13. STRING variables
UCSD PASCAL has a predeclared <type> STRING. A variable of <type> STRING is essentially a PACKED ARRAY[1..80] OF CHAR, with an associated length attribute of <type> INTEGER. The default length of 80 characters may be overridden by a declaration which specifies the desired maximum length within square brackets, as in:

```
TITLE: STRING[30];
```

where the absolute maximum length supported is 255 characters. The use of STRING variables is described extensively in this book.

14. WRITE and WRITELN
UCSD PASCAL differs from the standard in not supporting parameters of <type> BOOLEAN for WRITE and WRITELN statements. Parameters of <type> STRING produce the results described in the body of

this book.

15. Turtle Graphics
The Turtle graphics facilities described in this book and supported in UCSD PASCAL have no counterpart in the standard language.

Appendix B

GLOSSARY OF COMPUTER JARGON

This glossary presents a list of words and terms used in this book with meanings different from everyday usage. With each term is a very brief reminder about its meaning. For a more extensive discussion of the term, see the (<chapter> . <section>) referred to with each term. For example, (11.5) refers to Chapter 11 Section 5.

Activate (11.5)
: A procedure or function is said to be activated when it is called and begins executing. It is no longer active after it terminates normally, or via use of the EXIT statement. A recursive procedure or function may activate several "copies" of itself concurrently.

Actual Parameter (2.5)
: An actual parameter is a <variable> or <expression> supplied as part of a call to a procedure or function, thus replacing the *formal* parameter which appeared as part of the procedure or function declaration.

Address (5.4)
: The address of a word in the computer's memory can be thought of as the number of the register containing the word.

Algorithm (0.2)
: A statement describing a sequence of actions needed to perform a specific task.

Analog Computer (5.2)
: Term applying to a class of machines that use electrical signals, mechanical levers, pneumatic pressure, or other similar means to simulate the behavior of other systems.

Argument (4.9)
A data value to be used as an actual parameter.

Arithmetic Expression (2.9)
The PASCAL means of combining operands with numeric values to perform the arithmetic operations of addition, subtraction, multiplication and/or division.

Array (8.2)
A data structure which may contain many items (called "elements") of the same <type>.

ASCII (5.2)
The American national Standard Code for Information Interchange. An arbitrary assignment of numeric values to 96 displayable characters, and 32 control signals.

Assembler Language (5.3)
A method of programming a computer similar to using machine language, except that the user refers to each operation using an abbreviated descriptive identifier, rather than with numeric codes directly. Assembler language is translated into machine language by a program called an "assembler".

Assertion (6.5)
A statement of fact, the truth or falsehood of which will be tested within an algorithm.

Assign (2.7), Assignment Operator (2.8),
Assignment Statement (2.7)
Assignment of a value to a variable causes that value to replace whatever value, if any, was previously stored in the memory location named by the variable. The assignment operator (":=") is the PASCAL symbol identifying an assignment statement which calls for the variable on the left of the operator to be assigned a new value.

Backspace (7.4)
A key found on most keyboards. Generally used to indicate that the cursor pointing at the current text location should be backed up one space. Not all hard copy output devices support this feature. If the key is missing, <control-H> usually has the same effect.

Batch (7.3)
Term used to describe the manner in which programs are executed on a computer system (generally large) which accepts its input in the form of a deck of punched cards, and gives output to users in printed form on paper.

Binary Search (13.5)
A searching process in which the set of data items is cut roughly in half, then the half containing the item sought is cut in half, then the quarter containing the item sought is cut in half, and so on.

Bit (5.2)
A binary digit, whose value may be either 0 or 1.

Bit Map (12.6)
Term used to describe a graphic display device which creates images by providing a large number of positions where a program may turn a bright spot on or off.

Bug (1.10)
A logical error in a program, which causes the program to stop abnormally or to give incorrect results.

Built-In (2.11)
Adjective referring to pre-declared procedures and functions which are supplied as part of a software system.

Cal. :2.3)
The process whereby a portion of a program interrupts its own execution temporarily, and causes a named procedure to be executed.

Call-by-Name Parameter (4.7)
Same as Variable Parameter. An actual variable parameter is substituted for the formal variable parameter wherever the latter appears inside a procedure or function.

Call-by-Value Parameter (4.7)
A call-by-value parameter, or simply value parameter, is really a local variable whose value is initialized to the value of the actual parameter at the time a procedure or function starts execution.

Card Image (7.2)
A record containing the same information as punched into the corresponding computer punch card.

Case Statement (4.10)
The case statement allows selecting one of many statements to be executed. This contrasts with the IF statement which allows one of at most two statements to be controlled.

Central Processing Unit (5.3)
The main portion of the computer hardware which interprets and processes machine language instructions. Often called the "CPU".

Code (5.2)
A numeric value or sequence of bits used to stand for some non-numeric equivalent value. The term "code" often is used also to refer to a whole sequence of instructions in machine language.

Column (8.8)
A vertical grouping of entries in an array or table. May also refer to the position of a character in a line or row of text. The two meanings are really equivalent, since text is stored in the form of an array.

Command (2.1)
An instruction to a software system or program telling it to perform some action, or to cause the execution of a specific program unit.

Comment (1.4)
Part of a PASCAL program intended only for human understanding, and ignored by the compiler.

Communication (4.5)
Used in this book to refer to the manner in which information is passed from one part of a program to another, via parameters, and via global variables.

Compiler (0.9)
A large program which translates programs written in PASCAL (or some other programming language) into a form which can be interpreted directly by the computer hardware as a sequence of elementary operation instructions.

Compound Statement (3.2)
A group of statements enclosed between the reserved words BEGIN and END. A convenient way to cause all of the statements within the group to be controlled together.

Concatenate (2.11)
One <string> is concatenated to another by appending the first <string> to the end of the second. For example, if we concatenate "bird" to "big" we get "bigbird".

CONST, Constant (10.5)
Reserved word in PASCAL used to introduce a sequence of constant declarations, which associate specific identifiers with fixed values for use within the program.

Constructor (9.6)
This term is used in connection with the list of constant values enclosed within square brackets used to construct a new value for assignment to a Set.

Control Characters (3.5)
Non printing characters used to control output devices such as CRT terminals and line printers. Examples of control characters are carriage return, backspace, and rubout.

Control Variable (3.7)
An Integer, Character, or Scalar variable which is given an initial value and then counted up or counted down in controlling a FOR statement.

Conversational Computer (7.2)
A computer arranged to interact with the user by displaying or printing output messages, and receiving input messages, generally typed on a keyboard.

CPU (5.3)
See "Central Processing Unit".

Cursor (1.5)
A place marker indicating to a user his relative position within text which generally is displayed.

Cycle (5.4)
Used in this book to refer to one operational step in the CPU of a computer.

Data (0.2)
Information to be supplied to a computer program, where the task to be carried out generally will result in the data being altered, summarized, or used in making decisions.

Data Structure (8.2)
A logical organization for related variables which reflects relationships among various items of data.

Debug (1.10)
To debug is to discover and eliminate the logic errors ("bugs") from a program.

Declare, Declaration (2.3)
All user defined variables in a PASCAL program must be declared, using the prescribed syntax rules, in order to inform the compiler about detailed characteristics the variables are supposed to represent.

Delimit, Delimiter (1.11)
To delimit is to mark the places where an entity, such as a string or a comment, begins and ends. A delimiter is a symbol used as a marker for this purpose.

Difference (9.6)
In addition to its familiar definition as an arithmetic operation, the term "difference" also applies to Sets in PASCAL. Given the assignment statement S3:=S1-S2, the difference of S2 from S1 is assigned to S3. All set members of S1 that are not also members of S2 will be included in S3.

Digital (5.2)
A digital computer is one in which all operations are carried out using digits, usually the binary digits 1 and 0.

Display (0.5)
As used in this book, display refers to the presentation of output information from the computer on a visual device, often one similar to a television screen.

DIV (5.7)
PASCAL integer division operator. Requires integer operands, and returns the integer quotient as result.

Document (0.9)
To computer people, a document is quite often a written description of a computer or computer program including instructions on how to use the thing described.

Echo (7.2)
The term echo implies that each character typed on a keyboard will immediately appear on the display screen or typewriter device connected to the computer.

Edit (1.5)
To edit a program is to alter its contents. To computer people, an "editor" is usually a program used to assist one to edit other programs, rather than a human who does a lot of editing work.

Element (8.2)
The term element refers to a single data item, usually one item in an array of items.

Empty (1.9)
Implies an entity described by the syntax diagrams which may occur with no content at all, usually on an optional basis.

End Of File (EOF) (7.2)
The End Of File condition is reached when a program reads all of the available data from a file, where the term "file" applies to any external device.

Escape Character (7.11)
An escape character is a character used to act as a signal to a program that some action should be performed. Generally an escape character will appear in a context where the same character should never show up as part of normal data.

Exchange (14.4)
Describes the process where the data content of two variables is swapped.

Execute (1.4)
We say that a program or portion of a program is executed when it performs the actions or logical steps described by the program.

Exercise (0.2)
In this book, an exercise is a problem to be worked out by the reader for solution on a computer.

Exponent (5.6)
The portion of a floating point number that designates the power to which 2 or 8 should be raised.

File (1.5), (7.2)
The term file often applies to a collection of data stored on a magnetic disk or tape, on cards, or on some other medium that usually can be removed from the computer. The term also is often used in the narrow sense of referring to the logic mechanism through which data is communicated between a CPU and an external device under program control.

Field (5.6), (10.3)
A field is a contiguous group of bits or characters within a record, where the entire group represents the storage for a variable. A floating point number consists of several fields including the mantissa and the exponent.

Flag (7.11)
Used in this book in the same sense as an escape character. A logical device, usually an unlikely or impossible data value, used to serve notice that a program should take some specific action.

Floating Point (5.6)
A floating point number is one that is stored in the computer memory in such a way that the decimal point (or binary point) bears no fixed relationship to the bits of a memory word.

Floppy Disk (1.2)
A flexible magnetic disk used for data storage on small computers.

Flow Chart (3.3)
A diagram showing the logical sequence of processing that a program follows. One follows the sequence of action in a flowchart in much the same manner that one follows roads from town to town on a road map.

Formal Parameter (2.5)
An identifier declared to be a parameter in the heading line of a procedure or function declaration is called a "formal" parameter. When the procedure or function is called later, the parameter will be replaced by an "actual" parameter.

Format (7.2)
In computer jargon, a format is a specification written in a special language describing the conversion of characters to internal binary form on input, or the reverse of this on output. In PASCAL the format needed to translate a Real or Integer number from characters to binary, or vice versa, is inferred from the <type> of the variable or expression appearing in the Read or Write statement.

FORWARD (4.3)

A reserved word used in connection with the declaration of a procedure so that other procedures may refer to that procedure before the main "body" of the procedure appears in the program. Often used to make it possible for each of two procedures to call the other.

Function (2.11)

A procedure that is arranged to return a value when it completes its processing. A function is called by including the function identifier in an <expression>.

Global Variable (2.8)

A variable declared in the <block> of the main program is said to be "global" as a reminder that it can be referred to from within the main program or any procedure.

GO TO Statement (11.2)

A statement found in most programming languages which causes control of a program to jump from one place to another abruptly.

Hard Copy (0.5)

A hard copy is a printed record of computer output on paper. By contrast "soft" copy appears on a display screen, but it cannot be carried away from the computer in the user's hand.

Hardware (1.2)

The computer equipment that can be seen and touched. For example, a CPU, interactive terminal, disk drive, printer, or keyboard are all items of hardware.

Hard Wired (5.4)

Refers to the method of connecting items of computer hardware together by direct use of wires. Many of today's computers use very few hard wired connections, but instead rely on logical connections made using read-only memory devices that can easily be replaced.

Heading (2.6)
Term used in this book to refer to the portion of a procedure or function declaration that comes before the first CONST, TYPE, or VAR declarations in the same <block>.

Hierarchic Structure (6.5)
Another name for a "tree" structure. In a hierarchic structure, all logical connections branch from the root node, and no connections are allowed to loop back on themselves.

Higher Level (5.3)
The computer hardware generally can perform only simple primitive operations. A higher level operation is a sequence of these primitive operations designed to carry out a more complex action. A higher level programming language is one designed to call for higher level operations in readily understood terms.

High Order Bit (5.6)
The bit in a computer word having the highest place value. Usually represented as being at the left end in a picture of the bits in a word, just as the most significant digit in a number is at the left.

Histogram (12.6)
A "bar" graph in which each bar (usually vertical) represents the value of a single data item.

Identifier (1.8)
A name given to an entity in a program. Preferably the name should be a reminder about the purpose of the entity.

Indent, Indentation (3.11)
A line of program text is indented by inserting non-functional blank spaces at the left. By doing this appropriately, one can create a rough approximation to a diagram describing the structure

of a program in PASCAL.

Initialize (3.7)
When an initial value is assigned to a variable, we say it is "initialized".

Input/Output (5.3)
The process of transferring data to/from main memory from/to some external device.

Integer Constant (2.5)
A positive or negative whole number. Examples: -34, 109, 1, 3, 0, -102

Interactive (7.2)
An interactive computer system is one which can "converse" with the user by sending messages to the user via a display device or tele-printer, and by receiving messages via a keyboard.

Internal Form (7.2)
Within the computer, numbers are stored in an internal binary notation. On output, this form generally is converted into characters. On input, the reverse conversion takes place.

Interpreter (3.8)
A program which runs on a real "host" computer in such a way as to make the host appear to be a different logical computer.

Intersection (9.6)
The intersection of two sets is a set whose members include items that are members of <u>both</u> of the original sets.

Invalid Index (9.5)
A term describing an abnormal program termination which occurs when an attempt is made to: a) refer to an array location that has not been declared to be within the bounds of the array; b) assign a value to a subrange variable outside the bounds associated with its <type> declaration.

Inverse
The inverse of something is its opposite. The inverse of TRUE is FALSE, i.e. NOT TRUE. The inverse of I > J is I <= J, where I and J are Integer or Real variables.

Jump (11.2)
Term used to describe the process whereby a computer interrupts its normal sequence of processing instructions and abruptly commences processing from a different point in the program.

Key (13.6)
In a searching operation, the key is the item for which an instance is being sought in a list or file. In sorting, the key is a portion of the record specification to be used for comparison purposes to determine the order of the resulting list.

KEYBOARD File (7.7)
On the UCSD PASCAL software system, KEYBOARD is the name of the non-echoing equivalent of the standard INPUT file.

Label (11.3)
A marker designating a place in a program to which a GOTO statement will cause a jump to occur.

Leading Zeroes (5.9)
Zero digits which appear to the left of the most significant non-zero digit in a number.

Leaf Node (6.5)
A box in a structure diagram which has no branches to lower levels in the diagram. Also applies to similar boxes in any diagram constructed as a logical tree.

Listing (1.10)
A printed copy of a program or of the output of a program.

Local Variable (2.8)
A local <variable> is one declared within the same <block> where it is used.

Loop (3.3)
A term that originated when repeated execution of a series of program steps required use of the GOTO statement. This led to flow chart representations that looped back on themselves.

Machine Language (5.3)
The code values that the computer hardware interprets as instructions.

Main Frame (5.3)
The principal hardware components of a computer.

Main Memory (5.4)
A large number of storage registers grouped together and addressed according to the numeric order in which they appear. Main memory is where the values of variables are stored temporarily while a program is processing.

Mantissa (5.6)
Tne integer portion of a floating point number. On most computers, it is understood that the mantissa has a value equivalent to the integer value divided by 2 raised to the power N, where N is the number of bits in the mantissa field.

Maxi-computer (0.4)
A large computer capable of serving many users concurrently.

Memory (5.3)
See "Main Memory"

Merge (14.2)
The process whereby two (or more) sorted lists of data items are combined into one longer sorted list.

Micro-computer (0.4)
A small computer, usually costing no more than a few thousand dollars, and usually employing an integrated circuit microprocessor as its CPU.

Mini-computer (0.4)
A computer of small to medium size, which quite often is shared by many people simultaneously. In 1977, the term minicomputer applies to machines typically costing from $10,000 to $100,000.

Model (6.8)
This term is often applied to computer programs which simulate the operation of some system or process that occurs naturally or in everyday human affairs.

Module (5.3)
A logically separate portion of a larger program or piece of equipment. A "modular" system is one constructed of modules.

Monitor (13.4)
To monitor a program is to trace its flow of execution while it is running, generally displaying the content of selected variables as it goes.

Nesting (3.10)
Refers to a situation in which a logical construct has a similar construct within itself. For example an <expression> enclosed in parentheses may be nested inside a larger expression. A procedure may be nested within another procedure. A compound statement may be nested within another statement. And so on.

Node (6.5)
A branching point or leaf within a "tree" diagram.

Normalize (5.9)
The process of aligning the digits of a number in such a way as to satisfy the requirements of the addition/subtraction operation, or of information storage in memory to retain maximum accuracy.

Operand (5.4)
An item of information placed in a context in which it may be manipulated by the computer in any specified manner.

Operate (0.2)
To perform a sequence of actions upon operands in order to achieve a desired result.

Operator (2.10)
This term refers to the PASCAL symbols which call for certain operations to take place. For example the symbol ":=" calls for assignment of value to take place, and thus is called the "assignment operator".

Packed (8.7)
A packed array or (packed record) is one which occupies as little memory space as possible while retaining enough bits to store all possible values of the associated <type>(s).

Parameter (2.5)
A means of passing a message to a procedure or function from the place in the program where the procedure or function is called.

Parameter List (2.8)
The list of items in a procedure or function declaration heading which are declared to be the identifiers, and associated <type>'s, of the parameters to be used with the procedure or function.

Pass (2.5)
The value or name of a parameter is said to be "passed" (as a message) as part of the process of calling a procedure or function.

Pattern (2.11)
Term used to describe a <string> which will be used in scanning a second <string> for the purpose of determining whether the first <string> is contained in the second.

Peripheral Device (5.3)
A device which may be added to the main frame portion of a computer. Examples of devices considered to be peripheral include line printers, disk drive units, card readers, and interactive terminals.

Place Value (5.8)
The power of the "base" of the number system corresponding to the position of a digit. For example, the place value of the digit "2" in the number 234 is 100 in the decimal numbering system. The place value of the leftmost digit "1" in the binary number 0101 is 2 raised to the power 2, i.e. the equivalent of the decimal number 4.

Pointer (3.9)
As used in this book, the term "pointer" generally refers to an integer variable, the value of which points to a specific element of an array or <string> variable. PASCAL allows the use of variables of <type> pointer, the use of which is beyond the scope of this book.

Precedence (2.10)
In an <expression> containing several distinct operator symbols, the rules of precedence determine the order in which the corresponding operations will be carried out.

Predecessor (9.8)
In the definition of a Scalar <type> the predecessor of one item is the adjacent item occurring earlier in the list of items.

Problems (0.2)
The problems given with the earlier chapters of this book are designed to be worked out or answered using pencil and paper. They are to be distinguished from the Exercises, which are designed for solution using the computer.

Procedure (2.3)
A sub-program, i.e. a separate part of a program which may be called into execution by name.

Process, Processing (0.2)
The computer processes a program by carrying out the instructions in the program on a step by step basis. When a program, or part of a program, is processed we also say that it is "executed" or that it is "run".

Program (0.2)
A sequence of declarations of variables followed by executable statements or instructions which specify a logical sequence of computations to be performed.

Programming Language (0.2)
A set of rules and special words and symbols which are used together to construct a program.

Prompt (7.3)
A program displays a brief message to prompt a user to respond with desired input from the keyboard.

Prompt-Line (1.2)
In some computer systems such as the UCSD PASCAL system, prompt messages are normally displayed on a specific line of the display device.

Random Number (5.11)
A number chosen at random, as if it were chosen "out of a hat", from a specified set of numbers. Each time a new random number is drawn, it should (in principle) have no relationship to the previous number drawn.

Range (9.5)
Usually refers to the specified set of values that a variable may assume. The range is said to run from the lower bound (lowest possible value) to the upper bound (highest possible value).

REAL (5.6)
Pre-declared <type> in PASCAL designed for storing floating point numbers.

Record (7.2)
A data structure which may contain several related data items which may be of differing <type>'s.

Recursion, Recursive (4.2)
A recursive procedure or function is one which calls itself. Recursion is the process associated with recursive procedures and functions.

Register (5.4)
A group of binary storage devices used collectively. This term is most often applied to the very fast storage devices which are part of the CPU of a computer. Though main memory is composed of a large number of slower registers, the term register rarely is used in that case, and one normally refers to a memory location, element, or cell.

Reserved Word (1.8)
A word within a programming language which has a pre-defined meaning or special significance to the compiler program.

Return (2.11)
After it completes its processing, a procedure returns the sequence of program execution to the point in the program immediately following the point where the procedure was called. When a function returns, it leaves (i.e. "returns") a value in the place of its identifier within an expression.

Root (6.5)
Term used in this book to refer to the base node of a structure diagram or other tree structure.

Round (5.7)
To round a floating point number is to convert it to the nearest value that can be expressed within the limited number of bits that can be represented on the computer. The built-in function ROUND converts the value of a Real <variable> to the nearest Integer value.

Row (8.8)
A horizontal line of entries in a table, or in a tabular representation of an array.

Run-time (13.3)
Describes the period of time when a program is actually running on the computer. When the execution of a program terminates abnormally, we say that it has suffered a run-time error.

Search (13.2)
The process of examining a set of data in a systematic manner to determine whether a particular value may be present, and if so to locate its position.

Scalar Variable (9.2)
A <variable> in PASCAL which may take on any one of several non-numerical values represented by a list of identifiers in the declaration of the Scalar <type>.

Scale Factor (12.5)
A constant used to adjust the size of a graph to make the graph fill a display screen or printed page, while avoiding the loss of parts of the graph off the edges of the screen or page.

Scan (3.9)
Term used to describe the process of examining a string of characters to determine whether a particular pattern or character is present.

Semantics (7.4)
Set of rules which describe the actions or results to be expected when a programming language construct is used.

Series (5.10)
An arithmetic expression containing a large (possibly infinite) number of sub-expressions called "terms", all of which are constructed according to some logical rule.

Set (9.2)
In PASCAL a set is a variable constructed in a manner similar to an array containing only Boolean values. Each item in a set, when TRUE, is said to be a "member" of the set which is "present". A set may correspond to the possible range of values in a Scalar, Subrange, or CHAR <type>.

Side Effect (4.2)
The inadvertent change of the value of a variable by a procedure (in which the same identifier should have been declared locally) in such a way that other parts of a program behave incorrectly.

Signal (5.4)
An electrical impulse which causes some action to be taken by a portion of the computer's hardware.

Single Step (1.10)
The process of causing a program to be executed one instruction or one statement at a time.

Software (1.2)
A collection of large programs which make the primitive instructions of a computer's hardware handle more complex functions of use to humans.

Stack (4.2)
A list of data values arranged so that the first item that can be removed is the last item to be added.

State (5.4)
The state of a computer, or any logical device using binary logic, is described by the values of all the bits in all the binary registers. It is possible to return to any one state, from any other, by arranging all of the bits to be set once again to the values associated with that state.

Step-wise Refinement (6.6)
The recommended procedure for developing a program is to start with a rough description, then to refine that description by adding details step by step.

String (0.2)
A collection of characters which is interpreted as a single data item in PASCAL.

Structured Programming (0.3)
An orderly approach to computer programming which emphasizes breaking large and complicated logical sequences into smaller modules, each of which performs a task which is conceptually separate and distinct from other parts of the program.

Subrange (9.5), Subrange Variable (9.2)
A portion of the full range of values that a <type> of variables may assume. A subrange includes all of the values running from a specified minimum (lower bound) to a specified maximum (upper bound).

Subscript (8.4)
An index or pointer value used to access an element of an array.

Subscripted Variable (8.4)
A reference to an element of an array, consisting of the array identifier followed by one or more index expressions enclosed in square brackets.

Successor (9.8)
The successor of one item in the definition of a Scalar <type> is the item immediately following that item in the declaration.

Syntax (1.8)
The set of rules describing how correct programs may be written. A Syntax Diagram describes those rules in a concise way.

System (1.2)
A collection of interacting entities, often large. In this book, the term "system" generally applies to the collection of large software programs which comprise the means of developing and running PASCAL programs.

Terminal (7.2)
A device through which a user communicates with a computer, usually involving a display device or tele-printer plus a keyboard.

Term (5.10)
A specialized word applying to an item used in the syntax of arithmetic and Boolean expressions.

Top Down (6.6)
This term describes the process of algorithm and program development in which one starts at the root of the structure diagram, and then progressively adds more detailed nodes to the diagram.

Trace (2.4)
One can trace the logical path of steps that a program takes by inserting WRITELN statements at strategic points in order to show the values of selected variables when the program reaches those points. The program can be stopped temporarily so that the displayed values may be studied by adding a READLN statement following the WRITELN statement(s).

Transaction (8.8)
This term has its origin in business data processing. It applies to the sequence of processing steps which follow the input of one record of input data, and continue up until any immediately connected output has been completed.

Tree (4.10)
A branching logical structure having one and only one path to the root from any leaf node.

Truncation (5.7)
The process whereby the least significant bits of a binary number resulting from an arithmetic operation are lost because there is insufficient room in a memory word for all bits to be stored.

Truth Table (3.9)
A table showing the relationship between the value of a Boolean expression and the values of the variables comprising that expression.

Type (1.5)
Formal description of the kind of information that a variable may be used to store in a PASCAL program.

Undefined
The value of a variable is said to be undefined if no value has yet been assigned to it, or after conclusion of certain operations.

Union (9.6)
The union of two sets is a set whose members consist of all of the members of both of the original sets.

Update (14.5)
A record in an existing file is said to be updated when its content is changed to more up-to-date values.

User (7.3)
A user is a person who is running a program or otherwise working with a computer.

Validate (7.11)
Validation is the process of checking on the value of an input data item to determine whether that value is within reasonable limits, and thus probably not in error.

Value Parameter (4.7)
Same as "Call-by-value" parameter.

Variable (2.7)
A name given to a location in the computer's memory where a data value, or group of associated values, may be stored for later use.

Variable Parameter (4.7)
In the declaration of a procedure or function, identifiers of variable parameters are preceded by the reserved identifier "VAR". A variable parameter is a "dummy" name which is used in compiling, but which will be replaced by the idenfifier of the actual parameter when the procedure or function is called.

Variant (9.3)
A means whereby the last field of a Record declaration may have several different meanings.

Window Diagram (4.3)
A diagram used to illustrate the scope within which declared identifiers may be used within a PASCAL program.

Word, Word Size (5.4)
A collection of bits which form the content of a memory register. The word size is the number of bits contained in a word.

Workfile (1.7)
A temporary working copy of the program currently being altered using the Editor. The compiler takes its PASCAL program statements from the workfile when the R(un and C(ompile commands are used.

Appendix C

BUILT-IN PROCEDURES AND FUNCTIONS

1. ABS(X)

   Function which returns the absolute value of the Integer or Real parameter X. The <type> of the result is the same as the <type> of the actual parameter.

2. ATAN(X)

   Function which returns as a Real result the value of the arctangent(X), where X is Real. The value returned is Real in units of radians.

3. CHR(X)

   Function which returns a result of <type> CHAR the ordinal value of which is the Integer value of X. For example, the following two statements are equivalent:

   ```
     CH:=' ';    CH:=CHR(32)
   ```

   assuming that CH is a variable of <type> CHAR.

4. CLEARSCREEN

   A UCSD procedure which causes the screen on a CRT terminal with graphic facilities to be cleared, and the turtle left in its home postion at center of the screen.

5. CONCAT(S1, S2, ...)

   A UCSD function which returns a result of <type> STRING. The result string is the concatenation of all of the string parameters S1, S2, ..., where two or more actual parameters may be used.

6. COPY(SOURCE, INDEX, SIZE)

   A UCSD function which returns a result of <type> STRING. The actual parameter SOURCE is of <type> STRING, while INDEX and SIZE are of <type> INTEGER. The string returned is obtained by copying the first SIZE characters from the SOURCE string variable starting at the character SOURCE[INDEX].

7. COS(X)
   Function which returns as a Real result the cosine(x), where X is a Real actual parameter expressed in radians.

8. DELETE(SOURCE, INDEX, SIZE)
   A UCSD procedure which removes SIZE characters from SOURCE starting at SOURCE[INDEX]. SOURCE is of <type> STRING, while INDEX and SIZE are of <type> INTEGER.

9. EOF(F)
   Boolean function which returns TRUE after the <ETX> (end of file) character has been read for the file F. Otherwise FALSE is returned. If the file identifier F, and its enclosing parentheses, are missing, then the file INPUT is assumed by default.

10. EOLN(F)
    Boolean function which returns TRUE if the end of line character (<RET> or Carriage RETurn by default) has been read at the end of the most recent READ statement. Otherwise the function returns FALSE. If the file identifier F, and its enclosing parentheses, are omitted, then the file INPUT is assumed by default.

11. EXIT(P)
    A UCSD procedure which accepts the identifier of a procedure as its single parameter. The most recent activation of that procedure will be terminated normally. Results are not defined if P is not currently active, and an abnormal termination of the program will probably result.

12. EXP(X)
    Function which returns as a Real result the value of the mathematical constant "e" raised to the power of the Integer or Real parameter X.

13. INSERT(SOURCE, DESTINATION, INDEX)
A UCSD procedure which inserts the value of the variable SOURCE into the variable DESTINATION starting before the character DESTINATION[INDEX]. SOURCE and DESTINATION are of <type> STRING, while INDEX is of <type> Integer.

14. LENGTH(S)
A UCSD function which returns as an Integer result the number of characters contained in S, which is of <type> STRING.

15. LN(X)
Function which returns as a Real result the value of the natural logarithm of the Integer or Real parameter X.

16. LOG(X)
Function which returns as a Real result the value of the Logarithm to the base 10 of the Integer or Real parameter X.

17. MOVE(DISTANCE)
A UCSD procedure which causes the Turtle graphics cursor (the "turtle") to move DISTANCE screen units in its current pointing direction. DISTANCE is of <type> Integer.

18 MOVETO(XPOS, YPOS)
A UCSD procedure which causes the Turtle graphics cursor to move to the position (XPOS, YPOS) on the screen. This position is XPOS screen units to the right of center screen, and YPOS screen units above center screen. If XPOS is negative, the Turtle moves to the left rather than right. If YPOS is negative, the Turtle moves below the center screen, rather than above. Whereas MOVE causes the Turtle to move <u>relative</u> to the current position, MOVETO causes it to move to an <u>absolute</u> location on the screen.

19. ODD(X)
Boolean function which returns the value TRUE if the Integer parameter X has an odd value, otherwise it returns FALSE.

20. ORD(X)
Boolean function which returns as an Integer result the ordinal value of the parameter X. X must be of a Scalar <type> or of <type> CHAR or BOOLEAN.

21. PAGE(F)
Procedure which causes the next WRITE or WRITELN to the file F to appear on a new page of paper, if F is a file whose content is being sent to a printer. In the case of an interactive display terminal, PAGE will cause the screen to be cleared, and the cursor to be placed in the upper left corner.

22. PENCOLOR(COLOR)
A UCSD procedure used to alter the "color" of the "ink" used by the Turtle graphics cursor (i.e. the "turtle"). The parameter COLOR is of a Scalar <type> which can take on any one of the following values:

NONE: The Turtle does not write or disturb the contents of the screen as it moves. The Turtle's figurative pen is in the up position.

WHITE: The Turtle will now draw bright lines on the screen when moved.

BLACK: The Turtle will now draw lines by "turning off" bright dots on a bit-map display screen. (Applies only to bit-map devices.)

23. POS(PATTERN, SOURCE)
A UCSD function which returns as an Integer result the index in SOURCE where the first occurrence of the PATTERN is found. PATTERN and SOURCE are of <type> STRING. If no occurrence of the PATTERN is found, then the value returned is 0 (zero).

24. PRED(X)
Function which returns as its result the predecessor of the Scalar parameter X. If the value of X is the lower bound of the range of the Scalar <type>, then an invalid index termination will result.

25. ROUND(X)
Function which returns as an Integer result, the value of the Real parameter X rounded to the nearest Integer according to the following definition:

```
ROUND(X) = (TRUNC(X + 0.5) if X > 0
         = (TRUNC(X - 0.5) if X < 0
```

26. SIN(X)
Function which returns as a Real result the value of sine(X) where X is a Real parameter whose value if an angle expressed in radians.

27. SUCC(X)
Function which returns as its result the successor of the Scalar parameter X. If the value of X is equal to the upper bound of the declared range of the Scalar <type> then the program will terminate abnormally for an invalid index.

28. SQR(X)
Function which returns as its result the square of the Integer or Real parameter X. The result will be of the same <type> as the parameter.

29. SQRT(X)
Function which returns as a Real result the square root of the value of the Real parameter X.

30. TRUNC(X)
Function which returns as an Integer result the value of the Real parameter X truncated to the greatest Integer less than or equal to X for X > 0, or the least Integer greater or equal to X if X < 0.

31. TURN(ANGLE)
A UCSD procedure which causes the pointing direction of the Turtle to rotate through ANGLE degrees, where ANGLE is of <type> INTEGER. If ANGLE has a positive value, the rotation is in the counter clockwise direction, if negative then clockwise.

32. TURNTO(ANGLE)
A UCSD procedure which changes the pointing direction of the Turtle to the value of ANGLE explicitly. TURN makes a change <u>relative</u> to the present direction. TURNTO set the Turtle to an <u>absolute</u> direction.

33. WHEREAMI(XPOS, YPOS, DIRECTION)
A UCSD Turtle graphics procedure with three Variable (call by name) parameters into which the current position coordinate values and pointing direction of the Turtle are returned. All three actual parameters must be of <type> INTEGER. XPOS and YPOS are distances from the center of the screen. Direction is an angle in degrees measured in the counterclockwise direction from the horizontal direction to the right.

Appendix D

INDEX

Each entry refers to <chapter number> . <section number>. For example 2.5 refers to Chapter 2 Section 5. In general, this index contains only references to specific constructs of the PASCAL language. See the Glossary of terms, Appendix B for references to many additional terms.

Appendix E - SYNTAX DIAGRAMS

<identifier>

letter
letter
digit

<unsigned integer>

digit

<unsigned number>

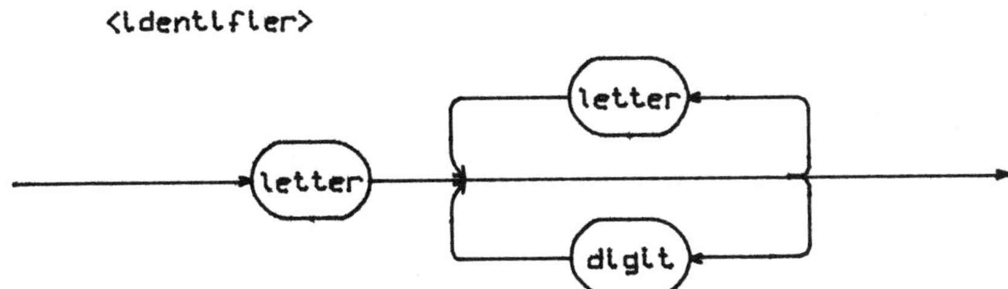

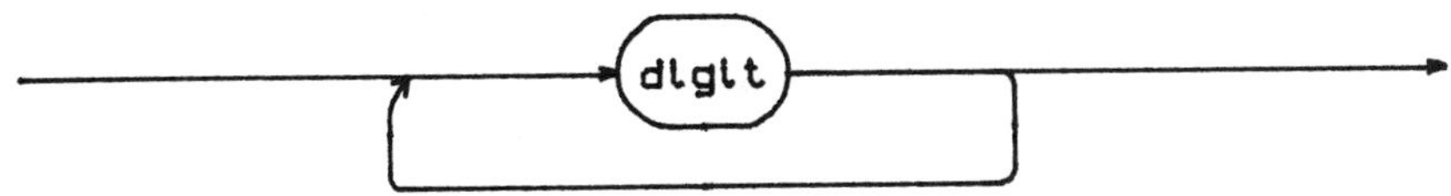

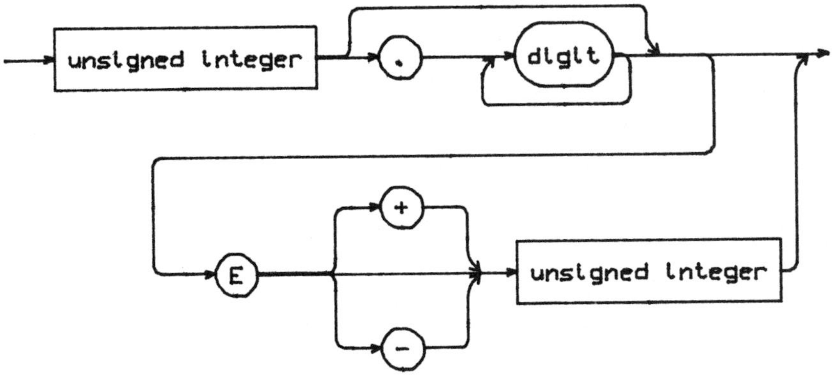

unsigned integer
.
digit
E
+
-
unsigned integer

<unsigned constant>

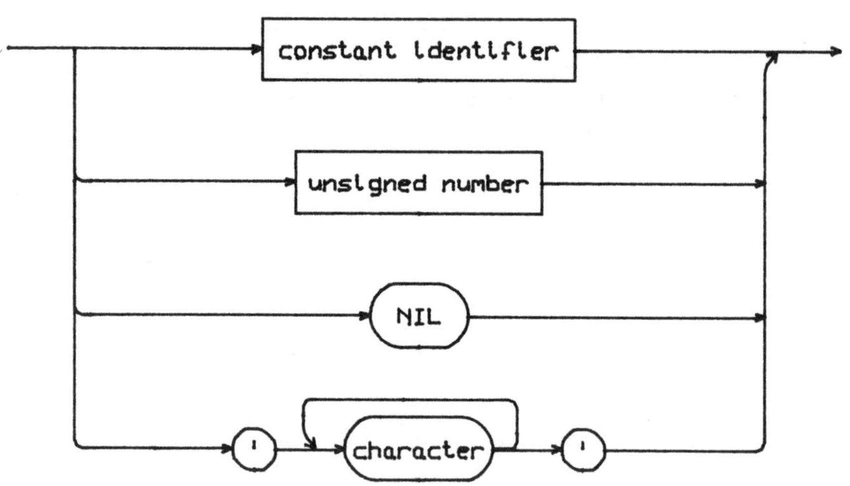

<constant>

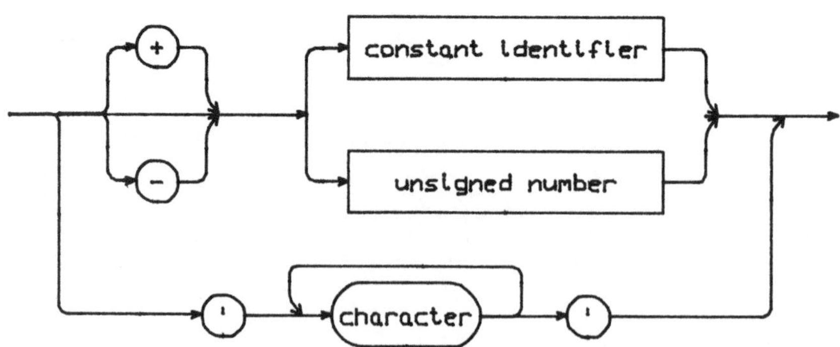

<simple type>

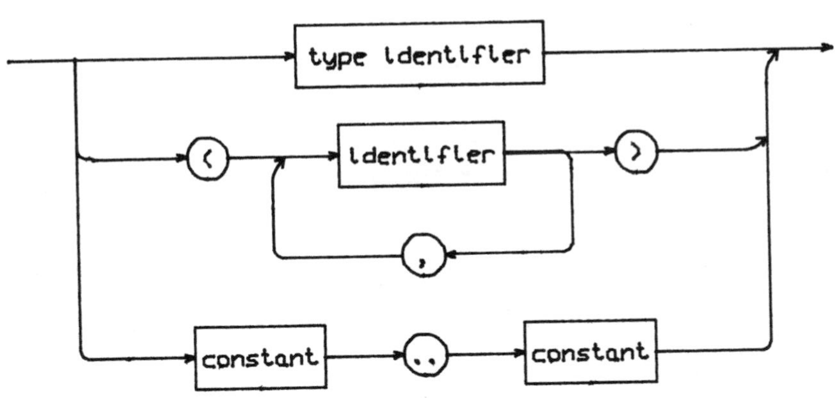

field list

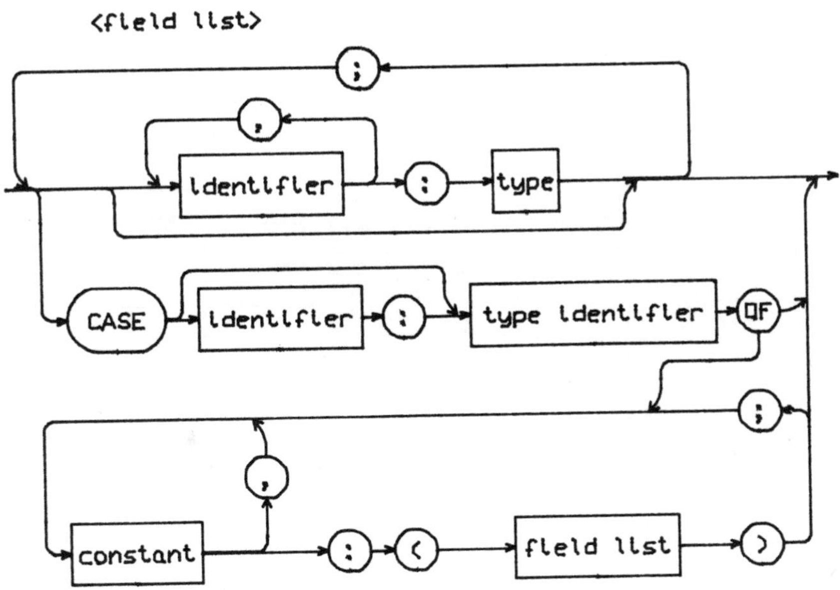

<type>

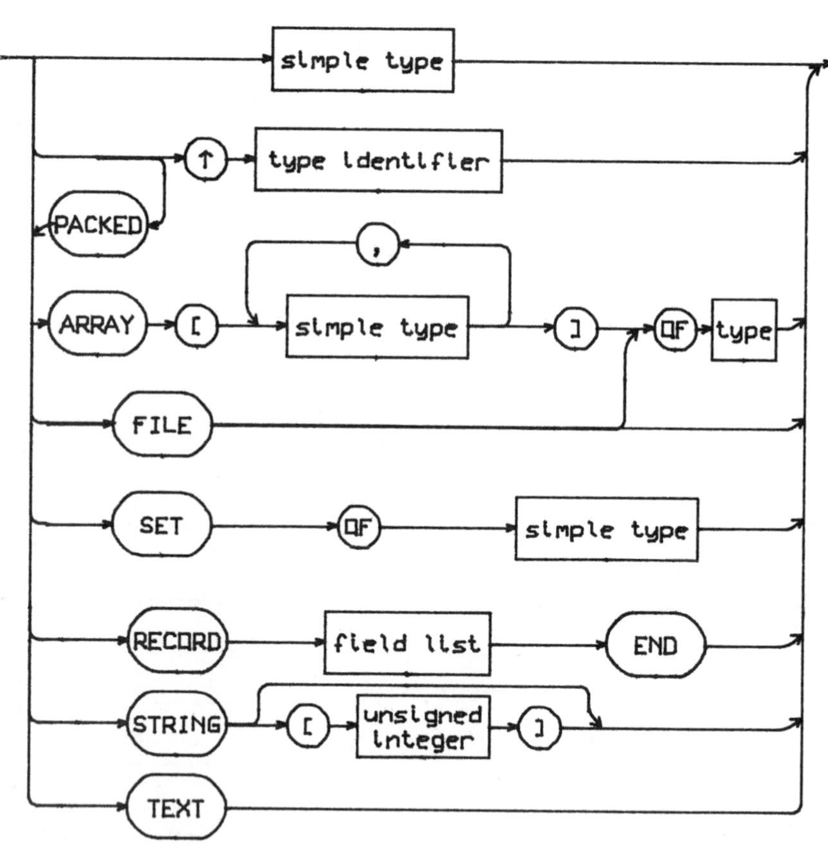
simple type
↑
type identifier
PACKED
,
ARRAY
[
simple type
]
OF
type
FILE
SET
OF
simple type
RECORD
field list
END
STRING
[
unsigned integer
]
TEXT

<variable>

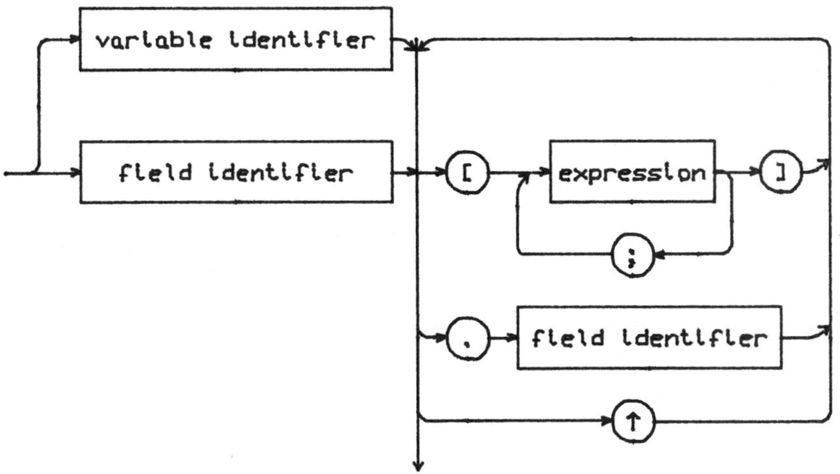

<simple expression>

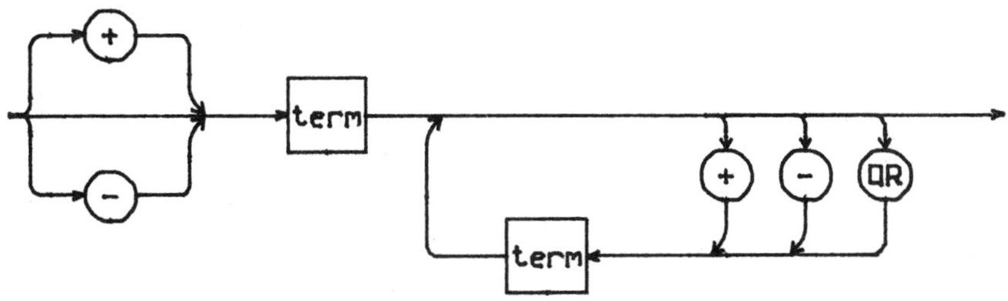

<term>

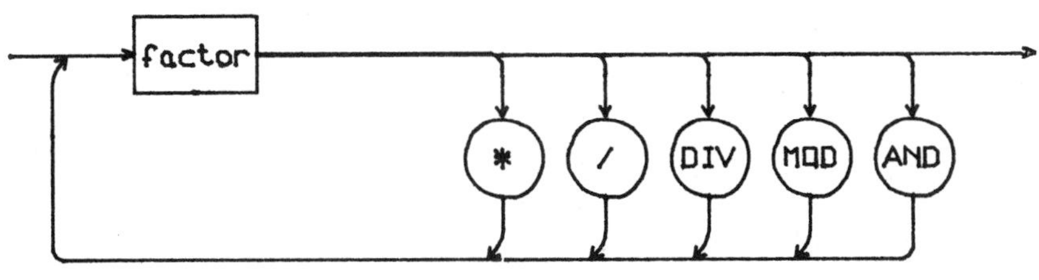

<factor>

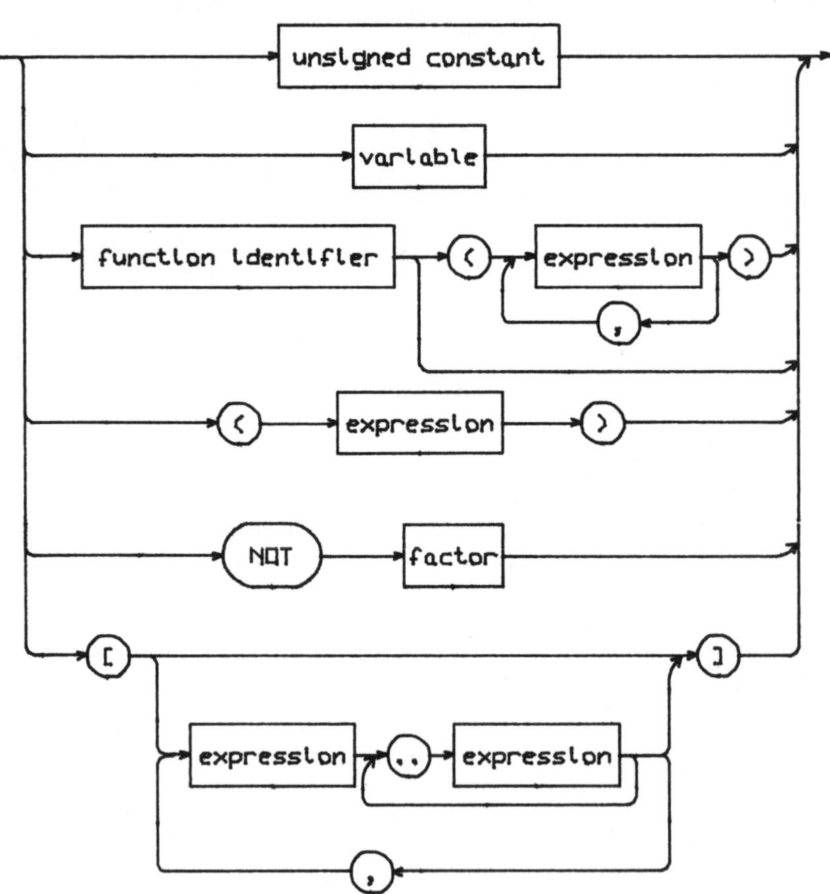
unsigned constant
variable
function identifier
(
expression
)
,
(
expression
)
NOT
factor
[
]
expression
..
expression
,

<expression>

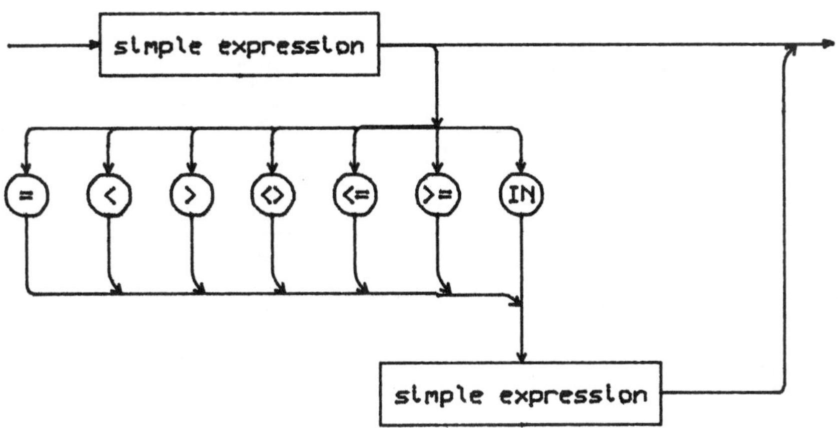

<parameter list>

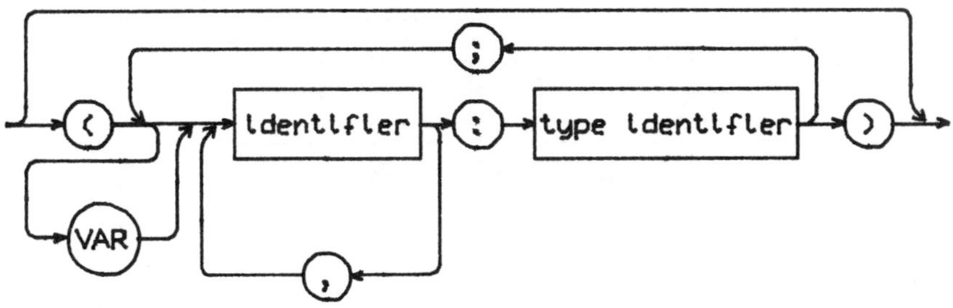

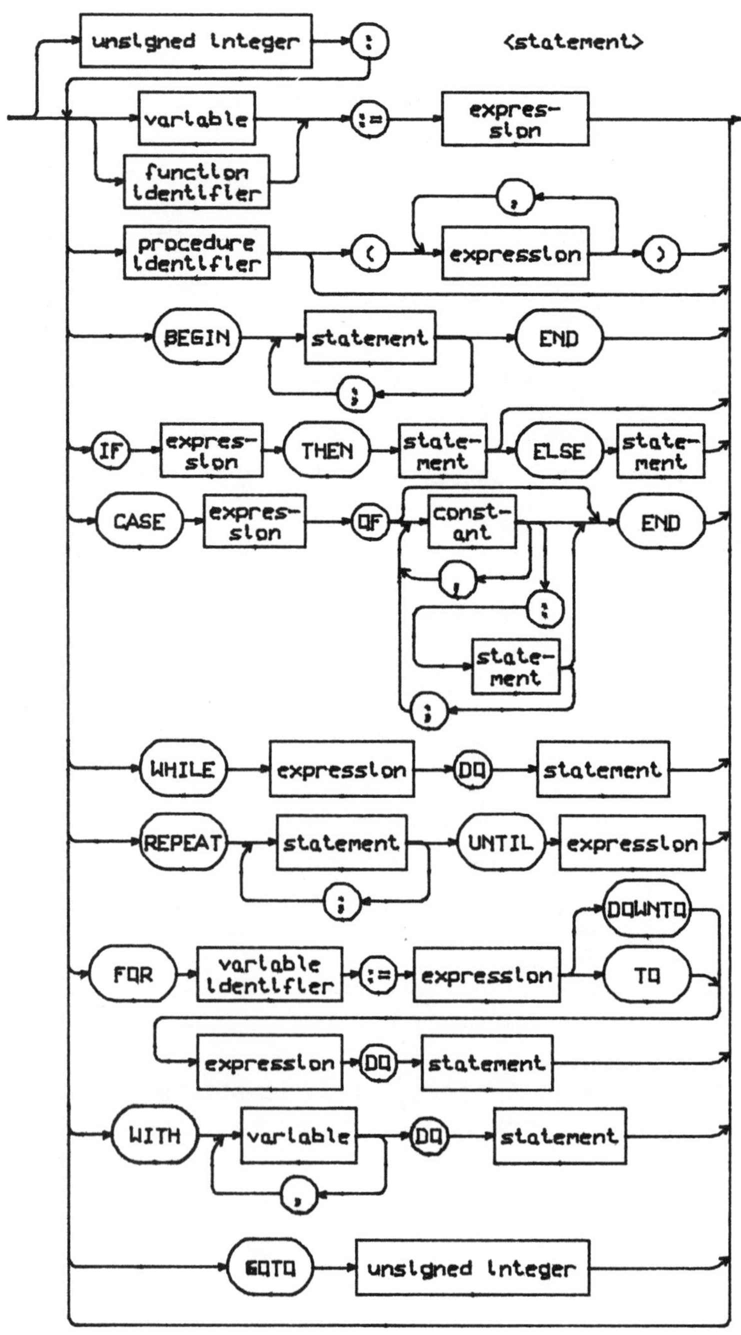

<statement>
unsigned integer
:
variable
function identifier
:=
expression
procedure identifier
(
,
)
BEGIN
statement
;
END
IF
THEN
ELSE
CASE
OF
constant
WHILE
DO
REPEAT
UNTIL
FOR
variable identifier
DOWNTO
TO
WITH
GOTO

<block>

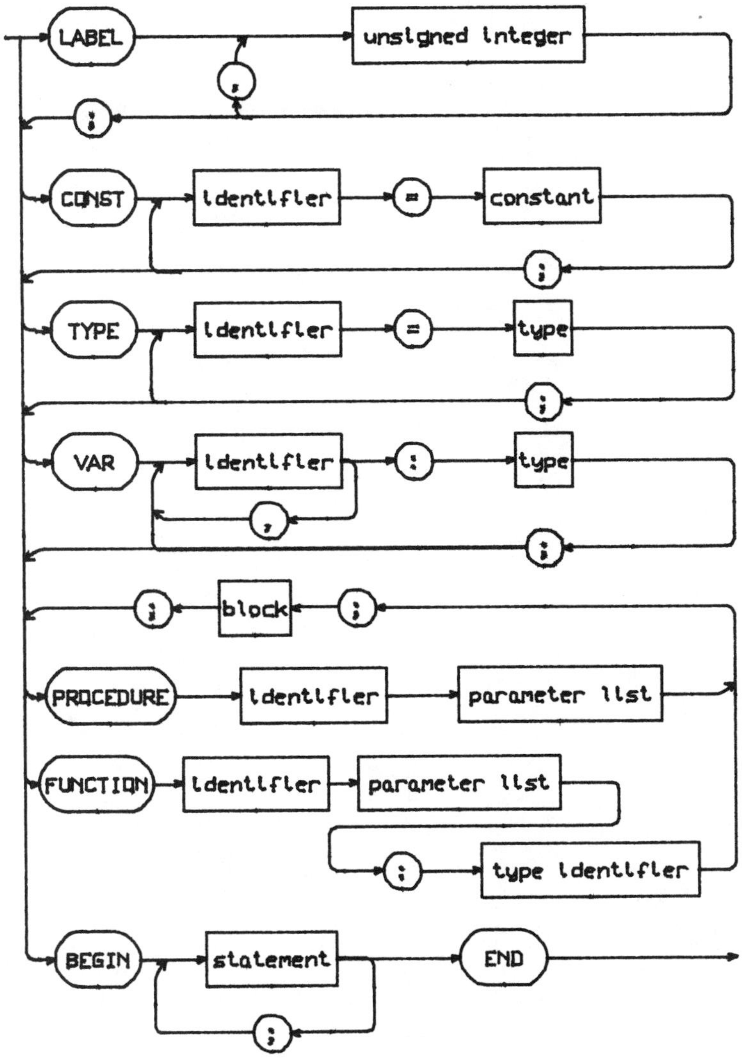

LABEL
unsigned integer
,
;
CONST
identifier
=
constant
;
TYPE
identifier
=
type
;
VAR
identifier
,
:
type
;
;
block
;
PROCEDURE
identifier
parameter list
FUNCTION
identifier
parameter list
:
type identifier
BEGIN
statement
;
END

<program>

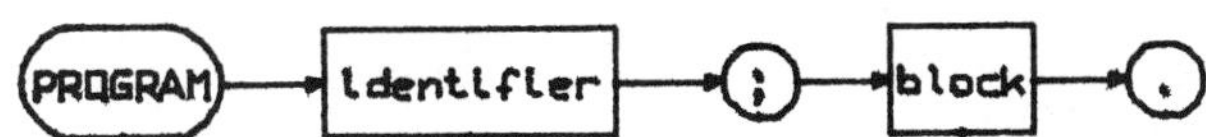

The Design of Well-Structured and Correct Programs

By **S. Alagić** and **M. A. Arbib**

1978. x, 292p. 68 illus. cloth
(Texts and Monographs in Computer Science)

In addition to providing a full treatment of the PASCAL programming language, this text synthesizes research in program design and proofs of correctness. The extensive, carefully chosen samples of algorithms—supplemented by many exercises—and the combination of the study of PASCAL with that of the tools to top-down program design and correctness, will provide the reader with a comprehensive knowledge of PASCAL.

A Concurrent PASCAL Compiler for Minicomputers

By **A. C. Hartmann**

1977. v, 119p. paper
(Lecture Notes in Computer Science, V. 50)

This book describes a seven-pass compiler for Concurrent PASCAL. Concurrent PASCAL is an abstract programming language for computer operating systems, which extends sequential PASCAL with the monitor concepts for structured concurrent programming. The author discusses basic terms, the pass breakdown, the virtual machine and implementation. Taken as a whole, this compiler is an engineering product that may serve as a prototype for industrial compiler writers; for this reason, the description of the compiler is relatively self-contained.